Ritual and Cult at Ugarit

Writings from the Ancient World
Society of Biblical Literature

Volume 10
Ritual and Cult at Ugarit
by Dennis Pardee
Edited by Theodore J. Lewis

Ritual and Cult at Ugarit

by
Dennis Pardee

Edited by
Theodore J. Lewis

Society of Biblical Literature
Atlanta

Library of Congress Cataloging-in-Publication Data

Pardee, Dennis.
Ritual and cult at Ugarit / by Dennis Pardee ; edited by Theodore J. Lewis.
p. cm. — (Writings from the ancient world ; no. 10)
Contains Ugaritic texts and Eng. translations.
Includes bibliographical references and index.
ISBN 1-58983-026-1 (pbk. : alk. paper)
1. Ugarit (Extinct city)—Religious life and customs.
2. Sacrifice—Syria—Ugarit (Extinct city) 3. Rites and ceremonies—Syria—Ugarit (Extinct city) I. Lewis, Theodore J. II. Title. III. Series.
BL1640 .P37 2002
299'.26—dc21

2002004828

Printed in the United States of America
on acid-free paper

Contents

Series Editor's Foreword

Writings from the Ancient World is designed to provide up-to-date, readable English translations of writings recovered from the ancient Near East.

The series is intended to serve the interests of general readers, students, and educators who wish to explore the ancient Near Eastern roots of Western civilization, or compare these earliest written expressions of human thought and activity with writings from other parts of the world. It should also be useful to scholars in the humanities or social sciences who need clear, reliable translations of ancient Near Eastern materials for comparative purposes. Specialists in particular areas of the ancient Near East who need access to texts in the scripts and languages of other areas will also find these translations helpful. Given the wide range of materials translated in the series, different volumes will appeal to different interests. But these translations make available to all readers of English the world's earliest traditions as well as valuable sources of information on daily life, history, religion, etc. in the preclassical world.

The translators of the various volumes in this series are specialists in the particular languages and have based their work on the original sources and the most recent research. In their translations they attempt to convey as much as possible of the original texts in a fluent, current English. In the introductions, notes, glossaries, maps, and chronological tables, they aim to provide the essential information for an appreciation of these ancient documents.

Covering the period from the invention of writing (by 3000 B.C.E.) down to the conquests of Alexander the Great (ca. 330 B.C.E.). the ancient Near East comprised northeast Africa and southwest Asia. The cultures represented within these limits include especially Egyptian, Sumerian, Babylonian, Assyrian, Hittite, Ugaritic, Aramean, Phoenician, and Israelite. It is hoped that Writings from the Ancient World will eventually produce translations of most of the many different genres attested in these cultures: letters—official and private—myths, diplomatic documents, hymns, law collections, monumental inscriptions, tales, and administrative records, to mention but a few.

The preparation of this volume was supported in part by a generous grant from the Division of Research Programs of the National Endowment for the Humanities. Significant funding has also been made available by the Society of Biblical Literature. In addition, those involved in preparing this volume have received financial and clerical assistance from their respective institutions. Were it not for these expressions of confidence in our work, the arduous tasks of preparation, translation, editing, and publication could not have been accomplished or even undertaken. It is the hope of all who have worked on these texts or supported this work that Writings from the Ancient World will open up new horizons and deepen the humanity of all who read these volumes.

Simon B. Parker
Boston University School of Theology

[Special Note: The texts included in this volume of the series pose particularly difficult problems of interpretation, both of their language and of their institutional context. For this reason the apparatus provided, both in the form of introductions to the texts and notes on them, is considerably more extensive and detailed than has been customary in the series. It is hoped that this will be appreciated by those who wish to understand something of the problems the texts raise, while not discouraging those whose intitial interest is more immediate.—S.B.P.]

Abbreviations

ALASP	Abhandlungen zur Literatur Alt-Syrien-Palästinas und Mesopotamiens
AO	Analecta Orientalia
AOAT	Alter Orient und Altes Testament
AuOr	*Aula Orientalis*
BA	*Biblical Archaeologist*
BASOR	*Bulletin of the American Schools of Oriental Research*
CBQMS	Catholic Biblical Quarterly Monograph Series
CRAI	*Comptes Rendus de l'Académie des Inscriptions et Belles-Lettres*
CTA	Herdner 1963
FAT	Forschungen zum Alten Testament
HS	*Hebrew Studies*
HSM	Harvard Semitic Monographs
HSS	Harvard Semitic Studies
JANES(CU)	*Journal of the Ancient Near Eastern Society (of Columbia University)*
JAOS	*Journal of the American Oriental Society*
JBL	*Journal of Biblical Literature*
JEOL	*Jaarbericht van het Vooraziatisch-Egyptisch Gezelschap (Genootschap) «Ex Oriente Lux »*
JNES	*Journal of Near Eastern Studies*
JNSL	*Journal of Northwest Semitic Languages*
JSOT	*Journal for the Study of the Old Testament*
JSOTSup	Journal for the Study of the Old Testament Supplement Series

MARI	*Mari, Annales de Recherches Interdisciplinaires*
MdB	*Le Monde de la Bible*
OBO	Orbis Biblicus et Orientalis
OLA	Orientalia Lovaniensia Analecta
OLP	*Orientalia Lovaniensia Periodica*
Or	*Orientalia*, nova series
RA	*Revue d'Assyriologie et d'Archéologie Orientale*
RB	*Revue Biblique*
RIH	Ras Ibn Hani (excavation number)
RS	Ras Shamra (excavation number)
RSO	Ras Shamra—Ougarit
SBLWAW	Society of Biblical Literature Writings from the Ancient World
SEL	*Studi Epigrafici e Linguistici sul Vicino Oriente Antico*
Sem	*Semitica*
SMEA	*Studi Micenei ed Egeo-Anatolici*
TCS	Texts from Cuneiform Sources
UBL	Ugaritisch-Biblische Literatur
UF	*Ugarit-Forschungen*

Explanation of Signs

{x}	spelling or reading in context, e.g., "{ʿnn} would be a scribal error for {ʿnt}"
italics	word or phrase where spelling is not the issue, e.g., "the interpretation of *šlm* is difficult in this passage"
all caps	root, e.g., "the most common term for sacrifice is DBḤ"
<x>	sign missing, e.g., "{ydb} is a mistake for {y<ʿ>db}"
⟨x⟩	extra sign, e.g., "{ủr⟨.⟩btm} is a mistake for {ủrbtm}"
[x]	sign entirely destroyed, e.g., {[ỉ]d . yph . mlk . ršp .}
⸢x⸣	sign partially preserved, reading not epigraphically certain but restorable from context, e.g., {⸢w⸣ ảlp l ảkl}
[-]	lacuna, estimated number of signs missing indicated by dash(es)
[ ]	lacuna of known length but the number of signs missing may not be estimated with any precision
[...]	lacuna of unknown length
....	unknown number of lines missing

Introduction

THE GOAL OF THIS VOLUME is to place before its readers those texts in the Ugaritic language that deal with the everyday contacts between the Ugaritians and their deities. This practical definition of ritual is not meant to deny that the better-known mythological texts may have had a ritual function. That function is, however, for the most part unknown. The texts dealt with here, on the other hand, all have an explicit or an implicit immediate link with daily religious practice in the kingdom of Ugarit. The texts fall into two primary categories: those that reflect directly the sacrificial cult as carried out in the various sanctuaries of the city of Ugarit (sections I–VII) and those that witness the infusion of ritual practice into life outside the sanctuary itself (sections VIII–XII). Both groups show a certain amount of diversity in form and function; these differences are reflected in the section divisions just indicated.

A previous volume in this series has provided a general introduction to the site of Ras Shamra and to the texts discovered there, and a comprehensive coverage of the mythological texts written in the poetic form of the Ugaritic language. For that reason, such an introduction is not judged necessary here.[1] Some of the texts dealt with here are poetry, but most are prose: virtually all of the texts in the first category described above are in prose, while those of the second are partially in prose, partially in poetry. It can be said in general that texts prescribing or describing the rituals that are performed in honor of the divine are in prose, while those that deal primarily or entirely with the acts of the gods are in poetry. Viewed from another perspective, the texts that deal with the sacrificial cult are quasi-administrative in form (though with the major difference that strictly administrative texts are for the most part descriptive in nature, rather than prescriptive) and are hence in prose; the divination texts are quasi-scientific in form[2] and are also in prose; the authors of texts that deal with the acts of the gods, on the other hand, tended to use the elevated language of poetry best known from the major mythological texts.

The reader must understand clearly from the beginning that the vast majority of the texts included here arise from royal concerns, either from the sacrificial cult, where the king himself was the primary actor, or from various groups that surrounded the king and who were the guardians and the transmitters of the royal ideology and its accompanying theology. Some are clearly identifiable with highly placed officials of the royal administration (text 48 with *ʾUrtēnu*, text 60 with *Šamumānu*); others may reflect the practices of persons lower on the sociopolitical ladder (in particular, those reflecting divinatory practice, texts 35–40). But with these few exceptions, the imprint of the royal family, primarily the king himself, is present virtually everywhere in this corpus.

The purview of these texts is the practical and theoretical concerns of daily religion. The texts in prose reflect, for the most part, a given situation, definable, in theory at least, in terms of time, place, and participants. Though many were found in what might be classified as "archives," none of these groupings constitutes a "library" of texts having to do with cultic practice. As nearly as we can judge from the texts as they have come down to us, there was no library of texts that a cultic official could consult to determine proper practice. The sacrificial texts are virtually all prescriptive, laying out a series of acts to be performed over a period of time that may extend from one day to two months. They appear, therefore, to reflect the impact on daily practice of an oral priestly tradition: someone dictated (or some talented priest wrote out himself) the cultic procedures to be followed during the upcoming period. Nothing in the texts, however, allows us to say what determined in one case that a rite for a single day should be written down, in another a rite for at least parts of two months. As with most of the textual genres from Ugarit, the texts that happen to have been preserved must reflect only a small fraction of the total number of texts that were inscribed.[3] The facts that (1) the texts were discovered at various places on the site and at the neighboring site of Ras Ibn Hani and that (2) more than one text may deal with a given slot in the cultic calendar lead to the conclusion that any given text reflects a single cultic situation—though it cannot be ruled out that a text generated for one series of rites may have been kept and reused the following year, or for a series of years. On the whole, however, it appears likely that the sacrificial texts reflect precise situations and that the vast majority of them date, therefore, to the last few years of the kingdom of Ugarit (i.e., to the years 1200–1185 in round figures).[4] These particular situations may be defined topographically as well as temporally: some texts (see, in particular, text 15 [RS 1.003]) reflect a significant number of changes of location, while others (e.g., text 18 [RS 1.005]) explicitly prescribe processions. But those texts that do not refer explicitly to a place or places may reflect the cultic practice of a particular sanctuary. Some of the texts in the second category described above were entirely circumstantial (e.g., the liver models that reflect a single consultation, the administrative texts in section XII); others reflect the gathering of data characteristic of scientific texts (e.g., the divinatory manuals [texts 42–45]); while others are more timeless in that they reflect the royal ideology linking the present king with his ancestors (texts 55–56); in one text the circumstantial and the timeless are intertwined in that it reflects the rite by which a king who has just died is enabled effectively to join his ancestors (text 24).

As will become clear from an examination of the texts that reflect daily religious practice, bloody sacrifice, that is, the slaying of a sacrificial animal, is at the very heart of the Ugaritic cult. The fact that no rules have come down to us that deal with the actual handling and disposal of the blood—nor, for that matter, of the meat or the by-products—is owing to the genre of texts that we have received: these are not treatises on the theory or the practice of sacrifice, but brief prescriptions for the carrying out of a given sacrificial rite. A. Caquot (1979: 1403; cf. Niehr 1999: 123) has referred to the sacrificial rituals as "*aide-mémoires,*" that is, essentially crib texts for priests. Contrary to one theoretical typology (del Olmo Lete 1992a, 1999a; cf. Gianto 1995), I find virtually no evidence for nonsacrificial "liturgies": virtually every cultic act prescribed in the prose texts translated below is preceded by, accompanied by, or followed by one or more sacrifices. For instance, though the "entry" itself by which the "entry rites" are defined (see text 18 [RS 1.005]) was not a sacrificial act, the rite is always accompanied by sacrifices and nonbloody offerings; though the "contemplation" of the "contemplation rite" (see texts 19–21) was not a sacrificial act, the rite is always accompanied by sacrifices; though the purification of the king was not a sacrificial act, it invariably takes place prior to and in preparation for the king's participation in a sacrificial rite; though prayer is not a sacrificial act, the clearest example we have of a prayer follows a sacrificial ritual and includes references to multiple sacrifices and offerings (see texts 13 and 46 [RS 24.266:26'-36']); though there was almost certainly a sacred banquet at which much wine was drunk, the wine for these banquets is defined as pertaining to the "royal sacrificial rites" (*dbḥ mlk* according to text 58 [RS 19.015:2])—it is simplistic and essentially incorrect to say that *dbḥ* in such a formula simply means "feast," as is shown by the actual rites to which text 58 refers (see notes below to this text and compare the actual texts of the various rites in those cases where the text has been preserved). In this respect, it is necessary to distinguish between ritual acts or elements of a liturgy and a complete rite or liturgy. Though anthropologists would certainly qualify the king's purification as a ritual act, it is accomplished, according to the texts that follow, solely to enable the king to participate in a sacrificial ritual. Its functional opposite is expressed by *ḥl*, the term by which the king's return to his noncultic functions is prescribed. It does not appear too strong to say that bloody sacrifice is the *sine qua non* of a complete ritual carried out in the official cult at Ugarit. Such a statement should not be taken as denying that individuals who worshiped far from this cult may have been forced by circumstances to adopt a "lesser" form of worship, one where the scarcity of cultic personnel and relative poverty did not allow for frequent sacrifice; but, judging from the texts at our disposal, the conclusion regarding sacrifice holds for the form of the cult that took place in the city of Ugarit by those who were situated at the peak of the social pyramid.

One final general point: if the reader compares the general organization of texts proposed herein as well as the specific treatment of several of them with the previous most complete study of these same texts, that of del Olmo Lete (1992a, 1999a), it will become apparent that I find far less textual evidence of the mortuary cult, that is, the cult of the dead,[5] at Ugarit than does my respected Spanish colleague. (For a relatively brief general statement, see Pardee 1996a.) My position is based (1) on the virtual absence of sacrifices prescribed for the divine entities that we would expect to be the beneficiaries of such a cult, viz., the *Rapaʾūma*, "shades of the dead," and the *Malakūma*, "(deceased) kings (i.e., former kings who now inhabit the underworld)," and (2) on the presence of the *ʾInāšu-ʾIlīma*, perhaps "men (who have become) divine (after death)," in the regular sacrificial cult—there appears to have been a regular provision for sacrifice to these underworld entities instead of a separate cultic institution in their honor. It is relatively clear from some of the poetic texts included here (in particular, texts 55–56) that the living king perceived his royal vigor as coming from his departed ancestors and that there were ceremonies intended to facilitate the transmission of this power. But, in the cultic texts at our disposal, there is very little evidence for a link between these ceremonies and the traditional sacrificial cult. It also appears likely, judging from the presence of a tomb under many of the houses in the city of Ugarit, that some form of cult of a family's ancestors was practiced; but, again, the texts at our disposal say virtually nothing about such ceremonies, not even those of the king himself, in an explicit manner. Moreover, no really clear archaeological evidence for such a cult has yet been unearthed in the many houses and tombs excavated to date (Pitard 1994). In sum, presently known texts provide data on a cultic system in which gods from the highest to the lowest, from the most ancient to the most recent, were honored in the sacrificial cult by a series of events defined by acts of which the primary parameters were time, place, and type of act. To date, a particular cultic event defined by specific time, place, or type of act devoted primarily to the cult of the dead is virtually unattested (see the brief references to a *pgr*-ceremony in texts 32 and 33). Such events appear, therefore, to have been for the most part incorporated into the regular sacrificial cult but on a minor scale. The situation is different with the funerary cult, that is, the events associated with the burial of a recently deceased person, for the details of such a ceremony are attested in text 24 (RS 34.126). Moreover, that text incorporates a mortuary element, for the shades of former kings are invited to participate in that festival. Indeed, as we will see below, the poetic texts referring to the king's gaining strength from the *Rapaʾūma* may reflect ceremonies linked to the inhumation of the deceased king and the enthronement of his successor. If such were the case, even these apparent allusions to a royal mortuary cult would belong to the category of funerary ceremonies rather than to that of the mortuary cult. Readers particularly interested in this question must, however, compare the treatments of del Olmo Lete and myself (particularly in Pardee 2000a, where much more extensive argumentation is provided) and come to their own conclusions.

Some remarks of a more practical nature having to do with how this book should be viewed in the context of current scholarship:

• With few exceptions, the interpretations offered here reflect conclusions reached in the course of preparing a new edition of the Ugaritic texts having to do with cultic practice (Pardee 2000a). For a full defense of the positions reflected in the translations and notes that follow, the reader must go to that edition. Specific references to that edition are supplied only exceptionally.

• In general, only texts that are well enough preserved to permit the translation of significant portions are included here. In all, more than forty fragmentary texts that may be found in the edition to which reference has just been made are not included here.

• Ugaritic texts are cited by excavation number ("RS . . ." or "RIH . . .") and by *editio princeps*, with the exception of texts included in this volume, which are cited by text number here and by excavation number, and of some of the well known mythological texts, which may be cited by *CTA* number alone.[6] A concordance of text numbers for the texts studied here has been provided to facilitate rapid location of a particular text.

• The reader who compares the texts proposed here with the original editions or with subsequent editions will find many differences. With only one exception (text 60 [RS Varia 14]), the transliterations offered here are based on new collations of the tablets. The present work in general notes only necessary corrections of the text on a given tablet. Readers wishing to know the bases for my differences from previous editions must consult the "*remarques textuelles*" in each chapter of Pardee 2000a.

• The same work should also be consulted for the history of discussion of each text. Most of the ideas found below do not, of course, originate with me but have arisen out of mind meeting mind over the course of the decades of study of these texts. Proper credits are indicated in the footnotes of my full edition and an attempt is made in the commentary to situate my interpretation with respect to my predecessors. I do cite more extensively here works that appeared subsequently to the last bibliographical updates in my edition (virtually nothing after 1996), principally, for the poetic texts, Parker, ed., 1997, and Wyatt 1998 (del Olmo Lete 1999a is an English translation of del Olmo Lete 1992a, which was taken fully into consideration in Pardee 2000a).

• Under a given "text" are sometimes grouped a series of tablets, which may include a partial text. The purpose of this organization is to put together all the witnesses to a given tradition, and only texts that reflect a particular ritual tradition are so grouped. In the cases of the deity lists, the multiple witnesses clearly reflect a single tradition with variants, while the sacrificial rituals so grouped reflect variants that are easily described on a superficial level but are much more difficult to account for in terms of actual ritual practice.

• Because the vast majority of the sacrificial ritual texts are prescriptive in nature, their primary structural feature is chronological, that is, a series of acts is prescribed to occur over a period of time, which ranges from a single day to portions of two months. The sacrificial rituals are organized below under headings that reflect these chronologically defined categories. The sections of the texts corresponding to different phases of the rites are indicated in the translation only; for charts and arguments supporting these structural analyses, see Pardee 2000a. The primary division of each text is chronological, if such data are present in the text, noted by Roman numerals; then the primary acts prescribed for a given time, whether sacrificial or other, are noted by capital letters; then the discrete elements, primarily sacrificial, of a given category of action, are set off in separate lines. The purpose of this organization of the translation is to provide an outline of the text for the reader in terms of time, of ritual categories, and of discrete elements of each category. Its intent is to make clear to the reader the structure of each text and the sequence of acts in each rite, as I understand them. For a detailed exposition on each text, see the section "*Structure du texte*" in each chapter of Pardee 2000a.

• All capital letters in the translation indicate either that the general meaning of a word may be determined in a broken passage but not its specific form and meaning (e.g., "EXIT," text 9 [RS 24.276:21']), that no English translation is proposed for a Ugaritic word (e.g., "KKD," text 6A [RS 1.009:16]), or that the vocalization of a proper name is unknown (e.g., "RM[?]," text 6A [RS 1.009:13]).

• Proper names, including divine names, are indicated in transliteration, rather than in the modern form (*ʾIlu* instead of El, *Baʿlu* instead of Baal). I began by only transliterating names that do not have modern equivalents, but there were too many ambiguities, and I decided that it was best to use a single system. Hebrew and modern equivalents are usually indicated in the glossary.

• In accordance with the editorial policy of the series, words considered necessary for a ready understanding of the English translation but not present in the Ugaritic are not placed in parentheses. Some examples are provided in the first note to the translation of text 6A (RS 1.009) and in the first note to the translation of text 42 (RS 24.247+).

• The glossary is divided into two sections, cultic terms and divine names. The purpose of the first is to decrease the number of explanatory footnotes by placing all general explanatory matter in a single place, valid for any text where a word occurs. Because the Ugaritic form and, if applicable, the Hebrew equivalent are provided in this glossary, it will also permit the interested reader to begin delving into the linguistic and comparative aspects of the usage of a word. The reader should keep in mind that some words that appear banal in English, for example, "ascend," "bird," "bull," "consume," "cow," "enter," have, because of their importance in the Ugaritic sacrificial cult, been included in this first section of the glossary as a handy reference to the form and meaning of the corresponding Ugaritic word. The purpose of the second section is to provide the most basic information on the various deities who are named as recipients of offerings and/or as actors in the poetic texts—it goes without saying that these descriptions are simplified in the extreme. A somewhat more detailed sketch of all these deities may be found in Pardee 2000a and much more detailed overviews on many in van der Toorn et al., eds., 1999.

Notes

1. Parker, ed., 1997.

2. On the use of the term "scientific" for these texts, see Rochberg 1999; Pardee 2001.

3. A modern myth regarding the Ugaritic texts is that they were purposely and regularly baked after inscription (see the recent example of Curtis *apud* Watson and Wyatt, eds., 1999: 11). In point of fact, this practice was extremely rare, and virtually all the tablets that have come down to us were baked in accidental fires, most in the final conflagration in which the Late Bronze city of Ugarit disappeared. This means that what we read today depends almost entirely on what happened to be in a given building when it burned and where the tablets happened to be stored and to fall with respect to the heat of the fire: tablets were in general kept in an upper story (see recently Bounni, Lagarce and Lagarce 1998: 23, for the case of the "Palais Nord" at Ras Ibn Hani) and the extent to which they were baked would depend on when and how that story burned and on where the tablets fell as the building collapsed.

4. For recent summaries, see Yon, Sznycer, and Bordreuil, eds., 1995; Freu 1999; Singer *apud* Watson and Wyatt, eds., 1999: 603–733.

5. On the distinction between "mortuary" and "funerary," see Schmidt 1994 and Pardee 1996a.

6. For a complete listing of texts by excavation number through those from 1986, see Bordreuil and Pardee 1989.

The Texts

Part One: The Sacrificial Cult

I

Deity Lists

THE DEITY LISTS are placed at the beginning of this presentation of Ugaritic ritual practice because it has become clear in recent years that these lists, which go by the conventional though inappropriate name of "pantheon texts," are directly related to sacrificial practice. The term "pantheon text" arose before the link with the sacrificial rituals was obvious, at a time when these texts appeared to have been formulated for purely "theological" reasons. The basis for the link between the deity lists and the sacrificial ritual was not established until 1968, when, in the same volume, J. Nougayrol published the syllabic version of text 1 (col. C [RS 20.024]) and C. Virolleaud the sacrificial ritual that corresponds thereto (text 1, col. D [RS 24.643:1–12]). It was not fully clear until the discovery of RS 92.2004 (text 3, col. A) that there existed a deity list that corresponded directly to the gods honored in the sacrificial ritual prescribed on the reverse of RS 24.643 (text 3, col. B).

It is unclear why these texts containing the simple lists, and only these (as far as is presently known), were generated separately from the sacrificial prescriptions, for it is possible to generate many lists of varying length from the sacrificial texts themselves,[1] and another is clearly present in one of the prayers translated below (text 47 [RS 24.271]). Nor has an explanation for the existence of the syllabic versions of these deity lists yet been proposed that is generally accepted. These are presently the only Sumero-Akkadian texts from Ugarit (in sharp contrast to contemporaneous Emar on the Euphrates) that manifest a direct relationship with the cult. The existence of several lists shows that the term "pantheon," at least in its narrow sense, is not suited to these texts; rather they constitute groupings of deities all of whom would have been members of the larger

Ugaritic pantheon. The only presently available evidence from Ugarit is provided by the lists themselves and the associated ritual texts. Comparisons with the *Phoenician History* of Philo of Byblos show that the first and third lists presented below almost certainly reflect cosmological speculation,[2] but we as yet have no "theological" or "mythological" texts from Ugarit that would provide the details of Ugaritic cosmological thinking. The very fact of the existence of these lists is nevertheless important, for they provide concrete data for the existence of such thinking and show that the various traditions had not been reduced to a single "theology" at Ugarit.

1. RS 1.017/RS 24.264⁺/RS 20.024/RS 24.643:1–9

The text in col. A was the first to be discovered, but its interpretation was impeded by its damaged state; its place in the sacrificial cult was unknown, because the corresponding sacrificial text was not to be discovered for another three decades. The four texts that attest to this divine list are here arranged vertically in columns to make the correspondences clearly visible by reading horizontally across the page. Columns A and B represent two versions of the list in Ugaritic. The first was discovered during the first campaign at Ras Shamra in 1929, but its damaged state meant that its importance was not recognized until the better-preserved versions were discovered. The syllabic version was discovered in 1956 (col. C), and its editor immediately realized that it corresponded to the Ugaritic version from the first campaign; indeed, because of a delay in publication, he was able to add a supplement (Nougayrol 1968: 63–64) to his comparison of the Ugaritic and syllabic versions based on knowledge of the new and more complete Ugaritic version discovered in 1961 (col. B [RS 24.264⁺]). The key for understanding that the deity lists directly reflect sacrificial practice was also discovered in 1961 and was published in 1968 (col. D [RS 24.643]; Virolleaud 1968: 580–82, 584). This text is a more-or-less standard sacrificial ritual, but the deities honored are virtually identical to those of the deity lists and they are mentioned in virtually the same order as the deities of the lists provided here in cols. A–C. The deities of col. D (RS 24.643:1–9) are, therefore, those of a sacrificial ritual, and the lists of deities presented here and below in text 3 are thus abstracted from the sacrificial text.

Besides the simple equivalences visible in a horizontal reading of the columns of text 1, there are other visual indicators that the deity lists were prepared for a specific sacrificial ritual. (The basic information follows, but for it to be truly meaningful, the interested reader should compare the deity lists with the sacrificial ritual translated as text 12 and go to the copies in Nougayrol 1968 and Pardee 2000a as cited below to observe the marks on the tablets.) That RS 24.264+ (col. B) was prepared as a sort of liturgical outline for a sacrificial rite corresponding closely to that of RS 24.643:1–12 is shown by the horizontal line inscribed after line 10 of the deity list (see copy in Pardee 2000a: 1284) and, even more specifically, by the "check marks" inscribed in the left margin of the deity list, for these were inscribed once, corresponding to the *šlmm*-rite in RS 24.643:1–9, then effaced, and finally reinscribed only before lines 1–10, corresponding to the *šrp*-rite in RS 24.643:10–12, which ends with the last of the seven manifestations of *Baʿlu*. Similar check marks are found in the right margin of the syllabic text RS 20.024 (see Nougayrol's copy: 1968: 379—there are clear indications on this tablet as well that the scribe wished to mark a break between lines 1–10 and the following lines, though the situation is not quite so clear as in the case of text 1B (RS 24.264+) and in that of the newly published RS 94.2518 (see below, text 56B).

That the deity list RS 24.264+ (col. B) may not have been prepared for the very same performance of the sacrificial liturgy as that reflected by RS 24.643:1–12 (col. D) is indicated, however, by the fact that the order of deities in RS 24.643 is not precisely identical to that of RS 24.264+. The order found on the tablet RS 24.643 is indicated here in column D; some of the names in the right-hand column do not, therefore, correspond directly to those in the left columns: a variant order is encountered in col. D, lines 5–6, omissions in col. D, line 9.

As should be clear from the introduction to these texts, there is no basis, other than the accident of discovery, on which to consider this list as constituting the "canonical 'pantheon'" (Nougayrol 1998: 170) or "the principal . . . canonical list" (del Olmo Lete 1999b: 308; see the cautionary remarks in Gianto 1995: 145 and Pardee 2000b: 61); for that matter, only the current status of the data allows us to speak of this text along with text 3 as the "principal" deity lists, as I occasionally do for the purpose of distinguishing them from the shorter lists.

Because of the difficulties of "translating" a list of divine names, a translation is not provided below, but in its place there is a vocalization, with a translation in parentheses where the superficial meaning of the name is transparent (this translation often reflects the more explicit syllabic version). For the functions of the deities whose name is not transparent in meaning, see part II of the Glossary. For a complete translation of RS 24.643, see below, text 12, and, for a detailed commentary on the list, Pardee 2000a: 291–319.

Text

A. RS 1.017	B. RS 24.264^{+}	C. RS 20.024	D. RS 24.643:1–9
(1) *ỉl ṣpn*			(1) *dbḥ ṣpn*[3]
(2) *ỉ⸢lỉ⸣b*	(1) *ỉlỉb*	(1) DINGIR-*a-bi*[4]	[*ỉlỉb*]
(3) *ỉ⸢l⸣*	(2) *ỉl*	(2) DINGIR^{lum}	(2) *ỉl*
(4) *dg⸢n⸣*	(3) *dgn*	(3) ^{d}*da-gan*	[*dgn*]
(5) ⸢*b*⸣*ʿl ṣpn*	(4) *bʿl ṣpn*	(4) ^{d}IM *be-el* ḪUR.SAG.*ḫa-zi*	[*bʿl ṣpn*]
(6) *bʿlm*	(5) *bʿlm*	(5) ^{d}IM II	(3) *bʿlm*
(7) *bʿlm*	(6) *bʿlm*	(6) ^{d}IM III	[*bʿlm*]
(8) *bʿlm*	(7) *bʿlm*	(7) ^{d}IM IV	[*bʿlm*][5]
(9) ⸢*bʿ*⸣*lm*	(8) *bʿlm*	(8) ^{d}IM V	(4) *bʿlm*
(10) [*b*]⸢*ʿ*⸣*lm*	(9) *bʿlm*	(9) ^{d}IM VI	⸢*bʿl*⸣[*m*]
(11) [*bʿl*]*m*	(10) *bʿlm*	(10) ^{d}IM VII	[*bʿlm*]
(12) [*ảrṣ*] *w šm*⸢*m*⸣	(11) *ảrṣ w šmm*	(11) ^{d}IDIM *ù* IDIM	(5) *ảrṣ w šmm*
(13) [*kṯr*]⸢*t*⸣	(12) *kṯ*⸢*r*⸣*t*	(12) ^{d}*sa-sú-ra-tu*$_{4}$	*kṯr*[*t*]
(14) […]	(13) ⸢*y*⸣*r*⸢*ḫ*⸣	(13) ^{d}EN.ZU	*yr*⸢*ḫ*⸣
(15) […]	(14) ⸢*ṣ*⸣*pn*	(14) ^{d}ḪUR.SAG.*ḫa-zi*	[*ʿṯt*]⸢*r*⸣ (?)[6]
(16) […]	(15) *kṯr*	(15) ^{d}*é-a*	(6) *ṣpn*
(17) […]	(16) *pdry*	(16) ^{d}*ḫé-bat*	*kṯr*
(18) […]	(17) *ʿṯtr*	(17) ^{d}*aš-ta-bi*	*pdry*
(19) […]	(18) *ǵrm* ⸢*w*⸣[*ṯhmt*]	(18) ^{d}ḪUR.SAG.MEŠ *u* A$^{\text{mu-ú}}$	*ǵrm* ⸢*w ṯhm*⸣*t*
(20) […]	(19) [*ảṯ*]*rt*	(19) ^{d}*aš-ra-tu*$_{4}$	(7) *ảṯrt*
(21) […]	(20) *ʿnt*	(20) ^{d}*a-na-tu*$_{4}$	*ʿnt*
(22) [*šp*]⸢*š*⸣	(21) *špš*	(21) ^{d}UTU	*špš*
(23) [*ả*]*rṣ*⸢*y*⸣	(22) *ảrṣy*	(22) ^{d}*al-la-tu*$_{4}$	⸢*ả*⸣*rṣy*
(24) [*ủ*]*šḫr*⸢*y*⸣	(23) *ủšḫry*	(23) ^{d}*iš-ḫa-ra*	*ʿṯtr*⸢*t*⸣
(25) [*ʿ*]*ṯtrt*	(24) *ʿṯtrt*	(24) ^{d}EŠDAR$^{\text{iš-tar}}$	(8) *ủšḫry*
(26) *ỉl tʿḏr bʿl*	(25) *ỉl* ⸢*t*⸣*ʿḏr bʿl*	(25) DINGIR.MEŠ *til-la-at* ^{d}IM	*ỉl tʿ*⸢*ḏ*⸣*r bʿl*
(27) *ršp*	(26) ⸢*r*⸣[*š*]*p*	(26) ^{d}GÌR.UNU.GAL	*ršp*
(28) *ddmš*	(27) *ddmš*	(27) ^{d}*dá-ad-mi-iš*	*ddmš*

(29) *pḫr ỉlm*	(28) *pḫr ỉ⌜lm⌝*	(28) ^{d}*pu-ḫur* DINGIR.MEŠ	(9) *pḫr ỉlm*
(30) *ym*	(29) *ym*	(29) ^{d}A.AB.BA	*ym*
(31) *ủṯḫt*	(30) *ủṯḫ⌜t⌝*	(30) $^{\text{d.dug}}$BUR.ZI. NÍG.NA	
(32) *knr*	(31) *knr*	(31) $^{\text{d.giš}}$*ki-na-rù*	[*k*]⌜*n*⌝*r*
(33) *mlkm*	(32) *mlkm*	(32) ^{d}*ma-lik*-MEŠ	
(34) *šlm*	(33) *šlm*	(33) ^{d}*sa-li-mu*	

Vocalization (Translation)[7]

(1) *ʾIlū Ṣapuni* (The gods of Mount Ṣapunu):
(2) *ʾIluʾibī* (The God-of-the-Father),
(3) *ʾIlu*,
(4) *Dagan*,
(5) *Baʿlu Ṣapuni* (*Baʿlu* of the Mountain *Ṣapunu*),
(6) *Baʿluma* (another manifestation of *Baʿlu*),[8]
(7) *Baʿluma* (another manifestation of *Baʿlu*),
(8) *Baʿluma* (another manifestation of *Baʿlu*),
(9) *Baʿluma* (another manifestation of *Baʿlu*),
(10) *Baʿluma* (another manifestation of *Baʿlu*),
(11) *Baʿluma* (another manifestation of *Baʿlu*),
(12) *ʾArṣu-wa-Šamūma* (Earth-and-Heaven),
(13) *Kôṯarātu* (Mistresses of Female Reproduction),
(14) *Yariḫu* (Moon),
(15) *Ṣapunu* (The Mountain *Ṣapunu*),
(16) *Kôṯaru* (Skillful),
(17) *Pidray* (Fatty),
(18) *ʿAṯtaru*,
(19) *Ǵūrūma-wa-Tahāmātu* (Mountains-and-Waters-of-the-Abyss),
(20) *ʾAṯiratu*,
(21) *ʿAnatu*,
(22) *Šapšu* (Sun),
(23) *ʾArṣay* (Earthy),
(24) *ʾUšḫaraya*,
(25) *ʿAṯtartu*,
(26) *ʾIlu Taʿḏiri Baʿli* (Auxiliary-Gods-of-*Baʿlu*),
(27) *Rašap*,
(28) *Dadmiš*,
(29) *Puḫru ʾIlīma* (Assembly-of-the-Gods),

(30) *Yammu* (Sea),
(31) *ʾUṯḫatu* (Censer),
(32) *Kinnāru* (Lyre),
(33) *Malakūma* (Kings),
(34) *Šalimu*.

2. RS 6.138

Only a small fragment of this text is preserved, and the reconstruction proposed below is, like any so extensive a reconstruction, hypothetical. Nevertheless, this beginning of a list appears worth presenting here because, according to the proposed reconstruction, the order of the first five deities named would have constituted a variation of the first list: Dagan and the seven manifestations of *Baʿlu* would have been omitted, and the omission would have been indicated by a horizontal line.

Text	***Reconstruction***	
Obverse		
(1) *ỉlỉb . ỉl .*	*ỉlỉb . ỉl .*	*ʾIluʾibī, ʾIlu,*
————		
(2) [--(-)]⌜-⌝	[*ảr*]⌜*ṣ*⌝	*ʾArṣu-*
(3) [---(-)]⌜-⌝	[*w šm*]⌜*m*⌝	*wa-Šamûma,*
(4) [ ]	[*kṯrt*]	*Kôṯarātu,*
(5) [--(-)]⌜-⌝	[*yr*]⌜*ḫ*⌝	*Yariḫu,*
....		
Reverse erased in antiquity		

Vocalization (Translation)

(1) *ʾIluʾibī* (The God-of-the-Father), *ʾIlu*,

————————

(2) *Arṣu-* (Earth-)
(3) *wa-Šamūma* (and-Heaven),
(4) *Kôṯarātu* (Goddesses of Female Reproduction),
(5) *Yariḫu* (Moon),

....

3. RS 92.2004/RS 24.643 reverse

As was the case with col. D of text 1, what is indicated here as col. B is abstracted from a sacrificial ritual in which the sacrifices are offered to a series of deities whose names correspond to those listed in the syllabic cuneiform text RS 92.2004 (col. A). No independent version of the list has yet been discovered in Ugaritic, and the syllabic version is, therefore, here presented in the left-hand column. This deity list, like the first, appears again below in the full translation of text 12 (RS 24.643), at least to the extent that the list is preserved there. A syllabic version of this list was first discovered in 1963 (RS 26.142, published by Nougayrol [1968, text 170]), but it was so badly damaged that its precise relationship to RS 24.643 reverse (here col. B and below text 12) could only be delineated after the discovery of RS 92.2004 (see Arnaud 1994; Pardee 2000a: 795–806).

Text

A. RS 92.2004[9]	B. RS 24.643:23–44	C. RS 1.017 (RS 24.264+)
(1) DINGIR-*a-bi*	(23) *ỉlỉb*	line 2
(2) ^{d}KI *ù* AN	(24) *ảrṣ w šmm*	line 12
(3) DINGIR^{lum}	(25) *ỉl*	line 3
(4) ^{d}NIN.MAḪ	*kṯrt*	line 13
(5) ^{d}KUR	(26) *dgn*	line 4
(6) ^{d}X *ḫal-bi*	*bʿl ḫlb*	absent[10]
(7) ^{d}X ḪUR.SAG.*ḫa-zi*	(27) *bʿl ṣpn*	line 5
(8) ^{d}*šar-ra-ši-ya*	(28) *ṯrṯy*	absent
(9) ^{d}XXX	(29) *yrḫ*	line 14
(10) ^{d}ḪUR.SAG.*ḫa-zi*	*ṣpn*	line 15
(11) ^{d}*é-a*	(30) *kṯr*	line 16
(12) ^{d}*aš-ta-bi*	*ʿṯtr*	line 18
(13) ^{d}*aš-ra-tu*$_{4}$	(31) [*ả*]⸢*ṯ*⸣*rt*	line 20
(14) ^{d}ḪAR *ù* GÌR	*šgr w ỉṯm*	absent
(15) ^{d}UTU	(32) [*šp*]*š*	line 22
(16) ⸢^{d}x⸣-*it-ri-ip-pí*	*ršp ỉdrp*	absent
(17) ⸢^{d}xx⸣-*nam-ṣa-ri*	(33) [----]⸢mṣ⸣r	absent
(18) [^{d}*da-ad-m*]*i-iš*	(34) [*ddmš*]	line 28
(19) [...]	[-(-)]*mt*	absent

A. RS 92.2004[9]	B. RS 24.643:23–44	C. RS 1.017 (RS 24.264+)
(20) [...]	(35) [...]	
(21) [...]	(36) [...]	
(22) [^{d}*iš*]-*ḫa-ra*	(37) [*ủšḫry*]	line 24
(23) [^{d}*nin*-]*urta*	(38) [*g̱tr* ?]	absent
(24) [^{d}]EŠDAR	[*ʿṯ*]⸢*tr*⸣[*t*]	line 25
(25) ^{d}SIRIŠ	(39) [*trṯ*]	absent
(26) ^{d}*ma-za-ra*	*mḏr*	absent
(27) DINGIR.MEŠ.URU.KI	(40) [*ỉl q*]⸢*r*⸣*t*	absent
(28) DINGIR.NITA.MEŠ *ù* DINGIR.MUNUS.MEŠ	*ỉl m*⸢-⸣[...]	absent
(29) ^{d}ḪUR.SAG.MEŠ *ù* ^{d}A.MEŠ	(41) [*ǵr*]⸢*m*⸣ *w* ⸢*t*⸣*hm*	line 19
(30) ^{d}A.AB.BA	[*ym*]	line 30
(31) ^{d}E.NI.TU.*ma-me-ri*	(42) [--]⸢*m*⸣*mr*	absent[11]
(32) ^{d}*su-ra-su-gu*-PI	*s*⸢*r*⸣[...]	absent
(33) ^{d}E.NI.ḪU.RA.UD.ḪI	[...]	absent[11]
(34) DINGIR.MEŠ *da-ad-me-ma*	(42–43) [*ỉl dd*]⸢*m*⸣*m*	absent
(35) DINGIR.MEŠ *la-ab-a-na*	(43) *ỉl lb*[-]⸢*n*⸣	absent
(36) ^{d}DUG.BUR.ZI.NÍG.DIN	⸢*ủ*⸣[*ṯḫt*]	line 31
(37) ^{d}GIŠ.ZA.MÍM	[(*knr*)][12]	line 32
(38) ^{d}X	[*bʿlm*]	lines 6–11
(39) ^{d}X	(44) *bʿlm*	lines 6–11
(40) ^{d}X	[*bʿlm*]	lines 6–11
(41) ⸢^{d}X⸣	[*bʿlm*]	lines 6–11
(42) [^{d}*ma-l*]*ik*-MEŠ		line 33[13]
(43) [^{d}]SILIM		line 34

Vocalization (Translation)[14]

(1) *ʾIluʾibī* (The God-of-the-Father),
(2) *ʾArṣu-wa-Šamūma* (Earth-and-Heaven),
(3) *ʾIlu*,
(4) *Kôṯarātu* (Mistresses of Female Reproduction),
(5) *Dagan*,
(6) *Baʿlu Ḫalbi* (*Baʿlu* of Aleppo),
(7) *Baʿlu Ṣapuni* (*Baʿlu* of the Mountain *Ṣapunu*),
(8) *Ṯarraṯiya*,

(9) *Yariḫu* (Moon),
(10) *Ṣapunu* (The Mountain *Ṣapunu*),
(11) *Kôṯaru* (Skillful),
(12) *ʿAṯtaru*,
(13) *ʾAṯiratu*,
(14) *Šagar-wa-ʾIṯum*,
(15) *Šapšu* (Sun),
(16) *Rašap-ʾIdrippi*,
(17) [---]MṢR,
(18) *Dadmiš*,
(19) [-(-)]MT,
(20) [...],
(21) [...],
(22) *ʾUšḫaraya*,
(23) *Gaṯaru* ?,
(24) *ʿAṯtartu*,
(25) *Tirāṯu* (Young Wine)
(26) *Maḏ(ḏ)ara*,
(27) *ʾIlū Qarîti* (Gods-of-the-City),
(28) *ʾIlū* M⸢-⸣[...] (Gods-of-Men and Gods-of-Women),
(29) *Ǵūrūma-wa-Tahāmātu* (Mountains-and-Waters-of-the-Abyss),
(30) *Yammu* (Sea),
(31) [--]⸢M⸣MR,
(32) *Su⸢ra⸣*[...],
(33) [...],
(34) *ʾIlū Dadmima* (Gods-of-the-Land-of-Aleppo),
(35) *ʾIlū* LB⸢-⸣N (Gods-of-*Labana*),
(36) *ʾUṯḫatu* (Censer),
(37) *Kinnāru* (Lyre),
(38) *Baʿluma* (another manifestation of *Baʿlu*),[15]
(39) *Baʿluma* (another manifestation of *Baʿlu*),
(40) *Baʿluma* (another manifestation of *Baʿlu*),
(41) *Baʿluma* (another manifestation of *Baʿlu*),
(42) *Malakūma* (Kings),
(43) *Šalimu*.

4. RS 24.246

This list was ruled by the scribe into two sections, and the contents of each section show the list to be truly bipartite: lines 1–14 correspond to a section of the sacrificial ritual text RS 1.001 (lines 13–19), translated below as text 17, while lines 15–28 constitute a separate and very distinctive list. That the names in the second list represent divinities is shown by the appearance of three of them in the sacrificial ritual RS 24.250+, also translated below (text 14). The entire list as such has not, however, appeared yet in a sacrificial ritual and, outside the case of text 14, none of the names has yet appeared separately. Moreover, the form of the names does not correspond to the general form of divine names in that these, like human names, contain a theophoric element, that is, the name of a deity, e.g., *ygbḥd* means "(the deity) *Haddu* is generous." On the other hand, these names differ from standard human names by the verbal form included in the name (e.g., /yargububaʿlu/, "*Baʿlu* is awesome," rather than /yargubbaʿlu/, "May *Baʿlu* be awesome" or "*Baʿlu* was awesome"). I have concluded that these names represent hypostases of the deity whose name furnishes the theophoric element, though any solution is presently very hypothetical (the reader should compare and contrast del Olmo Lete 1996 and Pardee 1998b; 2000a: 522–31). Note that a likely hypothesis regarding the divine elements in these names is that they represent hypostases of only two deities, *ʾIlu* and *Baʿlu*: the identification of *Baʿlu* as a title of *Haddu* has long been known, and such appears also to be the case of *Liʾmu*. *ʿAmmu* means "(divine) paternal uncle" and may refer to either *ʾIlu* or *Baʿlu*. Alternatively, there would be references to three divinities, with *ʿAmmu* constituting a reference to Dagan (this hypothesis is based on the prophetic formula *tūra Dagan*, "return O *Dagan*," known from the Mari texts, where the verb is another form of the same verb that occurs in *ʿAmmutāru*, "the Divine Uncle has returned"). If such were the case, these fourteen deities would represent hypostases of the deities occupying the second through fourth/tenth slots in the first list presented above (text 1, col. A [RS 1.017:3–11]). Because this second list consists of sentence names that have not yet appeared integrally in a sacrificial text, the names are translated below rather than transliterated. If this second list corresponded to a sacrificial ritual, that ritual had two major sections corresponding to the two sections that may be defined here by the repetition of names (note the semicolon after line 20 in the translation below). Or, if the names represent a divine genealogy, there are no repetitions of deities, only repetitions of names from one generation to another.

Text	***Vocalization (Translation)***
Obverse	
(1) *ỉl bt*	*ʾIlu-Bêti* (God-of-the-House),

(2) *ủšḫry*	*ʾUšḫaraya*,
(3) *ym . bʿl*	*Yammu* (Sea), *Baʿlu*,
(4) *yrḫ*	*Yariḫu* (Moon),
(5) *kṯr*	*Kôṯaru* (Skillful),
(6) *ṯrmn*	*Ṯarrumannu*,
(7) *pdry*	*Pidray* (Fatty),
(8) *dqt*	*Daqqītu*,
(9) *trṯ*	*Tirāṯu* (Young Wine),
(10) *ršp*	*Rašap*,
(11) *ʿnt ḫbly*	*ʿAnatu Ḫablay* (*ʿAnatu*-the-Mutilated),
(12) *špš pgr*	*Šapšu-Pagri* (*Šapšu*-of-the-Corpse),

Lower Edge

(13) ⌜*ỉ*⌝*ltm ḫnqtm*	*ʾIlatāma Ḫāniqatāma* (The Two Strangling-Goddesses),
(14) *yrḫ kṯy*	Kassite *Yariḫu* (Kassite Moon).

Reverse

---

(15) ⌜*y*⌝*gbḥd*	*Haddu* is generous,
(16) *yrgbbʿl*	*Baʿlu* is awesome,
(17) *ydbỉl*	*ʾIlu* is magnanimous,
(18) *yảršỉṣ*[16]	*ʾIlu* is concerned,
(19) *yrǵmỉl*	*ʾIlu* is compassionate,
(20) *ʿmtr*	*ʿAmmu* has returned;
(21) *ydbỉl*	*ʾIlu* is magnanimous,
(22) *yrgblỉm*	*Liʾmu* is awesome,
(23) *ʿmtr*	*ʿAmmu* has returned,
(24) *yảršỉl*	*ʾIlu* is concerned,
(25) *ydbbʿl*	*Baʿlu* is magnanimous,
(26) *yrǵmbʿl*	*Baʿlu* is compassionate,
(27) *ʿzbʿl*	*Baʿlu* is powerful,

Upper Edge

(28) *ydbḥd*	*Haddu* is magnanimous.

5. RS 4.474

An enigmatic text that has received a plethora of interpretations, RS 4.474 is divided into two principal sections by the presence of the preposition *b* ("by") before each of the entries in lines 12–18. Because of the formal characteristics in the first section that match it with the preceding deity lists and because the list in lines 1–4 matches the list of deities repeated in each paragraph of the sacrificial ritual in text 22 (RS 1.002), this text is here presented with the other deity lists. The deities in lines 1–4 represent a more-or-less standardized way of referring to *ʾIlu*'s immediate family, plausibly defined as he and his sons borne by *ʾAṯiratu*. This is borne out by the mention of "*ʾIlu* and *ʾAṯiratu*" after this standard list (line 5), the only mention of the couple as such in the ritual texts. Then follow five hypostases of *ʾIlu* in which his beneficence is stressed; the first three are expressed as abstractions, the last two as attributes (literally: "the solicitous god, the god who arises"). The first section closes with the mention of two hypostases of *Baʿlu* (though the reading of the first is disputed, it appears contextually certain), who was certainly not borne by *ʾAṯiratu* and may indeed have been viewed by the genealogists of Ugarit as a younger half-brother of *ʾIlu* (Pardee 1997a: 263 n. 190).

The second major section consists of a list of *ʾIlu*'s implements (apparently tools and weapons), with perhaps one abstract entity (the meaning of *ǵdyn*, the last element of the list itself, is uncertain). Each is specifically presented as agential by the prefixed preposition *b*, here interpreted as instrumental ("by"). The function of this second list is obscured by the uncertain reading of line 19 and, if the reading proposed be correct, by the ambiguity of the word *bn*: does it mean "sons of" or "he built"? In the former case, this would be the first attestation at Ugarit of a list of divinized implements, and the function of the prepositional formulation would be unclear; in the latter, the text may constitute one of the first specific references to *ʾIlu* as creator (cf. one of his titles in the mythological texts, *bny bnwt*, literally "he who builds descendants," usually taken as designating him as father of the gods).

Text	***Translation***
Obverse	
(1) *ỉl b⸢n⸣ ỉl*	*ʾIlu*, the sons of *ʾIlu*,
(2) *dr b⸢n⸣ ỉl*	the circle of the sons of *ʾIlu*,
(3) *mpḫrt bn ỉl*	the assembly of the sons of *ʾIlu*,
(4) *ṯrmn*[17] *w šnm*	*Ṯuk!amuna-wa-Šunama*;
(5) *ỉl w ảṯrt*	*ʾIlu* and *ʾAṯiratu*;
(6) *ḥnn ỉl*	the grace of *ʾIlu*,
(7) *nṣbt ỉl*	the solidity of *ʾIlu*,
(8) *šlm ỉl*	the well-being of *ʾIlu*;

(9) *ỉl ḥš ỉl* ⌜*n*⌝*dd*	solicitous ʾ*Ilu*, active ʾ*Ilu*;
(10) *b*ʿ?[18] *ṣpn b*ʿ*l*	*Ba*ʿ*lu* of *Ṣapunu*, *Ba*ʿ*lu*

Lower Edge

(11) *ủgrt*	of Ugarit;

Reverse

(12) *b mrḥ ỉl*	by ʾ*Ilu*'s blade,
(13) *b nỉt ỉl*	by ʾ*Ilu*'s axe,
(14) *b ṣmd ỉl*	by ʾ*Ilu*'s yoke,
(15) *b dṯn ỉl*	by ʾ*Ilu*'s crusher,
(16) *b šrp ỉl*	by ʾ*Ilu*'s fire,
(17) *b knt ỉl*	by ʾ*Ilu*'s foundation,
(18) *b ǵdyn* ⌜*ỉ*⌝*l*	by ʾ*Ilu*'s care

Upper Edge

(19) ⌜*b*⌝*n* ⌜*ỉl*⌝	did ʾ*Ilu* build.[19]

Notes

1. Pardee 2000a: 1091–1100 (Appendix II).
2.

RS 1.017 and parallels	RS 24.643:23-45 and parallels	Philo of Byblos
ỉlỉb	*ỉlỉb*	*Elioûn*
	ảrṣ w šmm	*Gê*, *Ouranos*
ỉl	*ỉl*	*Elos* = *Kronos*
	kṯrt	seven daughters
dgn	*dgn*	*Dagōn*

For the text of Philo of Byblos, see, e.g., Attridge and Oden 1981: 46–55. It has been claimed that the order of the elements in the divine name *ảrṣ w šmm* reflects Hurrian influence (see Archi 1993: 15) and that the very deity *ỉlỉb* owes his inclusion in the Ugaritic pantheon to Hurrian influence (ibid., 14–16); but since no Hurrian deity list reflects either of the orders attested in the two Ugaritic lists compared here, it appears more than likely that they represent Ugaritic rather than Hurrian theology.

3. *dbḥ ṣpn* is here clearly a heading (see the translation below of the sacrificial ritual [text 12] and the corresponding entry in text 58 [RS 19.015:3]) and so must be, therefore, the corresponding line of RS 1.017, which is to be translated "the gods of *Ṣapunu*," as most scholars have recognized (e.g., Koch 1993: 187).

4. Here and below, the {DINGIR}-sign is transliterated complete when it is used logographically (syllabic {DINGIR} = Ugaritic {ỉl} as part of the name) but with {^{d}} when it is used as a determinative (i.e., does not correspond to an ele-

ment of the name in Ugaritic). Syllabic signs used phonetically are in italics; those used as logograms or as determinatives are in roman script.

5. Because various scholars have adopted uncritically the restoration of only one token of {bˁlm} in this line, it is necessary to repeat here that there is no epigraphic reason for not restoring two: Pardee 1992: 160; 2000b: 67; forthcoming b.

6. Though the text of RS 24.643 is damaged here, it appears plausible that the same deities appear as in the parallel texts but in a different order, that is, *ˁṯtr* was placed after *yrḫ* rather than after *pdry*. In any case, this entry and the three following do not correspond to the facing entries.

7. The line numbers are those of col. 1.

8. The syllabic version of lines 6–11 may be translated "Weather-god 2," "Weather-god 3," etc.

9. This syllabic text is as yet unedited; the transliteration provided here was kindly provided to me by D. Arnaud in November of 1995. For a new translation of the much more fragmentary syllabic text RS 26.142, see Arnaud 1994.

10. *bˁl ḫlb* probably corresponds to one of the *bˁlm* in lines 6–11 of text 1A and B (RS 1.017/RS 24.264+).

11. {DINGIR.E.NI} corresponds surely to the Sumerian word for "god" (DINGIR) used as a determinative plus the Hurrian word *eni*, "god," which is written {ỉn} in the Hurro-Ugaritic bilingual texts (here as below, texts 25–28) and in the monolingual Hurrian texts written in alphabetic cuneiform (Laroche 1968). Because the Ugaritic entry has in each case disappered, it is impossible to know whether the word was transliterated as {ỉn} or translated into Ugaritic and written {ỉl}, as was done below in the case of the Sumerian logograms {DINGIR.MEŠ} (RS 92.2004:35 = RS 24.643:43 {ỉl}, restored on the same pattern in RS 24.643:42–43).

12. *knr* is here indicated in parentheses because the restoration cannot be considered certain in RS 24.643:43; that is, it must be judged possible that this name was omitted from that rite.

13. On the absence of the last two deities in RS 24.643 (middle column), see below, section II, n. 34.

14. The line numbers are those of col. 1, though the vocalization is that of the Ugaritic name, where it is known.

15. In contrast with the syllabic version of text 1 (col. C), where the additional manifestations of the weather deity followed immediately after *Baˁlu* of *Ṣapunu* and were numbered from "2" to "7," here the syllabic version omits the numeral, uses a different logogram for the divinity, and separates these four manifestations from the three who were named above (lines 6–8).

16. Read {yảršỉl}.

17. Read {ṯk!mn}.

18. The form of the third sign of this name is not proper for any one sign. The reading of {l} is from context.

19. The problems of this translation must be stressed: the reading of the line is uncertain, and the writing of a III-Y verb without {y} is not, though attested, common.

11

Prescriptive Sacrificial Rituals

THERE HAS BEEN A DEBATE whether the Ugaritic ritual texts are in nature prescriptive or descriptive. My definition of the vast majority of these texts as prescriptive in nature is based essentially on their grammatical and formal structure. Virtually all verbal forms are expressed imperfectively or imperatively rather than declaratively (Pardee 2000a: 189–90 [on RS 1.003:37 *ʿly*], 221–22 [on RS 1.005:1 *tʿrb*], 494–96 [on RS 19.015:1 *ykl*]) and, with rare apparent exceptions, the internal chronology of texts that are chronologically arranged is linear through a day, two days, a month, or two months (for the case that has been taken as a notable exception, see below text 15 [RS 1.003:38–48]). First, texts covering a month or two months are presented below, in the order of the months of the year, then those covering a shorter period, then those without an explicit or implicit time frame. The Ugaritic months of the Ugaritic year as presently known are:[1]

nql	Sept.–Oct.	Fall equinox
mgmr (*magmaru*)	Oct.–Nov.	
pgrm (*pagrūma*)/*dbḫ* (*dabḫu*)	Nov.–Dec.	
ỉbʿlt (*ʾibʿaltu*)	Dec.–Jan.	Winter solstice
ḫyr (*ḫiyyāru*)	Jan.–Feb.	
ḫlt (*ḫallatu*)	Feb.–Mar.	
gn	Mar.–Apr.	Spring equinox
ỉṯb	Apr.–May	
?	May–June	
?	June–July	Summer solstice

ʾiṯtbnm	July–Aug.
riʾš yn	Aug.–Sept.

These texts are characterized by their laconic formulations, by the occasionally bewildering reversal of the order of mention of the sacrifice and its divine recipient, and by the use of standard terms for offerings and for sacrificial categories. From this text and those that will follow, it is clear that the primary act of the Ugaritic cult was the offering of bloody sacrifices and other offerings to deities. Not stated, however, are (1) the details of how the offerings were performed, (2) from whose assets they originated and whose assets they became, and (3) the function of each offering and sacrificial category, that is, the "theology" of the cult. Most such details may only be deduced from the structure of the texts and from comparisons with other cultures.

RITUALS FOR A SINGLE MONTH

Under this heading are presented several texts that contain indications of a series of rites arranged in chronological sequence during a portion of a single month or the entirety thereof. If the beginning of the tablet is lost, we have no way of knowing whether the month name was present or with what day of the month the series began. If the end of the text is lost, we cannot know whether the chronological span was limited to a single month.

6. RS 1.009/RS 24.253/RS 24.284
(month name lost or never indicated)

These three texts are clearly related, but the detailed circumstances of the rites and the relationships of the rites represented by the three texts are impossible to determine. What is clear is that the best-preserved tablet, RS 24.253 (text B), never bore more than a portion of the monthly sequence (days 14, 15, and 17) and that RS 1.009 (text A), now only a fragment, once contained a longer series that probably covered the major festivals of a single month, while RS 24.284 (text C) represents only a full-moon festival that corresponds in general to the first six sections of the full-moon festival recorded in RS 24.253 (text B). The three tablets are presented here together because RS 1.009:10–17 once contained a text identical, or virtually so, to that of RS 24.253:1–14, while the basic structure of RS 24.284 is in its entirety parallel to that of RS 24.253:1–18, though not all details match.

A. RS 1.009[2]

Text

Obverse

(1) [ ]ṯ . slḫ . npš ṯʿ w ⸢ṯ⸣[n] ⸢k⸣bdm
(2) [ ]mm . ṯn šm . w ảlp . l [ʿ]⸢nt⸣ .
(3) [ ]š . ỉl š . bʿl š . dgn š
(4) [ʿṯ]⸢t⸣r . w ʿṯtpl . gdlt . ⸢ṣ⸣pn . dqt
(5) [ảl]⸢p⸣ ʿnt . gdlt . b ṯlṯ tmrm
(6) [ỉ]l š . bʿl š . ảṯrt . š . ym š . ⸢bʿ⸣l knp ⸢g⸣[…]
(7) [ ]⸢g⸣dlt . ṣpn . dqt . šrp . w šlmm
(8) [ả]⸢l⸣p . l bʿl . w ảṯrt . ʿṣrm . l ỉnš
(9) [ỉlm .]⸢t⸣ . l b b⸢t⸣m . gdlt . ʿrb špš w ḥl
(10) [mlk . b ảr]bʿt . ʿ[š]rt . yrtḥṣ . mlk . brr
(11) [b ym . ml]ảt . y⸢ql⸣n . ảl⸢pm⸣ . yrḫ . . ʿšrt
(12) [l bʿl . ṣ]⸢p⸣n . ⸢d⸣[q]⸢t⸣m . w ⸢y⸣[n]⸢t⸣ qrt
(13) [w mtnt]⸢m⸣[. w š]⸢l⸣ rm[š .] kbd . w š
(14) [l šlm . kbd . ảl]⸢p⸣ . w š . ⸢l⸣ bʿl . ṣpn
(15) [dqt l . ṣpn . šrp] . w š⸢l⸣mm . kmm
(16) [w b bt . bʿl . ủgrt .] ⸢k⸣k⸢d⸣m . w npš
(17) [ỉlỉb . gdlt . ỉl š . b]⸢ʿ⸣[l .] ⸢š⸣ . ʿnt ṣpn
(18) [ảlp w š … šrp]

....

Reverse[3]

....

(19') […]⸢-⸣r
(20') […]
(21') […]
(22') […]
(23') […]
(24') […]
(25') […]
(26') […]⸢-⸣
(27') […]
(28') […]
(29') […]⸢-⸣

(30') […]
(31') […]
(32') […]

(33') […]⌜-⌝
(34') […]
(35') […]
(36') […]*m*
(37') […]

Upper Edge

(38') […] . *ả*[*p* .] *w* ⌜*npš*⌝ […]

Translation[4]

IA. (1) […]Ṯ SLḪ, a neck as a *ṯ*ʿ-sacrifice.
B. And t[wo] livers (2) […].
C. […]MM[5]: two rams and a bull for [ʿ*A*]*natu*.
D. (3) […][6] a ram;
for ʾ*Ilu* a ram;
for *Baʿlu* a ram;[7]
for *Dagan* a ram;
(4) [… for ʿ*Aṯ*]*taru* and ʿ*Aṯtapal* a cow;
for *Ṣapunu* a ewe;
(5) [… a bul]l;
for ʿ*Anatu* a cow.
IIA. On the third day of the month : dates
(6) [… (for) ʾ*I*]*lu* a ram;
for *Baʿlu* a ram;
for ʾ*Aṯiratu* a ram;
for *Yammu* a ram;
for *Baʿlu-Kanapi* a c[ow;]
(7) […] a cow;
for *Ṣapunu* a ewe as a burnt-offering.
B. And as a peace-offering: (8) [… [8] a bu]ll for *Baʿlu* and ʾ*Aṯiratu*; two birds for the ʾ*Ināšu*-(9)[ʾ*Ilīma*.]
C. […]T within the temple a cow.
D. When the sun sets, [the king] will be free (of further cultic obligations).

III. (10) [On the fo]urt[e]enth day, the king will wash himself clean.

IVA. (11) [On the day of the full] moon, two bulls are to “fall” (be felled) for *Yariḫu*.

B. A feast (12) [for *Baʿlu* of *Ṣa*]*punu:* two e[we]s and a city-d[ov]e;
(13) [and two kidneys and a ram] for RM[Š];
a liver and a ram (14) [for *Šalimu*.

C. A liver (of?) a bul]l and a ram for *Baʿlu* of *Ṣapunu;*
(15) [a ewe for *Ṣapunu* as a burnt-offering.]

D. And as a peace-offering: the same.

E. (16) [And in the temple of *Baʿlu* of Ugarit:] some/two KKD and a neck;
(17) [for *ʾIluʾibī* a cow;
for *ʾIlu* a ram;
for *Ba*]*ʿlu* a ram;
for *ʿAnatu* of *Ṣapunu* (18) [a bull and a ram . . . as a burnt-offering.]

....

(19'-37') […]
(38') […] a sno[ut] and a neck[…]

B. RS 24.253

Text

Obverse

(1) *b ảrbʿt . ʿšr*[*t*]
(2) *yrtḥṣ . mlk .* ⸢*b*⸣[*rr*]
(3) *b ym . mlảt*
(4) *tqln . ảlpm .*
(5) *yrḫ . ʿšrt . l bʿ*[*l . ṣpn*]
(6) *dqtm . w ynt . qr*[*t*]
(7) *w mtntm .* ⸢*w*⸣ *š l rm*⸢*š*⸣
(8) *w kbd . w š . l šlm* ⸢*k*⸣*bd*
(9) *ảlp . w š . l bʿl ṣpn*
(10) *dqt l ṣpn . šrp . w šlmm*
(11) *kmm . w b bt . bʿl . ủgrt*
(12) *kkdm . w npš . ỉlỉb*
(13) *gdlt . ỉl š . bʿl š . ʿnt*

(14) *ṣpn . ảlp . w š . pdry š*
(15) *šrp . w šlmm ỉlỉb š*
(16) *bʿl ủgrt š . bʿl ḫlb š*
(17) *yrḫ š . ʿnt ṣpn . ảlp*
(18) *w š . pdry š . ddmš . š*
(19) *w b ủrbt . ỉlỉb š*

Lower Edge

(20) *bʿl . ảlp w š*

Reverse

(21) *dgn . š . ỉl tʿd̲r*
(22) *bʿl š . ʿnt š . ršp š*
(23) *šlmm .*

---

(24) *w šnpt . ỉl š*
(25) *l ʿnt . ḥlš . t̲n šm*
(26) *l gt̲rm . ǵṣb šmảl*
(27) *d ảlpm . w ảlp* ⌜*w*⌝ *š*
(28) *šrp . w šlmm kmm*
(29) *l bʿl . ṣpn b ʿrʿr*
(30) *pảmt t̲lt̲m . š l qẓrt*
(31) *t̲lḥn . bʿlt . bhtm*
(32) *ʿlm* ⌜.⌝ *ʿlm . gdlt . l bʿl*
(33) *ṣpn . ḫlb* ⌜*. w kb*⌝*d .* ⌜*d*⌝*[q]*⌜*t*⌝
(34) *l ṣpn* ⌜*. --(-)*⌝ *[.]* ⌜*b*⌝*ʿl . ủ*⌜*g*⌝*[rt ...]*
(35) *ỉlỉb . g*⌜*dlt .*⌝ *bʿ*⌜*l*⌝*[...]*
(36) *ủgr*⌜*t*⌝ *[-ˀ] [ʿ]*⌜*nt ṣ*⌝*pn [...]*
(37) ⌜*ʿ*⌝*š*⌜*l*⌜*-*⌝*[...]*

Translation

Obverse

IA. (1) On the fourteen[th day of the month] (2) the king will wash himself c[lean].

IIA. (3) On the day of the full moon (4) two bulls are to "fall" (be felled) (5) for *Yariḫu*.

B. A feast for *Baʿ[lu* of *Ṣapunu:]* (6) two ewes and a cit[y] dove; (7) and two kidneys and a ram for RM⌜Š⌝; (8) and a liver and a ram for *Šalimu*.

C. A liver (9) (of?) a bull and a ram for *Baʿlu* of *Ṣapunu;*
(10) a ewe for *Ṣapunu* as a burnt-offering.

D. And as a peace-offering: (11) the same.

E. And in the temple of *Baʿlu* of Ugarit: (12) some/two KKD and a neck;
for *ʾIluʾibī* (13) a cow;
for *ʾIlu* a ram;
for *Baʿlu* a ram;
for *ʿAnatu* of (14) *Ṣapunu* a bull and a ram;
for *Pidray* a ram (15) as a burnt-offering.

F. And as a peace-offering: for *ʾIluʾibī* a ram;
(16) for *Baʿlu* of Ugarit a ram;
for *Baʿlu* of Aleppo a ram;
(17) for *Yariḫu* a ram;
for *ʿAnatu* of *Ṣapunu* a bull (18) and a ram;
for *Pidray* a ram;
for *Dadmiš* a ram.

G. (19) And in the opening: for *ʾIluʾibī* a ram;
(20) for *Baʿlu* a bull and a ram;
(21) for *Dagan* a ram;
for the Auxiliary-Gods-of-(22) *Baʿlu* a ram;
for *ʿAnatu* a ram;
for *Rašap* a ram (23) as a peace-offering.

H. (24) And as a presentation-offering: for *ʾIlu* a ram.

I. (25) For *ʿAnatu*-ḪLŠ two rams;
(26) for the *Gaṯarūma* the left ǴṢB of (27) two bulls and a bull and a ram
(28) as a burnt-offering.

J. And as a peace-offering: the same;
(29) for *Baʿlu* of *Ṣapunu*, among the tamarisk(s), (30) thirty times;
a ram for the QẒRT (31) of the table of *Baʿlatu-Bahatīma*.

IIIA. (32) On the day after next: a cow for *Baʿlu* (33) of *Ṣapunu;*
one/some ḪLB and a liver (of?) a e[w]e (34) for *Ṣapunu;*
[X-offering for?] *Baʿlu* of Uga[rit ...].

B. (35) For *ʾIluʾibī* a cow;
for *Baʿlu* of (36) Ugarit [a ram;
for A]nat of *Ṣapunu* [X-offering] (37) ⸢ʿ⸣ ŠL⸢-⸣[...].[9]

C. RS 24.284[10]

Text

Obverse

(1) *b ym ảlpm* ⸢-⸣[...]
(2) *nbšt . yrḫ l b*ˁ⸢*l*⸣ [*ṣpn*]
(3) *dqtm* ⸢*w*⸣ *ynt qr*[*t*]
(4) *l* ⸢*ṯ*ˁ .⸣ *mttm . l* ⸢*ṯ*⸣ˁ
(5) *w kbdm . l k*⸢-⸣[...]
(6) *rmš š . w š šl*[*m*]

---

(7) *l b*[ˁ]*l ṣpn ảlp* ⸢*w*⸣ [*š*]
(8) *šr*⸢*p*⸣ *.* ˁ*ṣr l ṣp*⸢*n*⸣
(9) *w* ⸢*š*⸣[*lm*]⸢*m*⸣ *. l b*⸢ˁ⸣*l* ⸢*ṣ*⸣[*pn*]
(10) *ảl*⸢*p w*⸣ *š . l ṣp*[*n* ˁ*ṣr*]

---

(11) *bt* ⸢*b*⸣[ˁ*l*] ⸢*ủ*⸣*gr*⸢*t*⸣
(12) ⸢*l*⸣ [*ỉl*]⸢*ỉ*⸣*b . g*⸢*d*⸣[*lt*]

Lower Edge

(13) [...]
(14) [...]

Reverse

(15) ⸢*l*⸣ *š*⸢-⸣[...]
(16) *l b*ˁ[*l š*]
(17) *l* ⸢-⸣[...]
(18) *l* [ˁ*nt ṣpn*]
(19) ⸢*ả*⸣[*lp w š*]
(20) *l* [*pdr*(*y*)[11] *š šrp*]

---

(21) *w* ⸢*šl*⸣[*mm*]
(22) *l ỉl*⸢*ỉ*⸣[*b š*]
(23) *l b*ˁ*l* ⸢*ủ*⸣[*grt š*]
(24) *l b*ˁ⸢*l*⸣ *ḫlb* [*š*]
(25) *l yrḫ š*
(26) *l* ˁ*nt ṣpn*

Upper Edge

(27) *ảlp w š*
(28) *l pdr š*

Left Edge

(29) ⌜*l*⌝ *ddm*[!]⌜*š*.⌝ *š*

Translation

IA. (1) In the day,[12] two bulls [...] (2) (one/some/as) NBŠT[13] for *Yariḫu*.

B. For *Baʿlu* of [*Ṣapunu*] (3) two ewes and[?] a cit[y] dove— (4) it is a *ṯʿ*-sacrifice;
two kidneys, also as a *ṯʿ*-sacrifice;
(5) and two livers for K⌜-⌝[...];
(6) for RMŠ a ram
and a ram for *Šali*[*mu*.]

C. (7) For *Ba*[*ʿ*]*lu* of *Ṣapunu* a bull and [a ram] (8) as a burnt-offering;
a bird for *Ṣapunu*.

D. (9) And as a p[eace off]ering: for *Baʿlu* of *Ṣa*[*punu*] (10) a bull and a ram;
for *Ṣapu*[*nu* a bird.]

E. (11) In the temple of *Ba*[*ʿlu* of] Ugarit: (12) for [*ʾIlu*]*ʾibī* a c[ow;]
(13) [...]
(14) [...]
(15) [fo]r Š⌜-⌝[...]
(16) for *Ba*[*ʿlu* a ram;]
(17) for [...]
(18) for [*ʿAnatu* of *Ṣapunu*] (19) a b[ull and a ram;]
(20) for [*Pidar/Pidray* a ram as a burnt-offering.]

F. (21) And as a peace-o[ffering]:
(22) for *ʾIluʾi*[*bī* a ram;]
(23) for *Baʿlu* of U[garit a ram;]
(24) for *Baʿlu* of Aleppo [a ram;]
(25) for *Yariḫu* a ram;
(26) for *ʿAnatu* of *Ṣapunu* (27) a bull and a ram;
(28) for *Pidar* a ram;
(29) [fo]r *Dadm*[!]*iš* a ram.

7. RS 24.248

(month name lost or never indicated)

Because of the damaged state of this tablet and because of several peculiar features (e.g., the fact that the text begins with the word *i͗ršt*, "request"), it is impossible to determine just what rite is reflected here. It is included in this collection because of the certain mention in line 15 of "the tenth day," alongside the plausible readings/restorations of "the eighth day" in line 7 and possibly of the "ninth (day)" in line 11. The presence of the verb "to consume" in line 3 indicates that foodstuffs of some kind were involved, the mention of "outfits" may be taken as denoting rites of clothing the deities, the "lodges" as denoting a rite in which the deities are temporarily installed in "booths" (cf. text 15 [RS 1.003:50–51]).

Text

Obverse

(1) *i͗ršt*[...]
(2) *d i͗lm* . *p*⌜-⌝[...]
————x⌜-⌝[...]
(3) *d* . *ykl* . ⌜*b*⌝ [...]
(4) *ṯl*⌜*ṯ*⌝*m*⌜-⌝[...]
(5) ⌜*ʿš*⌝*r*[...]

---

(6) *w n*⌜*p*⌝*ṣ*⌜-⌝[...]
(7) *b ym* ⌜---⌝[...]
(8) *w spl* ⌜*b*-⌝[...]

---

(9) *w ṯt k*[...]
(10) *w a͗*⌜*rb*⌝[*ʿ* ...]

---

(11) *w b tš*⌜-⌝[...]
(12) *ytn š qd*⌜*š*⌝[...]
(13) *bt d*⌜-⌝*n w bt b*⌜-⌝[...]
(14) *w bt šr*

---

(15) *w b ym ʿšr*
(16) *tpnn* . *npṣm* . *ḫm*[*n*]*ḫ*

Lower Edge

---

(17) *w t<u>t</u>* ⌜.⌝ *ḫd<u>t</u>n*

Reverse

(18) *<u>t</u>nm . w ḫd<u>t</u>h*

(19) *tdn . ḫmt*

(20) *w tštn <u>t</u>nm*

---

(21) *w mbt ỉlm . <u>t</u>m*[...]

(22) *<u>t</u>mn . <u>t</u>mn* ⌜.⌝ *gml*[...]

(23) *<u>t</u>mn ủr*⌜-⌝[...]

(24) *w l p*[...]

---

(25) *w*[...]

(26) *<u>t</u>*⌜-⌝[...]

(27) *l*[...]

---

(28) *ḫ*⌜-⌝[...]

(29) *<u>t</u>l*⌜*<u>t</u>t*⌝[...]

Translation

I. (1) Request[...] (2) of the gods [...].

---

(3) What is to be consumed [...] (4) thirty [...] (5) ten/twenty[...].

II. (6) And an outfit[...] (7) on day eight[...][14] (8) and a *spl*-type pot [...].

---

(9) Two [...] (10) and fou[r ...].

III. (11) And in the nin[th? (day?) ...] (12) one must give a ram of/to the sanctuary[...]
(13) the temple of *Ditānu* and the temple of B[...] (14) and the temple of ŠR.[15]

IV. (15) And on day ten, (16) you will transfer the outfits to the ḪMN-sanctuary.

---

(17) You will again furnish (some), (18) twice (i.e., two of each); then again (19) you will bring them near (20) and you will place them twice (i.e., the two of them, each as appropriate).[16]

---

(21) And the seats/lodges![17] of the gods, eigh[t ...] (22) eight, eight GML (23) eight ʾUR[...] (24) and to P[...].

---

(25) And[...] (26) [...] (27) [...]

---

(28) [...] (29) three[...].

8. RS 24.256

(month name lost)

The series of rites prescribed in this text extended from the first day of the month to the seventeenth, and the king is said to be directly involved in most of them and probably participated in all (the directive to bathe on the thirteenth implies royal participation in the full-moon festival, even though that participation is not explicitly mentioned). On the first day of the month, the children of the king made up a procession that was repeated seven times. This, then, is one of the rituals most closely associated with the royal family, and it probably took place in the palace sanctuaries, though that is not stated explicitly. The deities honored during these rites are particularly associated with the royal house, two titularly (*Baʿlatu-Bahatīma*, "The-Lady-of-the-Palace," and *Bittu-Bêti*, "The-Daughter-of-the-House," perhaps *ʾIlatu-Magdali*, "The-Goddess-of-the-Tower," as well), others by association (*ʿAṯtartu-Ḫurri* and the *Gaṯarūma* ritually "enter" the royal palace, and the king is the principal officiant in text 18 [RS 1.005]), while the *ʾInāšu-ʾIlīma* plausibly represent the departed ancestors. As in text 18, so here statuettes of deities were moved from one location to another. It would be useful to know in which month the king was so involved in cultic activity, but, contrary to accepted opinion in recent years, the month name in line 1 cannot yet be restored.

Text

Obverse

(1) *b yrḫ* . ⸢-⸣[...]

---

(2) *ḥdṯ* . *ḫdrġl* . *r*[...]

---

(3) *ṯn šm* . *ḫmnh* . *w ṯq*⸢*l*⸣[...]
(4) *ksp* . *w ṣʿ rgbt* . *l bʿ*⸢*l*⸣[*t*]
(5) *bht*⟨.⟩*m š ʿṣrm l h*⸢*n*⸣[*š*][18]
(6) *ỉ*⸢*l*⸣*m* . *w bn mlk w b*⸢*n*⸣[*t*]
(7) *mlk* . *tʿln* . *pảmt šbʿ*
(8) *b ṯlṯ* . *tʿln* . *ỉlm b ḫmn*
(9) [*ʿ*]*rb špš w ḥl mlk* .
(10) [*b*] ⸢*š*⸣*b*⸢*ʿ*⸣ *ym* . *ḥdṯ* . *yrtḫṣ*
(11) [*ml*]*k* . *b*⸢*r*⸣*r* . *b ṯmnt* . *ỉy*⸢-⸣*m*
(12) *ảkl* . *ṯql ksp* . *w kd*
(13) *yn* . *l ʿṯtrt ḫr* . *b ʿšt*
(14) *ʿšrh* . *ṣbả špš w ḥ*

Lower Edge

(15) *l mlk* . *b ṯlṯt*
(16) *ʿšrt* . *yrtḫṣ m*

Reverse

(17) *lk* . *brr* . *b ảrbʿt*
(18) *ʿšrt* . *yrdn* . *gṯrm*
(19) *mṣdh* . *ṯn šm l gṯrm*
(20) *w rgm* . *gṯrm yṯṯb* .
(21) ⸢*w*⸣ *qdš* . *yšr* . *b ḫmš ʿ*
(22) ⸢*š*⸣*rh* . *šnpt* . *ỉl š* . *bʿ*⸢*l ṣ*⸣
(23) *pn š* . *bʿl ủgrt š* . *ṯ*⸢*n*⸣ [*šm*]
(24) *l ảṯrt* . *ṯn šm* . *l bt bt* [...]
(25) *ỉl*⸢*t mg*⸣*dl š* . *w ảġt*[...]
(26) *w šbʿ* . *gdlt* . *w ảr*⸢*b*⸣[*ʿ*]
(27) *ʿšrh* . *dqt* . *b ṯ*⸢*ṯ*⸣[*t ʿš*]
(28) *rt š l bt bt* . *w* ⸢-⸣[...]
(29) *b šbʿt ʿšr*[*t* ...]
(30) *ỉln* . *ṯ*⸢*lṯ*-⸣[...]
(31) ⸢-(?)--⸣[-]⸢---⸣[...]

Upper Edge

(32) *l*⌜-⌝[-(-)]*d*⌜-⌝[…]

Translation

IA. (1) In the month of [X, on the day of]

---

(2) the new moon, ḪḎRǴL R[…];[19]
(3) two rams in the ḪMN-sanctuary, and a shekel of (4) silver, and a bowl of dirt-clods[20] for *Baʿlatu*-(5)*Bahatīma;*
a ram and two birds for *ʾInāšu*-(6)*ʾIlīma*.

B. Then the sons of the kings and the daugh[ters of] (7) the king will ascend seven times.[21]

IIA. (8) On the third day, the gods ascend to the ḪMN-sanctuary.[22]

B. (9) When the sun sets, the king will be free (of further cultic obligations).

III. (10) [On the s]eventh day after the new moon, the [kin]g (11) will wash himself clean.

IV. On day eight?, two/some ʾIY[-],[23] (12) food (grain?), a shekel of silver, and a jar (13) of wine for *ʿAṯtartu Ḫurri*.

V. On the elev(14)enth day, when the sun rises, the (15) king will be free (of further cultic obligations).

VI. On the thir(16)teenth day, the [kin]g will wash (17) himself clean.

VIIA. On the four(18)teenth day, the *Gaṯarāma* will descend to the (19) MṢD;

B. two rams for the *Gaṯarāma*,

C. (20) and the recitation of the *Gaṯarāma* is to be repeated,[24]

D. (21) and the *qdš*-official will sing.

VIII. On the fift(22)eenth day, as a presentation-offering, for *ʾIlu* a ram;
for *Baʿlu* of *Ṣapu*(23)*nu* a ram;
for *Baʿlu* of Ugarit a ram;
two [rams] (24) for *ʾAṯiratu;*
two rams for *Bittu-Bêti* […];
for *ʾIlatu-Magdali* a ram, and ʾAǴT[…], (26) and seven cows and fou[r](27)teen ewes.

IX. On the six[teen](28)th day, a ram for *Bittu Bêti*, and[…].

X. (29) On the seventee[nth] day […] ʾILN, three/thirt[y …].
[…]

9. RS 24.276

(month name lost or never indicated)

This text is too badly damaged to permit a structural analysis. It is included here because of the clear indications of a chronological sequence (lines 15', 18', and 20') similar to that of the full-moon festival as prescribed in text 15 (RS 1.003/RS 18.056).

Text	***Translation***
Obverse	
(1') [...]⸢-*k*⸣[...]	
(2') [...]⸢*ả*⸣*n*⸢*p* .⸣[...]	
(3') [...]*ršp* . g⸢*d*⸣[*lt* ...]	[...] *Rašap* a c[ow ...]
(4') [...]⸢-⸣*by* . *bš*ʿ⸢-⸣[...]	
(5') [...]⸢-⸣ . *ršp* . *ả*[...]	[...] *Rašap* [...]
(6') [...]⸢-⸣*mt* . *yṣ*⸢*ỉ*⸣[...]	[...] he must exit[...]
(7') [...]	
(8') *š*⸢-⸣[...]	
(9') *k*[...]	
(10') *ḫ*[...]	
(11') ⸢-⸣[...]	
....	
Reverse	
....	
(12') [-]⸢*lỉ*⸣[...]	
(13') [-]⸢-⸣ . *ủ*[...]	
(14') [-]⸢*k*⸣*m*[...]	
(15') [*b ḫ*]*mš*[...]	[On the fi]fth day[...]
(16') [-]⸢-⸣*y* . *ỉ*[...]	
(17') ⸢*w*⸣ *ml*⸢*k*⸣[...]	And the king[...]
(18') *b ṯdṯ* . ⸢-⸣[...]	On the sixth day [...]
(19') ʿ*lyh* . ⸢-⸣[...]	in/to the upper room a [cow. The recitation][25]
(20') *yṯṯb* . *b š*[...]	will be repeated. On the se[venth day ...]
(21') *ym* . *w yṣ*[...]	the day. And EXI[T. X]
(22') ⸢*t*⸣*dn* . ʿ*r*⸢*b*⸣[...]	you will bring near. When [the sun] set[s ...]

(23') [-(-)]*tštn* . *ḫ*⸢-⸣[...]	[ ]you will place [...].

10. RS 24.298
(month name lost)

Only a fragment remains of this text, but, as it comes from the upper left-hand corner of the tablet and illustrates the common indication of the month name at the beginning of a series of sacrificial rituals, it is included here. Unfortunately, only a trace remains of the name itself, and it cannot be restored with any degree of certainty. If the sign is {n}, the restoration of {nql}, a known month name, would be likely, but the remaining head of a wedge may as well be read {ả}. Since the names of all the months of the year are not known, it is hazardous to settle on a single restoration. If the original text bore *nql*, this text would represent a sacrificial liturgy for the first month of the year distinct from the one indicated in text 15 (RS 1.003:48-55).

Text	***Translation***
Obverse	
(1) *b yrḫ* . ⸢-⸣[...]	In the month of[...]
(2) *ỉlỉb* . g⸢*d*⸣[*lt* ...]	*ʾIluʾibī* a c[ow ...]
(3) *py* . *ṯn* ⸢.⸣ [...]	PY two[...]
(4) *šrp* . ⸢*w*⸣ [...]	as a burnt-offering. And [as a peace-offering ...]
(5) *gd*⸢*l*⸣[*t* ...]	a c[ow ...]
(6) ⸢-*l*⸣[...]	

RITUALS FOR TWO MONTHS

Two of the texts classified under this heading, presented together as text 15 (RS 1.003/RS 18.056), explicitly refer to a following month, while the others, more fragmentary or without specific indications of extending over two months, are placed here for various structural reasons that will be indicated in the introduction to each text.

11. RS 24.249

(*ʾIbaʿlatu* ? – *Ḫiyyāru*)

One of the edges, either the upper or the lower, was broken from this tablet. This has removed one of the sets of data for determining the obverse-reverse orientation. Because the text on one of the surfaces begins *yrḫ* X, "In the month of . . . ," an apparent opening line for a monthly sacrificial liturgy, previous editors have identified that side as the obverse. Two principal features speak against this orientation, however: (1) what is here indicated as the obverse is the flatter of the two sides;[26] (2) in extending line 22' around the right edge of the tablet and onto the opposite surface, the scribe curved the signs so as to avoid the end of line 5', incised a line in the clay to separate these signs from the ends of lines 5' and 6', and wrote the last three signs squeezed in under the last two signs of line 6'. It is thus clear that what is here identified as the obverse was written before the text on the other side, which means that *yrḫ ḫyr b ym ḥdṯ*, "In the month of *Ḫiyyāru*, on the day of the new moon," in line 15' is, in some sense, in the middle of the text. One plausible interpretation of such a sequence is that the tablet once bore a series of rites meant to be enacted over the course of two months, in this case the two months following the winter equinox. Because, however, the first lines of the obverse have been lost, there is no way of determining with certainty the temporal context of the directives that have been preserved. The principal argument against the two-month interpretation is the presence of the deity *Ḫiyyāru* in the text on the obverse, for this name is best known as a month name. Sacrifices to the deity identified with the following month could only be interpreted as somehow leading up to that month. If such is the case, the sequence of days indicated on the obverse only by the repeated adverb *ʿlm . . . ʿlm*, "on the next day . . . on the day after that," would plausibly have occurred during the last days of the preceding month, that of *ʾIbʿalatu* (December–January).

Text

Obverse

(1') [-]*ǵb . ršp mḫbn š*

(2') *šrp . w ṣp ḫršḫ*

(3') *ʿlm . b ǵb ḫyr*

(4') *ṯmn l ṯlṯm ṣỉn*
(5') *šbʿ ảlpm*

(6') *bt . bʿl . ủgrt . ṯn šm*

(7') *ʿlm . l ršp . mlk* —-[27]

(8') *ảlp w š . l bʿlt*

(9') *bwtm š . ỉṯtqb*

(10') *w š . nbkm w . š*
(11') *gt mlk š . ʿlm*

Lower Edge
(12') *l kṯr . ṯn . ʿlm*
(13') *tzǵ⌜m⌝ . ṯn šm pr*
(14') *ḫz*

Reverse
(15') *yrḫ . ḫyr . b ym ḥdṯ*

(16') *ảlp . w š . l bʿlt bhtm*

(17') *b ảrbʿt ʿšrt . bʿl*
(18') *ʿrkm*

(19') *b ṯmnt . ʿšrt . yr*
(20') *tḫṣ . mlk brr*

(21') *ʿlm . tzǵ . b ǵb . ṣpn*

(22') *nskt . ksp . w ḫrṣ ṯt ṯn šm l bt bt*

(23') *ảlp . w š šrp . ảlp šlmm .*
(24') *l bʿl . ʿṣr l ṣpn*

(25') *npš . w š . l ršp bbt*

(26') ⸢ʿ⸣*ṣrm l* ⸢*ỉ*⸣*nš* ⸢*ỉ*⸣*lm*

(27') [---]⸢-⸣[ ]*dqt*⸢*m*⸣

....

Translation

I. (1') [In] the sacrificial pit of *Rašap*-MHBN: a ram (2') as a burnt-offering and a plated bowl?.

IIA. (3') On the next day, in the sacrificial pit of *Ḫiyyāru*: (4') thirty-eight sheep/goats (5') and seven bulls.

B. (6') In the temple of *Baʿlu* of Ugarit: two rams.

III. (7') On the next day, for *Rašap*-MLK (8') a bull and a ram; for *Baʿlatu* -(9')*Bah*!*atīma* a ram from *ʾIṯṯaqabu* (10') and a ram from *Nakabūma* and a ram from (11') *Gittu-Milki*, and a ram (of no particular origin).

IV. On the next day, (12') for *Kôṯaru* two (rams?).

V. On the next day, (13') as *tzǵ*-sacrifices: two rams and a young bull from (14') HZ.

VI. (15') In the month of *Ḫiyyāru*, on the day of the new moon: (16') a bull and a ram for *Baʿlatu-Bahatīma*.

VII. (17') On the fourteenth day, for *Baʿlu*, (18') offerings from the ʿRK-taxes.

VIII. (19') On the eighteenth day, the king will (20') wash himself clean.

IX. (21') On the next day: a *tzǵ*-sacrifice in the sacrificial pit of *Ṣapunu;*

(22') object(s) cast of silver, two shekels of gold, two rams for *Bittu-Bêti*.

(23') A bull and a ram as a burnt-offering;
a bull as a peace-offering (24') for *Baʿlu*.
A bird for *Ṣapunu;*
(25') a neck and a ram for *Rašap-Bibitta;*
(26') two birds for *ʾInāšu-ʾIlīma;*
(27') [...]two ewes
[...]

12. RS 24.643

(*ʾIbaʿlatu* ? – *Ḫiyyāru* ?)

The writing on the two principal surfaces of this tablet is oriented differently: the lines are parallel with the longest edges on the obverse, but parallel with the shortest edges on the reverse. Unfortunately, the obverse-reverse orientation is itself not certain: the obverse shows a large bulge in the middle; normally the obverse is the flatter. Because the tablet has gone through a rather hot fire, though, the bulge may not be important for determining which side was inscribed first. From the literary perspective, it is clear that the text on the reverse is independent of the preceding texts, for it consists of a sacrificial rite of which the order is that established by the deity lists presented above as text 3. Indeed, the texts placed on this tablet reflect, with the exception of the first two, a degree of independence from one another quite unparalleled in the ritual texts, and any decision as to the proper order of the text on the reverse with respect to the others would at this stage be arbitrary. The obverse-reverse order observed here has, therefore, no real claim to correctness and is simply that adopted by C. Virolleaud, the original editor of the text.

The only possible chronological indicator in these texts, that upon which the present classification as a ritual spanning two months is based, is the presence of the word *ḫyr* in the title of the text on the reverse: *ỉl ḫyr*, "the gods of (the month of?) *Ḫiyyāru*." That {ỉl} is a plural construct, "gods of" (not "the god"), is deduced from the parallel formula at the head of text 1A (RS 1.017): *ỉl ṣpn* there clearly means "the gods of *Ṣapunu*" and it finds its sacrificial equivalent in the title of the first rite in this text *dbḥ ṣpn*, "the sacrifices of *Ṣapunu*." It is, however, unclear why the present text shows *ỉl ḫyr* (line 23) rather than *dbḥ ḫyr* ("the sacrificial rite of the month of *Ḫiyyāru*") or even *dbḥ ỉl ḫyr* ("the sacrificial rite for the gods of the month of *Ḫiyyāru*"). Until a better interpretation emerges, the interpretation of *ḫyr* as a month name appears the most plausible. If that be the case, and if the obverse-reverse orientation adopted here is correct, and if the preceding rites occurred during the preceding month (all presently uncertain), then these rites stretched over the first two months following the winter solstice (roughly December 21–February 20 in modern terms).

The primary novelty of the presentation offered here as compared with my 1992 re-edition of the text has been made possible by a text discovered during the campaign at Ras Shamra that took place in spring of that same year (RS 92.2004): the order of deities there corresponds to all the preserved data in the sacrificial list on the reverse of this text, and there can be no doubt that the latter prescribes a sacrificial rite of which the order is that of the deity list (see above, text 3). Thus the first rites on the obverse (lines 1–12) correspond to the first deity list (RS 1.017 and parallels), while the rite on the reverse corresponds to RS 92.2004 and parallels; and, as in the case of lines 1–12, which may be reconstructed on the basis of RS 1.017 and parallels, so the lacunae in the ritual prescribed in lines 23–45 may be largely filled by reference to RS 92.2004.

The principal remaining doubts regarding the meaning of this text have to do with the interpretation of the enigmatic elements of the new deity list[28] and a fuller interpretation of the Hurrian section, lines 13–17, of which the lacunae are not presently reconstructable, but which appears to belong to the hymnic genre.

Text

Obverse

---

(1) *dbḥ . ṣpn* [...]
(2) *ỉl . ảlp . k*[29] *š*[...]
(3) *bʿlm . ảlp . w š* [...]
(4) *bʿlm . ảlp . w š* ⸢ *. bʿl*⸣[*m . ả*]⸢*lp*⸣[*. w š* ...]
(5) *ảrṣ . w šmm . š . kṯr*[*t .*] *š . yr*⸢*ḫ*⸣[.   ]⸢- . *š*⸣
(6) *ṣpn . š* ⸢.⸣ *kṯr . š . pdry . š . ǵrm .* ⸢*w thm*⸣t *. š*
(7) *ảṯrt . š . ʿnt . š . špš . š* ⸢. *ả*⸣*rṣy . š . ʿṯtr*⸢*t*⸣ *š*
(8) *ủšḫry . š . ỉl . tʿ*⸢*ḏ*⸣*r . bʿl . š ršp . š . ddmš* ⸢*š*⸣
(9) *pḫr . ỉlm . š . ym . š .* [*k*]⸢*n*⸣*r . š .* ⸢*ảl*⸣*pm . ʿṣrm* [.] *gdlt* ⸢-⸣[...]

---

(10) *w šlmm . ỉlỉb . š . ỉ*⸢*l*⸣[*. š .*] *d*⸢*gn*⸣ *.* ⸢*š*⸣ [.] ⸢*b*⸣*ʿb*⸢*l*⸣[30] *. ṣpn . ảl*[*p* ...]
(11) *bʿlm . kmm . bʿlm km*⸢*m*⸣[*. b*]*ʿl*⸢*m*⸣ *. kmm . bʿlm . kmm*
(12) *bʿlm . kmm . bʿlm . k*⸢*m*⸣[*m*]

---

(13) *ỉy . ṯlǵmd . pḏp . ḫlbǵ . ḫ*⸢---⸣[-]*ṯlǵlḏ . n*[ ]⸢*ḏ*⸣*ḏ .* ⸢-⸣[...]
(14) *ủmnḏ . ỉnḏ . md . kḏmr . ảr*⸢-⸣[-]⸢-⸣*ʿ . pnḏỉb*[...]
(15) *ṯlǵlḏ . pd . dld . ỉnḏ . ỉd*[-]⸢*ỉn-*⸣[-]⸢*š*⸣*t .* [...]
(16) ⸢*ỉ̱*⸣*t*⸢*g*⸣*ỉn . kwrt* ⸢.⸣ *ḫnn . ủštn .* ⸢-⸣[...]
(17) *tzǵ . ảrm . tṯb . ṯủṯk* ⸢.⸣ *ḫnz*⸢-⸣[...]

---

(18) *k tʿrb . ʿṯtrt . šd . bt . mlk*[...]

(19) *ṯn . skm . šbʿ . mšlt . ảrbʿ . ḫpnt .* ⌜-⌝[…]
(20) *ḫmšm . ṯlṯ . rkb . rtn . ṯlṯ . mảt .* ⌜*š*⌝[*ʿrt*…]
(21) *lg . šmn . rqḥ . šrʿm . ủšpǵtm . p*⌜*l*⌝[…]
(22) *kṯ . ẓrw . kṯ . nbt . šnt . w t*⌜*ṯ*⌝*n*⌜-⌝[…]

Reverse ?

---

(23) *ỉl . ḫyr . ỉlỉb . š*
(24) *ảrṣ w šmm . š*
(25) *ỉl . š . kṯrt . š*
(26) *dgn . š . bʿl . ḫlb ảlp w š .*
(27) *bʿl ṣpn . ảlp . w . š .*
(28) *ṯrṯy . ảlp . w . š .*
(29) *yrḫ . š . ṣpn . š .*
(30) *kṯr š* ⌜.⌝ *ʿṯtr . š .*
(31) [-]⌜-⌝*rt . š . šgr . w ỉṯm š*
(32) [--]*š*[-]*š . ršp . ỉdrp . š*
(33) [ ]⌜*mṣ*⌝*r . š*
(34) [ ]*mt .* ⌜*š*⌝ *.*
(35) [ ]⌜-⌝[…]
(36) […]
(37) […]
(38) [ ]⌜---⌝[…]
(39) [ ] *. mḏr . š*[…]
(40) [ ]⌜-⌝*t š . ỉl . m*⌜-⌝[…]
(41) [ ]⌜-⌝ *. w* ⌜*t*⌝*ḥmt* […]
(42) [ ]⌜*m*⌝*mr* ⌜.⌝ *š . s*⌜*r*⌝[…]
(43) [ ]⌜-⌝*m š . ỉl lb*[-]⌜-⌝ *š* ⌜. -⌝[…]
(44) [*ảl*]*p . w š . bʿlm ảl*[…]
(45) [*ả*]⌜*l*⌝*p . w* [.] ⌜*š*⌝ *.*

Proposed Restoration of Lines 1–12

(1) *dbḥ . ṣpn*[*. ỉlỉb . ảlp . w š*]
(2) *ỉl . ảlp . w*! *š* [*. dgn . ảlp . w š . bʿl . ṣpn . ảlp . w š*]
(3) *bʿlm . ảlp . w š* [*. bʿlm . ảlp . w š . bʿlm . ảlp . w š*]
(4) *bʿlm . ảlp . w š* ⌜*. bʿl*⌝[*m . ả*]⌜*lp*⌝[*. w š . bʿlm . ảlp . w š*]
(5) *ảrṣ . w šmm . š . kṯr*[*t .*] *š . yr*⌜*ḫ*⌝[*. š . ʿṯt*]⌜*r . š*⌝
(6) *ṣpn . š* ⌜.⌝ *kṯr . š . pdry . š . ǵrm .* ⌜*w ṯhm*⌝*t . š*
(7) *ảṯrt . š . ʿnt . š . špš . š* ⌜*. ả*⌝*rṣy . š . ʿṯtr*⌜*t*⌝ *š*
(8) *ủšḫry . š . ỉl . tʿ*⌜*ḏ*⌝*r . bʿl . š ršp . š . ddmš* ⌜*š*⌝
(9) *pḫr . ỉlm . š . ym . š .* [*k*]⌜*n*⌝*r . š .* ⌜*ảl*⌝*pm . ʿṣrm* [.] *gdlt* ⌜*š*⌝[*rp*]

(10) *w šlmm . ỉlỉb . š . ỉ⸢l⸣[. š .] d⸢gn⸣ . ⸢š⸣ [.] ⸢b⸣ ʿ⟨b⟩⸢l⸣ . ṣpn . ảl[p . w š]*
(11) *bʿlm . kmm . bʿlm km⸢m⸣[. b]ʿl⸢m⸣ . kmm . bʿlm . kmm*
(12) *bʿlm . kmm . bʿlm . k⸢m⸣[m]*

Proposed Restoration of Lines 31–45[31]

(31) *[ả]⸢ṯ⸣rt . š . šgr . w ỉṯm š*
(32) *[šp]š [.] š . division ršp . ỉdrp . š*
(33) *[----]⸢mṣ⸣r . š*
(34) *[ddmš . š . -(-)]mt . ⸢š⸣ .*
(35) *[ ]⸢-⸣[...]*
(36) *[...]*
(37) *[ủšḫry . š]*
(38) *[gṯr*[32] *. š . ʿṯ]⸢tr⸣[t . š]*
(39) *[trṯ . š] . mḏr . š*
(40) *[ỉl q]⸢r⸣t š . ỉl . m⸢-⸣[... š]*
(41) *[ǵr]⸢m⸣ . w ⸢t⸣hmt [. š . ym . š]*
(42) *[--]⸢m⸣mr ⸢.⸣ š . s⸢r⸣[--- . š . ... . š . ỉl]*
(43) *[dd]⸢m⸣m š . ỉl lb[-]⸢n⸣ š ⸢. ủ⸣[ṯḫt . š . (knr . š .)*[33] *bʿlm]*
(44) *[ảl]p . w š . bʿlm ảl[p . w . š . bʿlm . ảlp . w . š . bʿlm]*
(45) *[ả]⸢l⸣p . w [.] ⸢š⸣ .*[34]

Translation[35]

IA. (1) Sacrifice for the gods of Mount *Ṣapunu:*[36] [for *ʾIluʾibī* a bull and a ram];
(2) for *ʾIlu* a bull and! a ram;
[for *Dagan* a bull and a ram;
for *Baʿlu* of *Ṣapunu* a bull and a ram];
(3) also for *Baʿlu* (no. 2)[37] a bull and a ram;
[also for *Baʿlu* (no. 3) a bull and a ram;
also for *Baʿlu* (no. 4) a bull and a ram];
(4) also for *Baʿlu* (no. 5) a bull and a ram;
[also for *Baʿlu* (no. 6) a bull and a ram;
also for *Baʿlu* (no. 7) a bull and a ram];
(5) for *ʾArṣu-wa-Šamûma* a ram;
for the *Kôṯarā*[*tu*] a ram;
for *Yariḫu* [a ram];
for [*ʿAṯta*]*ru* a ram;
(6) for *Ṣapunu* a ram;
for *Kôṯaru* a ram;

for *Pidray* a ram;
for Mountains-and-the-Waters-of-the-Abyss a ram;
(7) for *ʾAṯiratu* a ram;
for *ʿAnatu* a ram;
for *Šapšu* a ram;
for *ʾArṣay* a ram;
for *ʿAṯtartu* a ram;
(8) for *ʾUšḫaraya* a ram;
for the Auxiliary-Gods-of-*Baʿlu* a ram;
for *Rašap* a ram;
for *Dadmiš* a ram;
(9) for the Assembly-of-the-Gods a ram;
for *Yammu* a ram;
for [*Kin*]*nāru* a ram;
two bulls, two birds, a cow: as a b[urnt-offering].[38]

B. (10) And as a peace-offering: for *ʾIluʾibī* a ram;
for *ʾI*[*lu* a ram];
for *Dagan* a ram;
for *Baʿlu*! of *Ṣapunu* a bul[l and a ram];
(11) also for *Baʿlu* (no. 2) the same;
also for *Baʿlu* (no. 3) the same;
also for [*B*]*aʿlu* (no. 4) the same;
also for *Baʿlu* (no. 5) the same;
(12) also for *Baʿlu* (no. 6) the same;
also for *Baʿlu* (no. 7) the sa[me].

C. (13–17) Hurrian hymn.

D. (18) When *ʿAṯtartu-Šadî* enters the royal palace:[39] [...] (19) two *sk*-garments, seven *mšlt*-garments, four *ḫpn*-garments [...], fifty-three RKB (of?) RTN, three hundred units of w[ool ...], a *lg*-measure of perfumed oil, two/some ŠRʿ, two *ủšpǵt*-garments, PL[...], a *kṯ*-measure of gum, a *kṯ*-measure of liquid honey.[40]

E. And you will reci[te ...].

II. (23) The gods of the month *Ḫiyyāru*: for *ʾIluʾibī* a ram;
(24) for *ʾArṣu-wa-Šamûma* a ram;
(25) for *ʾIlu* a ram;

for the *Kôṯarātu* a ram;
(26)for *Dagan* a ram;
for *Baʿlu* of Aleppo a bull and a ram;
(27) for *Baʿlu* of *Ṣapunu* a bull and a ram;
(28) for *Ṯarraṯiya* a bull and a ram;
(29) for *Yariḫu* a ram;
for *Ṣapunu* a ram;
(30) for *Kôṯaru* a ram;
for *ʿAṯtaru* a ram;
(31) for [*ʾA*]*ṯiratu* a ram;
for *Šaggar-wa-ʾIṯum* a ram;
(32) for [*Šap*]*šu* a ram;
for *Rašap-ʾIdrippi* a ram;
(33) [for ----]⌜MṢ⌝R a ram;
(34) for *Dadmiš* a ram;
[for -(-)]MT a ram;
(35) [for … a ram];[41]
(36) [for … a ram];
(37) [for *ʾUšḫaraya* a ram];
(38) [for *Gaṯaru*[42] a ram;
for *ʿAṯ*]*tar*[*tu* a ram;
(39) for *Tirāṯu* a ram];
for *Maḏ*(*ḏ*)*ara* a ram;
(40) [for the Gods-of-the-Ci]ty a ram;
for the Gods-of-M[en-and-of-Women a ram];[43]
(41) [for Mountain]s-and-the-Waters-of-the-Abyss [a ram;
for *Yammu* a ram];
(42) [for --]⌜M⌝MR a ram;
for S⌜R⌝[… a ram;[44]
for Door-bolt a ram;[45]
for the Gods-of-](43) [the-La]nd-of-Aleppo a ram;
for the Gods-of-*Lab*[*a*]*na* a ram;
for *ʾU*[*ṯḫatu* a ram;
for *Kinnāru* a ram;
also for *Baʿlu* (no. 4)][46] (44) [a bul]l and a ram;
also for *Baʿlu* (no. 5) a bul[l and a ram;
also for *Baʿlu* (no. 6) a bull and a ram;
also (for) *Baʿlu*] (no. 7) (45) [a bu]ll and a ram.

13. RS 24.266

(ʾIbaʿlatu - Ḫiyyāru ?)

The series of rites prescribed on the obverse of this tablet is stated twice to take place in the month of *ʾIbaʿlatu* (December–January, that is, the month that follows the winter solstice). They begin on the seventh of the month, skip immediately to the seventeenth, with nothing specified for the day of the full moon, and continue on the eighteenth, after which a break has removed a dozen or so lines of text. The next chronological data pertain to a series of days designated by numbers smaller than the last preserved on the obverse, viz., the fourth, the fifth, and the seventh. These may refer either to a festival that would have occurred during the last quarter of the month of *ʾIbaʿlatu* or to one of the festivals of the following month (*Ḫiyyāru*). Because the festival of the third quarter of the month in this version of the rites of *ʾIbaʿlatu* began only on the fourth day of that "week," with no full-moon festival per se, the rites prescribed on the reverse are perhaps those of the full moon of the following month, designated, as in text 15 (RS 1.003/RS 18.056), by the days of the third quarter of the month. This hypothesis supposes that events occurring on the first days of this "week" would have been prescribed in the part of the text that has disappeared in the lacuna between the two preserved portions. Both sections of the text are primarily in honor of *Baʿlu*, in two of his manifestations (*Baʿlu* and *Baʿlu* of Ugarit), or in all of them (*bʿlm*), and the prayer at the end is addressed to *Baʿlu*. *ʾIlu* is the only other principal deity mentioned here.

Text

Obverse

---

(1) *b yrḫ . i͗bʿlt* ⌜*. b*⌝ *y*⌜*m*⌝ [.] ⌜*šbʿ*⌝

---

(2) *š . l bʿl . r*ʿ⌜*k*⌝*t* ⌜*. b-*⌝[-(-)]⌜---⌝[…]

---

(3) *w bt . bʿl . u͗gr*[*t*] *. š*[---]⌜-⌝

---

(4) *ʿrb . špš . w ḥ*⌜*l mlk*⌝ [.] *b* ⌜*š*⌝*bʿt*

---

(5) *ʿšrt . yrtḥṣ mlk b*⌜*rr*⌝

---

(6) *gdlt . qdš ỉl* ⌜.⌝ *gdlt* ⌜.⌝ *l bʿlm*

---

(7) *gdlt . l ǵlm . dqtm . w glt*[47]

---

(8) *l ǵlmtm . bt . ṯʿy* ⌜.⌝ *ydbḥ*

---

(9) *w tnrr . b ʿd . bt bʿl*

---

(10) *lgrt*[48] *. ỉmr . w ynt . qrt*

---

(11) *l ṯʿ . b ṯmnt* ⌜.⌝ *ʿšrt . ỉbʿlt*

---

(12) *ảlp . l md*⌜*g*⌝*l bʿl . ủgrt*

---

(13) ⌜*ủ*⌝ *ủrm . ủ šnpt . l ydbḥ*

---

(14) *mlk . bt ỉl . npš . l ỉ*⌜-⌝[...]

---

(15) *npš . l bʿ*⌜*l*⌝[...]

---

(16) *w ʿr .* ⌜*l* -⌝[...]

---

(17) ⌜---⌝[...]

....

Reverse

....

(18') [--]*l .* ⌜---⌝[...]

(19') ⌜-⌝*tml . yk*⌜-⌝[...]

(20') *b rbʿ . ʿṣrmm . b ḥmš* [.] ⌜*ʿṣr*⌝

(21') *mm . w kbd . w . š šrp . l bʿ*⌜*l*⌝

(22') *ủgrt . b bt . b šbʿ . tdn*

(23') *mḥllm . ʿrb . špš .*

(24') *w ḥl m*⌜*l*⌝*k . hn . šmn . šlm*

(25') *bʿl . mtk . mlk*⸢*m* .⸣ *riʾšyt*
(26') *k gr ʿz . tǵ*⸢*r*⸣*km .* ⸢*q*⸣*rd*
(27') *ḥmytkm . ʿ*⸢*n*⸣*km . l* ⸢*b*⸣*ʿl tšuʾn*
(28') *y b*⸢*ʿl*⸣*m* ⸢. -- . *t*⸣*dy ʿz l* ⸢*ṯ*⸣*ǵrn*
(29') *y . qrd* [*l*] *ḥmytny . iʾbr y*
(30') *bʿl . n*⸢*š*⸣*qdš . mḏr bʿl*
(31') *nmluʾ* [. -]*kr b*⸢*ʿ*⸣*l . nš*[*q*]*dš*
(32') *ḥtp bʿ*⸢*l*⸣ [.] ⸢*n*⸣*mluʾ . ʿ*⸢*šr*⸣*t .* ⸢*bʿl*⸣ [.] ⸢*n*⸣[*ʿ*]
(33') *šr . qdš bʿ*⸢*l* .⸣ *nʿl . ntbt b*[...]
(34') *ntlk . w š*[*mʿ . b*]*ʿ*⸢*l* .⸣ *l* ⸢. -⸣*l*⸢--⸣[...]
(35') ⸢*y*⸣*dy . ʿz l tǵrk*[*m . qrd*]
(36') *l ḥmytk*⸢*m*⸣ [...]

Translation

IA. (1) In the month of *ʾIbaʿlatu*, on the seventh day: (2) a ram for *Baʿlu*-RʿKT[49] [...]

B. (3) and in the temple of *Baʿlu* of Ugarit [...].[50]

C. (4) When the sun sets, the king will be free (of further cultic obligations).

IIA. On the seven(5)teenth day, the king will wash himself clean.

B. (6) A cow in the sanctuary of *ʾIlu;*
a cow for the *Baʿlu*-deities;
(7) a cow for *Ǵalmu;*
two ewes and a cow (8) for ǴLMTM—the preceding beasts are to be sacrificed at the house of the *ṯāʿiyu*-priest.

C. (9) Next you shall illumine the ʿD-room of the temple of *Baʿlu* of (10) Ugarit: a lamb and a city-dove; (11) these belong to the category of the *ṯaʿû*-sacrifice.

IIIA. On the eighteenth of *ʾIbaʿlatu*, (12) a bull for the MDGL[51] of *Baʿlu* of Ugarit.

B. (13) A flame-sacrifice and a presentation-offering the king (14) must sacrifice at the temple of *ʾIlu*: a neck for *ʾI*[...];
(15) a neck for *Baʿlu*[...];
(16) and a donkey for [...]
(17) [...]
...
(18'–19') [...]

IV. (20') On the fourth day: birds.

V. On the fifth day: bir(21')ds and a liver and a ram as a burnt-offering for *Baʿlu* of (22') Ugarit in the temple.

VIA. On the seventh day: you shall bring (23') the purifiers near.

B. When the sun sets, (24') the king will be free (of further cultic obligations).

C. Behold the oil of well-being of (25') *Baʿlu*, libation-offering for the benefit of the *Malakūma*, of the best quality.[52]

D.[53] (26') When a strong foe attacks your gate,
a warrior (27') your walls,
You shall lift your eyes to *Baʿlu* and say:
(28') O *Baʿlu*, if you drive the strong one from our gate,
(29') the warrior from our walls,
A bull, (30') O *Baʿlu*, we shall sanctify,
a vow, O *Baʿlu*, (31') we shall fulfill;
a firstborn, O *Baʿlu*, we shall sanctify,
(32') a *ḥtp*-offering, O *Baʿlu*, we shall fulfill,
a feast, O *Baʿlu*, we shall (33') offer;
To the sanctuary, O *Baʿlu*, we shall ascend,
that path, O *Baʿlu*, (34') we shall take.
And *Baʿ*[*lu* will h]ear [your] prayer:
(35') He will drive the strong foe from your gate,
[the warrior] (36') from yo[ur] walls.

14. RS 24.250+

(*Ḥallatu* ? – *Gannu*)

In this text, several days of the month of *Gannu* (March–April) are mentioned, but the first, the reference to the eighth day, occurs only in line 18. This fact, in conjunction with the irregular form in which the ascription of the first offerings is couched, allows the hypothesis that this is only the second part of a text that would have been written on two tablets, only one of which has been recovered. The ritual sequence of this text is notable for including no provision for a full-moon festival: the mentioned rites skip from the eighth day to the twenty-second (that is, from the first day of the second quarter to the first day of the fourth). With the hypothesis that this text represents only the second part of a longer text, the fact that the first date mentioned includes the month name (line 18) may be taken as an indication that the series of rites in question covered two months. This classification is not adopted here only on account of that feature, however, for there is a clear case of a month name being mentioned twice in the same text (see text 13 [RS 24.266:11]). It is in no small part because of the extreme length of the rites that would have occurred during the first seven days of the month that this text is placed in this section. No example exists of the new-moon festival occupying an entire tablet and more as would be the case if the hypothetical text that preceded this one and the first seventeen lines of this text are assumed to have been devoted to that series of rites. If these two hypotheses regarding the original nature of this text are correct, the rites prescribed would have preceded and followed the vernal equinox, just as the rites of text 15 (RS 1.003/RS 18.056) preceded and followed the autumnal equinox. The absence of a full-moon festival during the month following the vernal equinox constitutes a difference with respect to RS 18.056, where a very brief rite occurs on the fifteenth day of what will be interpreted below as an intercalary month, but not with respect to RS 1.003, where the only rites mentioned occur on the first day of the following month.

Text

Obverse

---

(1) *l ršp . ḫgb . ʿṣrm*
(2) *l ỉnš . ỉlm . šrp*
(3) *ydbỉl . gdlt . yả*
(4) *ršỉl . gdlt*
(5) *ʿmtr . gdlt . n⸢pš⸣*
(6) *w š . l ršp . m⸢ḫ⸣[bn]*
(7) *šr⸢p⸣ . ⸢ʿ⸣ṣr⸢m⸣ [. l ỉnš]*
(8) *ỉl[m ...]*
(9) *bn⸢-⸣[...]*
(10) *mlk . b⸢t⸣ ml[k ...]*
(11) *š . l ⸢p⸣dr . ⸢y⸣[...]*
(12) *bt . m⸢lk⸣ . y⸢-⸣[--(-)]b*
(13) *ṣỉn . ḫmnḫ . ⸢š⸣ . qdšḫ*
(14) *ʿlyḫ . ⸢š ḫ⸣mnḫ . nkl*
(15) *š kbmḫ . w šr yšr*
(16) *šr . pảmt . l pn*
(17) *mlk . ptḫ yd . mlk*

Lower Edge

(18) *g⌜d⌝lt . b ṯmn . gn*
(19) *[n]pš . w ảrbʿ*

Reverse

(20) *ʿšrh . dqt*
(21) *w šbʿ . gdlt . w k*
(22) *l . šbšlt . dg . gnh*
(23) *ṯb . rgm . b gn . w ḥl*
(24) *mlk . b ṯn . l ʿšrm*
(25) *tủṣl . šlḥmt . b ḫmš*
(26) *l ʿšrm . yrtḥṣ . ml⌜k⌝*
(27) *brr . w l ll* ⌜.⌝ *tʿr*[-(-)]
(28) *ksủ . ʿlm . tṣủ . šl⌜ḥ⌝[mt]*
(29) *tšʿ . ṣỉn . w ảlp*[...]
(30) *w ủz . ỉ⌜š⌝m . ảr⌜-⌝*[...]
(31) *dqtm . w gdlt .* ⌜-⌝[...]
(32) *l ảrṣy . ṯṯb rgm*
(33) *w ḥl mlk*

Translation

IA. (1) ... for *Rašap-Ḥagab,*
two birds (2) for *ʾInāšu-ʾIlīma* as a burnt-offering.

B. (3) For *Yaddubuʾilu* a cow;[54]
for *Yaʾa*(4)*rrišuʾilu* a cow;
(5) for *ʿAmmutāru* a cow;
a neck (6) and a ram for *Rašap*-MHBN (7) as a burnt-offering.

C. Two birds [for *ʾInāšu*] (8) [*ʾIlīma* ...].

D. (9) Daughte[rs ...] (10) the king, the royal palace [...] (11) a ram for *Pidar*.

E. (12) In the royal palace [...] (13) sheep/goats in the ḪMN-sanctuary, a ram in the sanctuary, (14) in the upper room,
a ram in the ḪMN-sanctuary of *Nikkal*,
(15) a ram in the KBM.

F. And a singer shall sing (16) the song, several times,[55] before (17) the king.

G. Open the king's hand: (18) a cow.[56]

IIA. On the eighth day of the month of *Gannu*: (19) [a n]eck, four(20)teen ewes, (21) and seven cows, and a(22)ll the fish soup, in the garden.[57]

B. (23) The recitation having been repeated in the garden, then the (24) king will be free (of further cultic obligations).[58]

III. On the twenty-second day, (25) the foodstuffs are to be set aside.

IV. On the (26) twenty-fifth day, the king will wash himself (27) clean.

V. That night the throne is to be (28) prepared.

VIA. On the next day, the foodst[uffs] may be removed (lit. "they will exit");[59]

(29) nine sheep/goats and a bull [...], (30) a goose (of?) ʾI⸢Š⸣M, ʾAR⸢-⸣[?], two ewes and a cow [...] (31) for *ʾArṣay*.

B. Repeat the recitation (32) and the king will be free (of further cultic obligations).

15. RS 1.003 (*Raʾšu-yêni – nql* ?) **RS 18.056** (*Raʾšu-yêni – š*[...])

These two texts provide the most extensive examples of overlapping texts known in Ugaritic, let alone in the ritual texts: RS 1.003:1–49 and RS 18.056:1–53 are, as nearly as can be determined from their damaged state, virtual duplicates. (In addition, RS 1.003:12–19/RS 18.056:13–21 duplicate, with some variants, a portion of the rite for a day and a night translated below as text 17 [RS 1.001:3–10). Because, however, each text ends differently, I believe that they were prepared independently in order to reflect two different situations in the year. If the only month name that is preserved, *Raʾšu-Yêni*, "the first wine," is indeed the last month of the lunar calendar, it is plausible to deduce that the two texts represent rites for two different years, one in which the normal sequence of months was followed, the other a year requiring an intercalary month in order to readjust the lunar calendar to the solar year. This hypothesis fits the designation {yrḫ . š⸢-⸣[...]} in RS 18.056, for *nql* is the month that normally follows *Raʾšu-Yêni* (de Jong and Van Soldt). I have not, however, come up with a restoration for the word {š⸢-⸣[...]} that would, according to the hypothesis just mentioned, designate the intercalary month.

The list of personal names at the end of RS 18.056 plausibly reflects some form of participation by the individuals named in some part of the long rite just outlined, but the passage is too poorly preserved for this to be more than a hypothesis or to indicate what form that participation took. The very presence of the list is, however, sufficient to show that this text was prepared for a specific situation and was not a "canonical" text kept in some official's "library" for him to consult triennially when the liturgy for the intercalary month was needed. Indeed, I believe it not illegitimate to argue from this text that none of the tablets that have come down to us bears a "canonical" text from a priestly "library." If that be the case, the ritual cycle at Ugarit would have been a matter of oral tradition, and the tablets that have been discovered to date would have been dictated as an outline for an upcoming rite or sequence of rites.

In this festival of the last month of the year (RS 1.003:1–48/RS 18.056:1–52), roughly the last lunar month before the fall equinox, a very special place is accorded to the rites surrounding the appearance of the full moon, from the thirteenth through the twenty-first day of the month.[60] Vast numbers of sacrifices are offered (some 180 different items according to the texts in their present damaged state). The king is here, as in most rites for which a text has been preserved, the principal actor, indeed the only one mentioned explicitly. A fairly full panoply of divinities is honored: nearly thirty names are preserved. Manifestations of *ʾIlu* and *Baʿlu* are particularly favored; indeed a large proportion of the rites are either stated explicitly to have taken place (lines 38–54) in the temple of *ʾIlu* or may be assumed to have occurred there (lines 1–19).

The reference to the "day of the new moon" in RS 1.003:48/RS 18.056:52–53 marks this as a text outlining a two-month festival, or at least the festival of the last month of the year with a transitional festival to the new year. The new-year festival, similarly to that of the Hebrew Bible, appears to be a harvest festival, as may be surmised from the mention of "dwellings" for the gods made of "cut branches" (RS 1.003:51). It differs from the biblical version, however, in occurring on the first day of the month (at least there is no specific mention of a later day of the month in RS 1.003:50), rather than on the fifteenth day (the Israelite Festival of Booths began only after the Day of Atonement, which occurred on the tenth of the month). Relatively few specific rites are indicated for this day in RS 1.003, and it is likely that the details of the new-year festival would have been indicated separately. RS 1.003:50–55 deal essentially with getting the booths set up for the deities on the roof of the temple of *ʾIlu* and with getting the king safely back to the palace—all this occurs on the first day of the month. There is simply no way of knowing what the details of the new-year festival were, but the fact that the king was desacralized on that first day indicates that he did not play a major role for an interval of time thereafter.

The corresponding paragraph in RS 18.056 (lines 54–57), instead of dealing with this transition to the new year, outlines another full-moon liturgy, this one very brief. This correspondence of emphasis on the full moon in the main text and in this additional paragraph corroborates the hypothesis that {yrḫ . š⸢-⸣[...]} in RS 18.056:54 somehow expresses the fact of an intercalary month: in years when the lunar cycle had retarded by approximately a month with respect to the solar cycle, another last-month-of-the-year festival was observed. In the supplementary festival as in the regular festival of *Raʾšu-Yêni*, the appearance of the full moon is the principal focus of the rites. Instead of the transition to the new year, it thus marks the transition to the intercalary month, and no mention is made of the new-year festival, which would, in this case, have been outlined entirely on a different tablet.

Texts[61]

A. RS 1.003	Reconstruction of RS 1.003	B. RS 18.056
Obverse		
(1) *b yrḫ . […]*	*b yrḫ . [rỉš yn . b . ym . ḥdṯ]*	(1) *[b y]⸢rḫ⸣ [.] ⸢r⸣ỉš yn . b ym . ḥdṯ*
(2) *šmtr . ⸢ủ⸣[…]*	*šmtr . ⸢ủ⸣[ṯkl . l . ỉl . šlmm]*	(2) *[---]⸢r⸣ . ủṯkl . l ỉl . šlmm*
(3) *b ṯlṯt ʿ[šrt …]*	*b ṯlṯt ʿ[šrt . yrtḥṣ . mlk . brr]*	(3) *b [----] . ʿšrt . yrtḥṣ . mlk* (4) *br[r .]*
(4) *b ảrbʿ⸢t⸣[. ʿšrt …]*	*b ảrbʿ⸢t⸣ [. ʿšrt . rỉš . ảrgmn]*	*b ả⸢r⸣bʿt . ʿšrt . rỉš* (5) *ảrg[mn]*
(5) *w ṯn šm . ⸢l⸣[…]*	*w ṯn šm . ⸢l⸣[bʿlt . bḫtm . ʿṣrm . l ỉnš]*	*[ ]⸢-⸣ . šm . l bʿlt* (6) *bḫtm . ⸢ʿṣ⸣[rm . l ỉ]⸢n⸣š*
(6) *ỉlm . w š ⸢d⸣[d …]*	*ỉlm . w š ⸢d⸣[d . < šmn ? >*[62] *. ỉlš . š . ỉlḫm . w ? mlk]*	*ỉlm . w š* (7) *dd <. šmn ? > ỉlš . ⸢š⸣ [-----(-)] mlk .*
(7) *yṯb . brr[…]*	*yṯb . brr[. w mḥ-----⸢-⸣*[63] *- ⸢w q⸣ …]*	*yṯ⸢b⸣ . br*(8)*r . w mḥ[ ]⸢-⸣[-] ⸢w q⸣[…]*
(8) *ym . ⸢ʿ⸣lm . yʿ[…]*	*ym . ⸢ʿ⸣lm . yʿ[t]*	(9) *ym . ʿlm . ⸢-⸣[ ]* (10)*t .*
(9) *⸢k t⸣g⸢ml⸣[. -]s . w⸢--.⸣[…]*	*⸢k t⸣g⸢ml⸣[. -]s . w ⸢--.⸣[dqtm]*	*k ⸢-⸣[-]ml ⸢.⸣ [ ]* (11) *d⸢-⸣[-]⸢-⸣ .*
(10) *⸢w⸣ y⸢n⸣[t . q]rt . y⸢l⸣[…]*	*⸢w⸣ y⸢n⸣[t . q]rt . y⸢l⸣[…]*	*w ⸢-⸣[ ]* (12) *[ ]*
(11) *w ảl[p -] ỉl . w b ủ[…]*	*w ảl[p . l] ỉl . w b ủ[rbt…]*	*[ ]ả[ ]* (13) *[ ]*
(12) *ytk . gdlt . ỉlḫm . ⸢ṯ⸣[kmn . w šnm …]*	*ytk . gdlt . ỉlḫm . ⸢ṯ⸣[kmn . w šnm . dqt]*	*[ ]⸢--⸣[ ]* (14) *ṯkmn . w ⸢š⸣[nm]*
(13) *dqt [.] ⸢r⸣šp . šrp . w š[lmm . dqtm]*	*dqt [.] ⸢r⸣šp . šrp . w š[lmm . dqtm]*	*[ ]* (15) *w šlmm . ⸢-⸣[ ]*
(14) *ỉlḫ [.] ⸢ả⸣lp ⸢.⸣ w š [. ỉ]⸢l⸣ḫm . ⸢g⸣[dlt . ỉlḫm]*	*ỉlḫ [.] ⸢ả⸣lp ⸢.⸣ w š [. ỉ]⸢l⸣ḫm . ⸢g⸣[dlt . ỉlḫm]*	*[ ]* (16) *ỉlḫm . gd⸢l⸣[t]*

(15) bʿ⸢l⸣ [.] ⸢š⸣ . ảṯr⸢t⸣ [. š . ṯk]⸢mn w⸣ [šnm . š]	bʿ⸢l⸣ [.] ⸢š⸣ . ảṯr⸢t⸣ [. š . ṯk]⸢mn w⸣ [šnm . š]	[ ] (17) ṯkmn . w š⸢n⸣[m]
(16) ʿnt š [.] ršp š [...]	ʿnt š [.] ršp š [. dr . ỉl . w pḫr . bʿl]	[ ] (18) ỉl . w pḫr ⸢.⸣ [ ]
(17) gdlt . šl⸢m⸣[...]	gdlt . šl⸢m⸣[. gdlt . w b . ủrm . lb]	[(19) w b ủrm . l⸢b⸣
(18) rmṣt . ỉlh[m ...]	rmṣt . ỉlh[m . bʿlm . w mlủ . dṯt . w]	[ ] (20) bʿlm . w mlủ[ ]
(19) ksm . ṯlṯm . [--(-)]⸢mt .⸣[...]	ksm . ṯlṯm . [--(-)]⸢mt .⸣[mʿrb]	[ ] (21) ṯlṯm . w mʿr⸢-⸣[ ][64]
(20) d yqḥ [.] bt [. ml]⸢k⸣ . dbḥ [.] ⸢š⸣[mn . mr]	d yqḥ [.] bt [. ml]⸢k⸣ . dbḥ [.] ⸢š⸣[mn . mr]	[ ] (22) dbḥ šmn mr
(21) šmn . rqḥ [.] ⸢n⸣bt . mtn⸢t⸣[...]	šmn . rqḥ [.] ⸢n⸣bt . mtn⸢t⸣[. w ynt . qrt]	[ ] (23) mtnt . w ynt . ⸢q⸣[rt]
(22) w ṯn ḥ ṯ m . ⸢w⸣ b ǵr . ảrb[ʿ ...]	w ṯn ḥ ṯ m . ⸢w⸣ b ǵr . ảrb[ʿ . ʿšrh]	[ ] (24) w b ǵr . ảrbʿ . [ ]
(23) kdm . yn . prs . qmḥ . ⸢m⸣[ʿ ...]	kdm . yn . prs . qmḥ . ⸢m⸣[ʿ...]	[ ] (25) prs . qmḥ . mʿ[...]
(24) ⸢m⸣dbḥt . bt . ỉlt . ʿṣr[...]	⸢m⸣dbḥt . bt . ỉlt . ʿṣr[. l ṣpn . š]	(26) mdbḥt . bt . ⸢ỉ⸣[ ] (27) ṣpn š .
(25) l ǵ⸢l⸣mt . š . w l[...]	l ǵ⸢l⸣mt . š . w l[l yrḫ]	l ǵl⸢m⸣[t] (28) l yrḫ .
(26) gd[lt] . l nkl[...]	gd[lt] . l nkl[. gdlt . l bʿ lt . bhtm]	gdlt . l ⸢-⸣[ ] (29) ⸢-t . bhtm .
(27) ʿṣ[rm .] l ỉnš[. ỉlm ...]	ʿṣ[rm .] l ỉnš[ỉlm . gdlt]	ʿ⸣ṣrm . ⸢-⸣[...] (30) [ ]⸢-⸣
(28) ỉl[hm .] ⸢d⸣qt . š[pš . gdlt . rš]	ỉl[hm .] ⸢d⸣qt . š[pš . gdlt . rš]	ỉlh[...] (31) [ ][ ]⸢-⸣ . r[ ]
(29) [p .] ⸢š⸣r⸢p⸣ [.] w š⸢l⸣[mm ...]	[p .] ⸢š⸣r⸢p⸣ [.] w š⸢l⸣[mm . kmm . dqtm]	[ ] (32) [ ]dq[ ]

Lower Edge

(30) [ỉ]lh . gdlt[...]	[ỉ]lh . gdlt[. ỉlhm . gdlt . ỉlhm]	[ ] (33) ⸢ỉ⸣lh⸢m . gd⸣lt . ỉ⸢l⸣[ ]
(31) [d]⸢q⸣t . ṯkmn . w . ⸢š⸣[nm ...]	[d]⸢q⸣t . ṯkmn . w . ⸢š⸣[nm . dqt]	[ṯkm](34)n . w šnm . dqt ⸢.⸣

Reverse

(32) [--(-)] ⸢b⸣t . dqtm . ⸢b⸣ [nbk . šrp . w šl]	[ỉl] ⸢b⸣t . dqtm . ⸢b⸣ [nbk . šrp . w šl]	[ ] (35) bqtm[65] . b nbk . ⸢-⸣[ ]

(33) *[mm .] ⸢k⸣mm . gdlt . l . ⸢b⸣[ʿl . ṣpn]*	*[mm .] ⸢k⸣mm . gdlt . l . ⸢b⸣[ʿl . ṣpn]*	*[ ](36) kmm . gdlt . l ⸢-⸣[ ]*
(34) *⸢d⸣[q]⸢t⸣ . l . ṣpn . gdlt . ⸢l⸣ [. bʿl]*	*⸢d⸣[q]⸢t⸣ . l . ṣpn . gdlt . ⸢l⸣ [. bʿl]*	*[ ] (37) l ṣpn . gdlt . ⸢l⸣[ ]*
(35) *⸢ủ⸣[gr]⸢t⸣ . š . l . ⸢ỉ⸣[l]ỉb . g̀[…]*	*⸢ủ⸣[gr]⸢t⸣ . š . l . ⸢ỉ⸣[l]ỉb . g̀[-(-) l ảṯrt]*	*(38) ủgrt . š l ỉl⸢-⸣[ ](39)rt .*
(36) *⸢w⸣ [. ʿ]⸢ṣrm .⸣ l . rỉ⸢--⸣[…]*	*⸢w⸣ [. ʿ]⸢ṣrm .⸣ l . rỉ⸢--⸣[… pảmt]*	*w ʿṣrm . ⸢l⸣ […] (40) pảmt .*
(37) *⸢w⸣ [. b]⸢t⸣ . bʿlt . bt[m …]*	*⸢w⸣ [. b]⸢t⸣ . bʿlt . bt[m . rmm . w . ʿly]*	*w bt . [ ] (41) rmm . w ʿl⸢-⸣[ ]*
(38) *[m]⸢d⸣bḥt . b . ḫmš[…]*	*[m]⸢d⸣bḥt . b . ḫmš[. bt . ỉl . ṯql . ks]*	*[ ] (42) bt . ỉl . ṯq[ ]*
(39) *[--] kbd . w . db[ḥ …]*	*[p .] kbd . w . db[ḥ . k…]*	*[ ] (43) w dbḥ . k[…]*
(40) *[l] . ảṯrt . ʿṣr⸢m⸣[…]*	*[l] . ảṯrt . ʿṣr⸢m⸣[. l ỉnš ỉlm]*	*[ ] (44) ʿṣrm . l ⸢ỉ⸣[nš ỉlm]*
(41) *[-]⸢ṯ⸣b ⸢.⸣ mdbḥ . bʿl . g⸢d⸣[lt …]*	*[t]⸢ṯ⸣b ⸢.⸣ mdbḥ . bʿl . g⸢d⸣[lt . l bʿl . ṣpn]*	*[ ](45)bḥ . bʿl . ⸢-⸣[ ]*
(42) *dqt . l . ṣpn . w . dq⸢t⸣[…]*	*dqt . l . ṣpn . w . dq⸢t⸣[. l bʿl . ủgrt]*	*[ ](46) l ṣpn . w [ ]*
(43) *ṯn . l . ʿšrm . pảmt . ⸢š⸣[…]*	*ṯn . l . ʿšrm . pảmt . ⸢š⸣[…]*	*[ ](47)rm . pảm[t …]*
(44) *š ⸢.⸣ dd . šmn . gdlt . w . […]*	*š ⸢.⸣ dd . šmn . gdlt . w . [mlk . brr]*	*(48) š dd šmn[ ] (49) brr .*
(45) *rgm . yṯṯb . b . ṯdṯ . ṯn . […]*	*rgm . yṯṯb . b . ṯdṯ . ṯn . [šm . l šmn]*	*r[ ] (50) l šmn .*
(46) *ʿl⸢y⸣h . gdlt [.] rgm . yṯ⸢ṯ⸣[b . mlk . brr]*	*ʿl⸢y⸣h . gdlt [.] rgm . yṯ⸢ṯ⸣[b . mlk . brr]*	*ʿ⸢l⸣[ ] (51) brr .*
(47) *b . [šb]ʿ . ṣbủ . ⸢š⸣pš . w . ḥl ym . ʿ⸢rb⸣ [.] ⸢šp⸣[š]*	*b . [šb]ʿ . ṣbủ . ⸢š⸣pš . w . ḥl ym . ʿ⸢rb⸣ [.]⸢šp⸣[š]*	*b šb⸢ʿ⸣[ ](52) yt*[66] *. ʿrb šp⸢š⸣*
(48) *w[. ḥl .] mlk . ⸢w .⸣ b . ym . ḥdṯ . ṯn . šm*	*w[. ḥl .] mlk . ⸢w .⸣ b . ym . ḥdṯ . ṯn . šm*	*[b y](53)m . ḥdṯ . ṯn š⸢m⸣*
(49) *l . [---]t*	*l . [---]t*	*[------(-)]⸢-⸣*[67]

(50) *ỉ⌜d⌝ [. yd]⌜b⌝ḥ . mlk . l . prgl . ṣqrn . b . gg*
(51) *ả⌜r⌝[bʿ] ⌜.⌝ ảrbʿ . mṯbt . ảzmr . bh . š ⌜.⌝ š⌜r⌝[p]*
(52) *ảl[p .] ⌜w⌝ . š . šlmm . pảmt . šbʿ . k lbh*
(53) *yr[gm] ml⌜k .⌝ ṣbủ . špš . w . ḥl . mlk*
(54) *w . ⌜-⌝[-]⌜-⌝ . ṣpm . w . mḥ[--]⌜-⌝ . t[ṯ]ṯbn[...]*
(55) *b . [--] . w . km . ỉ⌜ṯ⌝ y[šủ] š⌜m⌝m . yd⌜h⌝[...]*

---

(54) *b yrḫ . š⌜-⌝[--- ả]⌜r⌝bʿt . ʿš*
(55) *rt . yr[tḥṣ . m]⌜l⌝k . brr*
(56) *ʿlm . š . š[r]⌜p⌝ . l [-]⌜-⌝ . ʿrb . šp*
(57) *š . w ḥ⌜l⌝ [. m]⌜l⌝k*

---

(58) *bn ảủ⌜p⌝[š .] ⌜w⌝ . bs bn hzpḫ ṯlṯt*
(59) *kṯr⌜ml⌝[k . w .] ⌜y⌝tr⌜n⌝ ḫm⌜š⌝t .*
bn gdả⌜ḫ t⌝š⌜ʿ⌝
(60) *kl⌜-⌝[----]⌜--⌝ ṯmnt . ⌜--⌝ w ⌜-⌝[...]*

Upper Edge
(61) ⌜-⌝*m*⌜-⌝[-]⌜-⌝*ṣpỉry*[-- *ṯ*]⌜*l*⌝*ṯ*⌜*t*⌝[...]

Translation[68]

I. (1) In the month of *Raʾšu-Yêni*, on the day of the new moon, (2) cut a bunch of grapes for *ʾIlu* as a peace-offering.[69]

II. (3) On the thirteenth of the month the king will wash himself cle[an].

IIIA. (4) On the fourteenth of the month: the best of the trib[ute][70] (5) and two rams for *Baʿlatu-Bahatīma;*
[two b]irds [for the *ʾI*]*nāšu*-(6) *ʾIlīma;*
a ram, a jar <of oil?> for *ʾILŠ;*
a ram for [the *ʾIlāhūma*.

B. And?] the king (7) will sit down while still clean[71] and someone will wip[e…] and […] (8) day.

IVA. On the next day, he/someone will […] (9) as TGML […];
two e[w]es (10) and a cit[y-d]ove someone will[…];
[…] (11) and a bul[l for] *ʾIlu*.

B. And in the o[pening…] (12) he/someone will pour.[72]

C. A cow for the *ʾIlāhūma;*
for *Ṯukamuna-wa-Šu*[*nama* a ewe];
(13) a ewe for *Rašap* as a burnt-offering.

D. And as a peace-offering: [two] e[wes] (14) for *ʾIlāhu;*
a bull and a ram for the *ʾIlāhūma*;
a co[w for the *ʾIlāhūma*];
(15) for *Baʿlu* a ram;
for *ʾAṯiratu* [a ram];
for *Ṯukamuna-wa-Šuna*[*ma* a ram];
(16) for *ʿAnatu* a ram;
for *Rašap* a ram;
[for the Circle] of *ʾIlu* and the Assembly of [*Baʿlu*] (17) a cow;
for Š*alimu* [a cow];
and in the flames the heart (18) as a roast-offering[73] for the *ʾIlāhū* [*ma*] and for the *Baʿalūma*,
full jars of [*dṯt*-grain and of] (19) emmer: thirty (also for the *ʾIlāhūma* and the *Baʿalūma* ?).

E. [ ]MT as an entry-offering (20) that one takes to the [ro]yal palace (or: that the king's palace will take): one *dabḥu*-sacrifice, oil perfumed with myrrh, (21) oil perfumed with various spices, honey, kidney(s), and a c[ity]-dove, (22) and two ḤṮ.

F. And in the ǴR, four[teen] (23) jars of wine, half a measure of flour [...]

G. [...] (24) altars of the temple of *ʾIlatu:* a bird [for] *Ṣapunu;*
a ram (25) for *Ǵalmatu;*
a ram and a *L*[--] for *Yariḫu;*
(26) a cow for *Nikkal;*
[a cow for *Baᶜ*]*latu-Bahatīma;*
(27) two birds for the *ʾInāšu*-[*ʾIlīma;*
a co]w (28) for the *ʾIlāhū*[*ma*];
a ewe for *Ša*[*pšu;*
a co]w for *Ra*[*š*(29)*ap*] as a burnt-offering.

H. And as a pe[ace]-offering[: the same;
two] ew[es] (30) for [*ʾI*]*lāhu;*
a cow for the *ʾIlāhūma;*
a cow for the *ʾIlā* [*hūma*];
(31) a [e]we for *Ṯukamuna-wa-Šunama;*
a ewe (32) for [*ʾIlu*]-*Bêti*.

I. Two ewes at the Spring as a bur[nt-offering.

J. And as a peace-(33)offering]: the same;
a cow for *Ba*[*ᶜlu* of *Ṣapunu*];
(34) a e[w]e for *Ṣapunu;*
a cow for [*Baᶜlu*] (35) of Ugarit;
a ram for *ʾIluʾibī;*
a Ǵ [-- for *ʾAṯi*]*ratu;*
(36) and two birds for RʾI⌜--⌝;
[X-number of] times (is this set of offerings to be performed).

K. (37) And (do the same?) at the temple of *Baᶜlatu-Bâtī*[*ma*]-*Rāmīma*, and in order to do so ascend (38) [the a]ltars.

VA. On the fifth day (of the festival of the full moon), in the temple of *ʾIlu:* one shek[el of sil(39)ver], a liver, and (one) *dabḫu*-sacrifice [...] (40) [for] *ʾAṯiratu;*
two birds for the *ʾI*[*nāšu-ʾIlīma*].

B. (41) [You] will return to the altar of *Baᶜlu:* a c[ow for *Baᶜlu* of *Ṣapunu*];
(42) a ewe for *Ṣapunu;*
and a ewe [for *Baᶜlu* of Ugarit];
(43) twenty-two times (is this set of offerings to be performed).

C. [...] (44) a ram, a jar of oil, a cow.

D. And [the king], still pure, (45) will repeat the recitation.

VIA. On the sixth day (of the festival of the full moon):

two [rams] for *Šamnu*; (46) in the upper room, a cow (also for *Šamnu* ?).

B. [The king], still pure, will repea[t] the recitation.

VIIA. (47) On the seventh day (of the festival of the full moon), when the sun rises, the day will be free (of cultic obligations);

B. when the sun sets, (48) the king will [be free (of cultic obligations)].[74]

VIIIA. And on the day of the new moon (of the following month): two rams (49) for [...]T.

B. (50) At that time, the king [will offer a sac]rifice to PRGL-ṢQRN on the roof,[75] (51) where there will be dwellings of branches, fo[ur] on one side, four on the other: a ram as a burnt-offer[ing].

C. (52) A bu[ll] and a ram as a peace-offering, to be repeated seven times.

D. According to what is in his heart (53) the king will sp[eak].

E. When the sun rises, the king will be free (of cultic obligations).[76] (54) [Someone will X] the *ṢP*s and someone will wi[pe] his [ ].

F. You will ta[ke] him back (55) to [the palace].

G. And when he is there he will [raise to] the heavens his hands.[77]

Translation of RS 18.056:54–61

IX. (54) In the month of Š [...,[78] on the fo]urteen(55)th day of the month, [the k]ing will w[ash himself] clean.

XA. (56) On the next day: a ram as a b[ur]nt-offering for [...].

B. When the sun sets, (57) the [ki]ng will be free (of further cultic obligations).

---

(58) *Binu* ʾAʾUP[Š] and BS son of HZPḪ : three;

(59) *Kôṯarumal*[*ki* and] *Yitrānu*: five; *Binu Gadduʾaḫi*: nine;

(60) KL[...]: eight; [...]

(61) *Mammiya* [...]: three[...].[79]

RITUAL FOR A SINGLE DAY: A ROYAL RITUAL

16. RS 24.260

Text

Obverse

(1) *ỉd ydbḥ mlk*
(2) *l ủš⌜ḫr ḫ⌝lm⌜ẓ⌝*
(3) *l b bt ⌜.⌝ ỉl bt*
(4) *š l ḫlmẓ*
(5) *w tr . l qlḥ*
(6) *w šḫl⌜l⌝ . ydm*
(7) *b qdš ỉl bt*
(8) *w tlḥm ảṯt*

---

(9) *š l ỉl bt . šlmm*
(10) *kl l ylḥm bh*

---

(11) *w l b bt šqym*
(12) *š l ủḫr*[80] *ḫlmẓ*

Lower Edge

(13) *w tr l qlḥ*

Reverse

(14) *ym ảḥd*

Translation

IA. (1) At that time,[81] the king is to sacrifice (2) to *ʾUšḫarâ Ḫulmiẓẓi* (3) inside the temple of *ʾIlu-Bêti:* (4) a ram for *Ḫulmiẓẓi*
(5) and a turtle-dove for QLḤ.[82]
(6) Purify the hands (of the participants) (7) in the sanctuary of *ʾIlu-Bêti;*
(8) the woman/women may eat (of the sacrificial meal).

B. (9) A ram for *ʾIlu-Bêti* as a peace-offering; (10) all may eat of it.

C. (11) (Again) within the temple:[83] libations;
(12) a ram for ʾU<š>ḫarâ Ḫulmiẓẓi.

D. (13) And a turtle-dove for QLḤ.
One day.[84]

RITUAL FOR A DAY AND A NIGHT

17. RS 1.001

The very first text discovered at Ras Shamra (14 May 1929) is ironically one of the most distinctive of the prescriptive sacrificial rituals. It represents the only text extant that prescribes an independent rite (as opposed to one that is part of a longer sequence) that occurs during a single day and the following night. There are good reasons to believe that such a rite would in fact have covered two days in the Ugaritic calendar, for the "day" probably began at sundown at Ugarit as in Israel (cf. Gen 1:5, 8, etc.).

Text

Obverse

(1) *dqt . ṯʿ . ynt . ṯʿm . dqt . ṯʿm*
(2) *mtntm w kbd . ảlp . š . l ỉl*
(3) *gdlt . ỉlhm . ṯkmn . w šnm . dqt*
(4) *⸢r⸣šp . dqt . šrp . w šlmm . dqtm*
(5) *[ỉ]⸢l⸣h . ảlp w š ỉlhm . gdl⸢t⸣ . ỉlhm*
(6) *[b]ʿl š . ảṯrt . š . ṯkmn w šn⸢m⸣ . š*
(7) *ʿnt . š . ršp . š . dr . ỉl w p[ḫ]r bʿl*
(8) *gdlt . šlm . gdlt . w b ủrm . ⸢l⸣b*
(9) *rmṣt . ỉlhm . bʿlm . dṯt . w ks̀m . ḫmš*
(10) *ʿ⸢š⸣rh . mlủn . šnpt . ḫṣth . bʿl . ṣpn š*
(11) *⸢tr⸣ṯ š . ỉlt . mgdl . š . ỉlt . ảsrm š*
(12) *w l ll . špš pgr . w ṯrmnm . bt mlk*
(13) *ỉ⸢lb⸣t . gdlt . ủšḫry . gdlt . ym gdlt*
(14) *bʿ⸢l⸣ . gdlt . yrḫ . gdlt . <kṯr>*
(15) *gdlt . ṯrmn . gdlt . pdry . gdlt dqt*
(16) *dqt . ⸢t⸣rṯ . dqt . <ršp . dqt>*

(17) ⌜š⌝rp . ʿnt . ḫbly . dbḥm . š[p]š pgr

Lower Edge

(18) [g]⌜d⌝lt . ỉltm . ḫnqtm . d⌜qt⌝m

(19) [y]rḫ . kṯy . gdlt . w l ǵl⌜mt⌝ š

Reverse

(20) ⌜w⌝ pảmt ṯlṯm . w yrdt . ⌜m⌝dbḥt

(21) ⌜g⌝dlt . l bʿlt bhtm . ʿṣrm

(22) l ỉnš ỉlm

Translation

I. (1) (At some time during the daylight hours.)[85]

A. (1) A ewe as a *ṯʿ* -sacrifice;
a dove, also as a *ṯʿ* -sacrifice;
a ewe, also as *ṯʿ* -sacrifice;
(2) two kidneys and the liver (of?)[86] a bull and a ram for *ʾIlu*.

B. (3) A cow for the *ʾIlāhūma;*
for *Ṯukamuna-wa-Šunama* a ewe;[87]
(4) for *Rašap* a ewe as burnt-offering.

C. And as a peace-offering: two ewes (5) for [*ʾI*]*lāhu;*
a bull and a ram for the *ʾIlāhūma;*
a cow for the *ʾIlāhūma;*
(6) for *Baʿlu* a ram;
for *ʾAṯiratu* a ram;
for *Ṯukamuna-wa-Šunama* a ram;
(7) for *ʿAnatu* a ram;
for *Rašap* a ram;
for the Circle of *ʾIlu* and the Assembly of *Baʿlu* (8) a cow;
for Š*alimu* a cow;
and in the flames the heart (9) as a roast -offering for the *ʾIlāhūma* and for the *Baʿalūma;*
dṯt -grain and emmer, (10) fifteen full measures of each (also for the *ʾIlāhūma* and the *Baʿalūma*?);[88]

D. As a presentation-offering, half of this (also for the *ʾIlāhūma* and the *Baʿalūma*?);
for *Baʿlu* of *Ṣapunu* a ram;
(11) for *Tirāṯu* a ram;
for *ʾIlatu-Magdali* a ram;
for *ʾIlatu-ʾ*ASRM a ram.

IIA. (12) And at night, *Šapšu-Pagri* and the *Ṯarrumannūma* being in the royal palace, (13) for *ʾIlu-Bêti* a cow;[89]
for *ʾUšḫaraya* a cow;
for *Yammu* a cow;
(14) for *Baʿlu* a cow;
for *Yariḫu* a cow;
for <*Kôṯaru* > (15) a cow;
for *Ṯarrumannu* a cow;
for *Pidray* a cow;
for *Daqqitu* (16) a ewe;
for *Tirāṯu* a ewe;
for <*Rašap* a ewe> (17) as burnt-offering.

B. For *ʿAnatu Ḫablay* two *dabḥu* -sacrifices (animal *ad libitum* $^{?}$);
for *Šapšu-Pagri* (18) a cow;
for *ʾIlatāma Ḫāniqatāma* two ewes;
(19) for Kassite *Yariḫu* a cow;
and for *Ġalmatu* a ram;
(20) and thirty times (is this set of offerings to be performed).

C. Then you will descend from the altars: (21) A cow for *Baʿlatu-Bahatīma;* two birds (22) for the *ʾInāšu-ʾIlīma* (as burnt-offering$^{?}$).

AN ENTRY RITUAL EXTENDING OVER (AT LEAST) TWO DAYS

18. RS 1.005

The "entry" ritual is an old Amorite practice, as is shown by its relatively frequent mention in the Mari texts, with similar rites attested at Emar (references in Pardee 2000a: 222 n. 21). From the Mari texts, it is clear that the "entry" could mark the deity's passage from a rural sanctuary into the city or even from another town to the city of Mari. Unfortunately, though the end point of the progress is, according to the Ugaritic texts, always the palace, no text states the starting point, and it is thus uncertain whether these rituals have only to do with the transfer of divine effigies from one sanctuary to another within the city or whether longer displacements were practiced. The deities named in the attested rites are *ʿAṯtartu-Ḫurri* (here only), *ʿAṯtartu-Šadî* (text 12 [RS 24.643:18] and text 58 [RS 19.015:10]), the *Gaṯarūma* (here below line 9), and the *Rašapūma* (RS 19.015:11). A fragmentary text (RIH 77/4+) refers to the "exit" of *Rašap-Guni*.[90] The only one of these deities whose name indicates a possible extramural residence is the second, whose name means "*ʿAṯtartu* of the Steppe Land"; but in point of fact such an interpretation would be purely etymological, since nothing is known about the location of her regular sanctuary. *Rašap* is a deity known for his multiple hypostases, one located as far away as Anatolia (*Rašap-Bibitta*). The *Gaṯarūma* constitute the most enigmatic of these divinities, apparently appearing as a plurality here but as a duality in text 8 (RS 24.256).

The two first sections clearly correspond to "entry" rituals accompanied by offerings to the deities who "enter" and to associated deities, while the last section prescribes the king's participation in a royal procession. It is the damaged sequence of ritual acts in the mid-part of the text, each set down in a single line separated from the next by a horizontal line, that has defied interpretation—and will continue to do so until a better-preserved version is discovered.

Text

Obverse

(1) *k tʿrb . ʿṯtrt . ḫr . g⸢b⸣*
(2) *bt mlk . ʿšr . ʿšr . ⸢b .⸣ -- ⸢.⸣ bt ỉl⸢m⸣*[91]
(3) *kb⸢kb⸣m . -trmt .*
(4) *lb⸢š⸣ [.] w ⸢k⸣tn . ủšpǵt*
(5) *ḫr⸢ṣ⸣ . ṯlṯt . mzn .*
(6) *drk . š . ảlp . w ṯlṯ*
(7) *ṣỉn . šlmm [.] šbʿ pảmt*
(8) *l ỉlm . šb⸢ʿ⸣ [.] l kṯr .*

---

(9) *ʿlm . tʿrbn . gṯrm .*
(10) *bt . mlk ⸢.⸣ ṯql . ḫrṣ .*
(11) *l špš . w yrḫ . l gṯr .*
(12) *ṯql . ksp ⸢.⸣ ṭb . ả⸢p⸣ w n⸢pš⸣*
(13) *l ʿnt⸢ḫ⸣ . ṯql . ḫrṣ .*
(14) *l špš [w] ⸢y⸣rḫ . l gṯr . ṯn*
(15) *[ṯ]⸢ql⸣[. ksp] ⸢.⸣ ṭb . ảp . w npš*
(16) *[ ]⸢-⸣bt . ảlp . w š*

---

(17) *[ ]m . l gṯrm .*

---

(18) *[ ] . l ʿntm .*

---

(19) [ ]⌜-⌝*rm* . *dkrm* .

Reverse

(20) [ ]⌜-⌝ . *l* ᶜ*ntm* .

---

(21) [ ]*l slm* .

---

(22) ⌜--⌝ [-(-)] ⌜-⌝*ry* . *ylbš* .

---

(23) *mlk* . *ylk* . *lqḥ* ⌜.⌝ *ỉlm* .

---

(24) *ảṯr* . *ỉlm* . *ylk* . *p*ᶜ*nm* .
(25) *mlk* . *p*ᶜ*nm* . *yl*[*k* .]
(26) *šb*ᶜ *pảmt* . *l klhm* .

Translation

IA. (1) When ᶜ*Aṯtartu-Ḫurri* enters the "mound"(-room) (2) of the palace: put on a feast in the temple of the (3) Star Gods.[92]
B. As a *tarūmatu*-offering: (4) a garment and a tunic, a *ủšpǵt*-garment, (5) three shekels of gold (in the form of) a traveler's (6) scale.[93]
C. A ram, a bull, and three (7) sheep/goats as a *šlmm*-sacrifice:
seven times (8) for the (Star?) Gods,
seven times for *Kôṯaru*.[94]

IIA. (9) On the next day, the *Gaṯarūma* will enter (10) the royal palace: a shekel of gold (11) for *Šapšu* and*Yariḫu;*
for *Gaṯaru* (12) a shekel of pure silver;
a snout and a neck (13) for ᶜ*Anatu*.[95]
B. A shekel of gold (14) for *Šapšu* and *Yariḫu;*
for *Gaṯaru* two (15) [sh]ekels of pure [silver];
a snout and a neck (16) [for x-deity;
for ʾ*I*]*lu-Bêti* a bull and a ram.

C. (17) [...]M for the *Gaṯarūma*.[96]

D. (18) […] for ʿ*Anatu* also.

E. (19) [… for] the male [*Ga*]*ṯarāma*.

F. (20) […] for ʿ*Anatu* also.

G. (21) […]to SLM.[97]

H. (22) ⸢--⸣[-(-)]⸢-⸣ will clothe.

I. (23) The king will go take the gods.

J. (24) Everyone will follow the gods on foot; (25) the king himself [will g]o on foot, (26) seven times for all of them.[98]

CONTEMPLATION RITUALS

The root PHY ("to see") occurs four times in three texts. Unfortunately, each of the texts is damaged, and it is not possible to define with any precision what the form and function of the "contemplation" was. That act was, however, linked with offerings and sacrifices, so there can be no doubt that the rite was fully integrated into the sacrificial cult. Text 20 (RIH 77/2B+) shows that the contemplation ritual could be part of a more complex series extending over two days, while text 21 (RIH 77/10B+) shows that two contemplation rites could follow one after the other, apparently on the same day. Moreover, the use of *ʾid*, "then, at that time," to introduce all or parts of these rites appears to indicate that they were integrated into a more complex liturgy. The state of the texts, however, is so poor that it is impossible to get a good idea of what longer sequences were typical. As to the PHY-rite itself, however, one finds in texts 19 and 21 (RS 19.013 and RIH 77/10B+) remarkable similarities in the offerings and the types of offerings (the relevant paragraph of text 20 [RIH 77/2B+] is too damaged to permit comparison—note, however, the similarity in structure between the second DBḤ-rite in this text and that of the PHY-rite in the other two texts). The fact that the two similar texts were found at such a distance from each other indicates that their resemblances do not reflect performance practice in a given sanctuary but that it was the royal ritual of "contemplating" a deity that required a similar liturgical setting.

19. RS 19.013

Text

Obverse

(1) *ỉd* [.] *yph* . *mlk*
(2) *r*⸢*š*⸣*p* . *ḫgb* . *ảp*
(3) *w* [-] ⸢*n*⸣*pš* . *ksp*
(4) *w* [-] *ḫrṣ* . *km*⸢*m*⸣
(5) *w* [-] *ḥ*⸢*ẓ*⸣ [.] ⸢*ả*⸣*lp*
(6) *w* [-] *š* . *l* [-]⸢--⸣*p*⸢-(-)⸣
(7) *w* [- *ʿṣ*]⸢*r*⸣[*m* . *l*] ⸢*ỉ*⸣*nš*
(8) *ỉ*[*lm* ...]
(9) *w*[...]
(10) *k*⸢-⸣[...]
(11) *ṯql*[...]

Reverse

(12) [...]
(13) [...]
(14) ⸢-⸣[...]
(15) ⸢-⸣[...]
(16) *ả*[...]
(17) [...]
(18) ⸢-⸣[...]
(19) ⸢-⸣[-]⸢-⸣*ḫ*⸢-⸣*šlm*
(20) [--]⸢- *š*⸣ [.] *l ảlỉt*
(21) [-]⸢-⸣ *ršp* . *š* .
(22) ⸢l⸣ [.] ⸢*š*⸣*lm* . *w mlk*
(23) *ynṣl* . *l ṯʿy* .

Translation

IA. At that time, the king must look upon (2) *Rašap-Ḥagab:* a snout (3) and a neck, a shekel of silver (4) and a shekel of gold.
The same, (5) plus an arrow, a bull (6) and a ram for *Rašap*-[...];[99]
(7) and [two bir]d[s] for *ʾInāsu*-(8)*ʾIlīma;*
(9) and [...] (10) [...] (11) a shekel [...]

B. (12–18) (Broken)
(19) [ ]*Šalimu*
(20) [ ] a ram for ʾALʾIT;
(21) [a ram] for *Rašap;*
a ram (22) for *Šalimu.*
C. And the king (23) will move away to perform the *ṯʿ*-sacrifice.[100]

---

20. RIH 77/2B+

This liturgy begins with two paragraphs that are introduced by the adverb *ỉd*, "at that time," marking a link with a larger set of rites (see introduction to the contemplation rituals). The third paragraph marks the passage to a second day, but thereafter the tablet is in such bad condition that it is impossible to determine whether there was a further chronological extension. After several sets of sacrifices on the first day mentioned, the "contemplation" rite occurs on the following day. The primary deities honored by the sacrifices are *ʾIluʾibī* and *ʾIlu*, but the indication of the deity who is the object of the contemplation rite has disappeared.

Text

Obverse

---

(1) *ỉd . ydbḫ . mlk . b ḫmn*
(2) [--]*š*⸢-⸣ *. w šỉn*⸢*m*⸣ *. l yšt*

---

(3) [*ỉ*]⸢*d .*⸣ *ydbḫ . mlk . l ỉlỉb*
(4) *b db . ảp . w npš . ksp .*
(5) *w ḫrṣ . kmm . ảlp . w š*
(6) *šrp . l ỉlỉb . w šl*⸢*m*⸣[*m*]

(7) *kmm . š . l il̓ . šrp .*
(8) *w šlmm . kmm . ʿṣ⌜rm⌝*
(9) *l šmn*

---

(10) *w ʿlm . b qr*⌜-⌝[...]
(11) [-]⌜*p*⌝*ḫ . mlk* ⌜-⌝[...]
(12) [--]*t* . ⌜-⌝[...]

....

Reverse

....

(13') [--]⌜-⌝*ql . ḫmš*[...]
(14') [-]*rḫ . npš . w str*[...]
(15') ⌜-⌝*m*[—]*šbʿ . kbkbm*
(16') *w ṯl*⌜*ṯ*⌝[*m* .] *ḫrṣ*

(17') *ri̓š . ả*[-]⌜-⌝*m . ḫmš*
(18') *ʿšrh . s*[-]⌜-⌝ .
(19') *w ảl . tṣủ* [.] ⌜-⌝*ṣủ .*
(20') *w ḫlt*

Translation

IA. (1) At that time, the king is to offer a sacrifice in the *ḫmn*-sanctuary (of?) (2) [...] and he will put his sandals (back?) on.

B. (3) At that time, the king is to offer a sacrifice to *ʾIluʾibī* (4) in the DB: a snout and a neck, a shekel of silver (5) and a shekel of gold.
C. The same plus a bull and a ram (6) as a burnt-offering to *ʾIluʾibī*.
D. And as a peace-offering: (7) the same.
E. A ram for *ʾIlu* as a burnt-offering.
F. (8) And as a peace-offering: the same;
two birds (9) for *Šamnu*.

IIA. (10) And on the next day, in the QR[...], (11) the king [must] look upon [X-deity] (12) [...].

....

Reverse[101]

....

B. (13') […] FALL FIVE[…] (14') in the [-]R a neck and STR[…] (15') […] seven star-ornaments (16') and thir[ty] shekels of gold.[102]

C. (17') HEAD [ ] fif(18')teen S[TR?].
D. (19') And they certainly must not be taken outside (lit. "exit").[103]
E. (20') But you will be free (of further cultic obligations).

21. RIH 77/10B+

Text

Obverse

---

(1) [*i͗*]*d . yph . mlk . ršp .*
(2) *ḫgb . a͗*⌜*p*⌝ [.] *w npš*
(3) ⌜*k*⌝*sp . w ḫ*⌜*rṣ*⌝ *. kmm*
(4) ⌜*w*⌝ *. t*⌜--⌝[ ]⌜-⌝ *š .*
(5) ⌜-⌝[-]*š*[ ]*šr*[…]
(6) *w š*⌜*l*⌝[ ]
(7) *kst*[ ]⌜-⌝*l* ⌜. -⌝[…]

---

(8) *i͗d .* ⌜*y*⌝*ph . mlk . ʿnt*
(9) *sl*⌜*z*⌝ *. a͗p* ⌜.⌝ *w npš . ksp*
(10) [*w .*] *ḫrṣ . kmm . a͗lp*
(11) ⌜*w*⌝ *š . šrp . l ʿnt*
(12) *w šlmm*

Lower Edge

(13) *kmm . š l* ⌜*ʿnt*⌝

Reverse

(14) [ ]⌜-⌝*nt*
(15) [*a͗*]⌜*l*⌝*i͗t . š*
(16) [ ]*šp .*
(17) [ ]⌜*d*⌝*m .*
(18) [ ] *. k*
(19) [ ]⌜*qb*⌝

(20) [...]
(21) [ ]⸢--⸣[-]⸢--⸣[...]
(22) [ ]⸢-(-)⸣*tr*⸢*d*⸣[?]⸢-⸣*ḥ*⸢*l*⸣
(23) [*m*]⸢*lk*⸣[ ]⸢-⸣*l*
(24) ⸢-⸣*m*[ ]*š*
(25) [-]*ỉ*⸢-⸣[ ]⸢-⸣

Translation

IA. (1) [At that] time, the king must look upon *Rašap*-(2)*Ḥagab:* a snout and a neck, (3) a shekel of silver (4) and a shekel of gold.
B. The same (4) plus an arrow!?, [a bull] and!? a ram (5) for? [-]Š[ ] as a burnt-[offering]?.[104]
C. (6) And as a pe[ace-offering ...].
D. (7) *kst*-garments [...].

E. (8) At that time, the king must look upon *ʿAnatu*-(9)SLZ/Ḫ:[105] a snout and a neck, a shekel of silver (10) [and] a shekel of gold.
F. The same plus a bull (11) and a ram as a burnt-offering for *ʿAnatu*.
G. And as a peace-offering (13) the same.
H. A ram for *ʿAnatu* (14) [...]
(15) [... ʾA]LʾIT a ram
(16–22) (Broken)
I. (22–23) The king will be free (of further cultic obligations).
J. (23–25) (Broken)

TEXTS WITH NO STATED TIME FRAME

Ritual for National Unity

22. RS 1.002

One fairly well preserved exemplar of this ritual is known (RS 1.002) while another is sufficiently preserved (RS 17.100A+B) to show that significant differences existed between performances. Four other fragments are too small to contain significant information regarding variants (RS 24.270A, RS 24.270B, RS 24.650B, RS24.652G+K). Judged too fragmentary for inclusion here, these other exemplars of the text type are nevertheless not without interest. The relatively large number of texts reflecting what is basically the same rite is without parallel at Ugarit, while the spread of find-spots and of scribal hands (the texts were found in the so-called High Priest's library on the acropolis, in the royal palace, and in the House of the Divination Priest on the south side of the tell) shows that the texts were not the product of a single school.

The ritual is unique also in its structure (originally three pairs of paragraphs grouped by reference to the male and the female inhabitants; each paragraph is designated below as a "section"), in its level of repetition (see charts in Pardee 1991 and 2000a: 99–100, 102), and in its concerns (much of the vocabulary is unique to these texts). The word "atonement" is often used in classifying this rite. I avoid the term because of its biblical connotations and because the Hebrew word that is customarily so translated (√KPR) does not occur here. Moreover, the combination of what I have called "horizontal" and "vertical" structural elements (i.e., those that run through each paragraph as opposed to those that provide the structure of the text as a whole—see Pardee 1991 and 2000a: 99–103, 140–42) may be taken to indicate that the rite was in fact intended as a response to three "theological" concerns, not just one. The key word is preserved only in the case of the third theme: it is *mšr* (lines 26' and 35'), "rectitude, uprightness," and that quality is assured by the slaughter of a donkey. This reflects an old Amorite practice, carried out particularly at moments of covenant making, where the donkey was "killed" (NKT expresses that general notion in this text).[106] Working backwards, the specific term designating the quality sought has disappeared from sections III and IV, but the nature of the rite as having to do with expiation may be deduced from the term ḤṬʾ ("sin"), with which the sacrificial act of ṮʿY, carried out on a ram, is associated on the vertical plane (ṮʿY appears between DBḤ and NKT in each paragraph, e.g., section IV, lines 23'-24'). Only the type of sacrifice associated with the first theme is known, and it is DBḤ, the first sacrificial type mentioned in each paragraph (e.g., section IV, l. 23'), the most general sacrificial term in the Ugaritic vocabulary. Because the overall concern of the text appears to be with unity among the various social groups within the kingdom of Ugarit and because DBḤ designates the sacrificial feast, the function of the first sections of the rite may have been to promote communion, both between the social groups named in the text and between humans and the deities honored (*ʾIlu* and his family). The three principal themes in order of appearance would thus have been communion between human classes as well as between humans and gods, expiation of sin, and "rectitude" in human and divine relationships.

Although the existence of multiple exemplars, with at least two variant versions, shows that the rite must have been performed with some regularity, there are no indications from the texts themselves as to frequency or, if annual, as to the moment in the year when the rite would have been carried out. Comparisons with the biblical Day of Atonement are tempting, but the important differences between the two sets of rites mean that only general similarities may be cited until chronological data on the Ugaritic liturgy are forthcoming.

Text

Obverse

Section ? (I or II)

(1') [...] ⸢*w*⸣ *n*⸢*py*⸣[...]
(2') [...] *npy . ủ*[*grt* ...]
(3') [...]*y . ủ l p .* [...]
(4') [...]⸢*ǵ*⸣*br . ủ* ⸢*l*⸣[*p* ...]
(5') [...]⸢--⸣[...]
....

Section II

(6') [*ṯʿ nṯʿ*]⸢*y*⸣
(7') [*d*]*r . b*⸢*n*⸣ ⸢*ỉ*⸣[*l*]
(8') [ ]

Section III

(9') [ ] ⸢.⸣ *w npy*
(10') [ ]*y . ủgr*⸢*t*⸣
(11') [*qṭ*]*y*
(12') [ ]⸢-⸣
(13') [ ]
(14') [ ]
(15') [*ndb*]*ḫ*
(16') [ ]⸢*yt*⸣[*šỉ*]
(17') [*mpḫ*]⸢*r*⸣*t* . [*bn . ỉl* *ṯkmn w šn*]*m hn š*

Section IV

(18') [*w n*]*py* . *g*⸢*r*⸣[. *ḫmyt . ủgrt . w np*]*y*

(19') [ ]⸢-⸣ . *w n*⸢*p*⸣[*y*]⸢-⸣ . *ủ tḫṭ*⸢*ỉ*⸣[*n . ủ l p . qṭy*]
(20') *ủ l p . ddmy . ủ l* ⸢*p*⸣ [. *ḫry . ủ*]⸢*l*⸣ *p . ḫty . ủ l p* [. *ảlṯy . ủ l p* .] *ġbr*
(21') *ủ l p . ḫbtkn . ủ l* ⸢*p*⸣ . *md*[*llk*]*n . ủ l p . q*[*rzbl*]
(22') *ủ tḫṭỉn . b ảpkn . ủ b* ⸢*q*⸣*ṣrt . npš*[*kn . ủ b qṭt*]
(23') *tqṭṭn ủ tḫṭỉn . l bḥ*⸢*m*⸣[107] *w l ṯʿ . d*[*bḥn . ndb*]⸢*ḥ*⸣
(24') *hw . ṯʿ . nṯʿy . hw . nkt . n*⸢*k*⸣*t . ytšỉ*[. *l ảb . bn ỉl*]
(25') *ytšỉ . l dr . bn . ỉl . l .* ⸢*m*⸣*pḫrt . bn* ⸢*ỉ*⸣[*l . l ṯkmn . w š*]*nm hn š*

Section V

(26') *w . šqrb . ʿr . mšr mšr* [.] ⸢*b*⸣*n . ủgrt .* ⸢*w*⸣ [*npy*] *ủgr*[108]
(27') *w npy . ymản . w npy . ʿrmt* ⸢. *w*⸣ *npy .* ⸢-⸣[ ]
(28') *w npy . nqmd . ủ šn . ypkm . ủ l p . q*[*ṭy . ủ l p . ddm*]*y*
(29') *ủ l p . ḫry . ủ l p . ḫ*⸢*t*⸣*y . ủ l p . ảlṯy . ủ* ⸢*l*⸣ [*p ġbr* .] ⸢*ủ*⸣ *l p*
(30') *ḫbtkm . ủ l p . m*⸢*d*⸣[*l*]*lkm . ủ l p . qrzbl . ủ* ⸢*šn*⸣ [.] *ypkm*
(31') *ủ b ảpkm . ủ b q*[*ṣ*]⸢*r*⸣*t . npškm . ủ b qṭt . tqṭṭ*
(32') *ủ šn ypkm . l d*[*b*]*ḥm . w l . ṯʿ . dbḥn . ndbḥ . hw . ṯʿ nṯʿy*
(33') *hw . nkt . nkt .* ⸢*y*⸣[*t*]*šỉ . l ảb . bn . ỉl . ytšỉ . l dr*
(34') *bn ỉl*[109] . *l ṯkmn* [. *w*] *šnm . hn . ʿr*

Section VI

(35') *w ṯb . l mspr . m*[*š*]⸢*r*⸣ *mšr . bt . ủgrt . w npy* ⸢.⸣ *gr*
(36') *ḥmyt . ủgrt . w* [*np*]*y* ⸢. *ả*⸣*ṯt . ủ šn . ypkn . ủ l p* ⸢.⸣ *qṭy*
(37') *ủ l p . ddmy . ủ l* [*p . ḫ*]*ry . ủ l p . ḫty . ủ l p . ảlṯy*
(38') *ủ l p* [.] *ġbr . ủ l p .* ⸢*ḫ*⸣[*bt*]⸢*kn . ủ l*⸣ *p . mdllkn . ủ l p* ⸢.⸣ *qrz*⸢*bl*⸣
(39') *l*[110] *šn ypkn . b ảp*⸢*k*⸣[*n . ủ b q*]⸢*ṣ*⸣*rt . npškn* ⸢.⸣ *ủ b q*⸢*ṭt*⸣
(40') *tqṭṭn . ủ šn . y*⸢*p*⸣[*kn . l dbḥm .*] *w l ṯʿ dbḥn*
(41') *ndbḥ . hw . ṯʿ n*[*ṯʿy . hw . nkt . n*]⸢*k*⸣*t .* ⸢*yt*⸣[*š*]⸢*ỉ* .⸣ *l ảb bn ỉl*

Reverse

(42') *ytšỉ . l* ⸢*d*⸣[*r . bn ỉl . l*] *mpḫrt . bn ỉl*
(43') *l ṯkm*⸢*n*⸣ [. *w šnm* .] *hn* ⸢*ʿr*⸣

Translation[111]

Section ? (I or II)

(1') […] and well-being […]
(2') [… well-being of U[garit…]

(3') […]Y; be it according to the statement of […]
(4') […] ʿBR, be it according to the state[ment of…]
(5') […] […]

Section II

(6') [the *ṯ*ʿ-sacrifice, it is offer]ed
(7') [to the Circl]e-of-the-Sons-of-ʾ*Ilu*
(8') [ ]

Section III

(9') [ ] and well-being
(10') [and well-be]ing of Ugarit
(11') [Qaṭ]ien
(12') [ ]
(13') [ ]
(14') [ ]
(15') [… is sacrific]ed
(16') [ ] May it be bor[ne]
(17') [assemb]ly [of the sons of ʾ*Ilu*, *Ṯukamuna-wa-Šuna*]*ma*: here is the ram.

Section IV

(18') [
we]ll-being[112] of the foreigner [(within) the walls of Ugarit,
and well-be]ing of (19') [ ]
and well[-being of];
whether you si[n:
be it according to the statement of[113] the Qaṭien],
(20') be it according to the statement of the DDMY,[114]
be it according to the statement [of the Hurrian,
be it] according to the statement of the Hittite,
be it according to the statement [of the ʾAlashian,
be it according to the statement of] ĠBR,
(21') be it according to the statement of your oppressed ones,
be it according to the statement of yo[ur] impo[verished ones],
be it according to the statement of Q[RZBL;]
(22') whether you sin:
be it in your anger,

be it in your [i]mpatience,
[be it in some turpitude] (23') that you should commit;
whether you sin:
as concerns the <sa>crifices
or as concerns the *ṯ*ʿ-sacrifice.
[The] sacrifice, it [is sacrific]ed,
(24') the *ṯ*ʿ-sacrifice, it is offered,
the slaughtering is done.[115]
May it be borne [to the father of the sons of *ʾIlu*],[116]
(25') may it be borne to the Circle-of-the-Sons-of-*ʾIlu*,
to the Assembly-of-the-Sons-of-*ʾI*[*lu*,
to *Ṯukamuna-wa-Šu*]*nama*:
here is the ram.

Section V

(26') Bring near the donkey of "rectitude": rectitude of the son of Ugarit: and[well-being of the foreigner within the walls] of Ugar<it>,
(27') and well-being of YMʾAN,
and well-being of ʿRMT,
and well-being of[ ]
(28') and well-being of *Niqmaddu;*
whether your "beauty"[117] be altered:
be it according to the statement of the Qa[ṭien,
be it according to the statement of DDM]Y,
(29') be it according to the statement of the Hurrian,
be it according to the statement of the Hittite,
be it according to the statement of the ʾAlashian,
be it according to the sta[tement of ǴBR,]
be it according to the statement of (30') your oppressed ones,
be it according to the statement of your im[pov]erished ones,
be it according to the statement of QRZBL;
whether your "beauty" be altered:
(31') be it in your anger,
be it in your im[pa]tience,
be it in some turpitude that you should commit;
(32') whether your "beauty" be altered:
as concerns the sa[cr]ifices
or as concerns the *ṯ*ʿ-sacrifice.

The sacrifice, it is sacrificed,
the ṯʿ-sacrifice, it is offered,
(33') the slaughtering is done.
May it be b[or]ne to the father of the sons of *ʾIlu*,
may it be borne to the Circle-of-(34')the-Sons-of-*ʾIlu*,
<to the Assembly-of-the-Sons-of-*ʾIlu* >,
to *Ṯukamuna-wa-Šunama*:
here is the donkey.

Section VI

(35') And return to the recitation of "rectitude": rectitude of the daughter of Ugarit: and well-being of the foreigner (36') (within) the walls of Ugarit,
and [well-be]ing of the woman/wife;
whether your "beauty" be altered:
be it according to the statement of the Qaṭien,
(37') be it according to the statement of DDMY,
be it according to the sta[tement of the Hu]rrian,
be it according to the statement of the Hittite,
be it according to the statement of the ʾAlashian,
(38') be it according to the statement of ǴBR,
be it according to the statement of your o[ppressed ones],
be it according to the statement of your impoverished ones,
be it according to the statement of QRZBL;
(39') whether (!) your "beauty" be altered:
be it in yo[ur] anger,
[be it in] your [impa]tience,
be it in some turpitude (40') that you should commit;
whether [your] "beauty" be altered:
[as concerns sacrifices]
or as concerns the ṯʿ-sacrifice.
The sacrifice, (41') it is sacrificed,
the ṯʿ-sacrifice, it is [offered,
the slaughtering] is done.
(42') May it be borne to the father of the sons of *ʾIlu*,
may it be borne to the C[ircle-of-the-Sons-of-*ʾIlu*,
to] the Assembly-of-the-Sons-of-*ʾIlu*,
(43') to *Ṯukamuna*-[*wa-Šunama*:]
here is the donkey.

A Ritual for the Gods of the Land

23. RS [Varia 20]

The title of this sacrificial liturgy was known long before the text itself came to light: according to the administrative text 58 (RS 19.015), excavated in 1955 and published in 1965, one of the "royal sacrifices" bears the name *ỉl bldn*, whereas the sacrificial text, though known from oral reports, was not formally published until 1993 (Bordreuil and Pardee 1993b). Its basic structure is simple: a burnt-offering followed by a peace-offering. It is not like any other text, however, in the following respects: (1) the first offering, *nskt qlʿ*, "a shield of precious metals," is otherwise unattested; (2) the order of deities honored by the peace-offering is otherwise unattested, and an otherwise unknown deity appears (*ảmšrt* in line 15); (3) the text of the last two lines, of which the interpretation is uncertain, is elsewhere unattested, and none of the three words is attested elsewhere in the ritual texts.

Text

Obverse

(1) *dbḥ ỉl bldn*

---

(2) *nskt qlʿ*
(3) *ỉlỉb ảlp w š*
(4) *šrp . w šlmm*

---

(5) *ṯn ảlp⸢m w⸣ ṯn*
(6) *šm l ỉlỉb*
(7) *l ḫl*[118] *š*
(8) *l bʿl š*
(9) *l dgn ⸢š⸣*
(10) *l yrḫ [š]*

Lower Edge

(11) *l ym ⸢š⸣*
(12) *l ỉl ⸢t⸣[ʿḏr]*

Reverse

(13) *bʿl š*

(14) *l ʿnt ḫbly* ⸢*š*⸣
(15) *l ảmšrt š*
(16) *l dr ỉl*
(17) *w pḫr bʿl*
(18) *gdlt*
(19) *l ṣpn gdlt*
(20) *w pảmt ṯn*
(21) *l ʿšrm*
(22) *mlsm mrkbt*
(23) *mtrn*

Translation

IA. (1) Sacrificial liturgy for the Gods-of-the-Land.

B. (2) A shield of precious metals[119] (3) for *ʾIluʾibī;*
a bull and a ram (4) as a burnt-offering.
C. And as a peace-offering: | (5) two bulls and two (6) rams for *ʾIluʾibī;*
(7) for *ʾI!lu* a ram;
(8) for *Baʿlu* a ram;
(9) for *Dagan* a ram;
(10) for *Yariḫu* a ram;
(11) for *Yammu* a ram;
(12) for the Auxiliary-Gods-of-(13)*Baʿlu* a ram;
(14) for *ʿAnatu Ḫablay* a ram;
(15) for ʾAMŠRT[120] a ram;
(16) for the Circle-of-*ʾIlu* (17) and the Assembly-of-*Baʿlu* (18) a cow;
(19) for *Ṣapunu* a cow;
(20–21) twenty-two times (is this set of offerings to be performed).[121]
D. (23) Whatever is left over (22) is for the chariot-runners.

A Funerary Ritual in Poetic Form

24. RS 34.126

This is the only explicitly funerary text from Ugarit. It was in all probability prepared for the ceremony at which the second-last known king of

Ugarit, the *Niqmaddu* known conventionally as *Niqmaddu* III and who died during the last decade of the thirteenth century B.C.E., was placed in the company of his ancestors. It is clear from the last lines that the new king who is about to take the throne is *ʿAmmurāpiʾ*, the last king of whom texts have survived. Also named there is *Ṯarriyelli*, a former queen of Ugarit whose function at the time was that of queen-mother.[122] Because this text was found in what is now known to be the House of Urtenu (Bordreuil and Pardee 1995: 31–32; Bordreuil and Pardee 1999–2000; Pardee 2000a: 816, 825), a high official in the queen's household, it is possible that this personage, whose Hurrian name would have been pronounced roughly as *ʾUrtēnu* in Ugaritic, was the political official in charge of the ceremony, though the liturgy itself would certainly have been in the hands of the clergy.

The text is unique as a funerary text and also unique as a poetic ritual. Though various texts associated with ritual are in poetic form (see texts 46–56), this is the only text with *dbḥ* in its title and with sacrifices as an integral part (lines 27–31) that is entirely in poetic form. This formal feature is surely to be explained, at least in part, by the content, viz., by the fact that deities participate directly in the ritual itself: the solar deity *Šapšu* plays an explicit role (lines 18–26), while lines 2–11 constitute an invitation for the *Rapaʾūma*, "the shades of the netherworld," to participate. Though the precise makeup of the *Rapaʾūma* is as yet unknown, they are generally accounted as belonging to the divine sphere. In any case, two former kings are invited among them here (lines 11–12), and deceased kings are identified explicitly in text 56 (RS 24.257 reverse, RS 94.2518) as divine. The poetic form of the text appears, therefore, to reflect the perception at Ugarit that talk about gods was to be poetic in form (as opposed to the essentially administrative talk about the care and feeding of the gods in their earthly sanctuaries that characterizes the prose ritual texts).

The principal sections, or sense-units, of this text are: (1) title (line 1); (2) invitation to the *Rapaʾūma* (lines 2–12); (3) call to mourn the king's absence at his throne and table (lines 13–17); (4) invitation to and participation of *Šapšu*, who pronounces the official invitation to the deceased king to descend among his ancestors (lines 18–26); (5) the sevenfold descent of the king accompanied each time by the offering of a *ṯʿ*-sacrifice (lines 27–30); (6) the offering of bird(s) to procure well-being for the queen-mother, the new king, and the city of Ugarit (lines 30–34). As is clear from this outline, the rite reflected by this text serves to allow the deceased king to join his ancestors. It is not this rite that accompanied the enthronement of the new king, and the rite in question is not, therefore, a "coronation," as some have held. Nor does the evocation of the deceased ancestors constitute an act of "necromancy" as others have held—these ancestors are called up to participate in and to effect the "*rapaʾum*-ization" of the newly deceased king, not to serve the immediate interests of those who call them up (on the function of "mantic" texts, see below, introduction to sections VI A and VI B). The rite is narrowly funerary, and the literary genre of the text is, therefore, that of a funerary text in poetic form. On the possibility that one or another of the poetic texts found in the "House of the Priest with Lung and Liver Models" may have had more to do with the new king's assumption of power, see below on texts 55–56.

Text	***Translation***
(1) *spr . dbḥ . ẓlm*	Document of the sacrificial liturgy of the Shades.[123]
(2) *qrỉtm ⸢. r⸣pỉ . ả[rṣ ...]*	You have been called, O *Rapaʾūma* of the Earth,
(3) *qbỉtm . qbṣ . d[dn ...]*	You have been summoned, O Assembly of *Didānu;*[124]
(4) *qrả . ủlkn . r⸢p⸣[ủ ...]*	ʿULKN the *Rapaʾu* has been called,
(5) *qrả . trmn . rp[ủ ...]*	TRMN the *Rapaʾu* has been called,
(6) *qrả . sdn . w ⸢.⸣ rd[n ...]*	SDN-*wa*-RDN has been called,
(7) *qrả . ṯr . ʿllmn[...]*	ṮR ʿLLMN has been called,
(8) *qrủ . rpỉm . qdmym[...]*	They have called the Ancient *Rapaʾūma*.
(9) *qrỉtm . rpỉ . ảrṣ*	You have been called, O *Rapaʾūma* of the Earth,
(10) *qbỉtm . qbṣ . dd⸢n⸣*	You have been summoned, O Assembly of *Didānu;*
(11) *qrả . ʿmṯtm⸢r .⸣ m⸢l⸣k*	King *ʿAmmiṯtamru* has been called,
(12) *qrả . ủ . nqm⸢d⸣ [.] ⸢mlk⸣*	King *Niqmaddu* has been called as well.
(13) *ksỉ . nqmd [.] ⸢ỉbky⸣*	O Throne of *Niqmaddu*, be bewept,[125]
(14) *w . ydmʿ . ⸢h⸣dm . ⸢p⸣ʿnh*	And may tears be shed over the footstool of his feet.
(15) *l pnh . ybky . ṯlḥn . ml⸢k⸣*	Before him they must[126] beweep the king's table,
(16) *w . ⸢y⸣blʿ . ủdmʿth*	Each must swallow down his tears:

(17) *ʿdmt . w . ʿdmt . ʿdmt*	Desolation and desolation of desolations!
(18) *ỉšḫn . špš .*	Be hot, O *Šapšu*,
w . ỉšḫn (19) *nyr . rbt .*	Yea, be hot, O Great Light.
ʿln . špš . tṣ⌜*ḥ*⌝	On high *Šapšu* cries out:
(20) *ảṯr* ⌜.⌝ [*b*]*ʿlk . l . ks*⌜*ỉ*⌝[127] .	After your lords, from the throne,
ảṯr (21) *bʿlk . ảrṣ . rd .*	After your lords descend into the earth,
ảrṣ (22) *rd . w . špl . ʿpr .*	Into the earth descend and lower yourself into the dust:[128]
tḥt (23) *sdn . w . rdn .*	Under SDN-*wa*-RDN,
tḥt . ṯr (24) *ʿllmn .*	Under ṮR ʿLLMN,
tḥt . rpỉm . qdm⌜*y*⌝*m*	Under the Ancient *Rapaʾuma*;
(25) *tḥt . ʿmṯtmr . mlk*	Under King *ʿAmmiṯtamru*,
(26) *tḥm*[129] *. ủ . nq*[*md*] *. mlk*	Under King *Niqmaddu* as well.
(27) *ʿšty . w . ṯ*⌜*ʿ*⌝[*y .*	Once and perform the *ṯʿ*-sacrifice,
ṯn .] ⌜*w .*⌝ *ṯʿ*[*y*]	Twice and perform the *ṯʿ*-sacrifice,
(28) *ṯlṯ . w . ṯʿy* [.]	Thrice and perform the *ṯʿ*-sacrifice,
⌜*ả*⌝[*rb*]⌜*ʿ*⌝ *. w . ṯʿ*[*y*]	Four times and perform the *ṯʿ*-sacrifice,
(29) *ḫmš . w . ṯʿy .*	Five times and perform the *ṯʿ*-sacrifice,
ṯ⌜*ṯ .*⌝ [*w .*] ⌜*ṯ*⌝*ʿy*	Six times and perform the *ṯʿ*-sacrifice,
(30) *šbʿ . w . ṯʿy .*	Seven times and perform the *ṯʿ*-sacrifice.
tq⌜*d*⌝*m ʿṣr* (31) *šlm .*	You shall present bird(s) of well-being:[130]
šlm . ʿmr[*pỉ*] (32) *w . šlm . bảh*[131] .	Well-being for[132] *ʿAmmurāpiʾ*, well--being for his house!;
šlm . [*ṯ*]*ry*⌜*l*⌝ (33) *šlm . bth .*	Well-being for *Ṯarriyelli*, well-being for her house;[133]
šlm . ủ⌜*g*⌝*rt* (34) *šlm . ṯǵrh*	Well-being for Ugarit, well-being for her gates.

Hurro-Ugaritic Bilinguals

A good many Hurrian texts have been found at Ras Shamra, some written in Sumero-Akkadian syllabic script, others in the Ugaritic alphabetic script. We have already seen, though not translated, the Hurrian paragraph of text 12 (RS 24.643:13–17) and there exist several Hurrian ritual texts in Ugaritic script that will not be presented here. It does appear proper, however, to include in this anthology the bilinguals. (For a succinct overview of the various forms in which the two languages are distributed in these texts, see Pardee 1996b.)

Sacrifices

25. RS 24.254

In this text, the sacrificial term *ảṯḫlm* is Hurrian as are the grammatical forms of the divine names expressing attribution of the offerings. The specific content of the offerings is not anywhere stated. The divine names are for the most part Hurrian, though *ʾIlu* and *ʿAnatu* are here present, adopted into this Hurrian grouping. The only purely Ugaritic linguistic element is present in the last line, where all three words are Ugaritic.

Text

Obverse

---

(1) *ảṯḫlm ỉn ṯlnd*

---

(2) *ỉn ảtnd*

---

(3) *ỉld . tṯbd*

---

(4) *kḏǵd ỉwrn prznd*

---

(5) *kmrwnd*

---

(6) *ỉyd . ảṯtbd*
(7) *ʿntd . ṯmgnd*
(8) *nkld*
(9) *ỉn ảrdnd*
(10) *nbdgd*
(11) *w pảmt šbʿ*

Translation[134]

I. (1) Sacrifice: for the god *T̲alanni;*
(2) for *ʾEne ʾAttanni* (the god, the father);[135]
(3) for *ʾIlu;*
for *Tet̲t̲ub;*
(4) for *Kud̲uǵ,*
for the lord of PRZ(N),
(5) for *Kumarwi;*
(6) for *ʾEya;*
for *ʾAt̲tabi;*
(7) for *ʿAnatu;*
for *T̲imegi;*
(8) for *Nikkal;*
(9) for the god *ʾArde;*
(10) for *Nubadig;*
(11) seven times (is this set of offerings to be performed).

A Three-Day Sacrificial Rite Followed by a Divine Betrothal Rite

26. RS 24.255

This is a truly remarkable text, both for the bilingual formulation of the sacrificial liturgies prescribed for the first day (only three words are preserved, all Ugaritic, of the rite for the second day), and for the unique divine marriage rite outlined for the third day, expressed entirely in Ugaritic. The deities mentioned in the first part of the text are for the most part identical to those of the preceding text, but here the sacrificial sequence is more complicated, with two sacrifices prescribed by the Hurrian term *ảt̲ḫlm* enclosing two expressed in Ugaritic, a burnt-offering and a peace-offering. The rite for the third day is expressed in terms of the bride-price (TRḪ) paid by (*ʿl*) *Milku*, king of the underworld, to the lunar deity *ʾIbbu*, apparently in view of her marriage to *ʿAt̲taru-Šadî*, probably an astral deity on the pattern of the other manifestations of *ʿAt̲tar*(*t*)*u*. Because the text is expressed in purely ritual terms, with no mythological commentary, we do not know the story behind this betrothal nor the relationship thought to exist between this betrothal and that of *Nikkal-wa-ʾIbbu* to *Yariḫu* in the poem translated as text 24 in Parker et al. 1997, there entitled "The Betrothal of Yarikh and Nikkal-Ib." We may surmise, however, that, whereas this latter text recounts the betrothal of West-

Semitic *Yariḫu* to Mesopotamian *Nikkal* (partially assimilated to *ʾIbbu*), the myth behind this ritual would have recounted the marriage of two West-Semitic deities, the astral god *ʿAṯtaru-Šadî* and the lunar goddess *ʾIbbu*. Again because of the absence of the myth, this brief section of a brief text does not allow us to say much about the correlation of myth and ritual; we might expect, nevertheless, that the myth was recited as part of this rite.

Text

Obverse

---

(1) *ỉl . prz . l md .*

---

(2) *ṯlṯ ymm . l lǵz yʿrb*

---

(3) *mlk . ảṯḫḫlm*[136] *ỉn . ảtnd .*

---

(4) *ỉld . tṯbd . kmrbnd .*

---

(5) *kd̲ǵd ỉn prznd*

---

(6) *nkld . šrpm . ʿṣrm .*

---

(7) *gd*⸢*t*⸣ *. klhn . š l yrḫ*

---

(8) *šmm*[137] *. ảṯḫlm . ỉn* ⸢*ả*⸣[*t*]⸢*nd*⸣ *.*

---

(9) *ỉld . tṯbd .* ⸢-⸣[…]

---

(10) *kd̲ǵd . š . ỉy*⸢*d*⸣ […]

---

(11) *ỉn ảr*⸢*dnd*⸣[…]

---

(12) *ṯmgnd .* ⸢-⸣[…][138]

Reverse

---

(13) *ʿlm* ⸢-⸣[…]

---

(14) *-ṯn . ảl*⸢*pm*⸣ [...]

---

(15) *b ṯlṯ . dqr ḫ*[...]

---

(16) *šbʿ . ảlpm* ⸢-⸣[139]
(17) *ỉl mlk . šbʿ .* ⸢-(-)⸣[140]
(18) *kmlt . d ʿṯtr š*
(19) *d . trḫt tảr*
(20) *š . lnh . w l ỉb*
(21) *tpt -* ⸢-(-)[141]⸣*l . hy bh*

---

(22) *mth . l tšlm .*
(23) ⸢ʿ⸣*ln .*

Translation[142]

IA. (1) The god PRZ.[143] For the space of (2) three days, the king enters the LǴZ.[144]
B. (3) Sacrifice: for *ʾEne ʾAttanni* (the god, the father);
(4) for *ʾIlu;*
for *Teṯṯub;*
for *Kumarbi;*
(5) for *Kuḏuǵ,*
for the god of PRZ(N),
(6) for *Nikkal.*
C. As burnt-offerings, birds (7) all cut into pieces.
D. A ram for *Yariḫu* (8) as a pe<ac>e-offering.
E. Sacrifice: for *ʾEne ʾA*[*tta*]*nni* (the god, the father);
(9) for *ʾIlu;*
for *Teṯṯub;*
for *K*[*umarbi*],
(10) for *Kuḏuǵ,*
a ram for *ʾEya;*
[for *ʾAṯtabi*];[145]
(11) for the god *ʾArde;*
[for ...];
(12) for *Ṯimegi;*
[for ...].[146]
II. (13) On the next day, [...] (14) two bulls [...].

III. (15) On the third day, DQR of Ḥ[...];
(16) seven bulls to the debit account of (17) the god *Milku;*
seven ew<es>, (18) perfect ones, of *ʿAṯtaru Šadî:*
(19) this is the bride-price that you will requ(20)st of him.[147]
And to *ʾIbbu* (21) you will transmit it in full.
As for her, from her (22) own cattle, she is not required to repay anything on this account.

Sacrificial Ritual of *ʿAṯtartu*

27. RS 24.261

This text has four sections as defined either by a sacrificial term and/or by a horizontal dividing line. The first two lines, in Ugaritic, introduce the text as a whole, more particularly the first two sections and the fourth: *Ṯaʾuṯka*, the Hurrian equivalent of *ʿAṯtartu*, receives an important part of these offerings, and she is the object of a special rite prescribed in line 9 in Ugaritic. In the long series of sacrifices in lines 10–29, introduced in Ugaritic but otherwise in Hurrian, *Ṯaʾuṯka* is mentioned, but only as one deity among others. The last section (lines 30–35), though gravely damaged, appears to have a structure at least similar to that of the first, for the name *Ṯaʾuṯka* appears near the beginning and is followed by several locative formulations. It is uncertain whether these locatives represent places in which offerings were presented to *Ṯaʾuṯka* or deified localities designated as recipients of offerings. The "house/temple" in which the second and third series of offerings occurs is not further identified; it could be either the royal palace or the temple of *ʿAṯtartu/Ṯaʾuṯka*.

Text

Obverse

(1) *dbḥ . ʿṯtrt*
(2) *qrảt . b grn*
(3) *ảṯḫlm . ṯủṯkd*
(4) *ảgndym ṯdndy*
(5) *ỉnmṯy . ỉnḫzzy*
(6) *kzǵd . ỉn ḫmnd*
(7) - - - - *nntd kltd*[148]
(8) *nbdgd . w l b btm*
(9) *ảṯḫlm . ṯủṯk tỉzr pnm*

---

(10) *w b bt . ảṯḫlm .*
(11) *ỉnṯt . ṯlnnṯtm*
(12) *ỉnṯt . ảtnṯ⸢t⸣m*
(13) *ỉld . tṯbd . [ṯ]ủ⸢ṯ⸣kd*
(14) *kmrbnd . kzǵd . ỉyd*
(15) *ảṯtbd . ỉn ảrdnd*
(16) *ỉn ḫmnd . nbdgd*
(17) *ʿntd . ṯmgnd*
(18) *pḏḏpḫnd*
(19) *⸢ḫ⸣btd . dqtd*
(20) *[ḫ]dnṯt ḫdlrṯt*
(21) *ỉšḫrd . ảlnb*[149]
(22) *nk⸢l⸣d . nntdm*
(23) *kltd . ảdmd kbbd*

Lower Edge

(24) *⸢p⸣ngnṯt*
(25) *⸢ṯ⸣hrṯt*

Reverse

(26) ⸢-⸣*nd*⸢*r*⸣*ṯt*
(27) *ủḏ*⸢*n*⸣[*d* …]
(28) [-]*bn*[----]⸢-⸣*d*
(29) [-]*n*[---]*dnd*

---

(30) [ ]⸢-⸣*m*
(31) [*ṯ*]⸢*ủ*⸣*ṯkd . nngy mlgy*
(32) ⸢-⸣[ ]⸢--⸣*rṯy*
(33) *p*⸢-⸣[ ]⸢-⸣*wrṯt*
(34) *n*⸢-⸣[*k*]⸢*l*⸣*td*
(35) -(-)[150] *bd*[…]

Translation

I. (1) Sacrifice of *ʿAṯtartu*, (2) gathering[151] at the threshing-floor.
A. (3) Sacrifice for *Ṯaʾuṯka:*
in the ʾAGND;
in the ṮDND;
(5) in the ʾINMṮ;

in the ʾINḪZZ;
(6) for *Kuzuǵ;*
for the god (of?) ḪMN;
(7) for *Ninatta;*
for *Kulitta;*
(8) for *Nubadig.*

B. And in the house/temple, (9) sacrifice.
As for *Ṯaʾuṯka*, you are to veil her face.

C. (10) And in the house/temple, sacrifice (11) for the gods *Ṯalanni;*
(12) for *ʾEnna ʾAttanna* (the father gods);
(13) for *ʾIlu;*
for *Teṯṯub;*
for [*Ṯa*]*ʾuṯka;*
(14) for *Kumarbi;*
for *Kuzuǵ;*
for *ʾEya;*
(15) for *ʾAṯtabi;*
for the god *ʾArde;*
(16) for the god (of?) ḪMN;
for *Nubadig;*
(17) for *ʿAnatu;*
for *Ṯimegi;*
(18) for *Piḏaḏapḫi;*
(19) for *Ḫebat;*
for *Daqqītu;*
(20) for the [*Ḫu*]*dena;*
for the *Ḫudellurra;*
(21) for *ʾIšḫara;*
for! *ʾAllani;*
(22) for *Nikkal;*
for *Ninatta;*
(23) for *Kulitta;*
for *ʾAdamma;*
for *Kubaba;*
(24) for the ⸢P⸣NǴ;
(25) for the ⸢Ṯ⸣HR;
(26) for the ⸢-⸣ND⸢R⸣;
(27) for *ʾUḏḏuni* [...];
(28) [for] [-]BN[?];

for [...]⸢-⸣
(29) [for] [-]N[?];
for [...]DN.

D. (30) [...]⸢-⸣M[152] (31) [...]for [*T̠a*]*ʾut̠ka:*
in the NNG;
in the MLG;
(32) ⸢-⸣[ ]in the ⸢ ⸣RT̠;
(33) P⸢-⸣[...];
in the ⸢-⸣WR;
(34) [for] *Nina*[*tta*];
for [*Ku*]*litta;*
(35) [for$^?$] *Nu$^?$badi*[g].

Three-Day Sacrificial Ritual for the Bed of *Pidray*

28. RS 24.291

The content and the bilingual character of this text differ from the three preceding texts in that, instead of simply listing the various divine recipients of the *ảṯḫlm*-sacrifices, the animal to be offered is each time indicated, always in Ugaritic. There are also more adverbial indicators in this text than in any of the preceding bilinguals, and such expressions are always in Ugaritic. The nature of the rite is debated, though most scholars believe that the explicit mention of a "bed" in the introduction may be interpreted as meaning that it represents either an incubation rite or a *hieros gamos*. Though such interpretations are certainly plausible, it must be stressed that no details are indicated beyond the preparation of the bed itself. It is not impossible, therefore, that these preparations are in view of a "contemplation" rite, of which the precise function is uncertain (see texts 19–21). The day on which the rite begins is stated as the nineteenth, though the month is not identified. This text belongs, therefore, to the group of texts that reflect only a segment of a full month's cultic activities. The three days of this text were the last of the third quarter of the lunar month and corresponded chronologically, therefore, to days 5 through 7 of the full-moon festival of the month of *Raʾšu-Yêni* known from text 15 (RS 1.003/RS 18.056). There is no reason to believe that all the activities of the unnamed month in which this rite took place were devoted to the incubation or the *hieros gamos*, of which these would be the culminating ceremonies; but without knowledge of the rest of this month's liturgy, any observations would be pure speculation. It appears more plausible, however, because of the clear segmentation of a monthly liturgy visible in RS 1.003/RS 18.056, to see this ceremony as the culmination of the full-moon festival; but even that less comprehensive view is uncertain, for we have seen one well-preserved monthly liturgy according to which nothing was prescribed for the day of the full moon (text 13 [RS 24.266]). This rite may be mentioned by name in text 58 (RS 19.015:7) as *pdry bt mlk*, "(the sacrificial rite that takes place when) *Pidray* is in the house of the king," and an allusion to the rite or to a part thereof (perhaps the ritual of "entry") may have been outlined in RS 24.300:13'–18' (not translated here).

Text

Obverse

(1) *b tšʿ ʿš⸢r⸣ḫ*
(2) *trbd . ʿrš [.] pd*
(3) *ry . b ⸢š⸣t . mlk*

---

(4) *ảṯḫ⸢l⸣[m . ỉ]n ṯlnd*
(5) *gd⸢l⸣[t .] ⸢ḫb⸣td . š*
(6) *šb[-]⸢d⸣ . gdlt*
(7) *dqtd . gdlt*
(8) *ḫdn ḫd⸢l⸣r dqtt*
(9) *ḫnnǵdṯt dqt*
(10) *nbdgd . d⸢qt⸣*
(11) *tgnd dqt*
(12) *kldnd . dqt*

Lower Edge

(13) *ʿlm . ṯn šm*
(14) *ḫbtd . w ỉ*
(15) *nš ỉlm*

Reverse

(16) *kmm . l pn*
(17) *ll . ʿṣrmm*

---

(18) *ỉn ṯlnd gdlt*

(19) *ảlnd . gdlt*
(20) *ḫbtd . glt*[153]
(21) *ỉnš ỉ⸢lm k⸣m⸢m⸣*

---

(22) *b ṯ⸢l⸣ṯ ỉn ṯlnd*
(23) *⸢ảl⸣nd ṯn šm*
(24) *ỉnš ỉlm . kmm*
(25) *pn ll . tnʿr*
(26) *ʿrš .*

---

(27) *ʿrb š⸢pš⸣*
(28) *w ḥl ml⸢k⸣*

Translation

IA. (1) On the nineteenth day of the month, (2) you are to prepare the bed of *Pid*(3)*ray* with the king's bed-covers.

B. (4) Sacrifice: for the god *Ṯalanni* (5) a co[w];
for *Ḫebat* a ram;
(6) for ŠB⸢R⸣ a cow;
(7) for *Daqqītu* a cow;
(8) for the *Ḫudena* (and) the *Ḫudellurra* a/two/some ewe(s);[154]
(9) for the ḪNNǴD a ewe;
(10) for *Nubadig* a ewe;
(11) for *Tagi* a ewe;
(12) for *Keldi* ewe.

IIA. (13) On the next day, two rams (14) for *Ḫebat;*
and for *ʾI*(15)*nāšu-ʾIlīma* (16) the same;
and, before (17) the night, birds.

B. (18) For the god *Ṯalanni* a cow;
(19) for *ʾAllani* a cow;
(20) for *Ḫebat* a c<o>w;
(21) for *ʾInāšu-ʾIlīma* the same.

IIIA. (22) On the third day, for the god *Ṯalanni* (23) (and) for *ʾAllani* two rams;

(24) (for) *ʾInāšu-ʾIlīma* the same.

B. (25) Before nightfall, you will remove (26) the bed.

C. (27) When the sun sets, (28) the king is free (of further cultic obligations).

Notes

1. Cf. de Jong and van Soldt 1987–88: 71 (here the correspondences with the modern calendar are shifted one step back; i.e., *riʾš yn* is indicated as the last month of the year, rather than the first; for my reasons, see commentary on RS 1.003:1 in Pardee 2000a: 156–59). Vocalizations are indicated here only if attested in Akkadian (syllabic script).

2. A reconstructed form of lines 10–18, based on RS 24.253:1–14, is indicated here below.

3. On the reverse, one finds to the right the traces of five lines of writing; the numbers indicated here for the other lines are calculated on the basis of the number of lines to be found on the corresponding sections of the obverse and must be judged to be hypothetical—their purpose is to give a rough idea of the length of the original text.

4. On the structure of the translation and its notation, see above, general introduction. For the detailed arguments supporting the divisions noted here and in the following texts, see Pardee 2000a. The reader should note that, in accord with the editorial policy of this series, English words required for a smooth translation but not present in the Ugaritic text are not placed in parentheses. Examples from this text: (1) "as a *ṯʿ*-sacrifice" (line 1): the Ugaritic phrase does not include a preposition corresponding to "as"; (2) "for *ʾIlu* a ram" (line 3): here also and in many similar cases of this syntactic structure the Ugaritic lacks a preposition and the ascription of the sacrifice was probably marked by the case vowel on the divine name (where such was present); (3) "On the third day of the month" (line 5): the days of the lunar month are normally expressed in Ugaritic by the use of the ordinal number alone, literally, "in third"; (4) "When the sun sets" (line 9): the Ugaritic phrase is nominal, "at the entering of the sun."

5. Though not certain, the restoration {[… šrp . w šl]mm}, "[… as a burnt-offering. And as a pe]ace-offering…," is plausible.

6. On the basis of text 23 ([RS Varia 20]:6–9), where the sequence *ỉlỉb*, *ỉl*, *bʿl*, *dgn*, appears, the restoration of *ỉlỉb* appears plausible here as the divine recipient. Before that name, there may have been an indication of the type of offering.

7. Note the order *Baʿlu-Dagan,* which is not that of the deity lists (where *Dagan* precedes *Baʿlu*) but is attested in other sacrificial texts (text 6B [RS 24.253:20–21], text 23 [RS Varia 20]:8–9], and in RIH 78/4:3–? [a text not translated here]).

8. Though not certain, the restoration {[kmm . w]}, "[the same; and]," is plausible.

9. Perhaps read {šl⌜m⌝[m]}, "as a peace [offering]," but the presence of a wedge, which appears to be {ʿ}, before this formula is unexplained.

10. Some of the readings as well as the pure reconstructions presented here are based on the similar text in 6B (RS 24.253).

11. It is uncertain whether {pdr} should be restored here, as below in line 28, or {pdry}, as in text 6B (RS 24.253:14).

12. On the basis of the comparison with text 6B (RS 24.253:3), "the day" here is the day of the full moon, though, because the relationship between the two rites is uncertain, it is not possible to say whether that day corresponded in this case to the fourteenth or to the fifteenth day of the month (the full moon can fall on either day as counted from the first visibility of the new moon).

13. The term *nbšt* does not appear at this point in text 6B (RS 24.253), nor does it appear elsewhere in these texts (though it may be a by-form of *npš*, "neck"), and it is therefore uncertain whether it designates a specific sacrifice or a type of offering.

14. Here and in line 15, the phrase denoting the day includes the word *ym*, "day" (except in the formulae for the "day of the new moon" and for the "day of the full moon," the day of the month is regularly expressed by the ordinal number alone). In line 11, on the other hand, one finds only {btš⌜-⌝ [...]}, which may be restored either as "on the ninth (day)" or as "in the temple (*bt*) of ... ."

15. The word *šr* may be either a common noun ("house of the singer") or a divine name ("temple of the god *šr*"). The same options exist for the corresponding word in the preceding phrase because it is broken (the restoration "*Baʿlu*," usually indicated here, is unlikely). I have indicated "temple" as the primary translation because the latter part of the texts deals with "gods."

16. This very obscure passage may refer to repeated clothing of the deities in "outfits," i.e., appropriate garments and symbols.

17. Most have emended (mbt) to read (m<ṯ>bt}, "place where one sits/dwells," on the analogy of RS 1.033 (*CTA* 47):4' and RS 2.002 (*CTA* 23):19. The second of these texts also contains the number "eight" and the two words together recall text 15 (RS 1.003:51), where "lodges of branches" are arranged "four by four."

18. There are two scribal errors in this line: a misplaced word divider in the second element of the divine name {bʿlt bhtm} and the writing of {ỉnš} with {h} instead of {ỉ} (only one wedge distinguishes these two signs).

19. The horizontal line present here between lines 1 and 2 does not appear to mark a structural break in the rite, though that is usually the function of such occasional lines (I am not referring, of course, to texts where a horizontal line separates each line of the text or each section thereof). Because the end of line 1 has broken away, however, this analysis of the line as nonfunctional (as in my translation) must remain hypothetical. The break at the end of line 2 also renders

unclear the function of *ḫd̠rǵl,* a Hurrian word that normally denotes a profession or an occupational category. This word occurs only here in the ritual texts, in which the mention of officiants or of their helpers is extremely rare.

20. If this be the correct translation of *rgbt*, the clods certainly had a symbolic function, unknown to us (see below, text 57 [RS 24.293]).

21. The destination of the ascension is not indicated explicitly; the only place that has been mentioned to this point is the ḪMN-sanctuary, which would for that reason be the logical candidate for the unnamed destination. This hypothesis is strengthened by the explicit mention of that destination in the next section. Here the sevenfold repetition implies a cyclical procession, while in the following section the deities are said to "ascend" one time only, which surely means that statuettes of the deities were deposited in the ḪMN-sanctuary for an unstated period of time.

22. Just the gods previously named (*Baʿlatu-Bahatīma* and *ʾInāšu-ʾIlīma*) or a broader group?

23. Both the reading and the interpretation of the end of this line are problematic: the number appears to be in the cardinal form (*t̠mnt*) instead of the expected ordinal (*t̠mn*), while the preserved signs of the last word do not correspond to anything known from these texts.

24. The identification of the *gt̠rm* constitutes one of the important problems of these texts. I once held that the form should be plural everywhere (Pardee 1993), but Tropper has shown (1997: 672) that the normal 3m.pl. prefix-conjugation form in prose is *tqtln* (as in the case of the *gt̠rm* in text 18 [RS 1.005:9]), not *yqtln*, as here. So, either the forms were not used consistently according to number or else the *gt̠rm* can appear either as a plurality or as a duality. In the latter case, one might posit that the duality here consists of *Šapšu*, the sun-deity, and *Yariḫu*, the moon-deity, for in RS 1.005 the plural form appears to refer to those two deities in association with *Gat̠aru* himself; another possibility is that the dual refers to *Gat̠aru* and *Yariḫu*, the two "male *Gat̠arāma*" mentioned in text 18 (RS 1.005:19). Such a rite involving the descent of the statuettes of the principal celestial deities would be particularly appropriate at the new-moon festival. Unfortunately, the meaning of the term expressing the goal of their descent (*mṣd*) is uncertain, though the consonantal spelling is identical to that of the word designating the home of *Ḥôrānu* in text 53 (RS 24.244:58).

25. Restore {⌜g⌝[dlt . dbr]}in line 19' on the basis of the similar sequence in text 15 (RS 1.003:46).

26. As these cushion-shaped tablets were inscribed, the soft clay would tend to settle; thus the latter side inscribed would be the rounder, and the first side, on which the tablet would have rested while the reverse was inscribed, the flatter.

27. At the end of this line, three signs were erased by the scribe.

28. RS 92.2004 and duplicates will be edited by D. Arnaud.

29. Read {w}.

30. The reading is reasonably clear but certainly faulty: correct to read {bʿl}.

31. Several of these restorations are based not on traces visible in RS 24.643 but on the deity lists RS 26.142/RS 92.2004 (see above, text 3). The reader should consult my edition of RS 24.643 (Pardee 2000a: 779–806) for the data and arguments behind the restorations.

32. This restoration is particularly speculative.

33. The parentheses are meant to express the uncertainty of this restoration: *ủṯḫt*, omitted above in line 9, appears to have figured in this offering list, so perhaps *knr* was omitted here.

34. Previous doubts that the text was incomplete, raised by the word divider at the end of this line and by the last named deity being {bˁlm} have been dispelled by RS 92.2004, for there lines 38–41 are identical and indicate the weather deity (see above, text 3). As in the case of the other deity list and the corresponding sacrificial list (here above, line 9), the last deities of RS 92.2004, the *Malkūma* and *Šalimu*, do not appear at the end of this sacrificial list.

35. The translation reflects the restorations of lines 1–12 and 31–45 proposed above.

36. The meaning of the phrase *ỉl ṣpn,* by which text 1A (RS 1.017) is headed, cannot be "the gods (who dwell on) *Ṣapunu,*" for that mountain is the dwelling of *Baˁlu* and several of these deities are known from Ugaritic sources to have dwelt elsewhere (see below, text 53 [RS 24.244]). The sacrificial rite must honor, therefore, a particular moment when these gods assemble on *Ṣapunu*." If my chronological hypotheses are of any value (see introduction to this text), the gathering would plausibly have occurred at the time of the winter solstice (or near the end of winter if the obverse-reverse orientation of the tablet is the opposite). The only concrete proposal for the function of the rite with which I am acquainted is to link it with *Baˁlu*'s vicissitudes when he was defeated by *Môtu* and buried on Mount *Ṣapunu* (Xella 1979–80: 147; cf. a different form of the hypothesis by de Moor 1971: 200–201). Though there are no explicit links between the mythological account and the sacrificial rite, it is not difficult to imagine a rite that would have brought the gods together to commemorate *Baˁlu*'s demise at the winter solstice (or to solicit his return a month before the vernal equinox, if this rite was in fact situated after *Ḫiyyāru* rather than before).

37. The numbers represent the device used in the syllabic texts to represent the multiple hypostases of *Baˁlu* (see above, text 1). The text on the reverse of this tablet names three of the hypostases (lines 6–8: *Baˁlu* of Aleppo, *Baˁlu* of *Ṣapunu*, and *Ṯarraṯiya*) leaving four unnamed (lines 38–41).

38. As compared with the corresponding deity list presented in text 1 (RS 1.017 and parallels), three divinities are omitted here: *ʾUṯḫatu*, the divinized censer; *Malakūma*, the deceased and divinized kings (see text 56); and *Šalimu* (the youngest of the offspring of *ʾIlu*, perhaps born of a human mother [Pardee 1997b]). In spite of the deities not being named, the three unascribed sacrifices were plausibly in their honor. Below, in the offering list corresponding to the second of the principal deity lists (text 3), the last two are also omitted (apparently

this time without mention of unascribed sacrifices), but *ʾUṯḫatu* appears to have been honored with a sacrifice. The omission of sacrifices explicitly offered to the *Malakūma* constitutes an explicit argument against the primacy of the "cult of the dead" at Ugarit. It is nonetheless likely that offerings were made to the *Malakūma,* and there are two indications of such activity in these texts: (1) text 13 (RS 24.266:25') may refer to a libation offering of oil to the deceased kings and (2) the "check marks" in the margin of text 56B (RS 94.2518) seem to indicate that this list of deceased and deified kings served as a checklist for a sacrificial ritual (see below on this text).

39. For the character of the "entry rituals," see below, introduction to text 18 (RS 1.005).

40. Because no specific ascriptions are indicated for the named items, it is assumed that they were all considered offerings for the goddess named in line 18.

41. All currently available texts (RS 24.643, RS 26.142, and RS 92.2004) are broken at this point, and no restorations are presently possible for lines 35 and 36 of RS 24.643. Because elsewhere in RS 92.2004 each line bears only one divine name, it appears probable that the corresponding lines in that text would also have borne only one name and that these two completely destroyed lines in RS 24.643 also contained only one entry each. Because, according to the preserved portions of this list, only manifestations of *Baʿlu* receive an offering consisting of anything but a ram, and because the expected seven manifestations of *Baʿlu* are accounted for elsewhere in this list, the restoration of a single ram as the offering in each of these lines appears likely.

42. A hypothetical restoration; that of {ʿṯtpr} or of {ʿṯtpl} appears less likely for reasons of space.

43. The syllabic entry (see RS 92.2004:28), in comparison with the beginning of the Ugaritic entry where {ỉl .} is plausibly the plural construct form of *ỉlm* meaning "the gods of," not "the gods who are," gives the above translation. The restoration of the Ugaritic is, however, uncertain (the partially preserved sign after {m} appears not to be {t}, and therefore the restoration {m⌜t⌝[m]}, "men," is not likely—at least on present evidence).

44. The Ugaritic and syllabic entries (text 3 [RS 92.2004:32]) obviously correspond, but the interpretation of the latter is uncertain.

45. RS 26.142:15' here contains the logogram for "door-bolt" (GIŠ.SAG.KUL; see Nougayrol 1968: 321 [line 2']; Arnaud 1994: 107), whereas RS 92.2004 contains a very different and presently unexplained entry. The Ugaritic has totally disappeared here.

46. By comparison with the lists in lines 3–4 and 11–12, these four unspecified manifestations of *Baʿlu* would correspond to the entries numbered 2 through 5; in terms of this list, where three manifestations of *Baʿlu* were named in lines 26–28, they constitute the manifestations that may be numbered 4 through 7.

47. Read {g<d>lt}.

48. Read {*ủ*!grt} (Loretz 1998).

49. {bˁl . rˁ⸢k⸣t} appears to be a hypostasis of *Baˁlu* (as opposed to a possible interpretation "lords/owners of RˁKT"), but the second part of the theonym has not been satisfactorily explained. The principal deity in the ritual sections of this text is *Baˁlu* of Ugarit, the hypostasis of the weather god associated principally with the city itself. In the prayer and in the last cultic act leading up to the prayer (the oil libation in lines 24'–25'), the deity is simply *Baˁlu*.

50. In the first lacuna a term designating a further offering may have disappeared, while in the second a specific offering to be made in the temple of *Baˁlu* of Ugarit was probably indicated.

51. This word is usually emended to {mgdl}, "tower" (or *mdgl* is given the same meaning). Because, however, the word *mgdl* is attested in Ugaritic meaning "tower," and because the reading {mdgl} here is quite clear, it is preferable to await further textual evidence before adopting one or the other of these solutions—Ugaritic may prove to have a word *mdgl* with a meaning distinct from *mgdl*.

52. The genitival phrase *šmn šlm bˁl* in lines 24'–25' apparently denotes an offering of oil meant to induce well-being from *Baˁlu*, while the *mtk mlkm*, "libation of the *Malakūma* (kings)," is offered either by living kings (and the plural would be generic, since Ugarit apparently had one living king at a time) or for the benefit of dead kings, i.e., the kings named in text 56 (RS 24.257/RS 94.2518) and/or those named in text 24 (RS 34.126)—if the reference is to dead kings, *mlkm* here corresponds to the entry *mlkm* in the deity lists (text 1 [RS 1.017:33], text 3 [RS 92.2004:42]).

53. This final section of the text contains a prayer addressed to *Baˁlu* (see below, texts 46 and 47); the prayer itself (lines 28'–34') is embedded in an introduction and a conclusion addressed to the worshipers.

54. The first three deities mentioned in this second sequence of burnt-offerings (lines 3–5) correspond to three of the names on the mysterious deity list of text 4 (RS 24.246 reverse); the order of mention of these three is not present in text 4.

55. On music at Ugarit, see now Koitabashi 1998 (with references to earlier studies, particularly those of A. Caubet). Given that the word *pảmt*, used in formulae expressing the number of "times" a cultic act is to be repeated, is usually accompanied by a number, the emendation of {šr} at the beginning of the line to {<ˁ>šr}, "ten," has been widely adopted; it is not impossible, however, that the number of repetitions was left to the singer.

56. The meaning of the rite of the opening of the hand, followed by the sacrifice of a cow, is unknown.

57. This portion of the festival of the month of *Gannu* takes place in the garden (*gannu*), where spring would be evident (the 8th of *Gannu* would be about the 1st of April). The garden in question is most likely the one that has been posited to have existed in the large open area designated courtyard III that was located in the southeast section of the palace (see Yon 1997: p. 47, fig. 20; p. 51, fig. 23; pp. 52–53).

58. The content of the recitation, literally, the "word," is unknown.

59. In text 20 (RIH 77/2B+), the exiting of items offered to the deity is forbidden on a given day. That prohibition, part of a liturgy that is not completely set down in the text in question, is explained by this text: certain objects must remain in the holy place and only be removed when so stipulated.

60. This description assumes that the mentions of the "fifth," "sixth," and "seventh" days of the month in lines 38–48 refer to those days of the full-moon festival, not of the new-moon sequence. Other scholars hold that this text is not chronologically ordered and that the references intend a return to the first quarter of the month and that the reference to the "day of the new moon" in RS 1.003:48/RS 18.056.52–53 intends a return to the first day of the month of *Raʾšu-Yêni*.

61. Under this rubric only the most obvious reconstructions are indicated, i.e., those that would be proposed if the two texts were not parallel. A plausible set of reconstructions based on the two texts is proposed in the middle column, expressed in terms of tablet RS 1.003. Rather than providing RS 18.056 in its own lineation, which would require some effort on the part of the reader to determine precisely which restorations were based on which readings in that text, I have divided that text up to match RS 1.003, with line numbers indicated. This arrangement shows at the very least that if one of these texts was copied from the other as some scholars think, the copyist made no attempt to observe the lineation of the tablet from which he was copying. (For separate presentations of each tablet and for the restored texts laid out as they would have appeared each on its own tablet, see Pardee 2000a: 143–213, 469–78.)

62. Below in line 44 and in RS 18.056:40, *dd* is preceded by the word *šmn*, "oil"; that word is certainly absent in the line corresponding to this one in RS 18.056, however, and the question is whether that text is faulty or reflects a different offering.

63. Half-brackets within brackets indicate that the corresponding reading in RS 18.056 is uncertain.

64. Though the broken state of the texts renders any decision uncertain, the data preserved indicate variant texts here. I posit that both texts had *mʿrb*, "an entry offering," but that another word preceded that word in RS 1.003. One possibility is that the offering designation was double, [*tr*]*mt mʿrb*, where the first word would be seen as cognate with Hebrew *tᵊrūmāʰ*.

65. A scribal error for {dqtm}.

66. A scribal error for {ym}.

67. The sign partially preserved at the end of this line cannot be a {t} as in RS 1.003:49; moreover, the space available in the preceding lacuna is large enough to have contained more signs than in RS 1.003. One must, therefore, posit variant texts here.

68. The text translated is the reconstructed text provided in the central column above. Though line numbers are indicated for RS 1.003, square brackets are here used only for textual material that is entirely reconstructed, i.e., present in neither RS 1.003 nor in RS 18.056.

69. This is the only case of the offering of grapes in these texts. The link with the offering and the month name and with the agricultural activity implied by the month name is obvious. The need to keep the agricultural cycle in synchrony with the solar year is particularly acute when the ritual cycle is so closely tied in with agricultural activities.

70. *ảrgmn* is known from the mythological texts as a gift from one deity to another (*CTA* 1 i 37) and in the administrative texts as the required tribute to the Hittite sovereign (see in particular RS 19.017—for a new epigraphic study of this text, see Pardee forthcoming g).

71. The directive for the king to "sit" in a state of purity (/barūra/) occurs only here. Neither the "throne" nor the place is mentioned. I have assumed that the place is the temple of *ʾIlu* (an inference from the nature of the first offerings) and that the command means that the king is to remain within that temple through the night from the fourteenth to the fifteenth day of the month, probably the night in which the moon is at its fullest, without in any way reducing his ritual cleanliness, so as to participate in a state of continuous cleanliness in the rites of the fifteenth day. Below, line 46, the king is required to pronounce a recitation in a state of purity.

72. The object of the verb "to pour" appears to have been lost in the lacuna at the end of line 11.

73. As in so many such cases in these texts, the provenience of the "heart" is not indicated.

74. The seventh day would have begun at sundown on the day before the sunrise mentioned here; the point of the two commands seems to be that, though no specific cultic activity is required, the king must remain in his holy state throughout the daylight hours; i.e., he may not go through the *ḥl*-process (on which, see text 13 [RS 24.266]:22'–24') until sunset, the end of the seventh day of the festival. By the chronological analysis adopted here, this brings us to the end of the third quarter of the lunar month; no cultic activities are scheduled for the fourth quarter or for the dark nights before the next new moon.

75. No contrary indication having been given, we may assume that the location is still that of the temple of *ʾIlu* (line 38), from which the king returns to his palace (lines 54–55). Rooftop sacrifices are known from the Kirta text (*CTA* 14 ii 73–79, iv 165–71).

76. Though the command to wash himself pure is not indicated above (the last reference was the *ḥl* at the end of the third quarter of the preceding month), the new *ḥl*-statement here implies that the king must have cleansed himself for the new-moon ceremonies. The activities enjoined in lines 50–52 seem to have occurred during the night of the sighting of the new moon; the king is allowed to return to his normal activities on the morning of the second day. This tablet says nothing about the continuation of the "feast of booths," though we may assume that it was not limited to a single night.

77. Certainly a gesture of prayer (compare *CTA* 14 ii 75–76); the ritual text,

one of the few to allude to prayer, places the act in a noncultic context (the king has become *ḥl* and has returned to his "home").

78. On my hypothesis that the partially preserved word here would have designated an intercalary month, rather than one of the regular months of the year, see the introduction to this text. By that interpretation, these lines enjoin for the intercalary month only a brief full-moon ceremony that is but a pale imitation of the lavish one observed during the regular last month of the year.

79. Unfortunately, only personal names and numbers are preserved in lines 58–61 and we have, therefore, no direct evidence for what was being counted.

80. Read {*ủ*<š>ḫr}.

81. The particle *ỉd* (cognate with Hebrew *ʿāz*) is here interpreted as an adverb and as indicating that the rite in question is part of a longer liturgy; compare text 15 (RS 1.003:50), where *ỉd* clearly links two stages of a series of rites taking place on the same day. The particle also appears in the first paragraph of the texts gathered below under the heading "Contemplation Rituals" (texts 19–21), both with the operative verb of those texts (PHY, "to see") and, as here, with DBḤ.

82. The deity QLḤ, whose characteristics are unknown, appears only in this text, as does the sacrifice of a dove (here and in line 13, again for QLḤ).

83.. The progress appears to have been from the principal altar in the temple of *ʾIlu-Bêti* to the particular sanctuary (*qdš*) of *ʾIlu-Bêti* within the temple, where a feast takes place, back to the principal altar of the temple.

84. This formula is attested only here, and its precise signification is unclear. The interpretation as "day one" (of a longer sequence) appears to be belied by the word *ỉd* at the beginning of the text, which already indicates that this rite is part of a longer series; in such a context "day one" could only mean "this is the end of cultic activity on day one; proceed to the following cultic act as appropriately designated chronologically." Interpreted as "one day," the essential function is the same, but the day in question is not defined as the first.

85. This heading is provided in parentheses in order explicitly to set off the contrast with the second major section of the text that begins in line 12 and which begins "And at night . . . ."

86. The Ugaritic syntax does not favor the interpretation of the phrase *mtntm w kbd* as genitivally attached to the following word, "bull." One often encounters in these texts the mention of body parts that must come from sacrificial victims but without a statement that would have made clear from which animal the parts are supposed to originate.

87. Because of the similar sequence of deities here in lines 2–3, in text 5 (RS 4.474:1–4), and in each paragraph of text 22 (RS 1.002), it appears plausible to identify the *ʾIlāhūma* as the sons in *ʾIlu*'s immediate family, most likely those by *ʾAṯiratu*. The identity of the deity designated below by the singular (line 5) is more difficult to determine for lack of contemporaneous data, though the form of the name is identical with Hebrew *ʾᵉlōᵃh* (Eloah) and Arabic *ʾal-ʾilāh* (Allah).

88. According to the interpretation of each of these terms offered above, the

ʾIlāhūma would be the sons of *ʾIlu*'s immediate family, the *Baʿalūma* the manifestations of *Baʿlu,* of which seven are enumerated in the first deity list given above, with probably the same number in the fourth list. Others take the *ʾIlāhūma* as attributive: "the *Baʿlu* deities."

89. This is the section of RS 1.001 in which the divine recipients correspond to the divine names in text 4 (RS 24.246:1–14). The deity *Ǵalmatu*, the last of this list, marked off from the others in the Ugaritic by the conjunction *w*, is not included in RS 24.246. The nature of all the deities named is in one way or another appropriate for a series of sacrifices that take place during the night; that is, they are all associated with darkness or the earth/underworld:

chthonic gods: *ỉl bt*, *ủšḫry*, *ym*, *kṯr*, *ršp*
gods of fertility: *bʿl*, *ṯrmn*, *pdry*, *dqt*, *trṯ*, *ʿnt ḫbly* (*pdry* both chthonic and a goddess of fertility),
nocturnal gods: *yrḫ*, *špš pgr*, *ỉltm ḫnqtm*, *yrḫ kṯy*

90.
(1') [ ]⸢-⸣[...]	
(2') [-] ⸢- r⸣šp . w l ll[...]	... *Rašap*. And at night[...].
(3') w ršp . gn . yṣản[...]	And *Rašap-Guni* must go forth[...].

---

91. This transcription is meant to express that two letters have been erased between {⸢b .⸣} and {⸢.⸣ bt ỉl⸢m⸣}. They have been imperfectly erased, however, and the traces after erasure could be read as {bg---bt} or as {-⸢m⸣-⸢ṯ⸣-bt}; I have been unable to make anything of these possibilities.

92. *ʿAṯtartu* herself, the goddess who represented the morning star, had an astral character.

93. This sequence of offerings would have been for *ʿAṯtartu* (who also, under the form of *ʿAṯtartu-Šadî*, received *ủšpǵt*-garments according to text 12 [RS 24.643:21]). The meaning of the phrase *mzn drk* is uncertain; if the interpretation offered here is correct, it is uncertain why *ʿAṯtartu-Ḫurri* would have needed a scale, other than the fact that she was traveling at this moment.

94. The problem of why *Kôṯaru* appears here is similar to that of *ʿAnatu*'s presence in the next sections. For the case of *Kôṯaru*, however, one can compare his function in text 55 (RS 24.252), where he and his "goodly companions" provide the music and dancing at a feast in honor of *Rapaʾu/Milku* and other deities, primarily chthonic.

95. Taking this passage at face value, the *Gaṯarūma* would here correspond to *Šapšu*, *Yariḫu*, and *Gaṯaru* himself. *ʿAnatu* does not seem to be included, if one may judge from lines 17–20, where *Gaṯarūma* (pl.) and *Gaṯarāma* (dual) alternate with that goddess. Her role would here, therefore, be analogous to that of *Kôṯaru* in the previous section, at least as regards the structure of the rite. According to this analysis, the "male *Gaṯarāma*" in line 19 would be *Yariḫu* and *Gaṯaru* (*Šapšu* is feminine at Ugarit). I am not convinced, as are some of my colleagues, that the {h} attached to the divine name *ʿAnatu* here is the 3m.s. pronominal suffix expressing *ʿAnatu*'s belonging to *Gaṯaru* (in addition to the commentary in

Pardee 2000a: 247–48, see Pardee 1995); if the *-h* is the adverbial morpheme, a similar structure is attested in text 29 (RS 1.019:9). Below in lines 18 and 20, the {m} attached to this divine name is probably also adverbial, rather than the dual morpheme, as some believe.

96. Because the left side of the tablet is broken from line 17 through line 22, any possible chronological indications have been lost. These ritual acts, each separated from the other by a horizontal line, are here indicated as occurring on the second day of the rite, the same as the entry of the *Gaṯarūma*, but they may have extended over several days.

97. The broken context precludes determining whether *slm* corresponds to the standard Semitic word for "stairs" or whether it is an entirely different word. Because of that difficulty, it is impossible to know whether line 21 constitutes the last element of the sacrificial sequence or the first of the processional sequence.

98. In the last stages of the liturgy, a clothing rite takes place (line 22), but the state of the text keeps us from knowing whether it is the officiants or the deities who assume certain garments. One possibility is to read the word before *ylbš* in line 22 as {⸢ḫ⸣ry} and to interpret it as a directive for the king to adopt Hurrian dress, plausibly in honor of *ʿAṯtartu-Ḫurri*. Next the king "takes" or "receives" the divine effigies (line 23), but no end point is indicated, so we again do not know what degree of displacement is involved. Wherever he goes with them, the other worshipers follow, all accomplishing a sevenfold circuit. The "gods" in question are either all the gods named in this text or, more plausibly, just the principal gods of the "entry" rituals: *ʿAṯtartu-Ḫurri*, *Šapšu*, *Yariḫu*, and *Gaṯaru*. The act of "taking" was prescribed either with reference to the procession itself (i.e., the king would have taken each deity from its temporary lodging and done a circuit within the palace, returning each deity to its temporary home at the end of his procession) or with reference to returning each deity to its regular "home" outside the palace.

99. The restoration of the divine name *Rašap* is very plausible here, either with no qualifier (cf. *ʿnt slḫ* ... *ʿnt* in text 21 [RIH 77/10B+:8–11]), in which case it is uncertain what was designated by the signs that follow the name, or *Rašap-Guni*.

100. The verb here is *ynṣl*, occurring only in this text, and of uncertain meaning. Usages in the other Semitic languages range from simple "displacement" through "saving" to "despoiling." Because of the broken state of the tablet, there is no way of knowing from where or what the king may have been moving. As is often the case in these texts, the king is named as the official in charge of the sacrificial act. It may be doubted, however, that he was the only one ever to wield the sacrificial knife.

101. As per convention, I indicate the cultic acts prescribed on the reverse as sequential to the last mentioned act on the obverse, but the lacuna is quite large (as many as eight to twelve lines may have disappeared between the preserved texts on obverse and reverse), and other chronological indications may have been present in the original text.

102. In buying power, thirty shekels of gold is a large amount of money: a horse, the Mercedes of the time, could be purchased for 70 to 200 shekels of silver, and each shekel of gold was worth four of silver. Contrary to common opinion, offerings of precious metals were relatively rare in the Ugaritic cult. The total amount of gold offered that is computable from the texts in their present state comes to only about fifty shekels, which makes this offering of thirty shekels all the more remarkable—and all the more unfortunate that the text is not well enough preserved to allow us to know to whom such a splendid offering was made. Elsewhere bulls are felled in honor of *Yariḫu* (text 6 [RS 1.009:11 and RS 24.253:4–5]), but such is not certainly the case here. The identification of the STR, which may constitute an offering mentioned again in line 18, there in the number of fifteen, is unknown.

103. Judging from text 14 (RS 24.250^{+}:28), the offering materials in question would have remained in the holy place for at least one night before being used/consumed. The officiant, however, is allowed to return to his noncultic activities (line 20').

104. The similarities with text 19 (RS 19.013) suggest the readings {ḥẓ}, "arrow," and {[ảlp] ⸢w⸣}, but the preserved traces do not fit these readings as well as one could wish. The space available for the divine name in line 5 is certainly longer than is the case in RS 19.013:6; one should perhaps reconstruct another manifestation of *Rašap* of which the second element is longer (e.g., {[r]š[p mhbn]}).

105. The sign appears to consist of two wedges only, but the presence of {slḫ} in RS 1.009:1 indicates a possible mistaken writing here. The sequence of offerings presented at the PHY-rite is relatively fixed, and the explanation of {sl⸢z⸣} here as an offering term thus appears unlikely, for there is no corresponding term in the other cases (interpreting *ḥgb* as an offering term is difficult because of the fixed order {ršp ḥgb}, attested four times in these texts and best taken as a compound divine name).

106. The link of *mšr* with the donkey sacrifice shows that this text is not simply "an adaptation of the Old Babylonian *mīšarum* edict" (Shedletsky and Levine 1999: 321), i.e., "a royal edict intended to redress grievances by declaring a moratorium on debt and certain other obligations" (ibid., 322). Quite to the contrary! This section much more plausibly reflects a properly old Amorite view of *mêšaru,* and the text more plausibly reflects a ceremony in three principal parts, of which only one was devoted to "rectitude."

107. Read {l <d>bḥ⸢m⸣}.

108. Read {ủgr<t>}.

109. After {l dr bn ỉl}, the scribe forgot {l mpḫrt bn ỉl }. Some literary units of this text contain variation from one section to another, others do not (see the charts in my previous publications to which reference is made here above, introduction). This one does not, a fact that seems to have gone unnoticed by Shedletsky and Levine, for they assert that the correction "is surely logical, but

not necessarily called for, since variations occur elsewhere in this text" (1999: 340 n. 8).

110. Read {ủ!}.

111. The first sections are too fragmentary to allow the translation to be set out according to the structure of the text. Sections IV–VI are set out appropriately, while the outline of the entire text has been indicated, as best can be done in view of the lacuna, in the charts to which reference is made in the introduction. Again because the first sections are so lacunary, notes on individual terms are given in sections IV and following, where they may be appreciated in context.

112. The term *npy* appears in each section immediately after the announcement of the theme; it declares the benefit to be produced for a series of persons from the offering of the animal named in the section in question, that series varying from two to five entries in the sections preserved. The word *npy* is here analyzed as an N-stem verbal noun from the root YPY, "to be beautiful," the same root that appears in another nominal form as part of what I have termed the "stimulus" in sections V and VI (Pardee 1991: 1191–94). I would like to have come up with an English term different from "well-being," which I also use to translate ŠLM, but no term so well sums up the function of *npy* and *yp* in this text, i.e., the sum of political, social, and economic unity and prosperity (Tropper [2000: 541–42] prefers German *Befriedigung* to his rendition of my English as *Wohlfahrt;* I sympathize with his concern, but none of the standard English equivalents of *Befriedigung* really works here, i.e., "satisfaction, fulfillment, gratification"). The identification of *npy* here with the garment by the same name serving to designate "a group or jurisdictional unit within the city of Ugarit" (Shedletsky and Levine 1999: 332) is not only a lexicographic *tour de force* but ignores the structural cohesion that the two terms *npy* and *yp*, both derived from the same root, lend to the text.

113. Another key expression is *ủ l p*, here taken as representing three words: the conjunction *ủ*, "whether . . . or," the preposition *l*, "to, according to," and *p*, "mouth, statement of" (/ʾô lê pî/). The negative stimuli are expressed as occurring "according to the mouth of" various ethnic and social minorities. The reference is apparently to complaints of mistreatment which are either direct (the men and women of Ugarit are accused of "sinning"—sections III–IV) or indirect (the men and women of Ugarit are said to see their "well-being change"—sections V–VI). The form and content of the first stimulus are unknown because no trace remains of the key term. The principal alternative interpretation of the signs {ủlp}, i.e., as a noun cognate with Hebrew *ʾallūp*, "clan chieftain" or "clan," encounters insurmountable syntactic difficulties in the formulae *ủlp ḫbtkm* and *ủlp mdllkm* that appear below: the tight structure of the texts shows that the phrases are genitival in nature, and, the word "clan" designating an ethnic group, "the clan or clan chieftain of your oppressed/impoverished ones" does not make a great deal of sense. The genitival phrase cannot, in any case, legitimately be translated "These are your robbed clans, your subjugated clans," as has recently been proposed

(Shedletsky and Levine 1999: 340); that interpretation would require that the second word be an abstract noun, not a participle, as the form *mdll* shows the form to be.

114. DDMY probably represents the inhabitants of the same region as the "Gods-of-the-Land-of-Aleppo" (see text 12 [RS 24.643:43]). Other terms represented in capital letters in this list are unexplained.

115. For the interpretation of the verbal forms as N-stem in cleft constructions, see Pardee 2000a: 125–27. The meaning "behold" does not exist in Ugaritic for *hw,* and such an interpretation is not, therefore, a legitimate basis for the interpretation of the verbs as active (Shedletsky and Levine 1999: 342). As we have seen in the preceding sacrificial texts, DBḤ and Ṯ˓Y are two of the standard sacrificial terms (both will appear again in RS 34.126, the funerary ritual translated below as text 24). On the other hand, NKT is not a standard term and was not in fact included in the two categories of sacrifice just mentioned (line 23') as contexts in which the committing of sin is possible on a regular basis. NKT denotes basic "slaughtering" and corresponds to the use of the West-Semitic verb *qatālu* and the Akkadian verb *dâku*, both meaning "to kill" and both used in the Mari donkey-sacrifice texts (texts cited in Pardee 2000a: 131–33). It is the sequential mention of these three verbs that suggested to me the "vertical" interpretation of this text as having to do with communion, expiation, and "rectitude" in covenant relationships (see above, introduction, and for a more detailed argument, Pardee 1991and 2001a: 99–103).

116. Apparently a circumlocution for "*˒Ilu*" (compare text 5 [RS 4.474:1], where "*˒Ilu*" and "the sons of *˒Ilu*" constitute two entries).

117. The word designating the well-being here is *yp*, cognate with Hebrew *yōpī*, literally "beauty," from the same root as *npy* (see above, n. 112 to this section); the reference appears to be to social and political well-being typified by the beauty of a well-fortified and prosperous city. Compare the uses of this root in Biblical Hebrew with reference to social and political entities: Isa 33:17; Ezek 27:3, 4, 11; 28:7, 12, 17; 31:8; Zech 9:17; Ps 50:2; Lam 2:15.

118. Read {i$^{?}$!l}.

119. Literally: "a cast thing, a shield." Compare *nskt ksp*, "an object or objects cast of silver," in text 11 (RS 24.249:22'). Given the imprecision of this latter text according to this interpretation, it is possible that *nskt* denoted a particular cast object. In that case, *nskt ql˓* here would mean "a *nskt*-object, a shield" (i.e., "a *nskt*-object and a shield"). For the appropriateness of an offering consisting of a shield, see Holloway 1998. Because the verb NSK is not used elsewhere for the simple presentation of an offering, del Olmo Lete's interpretation of the phrase as meaning "the offering of the shield" (1998: 173) is not to be preferred.

120. This divine name remains a mystery (see Bordreuil and Pardee 1993b: 51). Del Olmo Lete's proposal to see here "a scribal (hearing-)error/allophone of *aṯrt*" (1998: 169) finds no support in the texts; i.e., (1) no variant even vaguely like this of a divine name appears elsewhere; (2) it does not account for the {m} in the

name; and (3) *ʾAṯiratu*'s positions in the attested offering lists provide no basis for a putative appearance after *ʿAnatu Ḫablay* in this list (see Pardee 2000a: 1091–1100 [Appendix II]). More likely explanations of the first two signs exist (e.g., a noun derived from the same root as *ủm*, mother, or an Akkadianized form of the element /ʿammu/, "divine uncle"), but no convincing explanation of the element {šrt} has yet appeared.

121. The use of *pảmt* with a number to designate the number of repetitions of a particular cultic act is too frequent in these texts (text 6B [RS 24.253:30], text 8 [RS 24.256:7], etc.; list in Pardee 2000a: 1197) to allow for the interpretation of lines 20–22 as designating a sacrifice of twenty-two horses (del Olmo Lete 1998: 169–73; Holloway 1998: 353). The sacrifice would in any case be without parallel: the sacrifice of a single donkey is attested in these texts and at Mari (see text 22 [RS 1.002]), but not that of horses in any number. Finally, the term "runners" does not designate horses but the humans that accompany horse-drawn chariots, as is clearly shown by the use of *rāsīm* in Biblical Hebrew (see Bordreuil and Pardee 1993b).

122. On the identification of *Ṯarriyelli* as the queen-mother in *ʿAmmurāpiʾ*'s time (not "his queen" [Levine and Tarragon 1997: 357]), see, e.g., Freu 1999: 27; Singer 1999: 690–91, 696–700.

123. *ẓl* is used only here to designate the "Shades of the Dead." It appears to be a general term for *Rapaʾūma,* which is the technical term for the dead in the underworld. That these *Rapaʾūma* could on occasion revisit the world of the living is clear from this text; and that they were sources of blessing for the living is clear from text 55 [RS 24.252). Because most of our sources reflect royal ideology, the perspective that they provide on the *Rapaʾūma* is the royal perspective; we may suspect that corresponding theologies for the other strata of society existed.

124. The inviting of the deceased king's ancestors is expressed by perfective verbs, apparently functioning as "performative perfects"; i.e., they may be translated "you are hereby called," etc. (see Lewis 1989: 13). *Didānu* (or *Ditānu*) is a deity (see text 52 [RS 24.272]) and plausibly the eponymous ancestor of the old Amorite clan (Lipiński 1978) with which the Ugaritic kings identified themselves. Because Kirta is said to be exalted in the "Assembly of *Ditānu*" (*CTA* 15 iii 2–4), the deity/clan was thought to predate that already mythical hero. It would appear that the names in lines 4–6 belong to these pre-Kirta mythical times—at least these names do not appear in the lists of the "historical" kings of Ugarit (texts 56A and B [RS 24.257 and RS 94.2518]—for the hypothesis that these archaic names may have been present in the upper part of the left column of RS 24.257, see introduction to that text). No legend is presently known for any of these early ancestors; indeed the very vocalization of the names is unknown. If my interpretation of line 9 is correct, there were generations known as the "Ancient *Rapaʾūma*" who predated even these members of the Assembly of *Didānu*. Of the "historical" kings only two are named, *ʿAmmiṯtamru* and *Niqmaddu* (lines 11–12). Unfortunately, there was much repetition of names in the Ugaritic dynasty (see text 56

[RS 24.257]), and one may only speculate on which of the kings bearing these names were intended, though there is some agreement that the reference was to the two kings bearing these names sequentially in the fourteenth century (Bordreuil and Pardee 1991: 158; Arnaud 1998: 157). This hypothesis is borne out by the absence of the sequence *ʿAmmiṯtamru–Niqmaddu* among the earlier kings now attested in text 56B (RS 94.2518), though it may not be absolutely ruled out that the sequence may have occurred even earlier (for example in RS 24.257 I 22'–23').

125. The repetition of the name *Niqmaddu* in lines 12 and 13 has caused some confusion in modern scholarship. It appears more than likely that the *Niqmaddu* named in lines 12 and 26 was not identical to the one in line13, as some have thought, for this *Niqmaddu*'s throne is to be bewept according to this verse, while the former is in all likelihood the successor of *ʿAmmiṯtamru* in an earlier generation. Unless the throne of the earlier *Niqmaddu* was retained for funerary purposes, the *Niqmaddu* of line 13 would have been the king whose funeral is ordained in the present rite, viz., the last-but-one king of Ugarit, whose reign ended sometime during the last decade of the thirteenth century (for this interpretation, see Pardee and Bordreuil 1991: 158; for recent overviews of the last years of the history of Ugarit, see Freu 1999 and Singer 1999).

126. 3m.s. indefinite subject, as is shown by the suffix on *ủdmʿtb*, "his tears"; literally, therefore, "one must beweep" (/yabkiya/)—or "shall beweep," with indicative /yabkiyu/ (Tropper 2000: 456). A vocalization with a vowel at the end appears preferable to the jussive /yabkiy/, indicated in the vocalized text in Pardee 2000a: 819.

127. The lower left corner of the sign following {ks} is damaged, and either {ks⸢ỉ⸣}, "the throne," or {ksh}, which would be an error for {ksỉh}, "his throne," is a possible reading; the context indicates the former.

128. The singular suffix on "lords" (*-k* is 2m.s.) shows that it is the deceased king who is addressed. Though the formulation is in imitation of the mythological depiction of *ʾIlu* mourning *Baʿlu* (RS 2.[022]+ [*CTA* 5] vi 11–18) and of those who would go in search of the missing *Baʿlu* (ibid., line 24), its function here is verbally to convey the king from his earthly seat of authority to his place in the underworld. The word *bʿl* in such an interpretation, while a play on the divine name that appears in the mythological passages cited, does not have that precise meaning but is a reference to the deceased king's predecessors on the throne (Bordreuil and Pardee 1991: 160), though ultimately *Baʿlu*, by his own descent into the underworld, was the model of all the kings who would follow him. I have explained the use of the preposition "under" in lines 22–26 as a ritual descent of the newly deceased king into the bowels of the earth by means of the deep pit that is located between the two principal tombs in the royal burial area within the palace at Ugarit (Pardee 1996a: 274–75; Pardee 2000a: 823–24). The numeral adverbs in lines 27–30 show that the ritual descent would have been carried out seven times, each time marked by the offering of a *ṯʿ*-sacrifice. The animal is not

indicated, but, judging from text 22 (RS 1.002, Sections III–IV), it may have been a ram. Extrapolating from that same text, the function of these sacrifices would have been expiatory, i.e., to assure that the king was cleansed of any past misdeed on joining his predecessors.

129. Read {tḥt!}.

130. The word for "bird(s)" is in construct with the following word, and there is no way of determining from the written form whether it is singular, dual, or plural in form. Because the word is written *ʿṣrm* in other cases of bird-offerings in the prose rituals, one may expect this form also to have been dual (or plural). The form translated "well-being" is singular, *šlm*, rather than plural *šlmm*, the technical form used in the ritual texts for the "sacrifice of well-being," what I translate conventionally as the "peace-offering." It is uncertain whether *šlm* represents here a rare use of the singular for the sacrificial term (cf. Amos 5:22 and the Punic sacrificial tariff, Donner and Röllig 1966–69: text 69) or whether the expression is nontechnical.

131. Read {bt!h}, "his house," (or {bn!h}, "his sons").

132. The Ugaritic construction is genitival: "well-being of *ʿAmmurāpiʾ*."

133. *ʿAmmurāpiʾ* is the last known king of Ugarit, who took the throne during the last decade of the thirteenth century and appears to have remained on the throne until the destruction of the city in ca. 1185 B.C.E. *Ṯarriyelli* was the queen-mother, *ʿAmmurāpiʾ*'s mother or grandmother (see n. 122 to this section). At Ugarit, the principal wife of a king appears to have retained the title of queen and many of the accompanying perquisites until her death.

134. The horizontal line between each of the first six lines is not indicated here because the function of the line was clearly to separate lines of writing, not to set off discrete units of text.

135. The Hurrian word for "god" is indicated here as part of the name (rather than as a common noun as in some other entries) because this name corresponds to Ugaritic *ỉlỉb*, where *ỉl* is certainly part of the name.

136. Read {ảṯḫ⟨⟨ḫ⟩⟩lm}.

137. Usually corrected to {š<l>mm}.

138. A horizontal line and several signs were erased below line 12.

139. The partially preserved sign before {l} appears to have been either {ʿ} or a word divider.

140. The reading here is difficult, apparently either {n} placed over an erased sign or {ṯả}.

141. This damaged sequence could be read as {ṯg}, {m}, or {gm}; the translation below is based on the reading {tk!m!l}, i.e., taking the three wedges that the spacing requires first to be read {pt} as in fact representing {k}.

142. The horizontal line between each of the first sixteen lines is not indicated here for the same reason as in the case of the previous text.

143. Or: "The gods of PRZ."

144. The meaning of this term, of which the reading appears to me to be quite solid, in spite of other proposals, is unknown.

145. A conjectural but very plausible restoration based on text 25 (RS 24.254:6) and on the Hurrian lists of divine names (see Laroche 1968: 509).

146. Perhaps restore *Nubadig* at the end of line 11, as in text 25 (RS 24.254: 9–10) and *Nikkal* at the end of line 12, as in the same text, lines 7–8. These two restorations are perhaps less sure than that of *ʾAṯtabi* at the end of line 10 because they would involve the inversion of the order of these two sequences in this text as compared with text 25.

147. Because of the formal ambiguity of *tảrš*, it is uncertain whether the verb is addressed to the officiant on the human level, or is part of the negotiations envisaged as occurring on the divine level. The ritual character of the text indicates that the former is the more likely explanation; i.e., the officiating priest is to present the request for the bride-price to the priests of *Milku* and of *ʿAṯtaru Šadî,* who are to transfer the items in question to the priests of *ʾIbbu*. The function of the quasi-contractual language at the end is apparently to make clear that the items enumerated belong entirely to the category of bride-price and that the prospective bride, whose father is not mentioned, is under no obligation to return anything.

148. Four signs have been erased at the beginning of this line.

149. Read {ảlnd!} (Laroche 1968: 499).

150. Laroche (1968: 499) read {n} here, but the first wedge is longer than in other examples of {n} in this text, and the reading may be {tả}.

151. Literally, a "calling (together)"; compare the use of the verb QRʾ, "to call," in text 24 (RS 34.126:2–12).

152. The sign before {m} cannot be {l} and the restoration of {ảṯḫlm}, the Hurrian sacrificial term used in the preceding three sections cannot, therefore, be restored here.

153. Read {g<d>lt}.

154. The form {dqtt} is anomalous and it is uncertain whether it is a mistake for the singular ({dqt}) or for the dual (should have been {dqtm}), or an irregular plural.

III

Descriptions of Sacrificial Rituals

A Ritual Characterized by Bird-Offerings

29. RS 1.019

The tablet is poorly preserved, and the fragments were at one time poorly reassembled (Pardee 1988c). Even when the fragments are correctly oriented, the lacunae are still too important for a full interpretation of the text. It is quite certain that there were a good number of bird offerings, but less certain whether other offerings were included. It is also uncertain whether the text belongs here, above in section II (prescriptive rituals), or even with the administrative texts in section XII. The classification as a simple "record" (del Olmo Lete 1992a: 68–69; 1999a: 88–90) appears unlikely because of the variety of ways in which the ascription of the offerings is expressed, perhaps more characteristic of offering formulae than of economic transfer (for details, see Pardee 1988c: 190–91 and 2000a: 334–35). The principal problem with the interpretation as an offering text is the apparent ascription of offerings to non-divine entities (lines 14, 17–18, 19, perhaps in 15 as well). In these cases, it is necessary either to see the formulation as purely administrative in nature (i.e., the persons named received birds in a secular context) or to take the preposition as marking the human(s) in whose honor an offering was made to an unnamed deity. There is only one possible verbal form in the text in its present state, viz., {št} in line 9, and it is uncertain whether it is a suffix-conjugation form or an imperative; the former solution is chosen here because the verb appears at the end of the sentence.

Text	***A Possible Set of Reconstructions***
Obverse	
(1) [ ]⸢ʿ⸣*ṣrm*	[ ]⸢ʿ⸣*ṣrm*
(2) [ ]*ṯpḥ bʿl*	[*dbḥ*] *ṯpḥ bʿl*
(3) [*ṯ*]⸢*l*⸣*ṯ* . *ʿṣrm*	[*ṯ*]⸢*l*⸣*ṯ* . *ʿṣrm*
(4) [?]⸢-⸣ *bʿlt btm*	[*š* .] ⸢*l*⸣ *bʿlt btm*
(5) ⸢- - - - -⸣*n* . *l* . *dgn*	⸢*ṯlṯ* . *šả*⸣*n* . *l* . *dgn*
(6) ⸢-⸣[?]⸢-⸣ . *pỉ*⸢- - -⸣	⸢-⸣ [-] ⸢-⸣ . *p ỉ*⸢*pdm*⸣
(7) *ṯpš* . *šnʿ*⸢-⸣[-]⸢-⸣*qš*	*ṯpš* . *šnʿ*⸢*t*⸣ [.] ⸢*y*⸣*qš*
(8) *ṯr* . *bỉš*⸢-⸣	*ṯr* . *b ỉš*⸢*t*⸣
(9) *bʿlh* . *št*[?]	*bʿlh* . *št*
(10) *ḫqr*⸢ - . - -⸣[-(-)]*rt*	*ḫqr*⸢*n* . *pr*⸣ [*ảṯ*]*rt*
(11) *ṯn* [ ]*l r*⸢*d*⸣[-]	*ṯn* [ ] *l r*⸢*d*⸣[-]
(12) *ảḥt* . *ḫ*⸢*m*⸣[ ]⸢- -⸣[…]	*ảḥt* . *ḫ*⸢*m*⸣[*nh*] ⸢. *ṯ*⸣[*n*] /⸢*ṯ*⸣[*lṯ*]
(13) *b ym* . *dbḥ* . *ṯpḥ* […]	*b ym* . *dbḥ* . *ṯpḥ* […]
(14) *ảḥt* . *l* . *mzy* . *bn*⸢-⸣[…]	*ảḥt* . *l* . *mzy* . *bn* ⸢-⸣[…]
(15) *ảḥt* . *l* . *mkt* . *ǵ*⸢*r*⸣[…]	*ảḥt* . *l* . *mkt* . *ǵ*⸢*r*⸣ […]
(16) *ảḥt* . *l* . *ʿṯtrt* ⸢. *š*⸣[*d*]	*ảḥt* . *l* . *ʿṯtrt* ⸢. *š*⸣[*d*]
(17) *ảrbʿ* . *ʿṣrm*	*ảrbʿ* . *ʿṣrm*
Lower Edge	
(18) *gt* . *ṯrmn*	*gt* . *ṯrmn*
(19) *ảḥt slḥủ*	*ảḥt slḥủ*

Translation

I. (1) [X-number of$^?$] birds (2) [as a sacrifice] for the Family of *Baʿlu;*[1]
(3) [thr]ee birds (4) [and a ram fo]r *Baʿlatu-Bahatīma;*
(5) three pairs of sandals for *Dagan*; (6) [as well as one/some X] and two *ỉpd*-garments;[2]
(7) for *Šapšu* a bird-catching net;[3]
(8) a bull is put in fire (9) for *Baʿlu;*
(10) a ḪQRN and a young bull for [ʾ*Aṯi*]*ratu;*
(11) two [birds] for R⸢D⸣[…];[4]
(12) one bird in the Ḫ⸢M⸣[N-sanctuary];
two (or: three) (13) on the day of the sacrifice of the Family [of X-divinity];[5]
(14) one for (= in honor of$^?$) MZY son[of X];[6]
(15) one for the slaughter-offering of the Mountain;

(16) one for *ʿAṯtartu-Šadî;*
(17) four birds (18) (for = in honor of?) *Gittu-Ṯarrumanni;*[7]
(19) one (for = in honor of?) *Salḫu*.[8]

Rural Sacrifices

30. RS 13.006

Though of great potential interest for the history of sacrificial practice among the ancient West-Semitic peoples, this and the following text do not make as great a contribution as one would wish because of the state of preservation of this text and the difficulties of interpretation of both. Their great interest lies in the fact that they constitute descriptions of sacrificial acts that occurred outside the city of Ugarit, the source of virtually all the other data at our disposal for sacrificial practice in the kingdom. Both texts refer to a certain *Ṣitqānu* as slaughtering animals, the act expressed by DBḤ, "to sacrifice," in this text, by ṬBḪ, "to slaughter," in the other. The animals sacrificed are sheep and goats; the appearance of the goat (*gdy*, "kid," here; *ʿz*, "[nanny-]goat" in the following text) constitute a peculiarity because they are rarely mentioned in other prose texts.

Text

Obverse

(1) [...]*gt nṯṯ*
(2) [-]⸢--⸣[-]*šḫ w l y*⸢*t*⸣*n* ⸢*ḫsn*⸣
(3) *ʿbd ủlm ṯn ủn ḫsn*
(4) *gdy lqḥ ṣtqn gt bn nbk*
(5) *ủ mr* ⸢--⸣[-] ⸢g⸣*t n*⸢*ṯṯ*⸣ *ḫsn l ytn*
(6) *l r*⸢*ǵ-n d lq*⸣*ḥ ṣtqn*
(7) *bt qbṣ ủ*[-(-) g]⸢*t*⸣ *ỉlštmʿ dbḥ* ⸢*ṣ*⸣*tqn l*
(8) *ršp*

Translation

I. (1) [...] *Gittu*-NṮṮ[9] (2) [...] his ram. And *Ḫasānu* gave this, (3) who is the servant of *ʾUlmi*.
Ḫasānu pronounced a complaint.

(4) *Ṣitqānu* took a kid at the *Gittu-Banū-Nabaki* (5) and myrrh at the ⸢--⸣[-] of the *Gittu*-NṮṮ.
Ḫasānu gave this (6) to R⸢Ǵ-⸣N.
What *Ṣitqānu* had taken (7) at the house of QBṢ and [at] the *Gittu-ʾIlištamiʿ* he, *Ṣitqānu*, sacrificed to (8) *Rašap*.

Ritual Slaughter of Animals in a Rural Context

31. RS 15.072

The principal personage, *Ṣitqānu*, is the same as in the preceding text and one of the places mentioned, the *ʾIlištamiʿ*-hamlet, is also identical. In this case, however, *Ṣitqānu* is acting alone, without the participation of *Ḫasānu*, and his activities appear to be limited to a single household, that of a certain *ʾUbbinniyana*, on whose behalf he acted when outsiders raided the flocks and in whose household he remains throughout the period of shearing. Because the verb denoting the slaughter of the animals is here not DBḤ but ṬBḪ and because no divinity is named as recipient of the animals, it appears that *Ṣitqānu*'s role here is not so much that of a rural priest as that of one ritually empowered to slaughter animals outside a cultic context. The first act is, however, expressed by YTN, "to give," as in the preceding text, lines 2 and 5, and it may, despite the absence of an indirect object, have constituted the offering of a (living?) animal to the sanctuary of the principal local deity. The interpretation of ṬBḪ as denoting noncultic but ritually ordained slaughter is only an extrapolation by contrast with the preceding text, but it appears at least plausible. As such it provides a little background to the biblical texts that deal with noncultic slaughter of animals (cf. Lev 17, Deut 12:15–16). Without further data, however, the interpretation of *Ṣitqānu*'s double role as seen in these two texts must remain uncertain.

Text

Obverse

(1) *b gt ỉlštmʿ*
(2) *bt ủbnyn šḫ . d ytn . ṣtqn*
(3) *ṯủt ṭbḫ ṣṭq⸢n⸣*
(4) *b bz ʿzm ḥbḫ*^{10} *š⸢ḫ⸣*
(5) *b kl ygz ḥḫ*^{11} *šḫ*

Translation

I. (1) At the *Gittu-ʾIlištamiʿ*, (2) at the house of *ʾUbbinniyana*, was his (i.e., *ʾUbbinniyana*'s) ram, that *Ṣitqānu* gave.
(3) *Ṣitqānu* slaughtered a ewe.
(4) When the goats were raided, he slaughtered his ram.
(5) Throughout shearing-time, he slaughtered his ram.

Notes

1. This interpretation of the phrase {ṯpḥ bʿl} (cf. {ṯpḥ [...] below in line 13) assumes the irregular use of {ṯ} for /š/, as the word for "descendants, family" is normally written {špḥ} (cf. Hebrew *mišpāḥāʰ*). The same phenomenon appears to occur again in line 7, if {ṯpš} represents the deity *Šapšu*. Both cases involve the sequence /š-p/; other tokens of /š/ are written as expected.

2. The *ỉpd*-garment is the etymological forerunner of *ʾēpōd,* "ephod," in Biblical Hebrew, one meaning of which is to designate a priestly garment.

3. If this interpretation is accepted, the strangeness of the offering may be explained by the theme of the text, bird-offerings.

4. The form of the number "two," {ṯn} rather than {ṯt}, casts doubt on the restoration of {ʿṣrm}, which is clearly a feminine noun (cf. *ảḥt* below), but that restoration appears to be required by the following lines, where the feminine form of the number "one" is used quasi-pronominally to refer to "bird," and the word "bird" actually appears, as is expected, with the number "four" (line 17). The gender concord of the number nouns is not as consistent in Ugaritic as in the other ancient Semitic languages.

5. This temporal indication shows that the various offerings named did not all take place on a single day. Without any other such indicators, however, it is impossible to have any idea of the span of time covered.

6. The attempt to explain this line as expressing a sacrificial category (del Olmo Lete 1992a: 69; 1999a: 90) finds no etymological explanation for *mzy* (the meaning would be "libation," but the {z} shows that the word is unrelated to Hebrew NZH, Aramaic NDʾ) and leaves *bn* unaccounted for. On the other hand, it is uncertain whether "MZY son [of X]" expresses a sacrifice for the benefit of a man (the human in whose name a sacrifice is offered to a divinity is very rarely mentioned in these texts) or the divine recipient (divine names that consist of "X son of Y" are extremely rare and otherwise unattested in the sacrificial ritual texts).

7. The common usage in the sacrificial texts of ascribing offerings to deities with a grammatical rather than a lexical marker and the apparent structural unity

of lines 11–19 (i.e., number of birds + various designations of beneficiary) make it unlikely that lines 17–19 express two places whence these birds would have come (del Olmo Lete 1992a: 69; 1999a: 90). The claimed structural parallel with text 58 (RS 19.015) does not in fact exist. Particularly telling against that interpretation is the small number of birds indicated in lines 17–19; the function of the place-names in the second part of RS 19.015 is to indicate the origins of all the wine to be used in the feasts listed in the first part of the text. The small number of birds, only five, and the fact that the place of origin would be mentioned only here render a structural comparison with text 58 of little value.

8. The writing with {ủ} at the end of this word remains unexplained. The form may be built off the place name *slḫ* and the he /ʾ/ could be an adjectival ending ("a person from *slḫ*," probably a personal name) or this /ʾ/ could be a hypocoristic ending (cf. *tlmủ*, perhaps hypocoristic for *tlmyn*).

9. The word *gt* designates a small farming community or "hamlet." Some of these are owned by royalty, others by high officials of the kingdom, while some appear to have been leagued with nearby larger towns.

10. Read {ṭ!bḫ].

11. Read {ṭ!<b>ḫ}.

IV

Memorials of a Sacrificial Rite

TWO BRIEF TEXTS inscribed on stone stelae have survived that commemorate two occasions of the performance of an ancient Amorite rite known as the *pagrû* (*pagrāʾum* in the eighteenth-century texts from Mari). It appears to have been a rite in honor of the deceased members of the royal line in which all living members of the royal family were required to participate. If such was still the meaning of the rite in the late thirteenth century, and there is no reason to doubt such continuity, these stelae provide precious rare explicit data on the so-called cult of the dead at Ugarit (see below on texts 55, 56). A further link with the old Amorite tradition known from Mari is the dedication of both stelae to *Dagan*, for that god was closely linked with the Mari *pagrāʾum*-rite. The etymological meaning of the term *pagrû* is "having to do with a corpse, a cadaver (*pagru*)," and it is on the basis of this etymology that the modality of this sacrifice is assumed to have differed from that of the DBḤ, i.e., by the way in which the body of the slaughtered animal was treated: instead of being butchered in the common fashion (into cuts of meat for the divine and human participants, with the by-products fully utilized), the corpse of this sacrifice was probably disposed of more or less whole. In a later Babylonian purification rite, for example, a sheep was beheaded and its body was dragged through the sanctuary which was to be purified and the corpse was then thrown into a river (the example is purely heuristic, we presently have no indications as to precisely how the corpse was treated in the *pagrû*-rite). The two Ugaritic texts are very similar, but the syntax in which the word *pgr* occurs is different in each case: in the first text, the word for "stela" appears in first position and expresses the fronted object of the verb "to offer," whereas the *pagrû* assumes that position in the other text. Some of the terms vary as well: *Dagan* is described as the "lord" of the offerer in the second text and the bull offered for the feast is there designated as coming from the plowing stock, whereas the first, though not explicitly described, may be expected to have come from the herds of "fattened cattle" (*ảlpm mrủm*) that are often mentioned in the administrative texts.

The Mortuary Offering of *Ṯarriyelli*

32. RS 6.021

Text	**Translation**
Obverse	
(1) *skn . d šʿlyt*	Sacred stela that *Ṯarriyelli*[1]
(2) ⸢*ṯ*⸣*ryl . l dgn . pgr*	offered to *Dagan:* mortuary sacrifice;
(3) ⸢*w*⸣ *ảlp l ảkl*	and a bull for food.[2]

The Mortuary Offering of *ʿUzzīnu*

33. RS 6.028

Text	**Translation**
Obverse	
(1) *pgr . d šʿly*	Mortuary sacrifice that *ʿUzzīnu*[3]
(2) ⸢*ʿ*⸣*zn . l dgn . bʿlh*	offered[4] to *Dagan* his lord;
(3) [*w ả*]⸢*l*⸣*p . b mḥrṯt*	[and a b]ull with the plow.[5]

Notes

1. There is no reason to doubt that this *Ṯarriyelli* is the same as the queen-mother mentioned in text 24 (RS 34.126:32).

2. According to the interpretation offered here, the animal offered as the *pagrû*-sacrifice was not named (requiring the assumption that the species was fixed by tradition), whereas the bull was slaughtered for the feast that accompanied the *pagrû*-rite.

3. If this text is contemporary with the preceding one, this *ʿUzzīnu* was plausibly the *sākinu*, "governor, prefect," known from Akkadian texts, perhaps the same

as the ʿ*zn bn byy* who sent two letters to Ugarit (RS 17.063, RS 17.117 [Caquot 1978]) when he was abroad in his more youthful days.

4. A comparison of the two texts leads to the conclusion that the *pagrû*-sacrifice could be "presented" to the deity as could the stelae commemorating that sacrifice. Keeping in mind that ŠʿLY does not mean "to offer up a burnt-offering" (and is not, therefore, the equivalent of Hebrew *heʿelāh*, which means "to offer up the ʿ*ōlāh*"), the use of that verb with *pgr* as the fronted object shows that that offering was "presented (to the deity)," not "offered up as a burnt-offering."

5. The mention of the plow recalls the story of the call of Elisha (1 Kgs 19:19-21). The similar structure of this and the preceding text and the explicit indication in the preceding text that the bull was used as "food" may be taken as indicating that this bull also was intended to serve as the main course in the feast accompanying the *pagrû*-rite.

V

An *Ex Voto* Inscription

34. RS 25.318

Of the many inscribed objects discovered at Ras Shamra, only one bears a Ugaritic inscription explicitly defining the object as devoted to a divinity. The single text in this category is a drinking vessel in the form of a lion's head (photo Yon 1997:159; Pardee 2000a, cover of fascicle 2). The inscription consists of two lines, with a short horizontal line inscribed in the clay between the two. It begins under the handle and runs behind the right cheek; line 2 is 14 cm long, or about one-fourth the circumference of the vessel. Because one of the names is of the form "son of X," attempts have been made to make of line 1 a secondary addition intended to be inserted into the present line 2, either after {pn ảrw} or after {šˁly}. On the object itself, however, one finds no indication of this insertion, and it appears more likely that the horizontal line should be interpreted as explicitly indicating a break between the two lines, rather than as a joining of the two. For these reasons, I propose that the potter who created the object had his "name" (individuals are often designated as "son of X") placed in first position and that it is the commissioner and offerer of the work who is named in line 2. This *ʾAgapṯarru* appears again below in a text reflecting divinatory practice (text 35 (RS 24.312]), but it cannot be known whether the references are to the same person.

Text	***Translation***
(1) *bn ảgpṯr*	*Binu ʾAgapṯarri*.
——	
(2) *pn ảrw d šˁly nrn l ršp gn*	Lion's head (lit. "face") that *Nūrānu* offered to *Rašap-Guni*.

VI

Divination

VI A. PRACTICE

TWO TYPES OF DIVINATORY TEXTS are attested at Ugarit:[1] those that reflect daily practice and those that consist of collections of various types of phenomena interpreted as ominous.[2] The Ugaritic texts that reflect moments of divinatory practice are actually much rarer than are manuals in other Near Eastern archives and are for that reason particularly precious. The texts on clay models of animal livers reflect actual consultations, though their damaged state sometimes makes their meaning unclear.[3] An animal would have been sacrificed, and a specialist would have examined the liver and interpreted the formations present thereupon. In these texts reflecting actual practice, the "science" lay in the specialist's ability to interpret correctly the signs present on the organ examined; this skill would have been based on the specialist's knowledge of the tradition of interpretation. In the "manuals" translated below, the "science" lay in the collection of phenomena laying out the details of the tradition of interpretation. The models bear incisions representing schematically the features that were present on the animal liver that the model represents. In one case, that of text 35 (RS 24.312), the excellent state of preservation of the model allows a reasonable correlation of the text with the nonlinguistic marks to give a plausible global interpretation. The single lung model, that of a sheep or goat (text 40 [RS 24.277]), bears several texts that appear to reflect various cultic moments, not just divinatory consultations. The last of these texts refers rather clearly, however, to one set of circumstances under which a goat is to be sacrificed for the purpose of divination. The practical texts reveal clearly the functional aspect of divination: the rites are very narrowly mantic in that their purpose is to provide the inquirer with guidance from the world of the divine on how to conduct one specific aspect of life. The manuals, on the other hand, provide compendia of knowledge gained from consultations in one area of consultation, such as extispicy or astromancy.

Liver Models

35. RS 24.312

Text	*Translation*
(1) *l ảg*⌜*pṯ*⌝*r k yqny ǵzr* ⌜*d ả*⌝*lṯyy*	(This liver model is) for ʾ*Agapṯarri* when he was to procure the young man of the Alashian.[4]

36. RS 24.323

Text	*Translation*
(1) *dbḥt . bṣy . b*⌜*n*⌝ [...]	Sacrificial consultation[5] of BṢY, so[n]/daught[er][6] of
(2) ⌜*ṭ*⌝*ry . l* ʿ*ṯt*⌜*r*⌝[...]	ṬRY, to the ʿ*Aṯtaru*[...]
(3) *d .* ⌜*b* ʿ*ṯtr*⌝[*t*...]	who is in ʿ*Aṯtar*[*tu*].[7]

37. RS 24.326

Text	*Translation*
(1) *kbd . dt ypt*	This is the liver model[8] (pertaining to the consultation on behalf) of YPT,
(2) *bn ykn*ʿ	son of YKNʿ,
(3) *k ypth̩ . yr*⌜*ḫ*⌝ *hnd*	when this month was about to begin (lit., "open").

38. RS 24.327

Text	***Translation***
(1) [ ]*l*	[...]L
(2) *d* ⌜*yb*⌝*nmlk*	of *Yabnimilku*
(3) *l ḫpṯ*	with regard to *ḫpṯ*.[9]

39. RS 24.654

Text	***Translation***
(1) *k*⌜*bd*⌝ *ḫ*[...]	This is the liver model (pertaining to the consultation on behalf) Ḫ[...]
(2) *k ymmr*[...]	when [...][10]
(3) *ym š*⌜*ḫ*⌝[...]	on a/the day of [...].

A Lung Model

40. RS 24.277

This clay model of an animal lung (representing the lung of a sheep or goat, judging from its size) has three long broad sides on which inscriptions have been placed in fields delimited by strokes in the clay. Though it is possible in some cases to determine in which order the fields on one of the surfaces were inscribed, it is not possible to determine the order of inscription of the three principal surfaces. This means that any modern lineation is in part arbitrary, a fact indicated in my transliteration by priming on the numbers (this device usually indicates an uncertain number of lines owing to breakage, rather than to an uncertain order of lines). The texts, and the phrases within the texts, are very brief, with the result that even a small amount of damage can render the text incomprehensible. Because of the brevity of the texts and uncertainty as to the circumstances to which they refer, I have for the most part translated the nominal phrases without indicating a predicate in English. The first three texts refer explicitly to sacrifices, but, because no divinatory terminology is used, it is impossible to say for sure whether the presence of these texts on an organ model is enough to permit us to classify the function of these sacrifices as divinatory. Moreover, since several sacrifices are mentioned, there can have been no link between this object and a single act of sacrificial divination such as we have seen in the case of the liver models. In any case, the size of the model is too small for the bull mentioned in line 20'. Because of the apparent "theoretical" importance of the last three inscriptions on Surface 3, which appear to be syntactically linked and in which a goat is twice mentioned, it is tempting to identify the model lung as that of a goat and to see the motivation for the creation of the inscribed model as coming from a desire to place the text on an appropriate object. Unfortunately, that surface of the tablet is too damaged to provide any certainty for such a fragile hypothesis.

Text	***Translation***
Surface 1, Inscription 1	
(1') *dbḫ kl yrḫ*	Sacrifices of the entire month.
(2') *ndr*	An object vowed,
(3') *dbḫ*	a sacrifice.
Surface 1, Inscription II	
(4') *dt nảt*	Sacrifices offered by Nʾ AT
(5') *w ytnt*	and gifts for
(6') *ṯrmn w*	(the deity) *Ṯarrumannu* and
(7') *dbḫ kl*	a sacrifice offered by all;
(8') *kl ykly*	all will eat this sacrifice until it is consumed,
(9') *dbḫ k . sprt*	in accordance with the documents.
Surface 1, Inscription III	
(10') *dt nảt*	Sacrifices offered by NʾAT
(11') *w qrwn*	and *Qurwanu;*
(12') *l k dbḫ*	(these will be done) like the (preceding) sacrifice.
Surface 1, Inscription IV	
(13') [...]⸢*r*⸣*bt*	[...]RBT
(14') [...]*bnš*	[...]personnel.
Surface 2, Inscription V	
(15') *š* ⸢*š*⸣[...]	A ram Š[...]
(16') *w* ⸢-⸣[...]	and [...]
(17') *d*[...]	D[...]

Surface 2, Inscription VI

(18') *ypy*[...]	YPY[...]
(19') *w s*⸢-⸣[...]	and S[...]

Surface 2, Inscription VII

(20') *ṯr dg*⸢*n*⸣[...]	A bull for *Dagan* [...]
(21') *b bt k* . ⸢-⸣[...]	in the house, according to the do[cuments],
(22') *w l db*⸢*ḥ*⸣[...]	and to/surely the sacrifice [...].

Surface 3, Inscription VIII

(23') *hm qrt tủḫd . hm mt yʿl bnš*	If the city is about to be seized, if some-one (lit., "a man") attacks, the (male) personnel[11] (of the city)

Surface 3, Inscription IX

(24') [...]⸢-⸣ *ảṯt yqḥ ʿz*	[...] the women, they will take[12] a goat [...]
(25') [...]⸢--⸣	[...]

Surface 3, Inscription X

(26') *bt hn bnš yqḥ ʿz*	in/with regard to the house, the (male) personnel will take a goat
(27') *w yḥdy mrḥqm*	and see afar.[13]

An Astrological Report

41. RS 12.061

This very brief text has caused a great deal of ink to flow because of various attempts to interpret it as reflecting a solar eclipse. I am convinced that this approach is untenable and have proposed with N. Swerdlow (Pardee and Swerdlow 1993) that it refers to a repeated sighting of Mars (= *Rašap*) at sundown for six days in a row, after which the planet would no longer have been visible at sundown. In other words the so-called heliacal setting of Mars would have occurred on the sixth day after five continuous days of visibility at sundown, starting with the evening before the sighting of the new moon. The two lines on the reverse of the tablet are epigraphically uncertain, and it is unclear whether livers are being consulted (reading {⌜kb⌝dm} at the beginning of line 5) or whether the men of the city are seeking out the governor (in order that he appoint specialists to investigate the meaning of the sighting), as I translate below.

Text	***Translation***
Obverse	
(1) *b t̠t̠ . ym . ḫdt̠*	During the six days of the new-moon festival[14] of
(2) *ḫyr . ʿrbt*	the month of *Ḫiyyāru*, the sun (*Šapšu*)
(3) *špš* ⌜.⌝ *t̠ǵrh*	set, her gatekeeper being
(4) *ršp*	*Rašap*.[15]
Reverse	
(5) ⌜*w ảdm* ⌝ ⌜.⌝ *tbqrn*	The men (?) shall seek out
(6) *skn*	the governor.

Notes

1. Most of the divinatory texts were found in the "House of the Priest with Lung and Liver Models" (see Courtois *apud* Pardee 1988a: 5–12).

2. In addition to the reeditions of these texts in Pardee 2000a, see my English translations (with more extensive notes than can be offered here) in Pardee 1997c and 2001; for more detailed studies of the technical details and of the history of the genre, see Meyer 1987 and 1993; on the nature of these texts as "scientific," see above, "Introduction."

3. Also discovered at Ras Shamra were a large number of fragments of inscribed liver models carved from ivory. These texts are too fragmentary to be included here. For the publication of these objects, see Pardee forthcoming c. There I comment on forty-five fragments; some bear parts of more than one inscription (i.e., discrete texts on a single object, as in the case of the lung model [here below text 40]). Though we can say little about the content of the texts they bear, such a large number of texts inscribed on a relatively precious matter testifies to the importance of divination and the preservation of its verbalized results.

4. According to J.-W. Meyer 1987: 220, the specialist in these matters, the response to the question of whether or not to proceed with the procurement of the boy, in all probability as a servant, was positive.

5. By the presence of a word derived from the root DBḤ, "to sacrifice," this text establishes explicitly the link between sacrificial and divinatory practice.

6. The name BṢY does not reveal the gender of its bearer, and the last partially preserved sign could be either {n} or {t}, allowing the readings {b⌜n⌝}, "son," or {b⌜t⌝}, "daughter."

7. The last name is taken here as the village name known elsewhere as *gt ʿṯtrt*, "the *ʿAṯtartu*-farm." The name *ʿAṯtaru* in the preceding line is translated as the male deity who would have been particularly venerated in that village. These signs could, however, represent the first part of a personal name, in which case the preceding *l* would denote the person for whom the consultation was effected, rather than the deity in whose honor the animal was sacrificed.

8. As stated in the introduction, the liver model in each case represents an individual liver drawn from a sacrificed animal.

9. *ḫpṯ* elsewhere refers to a type of service, manual labor, or military duty; this text is too brief and too poorly preserved to allow us to determine the meaning of the term here.

10. Perhaps *k ym mr*, "according to a bitter day."

11. Cultic personnel are counted among the "personnel of the king" (*bnš mlk*), and it is possible that this reference is to the members of the personnel who specialize in divination. There appears to be a contrast between males here and women in the following text, but the term there is generic, meaning simply "women," with no indication that they may have a particular function in divination. The contrast there may, therefore, only be between the male and female inhabitants of the city, as in text 22 (RS 1.002 and parallels).

12. This verb form is not marked for feminine gender, and it is not, therefore, the women who are taking the goat. The verb is 3m.sg. or pl., indicative or jussive (/yiqqaḥ/, "let one take," /yiqqaḥu/, "one will take," or /yiqqaḥū/, "let them take"). Cf. *bnš yqḥ* in line 26'.

13. It is uncertain whether this formulation is locative, as is expected from its form, that of a *m*-preformative noun, with the phrase meaning perhaps "see (the enemy) far off," or temporal, with the connotation of "see into the future."

14. The importance of the new moon festival as seen in the sacrificial texts indicates that this text also probably had a ritual dimension. The sighting would have been done by specialists in astrological divination, who in turn would have been part of a larger group including (or identical with) specialists in sacrificial divination.

15. The Ugaritic terminology, in this respect similar to the Hebrew (√BWʾ, "to enter," expresses the setting of the sun; *ʿereb*, "evening," constitutes a remnant of the usage of ʿRB, as in Ugaritic, to express that notion); the idea is that the sun "enters (the underworld)" when it sets. *Rašap*, one of the principal West-Semitic deities of the underworld, is thus depicted as opening the gates of that realm to allow the sun to enter. As god of the army (*Rašap Ṣabaʾi*) and of the underworld, *Rašap* may correspond to classical Mars.

VI B. DIVINATION: MANUALS

OMINOLOGY WAS ONE of the most important of the "sciences" practiced in Mesopotamia, where large compendia of phenomena were gathered in collections organized according to the aspect of life in which the phenomena could occur (unnatural fetuses, aspects of the moon and other astral bodies, dreams, etc.). This fact and the further fact that the origins of these collections in Babylonia go back quite early indicate that the Ugaritians did not invent the genre. On the other hand, the purity of the Ugaritic language in these manuals, with few loanwords from Akkadian or Hittite, indicates the tradition was probably an old one in the West. Indeed, it is not improbable that it goes back to the Amorite heyday nearer the beginning of the second millennium B.C.E. when the Amorite ancestors of the thirteenth-century Ugaritians enjoyed political dominance all along the Fertile Crescent, from Babylon to Hazor. If the Mesopotamian view of the Amorite rise to power had some truth to it, the early Amorites were uncouth country folk who became great assimilators of Mesopotamian urban civilization. It is only a step to say that they may have been responsible for the cultivation and spread of the Mesopotamian "science" of divination toward the Levant. One further feature of the Ugaritic texts deserves mention at this point: not only do the Ugaritic versions not correspond to a known Mesopotamian or Anatolian text tradition, but they differ structurally from any previously discovered tradition by the fact that they appear to reflect an attempt to provide a relatively reasoned overview of the possibilities. For example, even the earliest Mesopotamian texts of omens based on malformed animal births contain repeated ominous phenomena, each with a different possible value (e.g., a calf born with five legs may have two different interpretations in a given text). In none of the Ugaritic texts discovered to date—to be sure few in number and poorly preserved—does such repetition of ominous phenomena occur.

These texts are classed as "scientific" because of their overtly observational form ("If such-and-such a phenomenon is observed, such and such an event will result") and because of the formal similarity with the empirical "science" of medical texts ("If such-and-such a symptom occurs, give such-and-such a remedy").[1] Because the "knowledge" gathered in these compendia is mantic in nature, the texts are not "scientific" in the sense of the term as used in modern Western society; but for the ancients the data appear to have been considered to be as valid and useful as those in a modern scientific handbook.

Malformed Animal Fetuses

42. RS 24.247+

The Akkadian series known conventionally by the opening words of an omen expressed in explicitly conditional terms, i.e., *šumma izbu*, "if a fetus (presents such-and-such a form)," is one of the best known because it is relatively well preserved and has been the object of a reliable modern edition in accessible form (Leichty 1970). The tradition goes back to the Old Babylonian period but is best known from the long compilations done in the Neo-Assyrian period. The "science" represented is that of "teratology," i.e., the study of "monsters," in this case, monstrous births, or, more properly, "teratomancy," the science of divination by monstrous births. The single Ugaritic text cannot compare in volume with the twenty-odd tablets of the later Akkadian series. It is nonetheless important, both as a witness to this full assimilation in the west and in a western language of a literary tradition best known from Mesopotamia and as a form of the tradition as yet unknown in the east, i.e., as a brief list of malformations apparently intended to represent the major possibilities of malformation of the various parts of the body. As regards this latter feature, though the text does not proceed systematically from one region of the body to another, the absence of repeated omens, the fact that head, trunk, legs, and internal organs are all covered, and the occasional grouping of omens from one region of the body (e.g., lines 30'–38': nostrils, tongue, lip, face, ears), all seem to reflect a conscious desire to be comprehensive. In form, the text appears to belong to the category in which the protasis is not markedly conditional (the temporal conjunction setting up the general situation, though not the specific omen, is here restored in line 1); the omens are, therefore, presented simply as nominal phrases, e.g., "and there is no right ear" (line 35'). The apodosis (the interpretation) is, on the other hand, usually in the form of a verbal phrase expressing what may be expected to happen. As a glance at the following transliteration will show, the tablet where preserved is usually quite legible, but large fragments were never found, including the entire lower portion, which probably contained some twelve to fifteen lines.

Text

Obverse

---

(1) *t̲ảtt ṣỉn* ⌜-⌝[--]⌜-⌝*dảt . ảbn . mảdtn tqln b ḥwt*

---

(2) *ˤṣ . hn*⌜-⌝[--(-)]⌜*y*⌝ *ảt̲r yld . bhmth t*ˤ⌜--⌝[...]

---

(3) *gmš š*[ ]*n ykn b ḥwt*

---

(4) *w* ⌜*ỉ*⌝[*n*]*ḥwtn tḫlq*

---

(5) ⌜-⌝[ ]*rǵbn ykn b ḥwt*

---

(6) [ ]⌜-.⌝ *w ḥr ảpm . ḥwt*⌜*n*⌝[----(-)]⌜*m*⌝*t̲n rgm*

---

(7) [*w*] ⌜*ỉn*⌝[ ]⌜*m*⌝*lkn yỉḫd ḥw*[*t ỉbh w*?] *mrḥy mlk* ⌜*t*⌝*dlln*

---

(8) [-]⌜-⌝*h . m*⌜-⌝[----]⌜-*m*⌝*ḥt . bhmtn*[-------]⌜-⌝

---

(9) ⌜*w*⌝ *ỉn šq .* [*šmảl*] ⌜*b*⌝*h . mlkn* ⌜*y*⌝[-----(-)]⌜*ỉ*⌝*bh*

---

(10) ⌜*w*⌝ *ỉn qṣr*[*t šm*]⌜*ả*⌝*l . mlk*⌜*n*⌝[------(-) *ỉ*]⌜*b*⌝*h*

---

(11) *w qrn šỉ*⌜*r*⌝ [. *b*] ⌜*p*⌝*ỉth . š*⌜*mả*⌝[*l*]*n*

---

(12) *t̲ḫl . ỉn . bh*[--]⌜-⌝*dn .* ⌜-⌝[ ] ⌜*m*⌝*t̲*⌜*n*⌝ [...]
(13) *mlkn . l ypq* ⌜*š*⌝[*p*]*ḥ*

---

(14) [*w*] *ỉn* ʾ*uškm b*⌜*h* .⌝ *d̲*⌜*r*⌝[ˤ]⌜-⌝

---

(15) ⌜*w*⌝ *ỉn . kr*ˤ *y*⌜*d*⌝*h* ⌜-⌝[ ]⌜*y*⌝*ḫlq bhmt* [--]⌜-⌝

---

(16) [-]⌜-⌝[-]⌜-⌝[ ] . *ỉbn yḫlq bhmt* ⌜*ḥw*⌝*t*

---

(17) [ ]⌜-⌝ . *t̲nn* ˤ*z yủḫd ỉb mlk*

---

(18) [ ]*ḫlq . mt̲n rgm*

---

(19) [ ]rǵb . w tp . mṣq⸢t⸣

---

(20) [ ]⸢y⸣ʿzzn

---

(21) [ ]rn

---

(22) [ ]bh

---

(23) [ ]⸢t⸣p⸢š⸣[...]

....

Reverse

....

(24') [ ]⸢- . l⸣[...]

(25') [ ]⸢ỉ⸣r . lk⸢-⸣[...]

(26') w ỉn . šq ymn . b⸢h⸣[...]

(27') w ỉn . ḫrṣp . b k⸢-⸣[...]

(28') w ỉn . krʿ . ydh[...]
(29') l ypq špḥ

(30') w ỉn . ḫr ảpm . kl[...]

(31') w ỉn . lšn bh . r[...]

(32') šptk . tḫyt[2] . k⸢-⸣[...]

(33') pnh . pn . ỉrn . ủ⸢-⸣[ ]⸢-⸣tqṣrn[...]
(34') ymy . bʿl hn bhm[t ...]

(35') w ỉn . ủdn . ymn . ⸢b⸣[h ỉbn y]šdd ḥwt
(36') [w y]ḥslnn

(37') w ỉn . ủdn šmảl . ⸢b⸣[h .]⸢mlkn⸣[y]šdd ḥwt ỉ⸢b⸣[h]
(38') w yḥslnn

(39') *w qṣrt . pʿnh . bʿln ygt*⸢*r*⸣ [. *ḫ*]*rd . w ủḫr*
(40') *y . ykly* ⸢*rš*⸣*p*

(41') ⸢*w*⸣ *ả*⸢*ph*⸣ *. k ảp . ʿṣr . ỉlm . tbʿ*⸢*rn*⸣ *. ḥwt*
(42') [ ]⸢-⸣*št . w ydủ*

(43') [ ]⸢.⸣ *l rỉšh . d̲r*⸢*ʿ*⸣ [.] ⸢*m*⸣*lk hwt*
(44') [-------]⸢*ḫ*⸣

(45') [------]⸢*d*⸣*rh . yṣủ . špšn . tpšlt ḥ*
wt hyt

(46') [------]*mlkn . yd . ḫrdh . yddll*

(47') [-----]⸢*l*⸣ *. ủšrh . mrḫy . mlk tnšản*
(48') [-----]⸢-⸣*b . ydh*

(49') [----]⸢-⸣ *ảṯrt . ʿnh . w ʿnh b lṣbh*
(50') [*ỉbn y*]*rps ḥwt*

(51') [---]*bh . b ph . yṣủ . ỉbn . yspủ ḥwt*

(52') *w* [*ỉn*] *pʿnt . bh . ḫrdn . yhpk . l mlk*

(53') *w* [--] *lšnh . ḥwtn tprš*

(54') *b*⸢-⸣[--]⸢-⸣*ḫrh . b pỉth . mlkn . yšlm l ỉbh*

(55') *w ỉ*[*n* -]⸢*k*⸣*bm . bh . d̲rʿ . ḥwt . hyt . yḫsl*

Upper Edge

(56') *w ʿ*⸢-⸣[-] *. ỉlm . tbʿrn ḥwt . hyt*

(57') *w ʿnh* [*b*] ⸢*l*⸣*ṣbh . mlkn yʿzz ʿl ḫpṯh*

(58') *w ḫr .* ⸢*w* -⸣*r . bh . mlkn ybʿr ỉbh*

(59') *w ỉn yd š*⌜*mả*⌝*l bh . ḫwt ỉb tḫlq*

Translation[3]

(1) As for the ewes of the sheep/goats, [when t]hey give birth!:[4] If it is a stone, many will fall in the land.
(2) If it is a piece of wood, behold [ ]⌜Y⌝ ʾAṮR YLD, its cattle will be destroyed.
(3) If the fetus is smooth, without h[air?], there will be [...] in the land.
(4) And if i[t has no], the land will perish.
(5) [ ] there will be famine in the land.
(6) [ ] nor nostrils, the land [;] ditto.
(7) [And] if it has no [ ], the king will sieze the lan[d of his enemy and?] the weapon of the king will lay the land low.
(8) [ ] [ ] cattle [will peri]sh.?
(9) And if it has no [left] thigh, the king will [ ] his enemy.
(10) And if there is no lower left leg, the king [will] his enemy.
(11) And if there is a horn of flesh [in] its lef[t te]mple, [ ].
(12) If it has no spleen [ ] [;] di[tto;] (13) the king will not obtain offspring.
(14) [And] if it has no testicles, the (seed-)gra[in].[5]
(15) And if the middle part of its foreleg is missing, [ ] will destroy the cattle [ ].
(16) [ ] the enemy will destroy the cattle of the land.
(17) [ ] the mighty archers will seize the enemy of the king.
(18) [ ] perish/destroy;[6] ditto.
(19) [ ] famine, hard times will disappear.
(20) [ ]will become powerful/strengthen him.
(21) [ ]
(22) [ ] his [?]
(23) [ ]

Reverse

(24') [ ] [...]
(25') [ ] [...]
(26') And if it has no right thigh[...].

(27') And if there is no ḪRṢP in [its?] K[...].
(28') And if it has no middle part of the [right?] foreleg[...] (29') will not obtain offspring.
(30') And if [it has] no nostrils [...].
(31') And if it has no tongue [...].
(32') If its lo<w>er lip [...].
(33') If its face is that of a ʾIRN, [ ] will shorten/be shortened (34') the days of our lord; behold, the catt[le ...].
(35') And if it has no right ear, [the enemy will] devastate the land (36') [and will] consume it.
(37') And if [it] has no left ear, the king [will] devastate the land of [his] enemy (38') and will consume it.
(39') And if its (rear?) legs are short, our lord will confront the *ḫurādu*-troops and (40') *Rašap* will consume the progeny.
(41') And if its nose is like the "nose" of a bird, the gods will destroy the land (42') [ ] will fly (away?).
(43') [ ]to/on its head, the (seed-)grain of that king (44') [will ...].
(45') [ ] its [-]DR protrudes, the Sun/*Šapšu* will abase! that land.
(46') [ ] the king will lay low! the power (lit. "hand") of the *ḫurādu*-troops.
(47') [ ] its penis, the weapon of the king will indeed be raised (48') [...] his hand.
(49') [ ] in place of (?) its eyes and its eyes are in its forehead, (50') [the enemy will] tread the land under.
(51') [And if] its [--]B protrudes from its mouth, the enemy will devour the land.
(52') And if it has [no] (rear?) legs, the *ḫurādu*-troops will turn against the king.
(53') And if it has [two?] tongue(s?), the land will be scattered.
(54') If [its?] B-[(-) and?] its ḤR are in its temples, the king will make peace with his enemy.
(55') And if it has n[o] [-]KB, the (seed-)grain of that land will be consumed.
(56') And if ʿ⸢-⸣[-], the gods will destroy that land.
(57') And if its eye(s) is/are [in] the forehead, the king will become more powerful than his *ḫupṯu*-troops.
(58') And if it has ḤR and? [-]R, the king will destroy his enemy.
(59') And if it has no left (fore?)leg, the land of the enemy will perish.

Malformed Human Fetuses

43. RS 24.302

Though only a tiny fragment, this text is important for the history of Ugaritic "science," for it testifies to a teratological tradition based on the study of malformed human fetuses. This sub-genre corresponds to the Akkadian series *šumma sinništu*, "If a woman (gives birth to a fetus with such-and-such a deformity)." The basic form and presuppositions are identical to those of the *šumma izbu* series. At the level of expression, however, there is one important difference: here the temporal/hypothetical conjunction *k*, "when, if," is repeated at the beginning of each omen, with one exception (lines 12'–13'). The act of giving birth was, therefore, explicitly stated in most cases; this would have been followed by the observed deformity ("and such-and-such a condition exists"), which is in no case preserved; the final element would have been the interpretation, of which elements are here preserved, most identifiable from the preceding text, better preserved.

Text	***Translation***
Obverse	
(1') *k* ⸢*t*⸣[*ld ảṯt* ...]	When [a woman] g[ives birth ...]
(2') *ḫw*[*t* ...]	the lan[d ...].
(3') *k tl*⸢*d*⸣[*ảṯt* ...]	When [a woman] giv[es birth ...]
(4') *yʿzz ʿ*⸢*l*⸣[...]	will become more powerful th[an ...].
Lower Edge	
(5') *k tld* ⸢*ả*⸣[*ṯt* ...]	When a wo[man] gives birth [...]
(6') *ḫwt ỉb* ⸢*t*⸣[...]	the land of the enemy will [...].
Reverse	
(7') *k tld ả*[*ṯt* ...]	When a wo[man] gives birth [...]
(8') *ʿḏrt tk*⸢-⸣[...]	aid will [...].
(9') *k tld* ⸢*ả*⸣[*ṯt* ...]	When a wo[man] gives birth [...]
(10') *mrḫ*⸢*y*⸣[...]	the weapon of [...]

(11') *l yp*[*q špḫ* ...]	will not ob[tain offspring ...].
(12') *bh* ⌜-⌝[...]	If it has [...]
(13') *t*⌜-⌝[...]	will [...].
(14') ⌜-⌝[...]	

Lunar Omens

44. RIH 78/14

This Ugaritic text corresponds to the series called *Sin* after the name of the Mesopotamian lunar deity, a sub-set of the larger series *Enuma Anu Enlil*, though again there are no specific correspondences between the few protasis-apodosis sets preserved in the Ugaritic text and sets attested in the Mesopotamian, Anatolian, or Syrian traditions. Again, the text is badly damaged and its principal contribution is to provide proof of the existence of the sub-genre in Ugaritic. The basic format is here identical to that of the preceding texts in this section but, instead of the omen consisting of a monstrous birth, it is an aspect of the moon that is ominous. Again, however, there is a difference at the level of expression: here the primarily hypothetical particle *hm*, "if," introduces all extant omens. The text is too poorly preserved to allow much to be said about its structure. There is here one repeated phenomenon, viz., the redness of the moon (lines 2–3, 6–7), but as that feature may have been linked with a different second feature, we cannot say whether there were in this text repeated identical omens. It seems fairly clear that the text is not organized as a simple sequence from lunar events that may occur at the time of the new moon to the dark of the moon, for the word *ḥdṯ*, "new," appears on the reverse of the text in conjunction with *yrḫ*, "month." On the other hand, the text does begin with the mention of the new moon and end with that of the thirtieth day, the last possible before the appearance of the new moon, so the text is at least partially organized sequentially and we seem again, therefore, to have before us a text organized according to a set of logical possibilities rather than a random collection.

Text

Obverse

---

(1) ⌜*h*⌝*m* . *b ḥd*[*ṯ*] . *y*[-] ⌜. -⌝ [-(-)]⌜—*r*⌝*šn* . *ykn*

---

(2) *hm . yrḫ . b ʿ⌜l⌝[y]⌜h⌝ . w pḥm*
(3) *nʿmn . y⌜kn⌝ [-]h*

---

(4) *[hm .] ⌜yr⌝ḫ . b ʿlyh . ⌜yr⌝q*
(5) *[ ]⌜b⌝hmtn . tḫlq*

---

(6) *[ ]⌜-⌝y⌜h⌝ . w pḥm*
(7) *[ ]⌜-⌝ qbṣt*

....

Reverse

....

(8') *[ ]⌜ḫ⌝l⌜q⌝*

(9') *[ ]⌜-⌝ ḥdṯ . yrḫ . bnšm .*
(10') *[ ]⌜.⌝ w thbẓn*

(11') *[ ]ym . ⌜y⌝h . yrḫ . kslm . mlkm . tbṣrn*

(12') *[hm .] ṯlṯ . ỉd . ynphy . yrḫ . b yrḫ . ảḫrm*
(13') *[--]lt . mẓrn y⌜l⌝k*

(14') *[hm .] ⌜k⌝bkb . yql . b ṯlṯm . ym . mlkn . ⌜---⌝*
[...]

Translation[7]

(1) If at the time of the new moon [ ], there will be [po]verty.
(2) If the moon, when it rises, is red, (3) there will be prosperity [during] that month.
(4) [If] the moon, when it rises, is yellow-green (5) [ ], the cattle will perish.
(6) [If the moon, when it ri]ses, is red, (7) [ ] assembly.

....

(8') [will p]erish.
(9') [If] newness of the moon, the personnel (10') [ ] and will be put down.
(11') [If]YM YH YRḪ KSLM,[8] the kings will keep an eye on each other.

(12') [If] three times a moon is seen in a moon/month[9] and thereafter (13') [ ]LT, there will be rain.
(14') [If] a star falls on the thirtieth day, the king […].

Dream Omens

45. RS 18.041

The state of this tablet precludes a certain interpretation,[10] but at least one possibility is that it refers to omens consisting of items and events seen in dreams.[11] Formally, it differs from the preceding examples of divinatory manuals by beginning with the word *spr*, "document." At least a partial precedent for such a title is, however, provided by the hippiatric texts, which begin with this word and have the protasis-apodosis structure of the omen texts. If such be the case here, the structure of the individual omens would have resembled that of text 42 (RS 24.247^{+}) in that no temporal or hypothetical particle introduces the omen. It would seem, on the other hand, to differ from any of the manuals known to date by the fact of including more than one item from a particular class of animals or objects in a single omen, rather than devoting one omen to each item. This may perhaps be seen again as reflecting a reasoned structure rather than a random collection. A further possible difference is the presence of the word *dbr*, "word," in these texts, possibly indicating the interpretation to follow; no such lexical indicator of the interpretation exists in the other manuals and the phenomenon would be more reminiscent of the Qumranian use of *pšrw*, "its interpretation," than of the Mesopotamian and Ugaritic omen manuals.

Text

Obverse

---

(1) ⸢*s*⸣[*p*]⸢*r*⸣ [.] *ḫlmm* . ⸢*ả*⸣*lp* ⸢.⸣ *šnt* . ⸢*w*⸣ […]
(2) *šntm* . ⸢*ả*⸣*lp* [.] *dkr* . *rg*⸢*m*⸣ […]

---

(3) *ảlp* . *pr* . *bʿl* . ⸢--⸣ . *r*⸢*b*⸣[…]
(4) *w prt* . *tkt* . [ ] ⸢-⸣ […]
(5) *šnt*

---

(6) *s̀s̀w . ʿṯtrt . w s̀s̀w [.] š⸢-⸣[...]*
(7) *w hm . y⸢h⸣pk . s̀s̀w . rgm . [...]*
(8) *d ymǵy . [-] ⸢b⸣nš . ⸢-⸣[...]*

---

(9) *w ḥm⸢r⸣[--]⸢-- ḥ⸣mr ⸢.⸣ ⸢-(-)⸣[...]*
(10) *w mṯn[ ]⸢r⸣ [?] ⸢b-⸣[...]*
(11) *w bn⸢-⸣[ ]d ⸢. ả⸣m⸢-⸣[...]*
(12) *l bnš . ḫ⸢mr⸣[ ]d l [?] n⸢-⸣[...]*
(13) *w d . l mdl . r[ ]⸢-š⸣[...]*

---

(14) *w ṣỉn . ʿz . b⸢-⸣[...]*
(15) *llủ . bn m⸢-⸣[...]*
(16) *ỉmr . ḫ⸢p? --⸣[...]*
(17) *⸢-⸣n . b⸢ʿl⸣[...]*

....

Reverse

(18') *[--]n [.] ả⸢mt-⸣[...]*
(19') *⸢-⸣m[ ]⸢.⸣ rḥ⸢--⸣[...]*

(20') *n⸢ỉt⸣[--]d . b⸢n⸣[...]*
(21') *ỉdk [?] nỉt[...]*
(22') *trg[-] [?] ⸢ʿb⸣dk [?] y[...]*

(23') *mʿbd . ḫrm⸢ṯt⸣ [?] ⸢-⸣[...]*

(24') *w ks̀t . šqy⸢-⸣[ ]⸢-⸣[...]*
(25') *bn . šqym . ⸢q⸣[...]*
(26') *kbdt . b⸢nš⸣[...]*

(27') *šỉnm . n[-]⸢-⸣[--]⸢-⸣[...]*

(28') *b ḥlm . ả⸢ṯ⸣[-----(-)]np⸢-⸣[...]*
(29') *pn ⸢. -⸣[-]⸢-⸣ [?] ⸢y⸣[-]⸢-⸣[-]⸢-⸣[...]*

(30') *⸢bnš⸣m . ảṯt . ⸢k⸣[—(-)]ʿnp . ʿ[...]*
(31') *⸢šʿ⸣rm . ⸢bǵ⸣[----(-)]⸢—⸣ảr . [...]*

(32') *w ⸢b--⸣[ ]⸢--⸣[ ]⸢-š--⸣[...]*

(33') *b m*[...]
(34') ⸢-⸣[...]

Translation[12]

(1) Document of dreams.
A year-old bull and [...] (2) two years; the mature bull: the word (= interpretation?) [...].

---

(3) The bull: the young bull of *Baʿlu* [...] (4) the heifer about to be slaughtered [...]
(5) one year.

---

(6) The horse of *ʿAṯtartu* and the horse of Š[...] (7) and if the horse turns over: the word (= interpretation?) [...] (8) that arrives where the man is [...].

---

(9) And the donkey [ ] donkey [...] (10) and ditto [...] (11) and BN [...] (12) to the member of the personnel, the donkey [...] (13) and that to the harness [...].

---

(14) And the sheep/goats: the goat [...] (15) the kid, offspring of [...] (16) the lamb [...] (17) son(s) of *Baʿlu*? [...].

....

Reverse

....

(18') [...] the servant-girl [...] (19') [...].

(20') The axe [...] (21') then the axe [...] (22') SPE[AK], servant KY[...].

(23') The worker (or: the work) (with) the *ḫrmṯt*-tool [...].

(24') And the cups of ŠQYM/T [...] (25') the sons of the cup-bearers [...] (26') KBDT the personnel [...].

(27') The sandals [...].

(28') In a dream [...] (29') face of [...].

(30') The male personnel, the women [...] (31') barley [...].

(32') And [...] (33') in [...] (34') [...] ...

Notes

1. This genre is, for the present, attested in Ugaritic only in the hippiatric texts, manuals for caring for sick horses (for the most recent treatment, see Cohen 1996).

2. Read {tḥ<t>yt}.

3. The horizontal line between omens is not indicated in the translation. The reader should also note that, although each omen is set off by a horizontal line from the next, an explicit word for "when/if" is not repeated but is supplied in the English translation. Contrast this usage with that of the following text, where all entries but one begin with the word *k*, "when," and with the lunar-omen text (RIH 78/14 [text 44]), where each omen is introduced by *hm*, "if."

4. This translation is based on reading the three horizontal wedges {ảt} as {n} and on restoring the preceding signs as {⸢.⸣ [k t]⸢l⸣}, hence *k tldn*, "when they give birth."

5. This line provides one of the few cases where the apodosis contains a word-play on the omen: the word for "(seed-)grain" is identical to that for "semen" (the meaning of "seed-grain" for *dr*ʿ is determined at least for line 55', where the use of the verb ḤSL shows, in comparison with Deut 28:38, that the "seed" in question is "grain," not "semen"). In Ugaritic, the distinction was not made between "grain" specifically designated for sowing and "grain" intended for use as food: both were simply *ḏr*ʿ, "seed."

6. Without the preceding words, it is impossible to determine whether ḪLQ is stative or in a transitive verbal stem.

7. The horizontal line between omens is not indicated in the translation.

8. It is tempting to take the last two words of this sequence as meaning "the month of Kislem" (Akkadian *kislimu*), but the general rarity of Akkadian words in these texts and the possibility of a Ugaritic etymology prevent me from adopting that interpretation until further data become available.

9. I have been unable to locate a parallel in the Mesopotamian literature that would elucidate whether this omen refers to reappearances of the moon during a span of days that would normally correspond to a single lunation, or to one moon appearing to be superimposed upon another.

10. Not only is the surface of the tablet as preserved in very bad condition, but the right side is broken away and the bottom of the tablet, where as many as fifteen to twenty lines may have existed, was never discovered.

11. The other principal interpretation of this text, based on taking *ḫlmm* in line 1 as "fattened animals" (references in Pardee 2000a: 462 n. 10) accounts neither for the presence of other categories on the reverse of the tablet nor for the phrase *b ḫlm* in line 28', preceded by a paragraph devoted to "sandals" (line 27') and followed by one dealing with "male personnel" (line 30').

12. Cf. Pardee 1997d; 2001: 242–43.

VII

Prayers

THE USE OF SONG IN THE CULT is attested by the appearance of ŠR in various forms, but no specific word for prayer is attested; its use is only rarely indicated by use of other formulae (e.g., DBR, "to speak," or the king lifting his hands to the heaven according to text 15 [RS 1.003:55]); and actual prayers are extremely rare. The clearest example is that of the brief prayer to *Baʿlu* that was appended to RS 24.266 (presented here as texts 13 and 46) without an explicit link to that sacrificial text, while text 47 (RS 24.271) may provide an example of a prayer for well-being addressed to a much larger group of deities.

A Prayer Appended to a Sacrificial Ritual
46. RS 24.266:26'–36'

For the context supplied by the sacrificial text, see text 13 above. Here I indicate the poetic lineation in the Ugaritic text as well as the restorations reflected in the translation. This is one of the rare examples of a text formally addressed to humans that is in poetry, apparently because the long embedded text, the prayer itself, is addressed to a divinity.

Text	***Translation***
(26') *k gr ʿz . ṯǵ⌜r⌝km .* ⌜*q*⌝*rd* (27') *ḥmytkm .*	When a strong foe attacks your gate, A warrior your walls,
ʿ⌜n⌝km . l ⌜b⌝ʿl tšủn	You shall lift your eyes to *Baʿlu* and say:

(28') *y b⌜ʿl⌝m ⌜. hm . t⌝dy*	"O *Baʿlu*, if you drive the strong one
ʿz l ⌜ṯ⌝ǵrn(29')*y .*	from our gate,
qrd [*l*] *ḥmytny .*	The warrior from our walls,
ỉbr y (30') *bʿl . n⌜š⌝qdš .*	A bull, O *Baʿlu*, we shall sanctify,
mḏr bʿl (31') *nmlủ*	A vow, O *Baʿlu*, we shall fulfill;
[*. b*]*kr b⌜ʿ⌝l . nš*[*q*]*dš*	A firstborn, O *Baʿlu*, we shall sanctify,
(32') *ḥtp bʿ⌜l⌝* [.] *⌜n⌝mlủ .*	A *ḥtp*-offering, O *Baʿlu*, we shall fulfill,
ʿ⌜šr⌝t . ⌜bʿl⌝ [.] *⌜n⌝*[*ʿ*](33')*šr .*	A feast, O *Baʿlu*, we shall offer;
qdš bʿ⌜l .⌝ nʿl .	To the sanctuary, O *Baʿlu*, we shall ascend,
ntbt b[...] (34') *ntlk .*	That path, O *Baʿlu*, we shall take."
w š[*mʿ . b*]*ʿ⌜l .⌝ l ⌜. ṣ⌝l⌜tk⌝*[*m*]	And *Ba*[*ʿlu* will h]ear [your] prayer:
(35') *⌜y⌝dy . ʿz l ṯǵrk*[*m .*	He will drive the strong foe from you[r] gate,
qrd] (36') *l ḥmytk⌜m⌝* [...]	[The warrior] (36') from yo[ur] walls.

A Prayer for Well-Being

47. RS 24.271

The identification of this text as a prayer cannot, because of the lacunae at the beginning and the end, be judged certain. The interpretation of *šlm* (in lines 1–3 and 28'–33') that presents the fewest difficulties is, however, as a series of imperatives addressed to the gods named; by implication all the gods named in the intervening lines would be objects of the same request for blessing. This structure, if correctly perceived, is therefore superimposed on a deity list, though a very peculiar one: (1) virtually all of the deities, where determinable, are listed as pairs, whether or not they are identifiable as "double deities" (e.g., *Kôṯāru-wa-Ḫasīsu*); (2) the only parallel for this list is very partial, viz., all but two of the male divinities of the anti-serpent text RS 24.244 (translated below as text 53) are present here.[1] Because this latter text clearly incorporates an important geographical component (the messenger is directed to travel to the principal seat of each of the gods named), it is perhaps plausible to see in this list a more comprehensive overview of the gods worshiped at Ugarit who were considered to be sons of *ʾIlu*, whatever their geographical spread (the geographical details are not indicated here). The listing by twos even finds a parallel in the second of the serpent-incantation texts (text 54 [RS

24.251]), for there the gods who were named singly in text 53 are grouped by pairs in various more or less artificial fashions.

Text	***Translation***
Obverse	
(1) [*šlm*] *ảb . w ỉl*⸢*m*⸣[…]	Give well-being, O Father and the gods,
(2) [*w*$^{?}$] ⸢*š*⸣*lm . šlm ỉ*[*l* …]	[yea] give well-being, give well-being, O ʾ*I*[*lu* and ?],[2]
(3) ⸢*š*⸣*lm . ỉl šr .*	give well-being, O princely ʾ*Ilu*,
(4) *dgn . ẉ bʿl .*	*Dagan* and *Baʿlu*,[3]
(5) *ṯ*$^{?}$*ẓ w kmṯ*	*Ẓiẓẓu*[4] and *Kamāṯu*,
(6) *yrḫ w ksả*	*Yariḫu* and *Kasʾa*,
(7) *yrḫm* ⸢.⸣ *kṯy*	also the Kassite *Yariḫu*,[5]
(8) *ṯkmn w šnm*	*Ṯukamuna* and *Šunama*,
(9) *kṯr w ḫss*	*Kôṯaru* and *Ḫasīsu*,
(10) *ʿṯtr ʿṯtpr*	*ʿAṯtaru* (and) *ʿAṯtapar*,
(11) *šḫr w šlm*	*Šaḫru* and *Šalimu*,
(12) *ngh w srr*	NGH and SRR,[6]
(13) *ʿd w šr*	ʿD and ŠR,
(14) *ṣdq mšr*	*Ṣidqu*, *Mêšaru*,
(15) *ḥnbn ỉl dn*[…]	ḤNBN ʾIL DN[…],
(16) ⸢*k*⸣*bd w* ⸢*n*⸣*r*[…]	KBD and NR[…],
…………………………………	

Reverse

....

(17') [ ]⌜--⌝[...]	
(18') [--]⌜-*p*⌝ *ỉl*[...]	
(19') [-]*lmtmrd*[...]	
(20') *qdš mlk ỉ*[...]	QDŠ, king of/*Milku* (of) [...],[7]
(21') *kbd d ỉl* g⌜-⌝[...]	KBD of/who god [...],
(22') *mrmnmn*	MRMNMN,
(23') *brrn ảryn*[...]	BRRN ʾARYN[...],
(24') *ảṭḫn tlyn*[...]	ʾAṬḪN TLYN[...],
(25') *ảtdb w ṯ?r*	ʾATDB and Ṯ?R,[8]
(26') *qdš w ảmrr*[...]	*Qudšu* and ʾ*Amrur* [...],
(27') *ṯḫr w bd*	ṮḪR and BD.
(28') ⌜*k*⌝*ṯr ḫss šl*⌜*m*⌝[...]	O *Kôṯaru*, O *Ḫasīsu*, give well-be[ing ...],
(29') *šlm ỉl bt*	give well-being, O ʾ*Ilu-Bêti*,
(30') *šlm ỉl ḫš*⌜-⌝[...]	give well-being, O god of Solicitu[de ...],
(31') *ršp ỉnš* ⌜*ỉ*⌝[*lm* ...]	*Rašap*, ʾ*Ināšu*-ʾ*Ilīma*,[9]
(32') ⌜*dr*⌝*m ỉl*⌜*m*⌝[...]	generations (of gods), god[s ...]

Upper Edge

(33') [*w ỉ*]⌜*l*⌝*m šlm*[...]	[yea O go]ds, give well-being[...].

Notes

1. *Baʿlu, Dagan, Yariḫu, Rašap, Ẓiẓẓu-wa-Kamāṯu, Kôṯaru-wa-Ḫasīsu,* and

Šaḫru-wa-Šalimu. Not present in this text, at least in its present state, are *Milku* and *Ḥôrānu* (*Milku* may be in line 20', but that interpretation is not obvious).

2. Restore perhaps "gods" (or "goddesses") on the pattern of line 1.

3. Here, as in the two long deity lists for which corresponding sacrificial rites exist (texts 1 and 3 above), *Dagan* is placed before *Baʿlu*. In the serpent-incantation texts, on the other hand, *Baʿlu* precedes *Dagan*, either sequentially in the narrative (text 53 [RS 24.244]) or in a paired mention of the two deities (text 54 [RS 24.251]) such as here. In none of the deity lists preserved as such is the order *Baʿlu-Dagan* attested, though there are texts where *Baʿlu* appears but not *Dagan* (texts 4 and 5 above) and there are sacrificial sequences where *Baʿlu* appears before *Dagan* (see above on text 6A [RS 1.009]).

4. A rough circle is inscribed around the first sign of this name, probably indicating that the {ṯ} is incorrect, for elsewhere the name is written {ẓẓ}.

5. This is the only entry in lines 4–14, and perhaps beyond (the damaged text and uncertainty of interpretation in many subsequent cases oblige us to leave the question of singularity or duality open in all uncertain cases), in which a single deity is named: the second element here is an adjective rather than a divine name. The *-m* on *yrḫm* is "enclitic," expressing a connection with the preceding line.

6. From here on, the "translation" of many of the divine names is indicated only in capital letters. In these cases, either the interpretation is unclear, or the reading is uncertain owing to damage to the tablet, or both factors together leave the name obscure. In the case of this entry, the first element is in all likelihood related to the Semitic root NGH, with consonantal /h/, denoting brightness; the possible origin of the second element is, however, less clear, and the pair is otherwise unattested.

7. The standard pairing of *qdš* with *ảmrr* (this double-deity functions as *ʾAṯiratu*'s messenger in the mythological texts) appears below in line 26', and it is thus unclear whether *mlk* here is a title of this divinity or part of a binomial of which the second element would itself be a compound name (*Milku* + another element).

8. Like the {ṯ} of line 5, this {ṯ} also has inscribed around it a rough circle. Because, however, this binomial is otherwise unknown, it is unclear whether the circle here denotes a mistake, as appeared to be the case in line 5, and, if a mistake is indicated, what the correct reading was.

9. Though *Rašap* is the god of the underworld and the *ʾInāšu-ʾIlīma* plausibly one of the principal components of the underworld population, the two are not associated as often as one might expect: both entities appear rather often in the ritual texts, but they are placed in immediate proximity only three other times and each time a particular manifestation of *Rašap* is named (in text 11 [RS 24.249:25'–26'] it is *Rašap-Bibitta;* in text 14 and again in text 11 [RS 24.250:1–2 and RS 24.294:9'–10'] it is *Rašap-Ḥagab*).

The Texts

Part Two: Ritual Activity Outside the Sacrificial Cult

VIII

Incantations

THE INCANTATORY GENRE is poorly represented in Ugaritic, and its forms are only beginning to be understood. In part, this may be owing to accidents of preservation, for other texts contain incantatory elements, e.g., text 53 (RS 24.244), translated below as one of the historiolae; the function of other badly damaged texts may also have been incantatory (cf. RS 15.134, particularly the treatment in del Olmo Lete 1999a: 373–78). The three examples provided here show that the incantation in the narrow sense of the word, while it may contain references to divine entities, does not consist formally of a mythological text with incantatory elements. Rather, it contains formulae that were believed to hold their own effective power, and it may refer to ritual acts that would have accompanied the pronouncement of the formulae. These three clear examples are all couched in poetry, as is the case with all ritual texts other than those dealing with the sacrificial rites.

Some of the more important of the contributions of these texts to our understanding of the genre are the following:

1. Text 48 (RS 92.2014) illustrates explicitly the association of acts and words.

2. They attest to the principal terms designating the actors: the protective incantation was directed against the verbal attackers, known as the *dbbm*, the "talkers." Text 49 (RS 22.225) adds the "evil eye" as an offensive entity, and five categories of persons are named who may attack by the evil eye: the agent of attack was the sorcerer, the *kšp; ǵlm dᶜtm*,

"familiars," and *ḫbrm*, "companions," could be associated with the sorcerer; at least one agent in acting and speaking on behalf of the attacked party was a type of priest, the *ṯʿy;* and the beneficiary of the incantation could be a private individual, *ʾUrtēnu* in RS 92.2014, the owner of the house in which the tablet was found.

3. The use of *dbbm* to designate one of the principal enemies shows that the offensive instruments could be words, which caused venomous reptiles to attack and which could bring on illness (a description of negatively effective acts is not yet attested, though such certainly were performed); in text 49, the "evil eye" acts as an independent offensive entity.

4. The poetic form of these texts leaves no doubt that the genre conforms to the name given to it in modern parlance, which derives, of course, from classical usage ("incantation" is defined as "the chanting of a magic formula").

5. In text 49 (RIH 78/20), *Ḥôrānu*, long known as a powerful force against magic attack, is invoked as a divine agent in defending against the sorcerers; the goddess *ʾAṯiratu* is also named near the end of the preserved portion of that text, but the state of the text prevents us from knowing precisely what her role was.

An Incantation against Snakes and Scorpions

48. RS 92.2014

This is the first fully preserved incantation in the Ugaritic language, and its contributions to our understanding of the genre in its West-Semitic form near the end of the Late Bronze Age are thus enormous, in spite of its brevity.[1] The first part of the text is phrased explicitly in terms of warding off serpents and scorpions,[2] the second in terms of rendering harmless the verbal attacks of the enemy (*ršʿ // bn nšm*) and the sorcerers (*dbbm kšpm . . . kšpm dbbm*) who instigate the venomous creatures to attack. The text is formulated as a dialogue between the practitioner of white magic ("I"), who will turn back the evil attacks, and his client ("you"), the object of the attacks ; all the evil entities are referred to in the third person. The incantation itself is general, potentially valid for anyone who seeks the services of this practitioner. According to the last two lines, on the other hand, this particular writing down of the incantation was intended for Urtenu.

Text	***Translation***
(1) *dy . l . ydʿ . yṣḥk . ủzb*	When the unknown one calls you and begins foaming,
(2) *w . ảnk . ảṣḥk .*	I, for my part, will call you.
ảmrmrn (3) *ʿṣ . qdš .*	I will shake pieces of sacred wood,
w . ʿlk . l . (4) *tʿl . bṯn .*	So that the serpent not come up against you,
w . tḥtk (5) *l . tqnn . ʿqrb*	So that the scorpion not stand up under you.
(6) *ʿly . l . tʿl . bṯn . ʿlk*	The serpent will indeed not come up against you,
(7) *qn . l . tqnn . ʿqrb* (8) *tḥtk .*	The scorpion will indeed not stand up under you!
km . l . tủdn (9) *dbbm . kšpm .*	So may the tormenters, the sorcerers not give ear
hwt (10) *ršʿ .*	To the word of the evil man,
hwt . bn nšm	To the word of any man (lit. "son of the people"):
(11) *ghrt . phm . w . šptḥm*	When it sounds forth in their mouth, on their lips,
(12) *yšp⌜k⌝ . kmm . ảrṣ* (13) *kšpm . dbbm*	May the sorcerers, the tormenters, then pour it to the earth.
(14) *l . ủrtn . l . gbh* (15) *l . tmnth .*	For *ʾUrtēnu*, for his body, for his members.[3]

An Incantation against Male Sexual Dysfunction

49. RIH 78/20

Discovered in 1978 and published soon thereafter (Bordreuil and Caquot 1980: 346–50), this text has engendered a great deal of discussion. The similarities of vocabulary between this and the preceding text are sufficient to permit the classification as incantatory rather than mythological. On the other hand, the differences between the two texts show that the genre was not frozen into a set form: this text contains both more poetic imagery connected with the act of expulsion itself and material of a quasi-moral nature (lines 5–8) explaining how a man can open himself up to attack.

Text	***Translation***
(1) *ydy . dbbm . d ǵzr ..*	This recitation casts out the tormenters of a young man:
tg ḫṭk . r[--(-)]	The pain of your rod it has banished,[4]
(2) *bʿl . tg ḫṭk .*	The producers of the pain of your rod.
w tṣủ . l pn . ql . ṯʿy	It goes forth at the voice of the *ṯāʿiyu*-priest,
(3) *k qṭr . ủr⟨.⟩btm .*	Like smoke from a window,
k bṯn . ʿmdm	Like a serpent from a pillar,
(4) *k yʿlm . ẓrh .*	Like mountain-goats to a summit,
k lbỉm . skh	Like lions to the lair.
(5) *ḫṭ . nqh .*	The rod has recovered,
ủ qrb . ḫṭ .	Yea the rod has approached.[5]
tḫṭả . l gbk	Should you sin against your body,[6]
(6) *w tršʿ . l tmntk .*	Should you commit evil against your body,
tlḥm . lḥm (7) *ẓm .*	You must eat moldy bread,
tšt . b ḫlṣ . bl . ṣml .	Drink fig-juice in oppression,
b mrmt (8) *b mỉyt .*	On the heights, in the well-watered valleys,
b ẓlm . b qdš .	In the shadows, even at the sanctuary.
ảphm (9) *kšpm . dbbm .*	Then, as for the sorcerers, the tormenters,
ygrš . ḥrn	*Ḥôrānu* will drive them out,
(10) *ḥbrm . w ǵlm . dʿtm . lk*	Even the companions and the "lads of knowledge" he will drive out for you.
(11) *l ẓtm . ảl . tmk .*	With respect to heat, do not sag,
ảl . tʿlg (12) *lšnk .*	May your tongue not stutter,
ảl . tảpq . ảpq .	May your canal not be decanalized.[7]
lbš (13) *ỉl . yštk .*	The god can clothe you,
ʿrm . ỉl . yštk	The god can make you naked.

(14) *l ảdm . wd*[8] *. ḫṭm .*	For the man, descend from the rod
l ảrṣ . zrm	To the earth, O flow;
(15) *l bn . ảdm . b ảnšt . npẓl*	For the son of man, from illness he is delivered.
(16) ⸢*h*⸣*n . b npš . ảṯrt . rbt .*	Behold, in the throat of Lady ʾ*Aṯiratu*
bl (17) [---]*rk . l ṯtm .*	Do X with juice to regale her.
ỉtbnnk (18) [-----]	I will recognize you [...]
⸢*b*⸣*t . ủbủ . ảl . tbỉ*	The house I enter you must not enter[9]
(19) [...]⸢-⸣ *. ảl tṯbb . rỉš*	[...] Do not turn your head
(20) [...]*r*ʿ*tm . k*⸢-⸣[-]	
(21) [...]⸢*m*⸣ *. kn* ⸢. -⸣[...]	
(22) [...]⸢-⸣*r*[...]	

The Attack of the Evil Eye and a Counterattack

50. RS 22.225

The general meaning of this text as having to do with the "evil eye" has only become apparent in recent years (del Olmo Lete 1992a: 255; 1992b; 1999a: 379–84; Ford 1998; Wyatt 1998: 375–77). The reading of the first word as {ʿnn}, rather than the editor's {ʿnt}, that is, the goddess ʿ*Anatu* (Virolleaud 1960: 182), was first proposed in Dietrich, Loretz, and Sanmartín 1976: 105, but they followed the interpretation of the editor to the extent of suggesting that {ʿnn} should be a scribal error for {ʿnt} (this emendation constitutes the basis of the recent interpretation of the text by Dietrich and Loretz [1997], convincingly refuted by Ford [1998: 253–56], reaffirmed in Dietrich and Loretz 2000: 234, 239).[10] Del Olmo Lete (1992a) was the first to take the reading {ʿnn} seriously and to propose an overall interpretation of the text based on it. Since this ground-breaking study, the reading {ʿnn} has been confirmed and illustrated both by photographs and a hand copy (Lewis 1996). Each of the treatments cited above has added to our understanding of the text.[11] The most convincing new proposal in Ford's analysis is to take the forms {tp-} as from the root PHY, "to see."[12] Another key element of the interpretation is to see in the "brother" (line 2) not the brother of the eye itself (which, being feminine, should have a sister, rather than a brother) but the "brother" of the manipulator of the evil eye, that is, the person whom the eye attacks.[13]

Though the meaning of the text is becoming ever better understood, a remaining enigma is the fact that it is perhaps a simple scribal exercise, for the other side of the tablet bears a syllabic lexical text (Bordreuil and Pardee 1989: 284; van Soldt 1995: 183–84, 195). This factor is in addition to the absence of the end of the tablet, which makes it impossible to know whether this incantation, scribal exercise or not, bore a colophon. It lacks, therefore, the precise life setting of text 48 (RS 92.2014) and even the less precise setting of text 49 (RIH 78/20) of which the end has disappeared and with it any possible colophon such as that of text 48 but which was provided with a title.

Text	***Translation***
(1) *ʿnn . hlkt . w šnwt*	The Eye[14] goes, yea it runs;[15]
(2) *tp . ảḫh . k nʿm .* *ảḫh* (3) *k ysmsm .*	It has seen its brother, that he is good.[16] Its brother, that he is lovely;
tspỉ . šỉrh (4) *l bl . ḫrb .*	It has begun to devour his flesh without a knife.
tšt . dmh (5) *l bl . ks .*	To drink his blood without a cup;[17]
tpnn . ʿn (6) *bṯy .*	It is the eye of a BṮY-man[18] that has seen him (i.e., the brother),
ʿn bṯt . tpnn	The eye of a BṮY-woman that has seen him,
(7) *ʿn . mḫr .* *ʿn . pḫr* (8) *ʿn . ṯǵr .*	The eye of a price-setter,[19] The eye of an assembler, The eye of a gate-keeper.
ʿn ṯǵr (9) *l ṯǵr . tṯb .*	The eye of the gate-keeper, to the gate-keeper let it return!
ʿn . pḫr (10) *l pḫr . tṯb .*	The eye of the assembler, to the assembler let it return!
ʿn . mḫr (11) *l mḫr . tṯb .*	The eye of the price-setter, to the price-setter let it return!
ʿn . bṯy (12) *l bṯy . tṯb .*	The eye of the BṮY-man, to the BṮY-man let it return!
ʿ⌜n .⌝ [*bṯt*] (13) *l bṯt .* ⌜*t*⌝[*ṯb*]	The eye of the BṮY-woman, to the BṮY-woman let it return!
[...]	

Notes

1. I have previously provided an English translation of this text in Pardee 1997f and a fuller version in 2000a: 829–33. The official *editio princeps* will appear in Bordreuil and Pardee forthcoming a. For lexical notes on the translation that follows, see the publications just cited.

2. By 1200 B.C.E., it was already an old tradition to formulate incantations against snakes and scorpions: for the examples from Ebla, a millennium and more older, see Catagnoti and Bonechi 1998, esp. pp. 18–23, 32–34.

3. The terms *gb* and *tmnt* occur also in the next text.

4. Restoring {r[ḥq]}, taken as a D-stem, "it has put far away." The word *ḫṭ*, "staff, rod," is here taken as a metaphor for the male member, and the text as a whole as an incantation against male sexual dysfunction caused by sorcery.

5. "Approached, come near" apparently expresses here the resumption of normal sexual activity.

6. This and the following two bicola seem to introduce the notion of sin as a factor that weakens the body, making it more susceptible to attack by sorcery; hence the person so attacked must do penance in order for *Ḥôrānu* to intervene. The inclusion of the "sanctuary" in the list of places the sick man must visit shows that the formulae do not express punishment, but acts of contrition and of seeking after healing.

7. This tricolon is taken as containing three metaphors for male sexual function: heat, the flow of words used as a metaphor for the flow of semen, and the seminal canal being unblocked.

8. Read {r!d}.

9. As is shown by the identical formula in Arslan Tash I 5–6 (Donner and Röllig 1966, 1968, 1969: text 27; cf. Pardee 1998c), these words are addressed to a malefic entity.

10. It will be clear from my transcription below that I agree with Ford that the text may best be understood as it stands, without emendation. For the case of {knʿm} (line 2), which Dietrich and Loretz read as {w nʿm} but emend to {k nʿm}, see Ford 1998: 202, 255.

11. I collated the tablet in 1981, and this collation confirmed the reading of {ʿnn}; but I published neither my collation nor a philological study of the text. Influenced, however, by the common acceptance of the text as containing at least mythological allusions, I did not include it in Pardee 2000a. This tradition was followed also, though hesitantly, by Smith (*apud* Parker et al. 1997: 224–28) and, without hesitation, by Dietrich and Loretz (2000: 225–56). I should add that there is no epigraphic basis for the assertion that the scribe changed the third sign from an original {t} to {ʿ} (Pope *apud* Smith 1998: 651–52): the argument adduced—viz., that the word divider touches the tip of the {n}—cannot be taken as proof that the sign was rewritten, for word dividers are often placed on the tip

of a preceding horizontal wedge—indeed the phenomenon recurs several times in this text, as a glance at any of the published photographs will show. Nor can it be proven that this word divider "is partially overridden by the last wedge of the final *n*" (ibid.). I saw nothing to confirm this when I collated the tablet, and I can see nothing to corroborate it on my photograph or on those that have been published: the overlap of the two wedges has not produced crinkling on one or the other of the edges that would indicate which wedge was placed first.

12. Previous commentators took *tp* as a *t*-preformative noun from the root YPY meaning "beauty." Dietrich and Loretz have recently proposed to emend to {tp<nn>} on the basis of the presence of {tpnn} in line 5; the form is interpreted as "wandte sich . . . zu" from the root PNY (2000: 234, 241–42). According to Ford's identification, the G-stem prefix conjugation lost the /h/, perhaps by assimilation to the preceding root consonant (Ford 1998: 229), something like /tiphay/ → /tippay-/ → /tippa/. Similar simplifications have occurred in the root ṮWY (attested in the letters RS 17.117:6–7 [Caquot 1978] and RS 18.031:24 [Virolleaud 1965: text 59] and elsewhere). This analysis speaks directly in favor of the identification of the root meaning "to see" (one for which there are no clear etymological parallels in the other Semitic languages) as III-Y rather than *mediae infirmae*, for only if the /h/ was in immediate contiguity with the /p/ will it have assimilated to it (cf. Coote 1974).

13. Wyatt explicitly took the "brother" to be "the other eye of the pair" (1998: 375–76); for Ford, the expression reflects the personification of the evil eye (1998: 230: ". . . the evil eye has been conceptualized as a separate . . . entity on equal footing with the victim"). In the second of the Arslan Tash inscriptions, the only other incantation against the evil eye of the pre-Christian periods that is in a West-Semitic language, the presentation passes explicitly, at the very end of the incantation, from the single big round eye borne by the demon depicted on the reverse of the plaque to the two eyes that the sorcerer must in fact possess (for the new reading of the key term *ʿnm*, "two eyes," see Pardee 1998c). This bit of human *realia* is not, on the other hand, expressed in the Ugaritic text, where the "brother" is the victim of the demon/sorcerer whom the evil eye has chosen as its prey rather than the second of the sorcerer's two eyes.

14. {ʿnn} probably consists of the singular noun to which an enclitic *-n* has been attached (/ʿênuna/) rather than being a derived form of the noun (/ʿênānu/), for the grammatical gender of nouns with the *-ān* ending is usually not feminine (the accompanying verb forms, *hlkt* and *šnwt*, show that *ʿnn* is of feminine gender).

15. The verbal forms in lines 2, 3, and 4 (*tp* . . . *tspiʾ* . . . *tšt*) are marked *yaqtulø* forms (i.e., marked for either perfectivity or jussivity), whereas *hlkt* and *šnwt* may be either suffix-conjugation forms (*halakat* . . . *šanawat*), perhaps D-stem expressing iterativity (*hallakat* . . . *šannawat*) or G-stem participles (*hālikatu* . . . *šāniwatu*). There are reasons to believe that the participle played an important role in some poetic texts (for the case of the "para-mythological" texts, see Pardee

1988a: 26–27, 205–6). Because the structure of the text shows that the forms in lines 2–6 cannot be jussives (i.e., the meaning of these forms cannot be "let it see his brother," etc.), the analysis of *hlkt . . . šnwt* as participles leads to a translation of these *yaqtulø* forms as English present perfects rather than preterites (the option chosen by Ford 1998: 202). The acts of lines 2–8 are thus expressed perfectively (with, perhaps, the added notion of inchoativity in lines 3–4, as tentatively translated below), whereas the combination of participial and perfective forms may lend immediacy to the presentation of the demon in lines 1–8. As this text is clearly poetic in form, there is in any case no reason to doubt the analysis of the *yaqtulø* forms as perfectives/preterites (cf. Ford 1998: 256 n. 182).

16. Linguistically speaking, the conjunction *kī* introduces a nominal object clause of the verb of perception; it has no particularly emphatic function (contra Ford 1998: 202, 221–22, and other scholars cited by Ford as regards the corresponding construction in Biblical Hebrew, e.g., in the type passage Gen 1:4: *wayyarʾ ʾᵉlōhīʸm ʾet-hāʾōʷr kīʸ-ṭōʷb*, "God saw the light, that it was good").

17. The theme of this bicolon is certainly "the violent, voracious, and inhuman manner, much like that of a beast of prey, in which the demon . . . feeds on its victim" (Ford 1998: 234), not that of the absence of bloodshed (del Olmo Lete 1992a: 257). This is confirmed by Arslan Tash II, where the ogre bearing the evil eye is depicted in the process of devouring its victim whole, that is, without the aid of knife or cup (see the new copy of the representation and references to previous studies in Pardee 1998c).

18. This key term is unattested elsewhere in Ugaritic and has found no certain etymological explanation: del Olmo Lete's comparison with a Sumerian formula for "evil person" (1992b: 11–12) is generally cited, while his comparison with Akkadian *bīšu* has correctly been described as "problematic" (Ford 1998: 243 n. 138). The comparison of the masculine and feminine forms indicates that the {y} of the masculine form is more likely a root letter than the gentilic ending, for the gentilic /y/ may have been retained in the feminine gentilic, which was historically /-iyyatu/. Whereas only masculine forms are given for the following three categories, the use of masculine and feminine forms here may favor the interpretation as a general term denoting evil persons, probably the enemy who has invoked the evil eye against the beneficiary of the incantation and thus the functional equivalent of *ršʿ // bn nšm* in text 48 (RS 92.2014:10). If so, perhaps this is a by-form of the hollow root BṮ, "to be ashamed, shameful," perhaps with a more active meaning than the well-known Hebrew root BWŠ. Ford points out the explicit reversal expressed in the last line by the two words *bṯt* and *ṯṯb*. Whatever the precise meaning of the terms *bty . . . ṯǵr*, Ford's general interpretation (1998: 237–43) according to which they designate "possessors" rather than victims of the evil eye, is surely to be preferred.

19. The three new nouns in this and the following verse have been given mundane interpretations (tax-collector/merchant, potter, gate-keeper). Because, however, the first two are unattested in the Ugaritic administrative texts, where the

mention of categories of personnel occurs relatively frequently, I wonder if they do not belong to the world of magic. Along those lines, I propose translations for the first two more in keeping with their known Ugaritic cognates (*mḫr* elsewhere means "price"; *pḫr,* "assembly"). The price-setter would be the one who sets the price of divination; the assembler the one who gathers the materials; and the gate-keeper the one who keeps them under lock and key and is responsible for releasing them. This interpretation corresponds well to the order of presentation in the text, where the gate-keeper is the last mentioned in the section devoted to the propagators of the evil eye, the first in the incantational recall of this eye—the releaser and the one who locks back up are one and the same. For the structure of this section, see Ford 1998: 248–51, with references to preceding studies.

IX

Historiolae

SEVERAL SUB-GENRES OF RELIGIOUS TEXTS are attested in which mythological elements are mixed with more practical elements or in which mythological elements are juxtaposed for purposes apparently different from the creation of the mythological texts themselves. A text that links myth with magic has been named a historiola (Frankfurter 1995), and the four texts translated in this section reveal reasonably clearly such a form and motivation.[1]

The six texts in this and the following section were all discovered along with many texts reflecting the sacrificial cult in the "Maison du Prêtre aux Modèles de Poumon et de Foies" (The House of the Priest with Lung and Liver Models) during the 1961 campaign (see Courtois *apud* Pardee 1988a: 4–12). Placing these texts in juxtaposition with the sacrificial texts brings out the riches of this collection of tablets for our understanding of Ugaritic religion.

***ʾIlu*'s *Marziḥu* and a Recipe for Hangover**

51. RS 24.258

Though a significant portion of the middle of this first text has disappeared, the beginning and the end are preserved, and it provides the clearest example of a mythological text followed by a practical application: in the myth, *ʾIlu* falls dead drunk and requires a restorative while the practical section contains a recipe for cure from alcoholic prostration. This text also provides the clearest indication of the relationship between the *marziḥu* and the sacrificial cult: in the first part of the text, *ʾIlu* slaughters animals (the verb is DBḤ, translated "to sacrifice" in the cultic texts above) for the divine banquet, while in the second (lines 14–16), he convenes the *marziḥu,* where the sole activity is drinking. Then he proceeds to his house. I have attempted (1988a: 57–59) to localize the three activities by comparing this text with the Temple of Baʿalshamin at Palmyra, where inscriptions designate a *marziḥu*-room next to the principal sanctuary and at a distance from the sacrificial altar. By extrapolation from this text and from the ideal form of a sanctuary painted in the Hebrew Bible, we may surmise that *ʾIlu* "sacrificed" in an open courtyard in front of his private apartments, that the banquet took place either there or in an adjacent hall, that he then convened the *marziḥu* in a special room,[2] and that the "house" to which he returned according to lines 17–22 would have been his private living quarters, corresponding to the "the holy of holies" of a sanctuary.[3]

Text	***Translation***
Obverse	
(1) *ỉl dbḥ . b bth . mṣd*	*ʾIlu* slaughters ("sacrifices")[4] game in his house,
ṣd . b qrb (2) *hklh .*	Prey within his palace,
ṣḥ . l qṣ . ỉlm .	He invites the gods to partake.
tlḥmn (3) *ỉlm . w tštn .*	The gods eat and drink,
tštn y<n> ʿd šbʿ	They drink wi<ne> to satiety,
(4) *trṯ . ʿd ⸢škr⸣ .*	New wine to drunkenness.
yʿdb . yrḫ (5) *gbh .*	*Yariḫu* prepares his goblet,[5]
km . ⸢k⸣[l]⸢b⸣ . yqṯqṯ .	Like a dog he drags it
tḥt (6) *ṯlḥnt*	Under the tables.
ỉl . d ydʿnn	Any god who knows him
(7) *yʿdb . lḥm . lh*	Prepares him a portion of food;
w d l ydʿnn	But one who does not know him
(8) *ylmn . ḫtm .*	Strikes him with a stick
tḥt . ṯlḥn	Under the table.
(9) *ʿṯtrt . w ʿnt . ymǵy*	He goes up to *ʿAṯtartu* and *ʿAnatu;*[6]
(10) *ʿṯtrt . tʿdb . nšb lh*	*ʿAṯtartu* prepares him a *nšb*-cut of meat,
(11) *w ʿnt . ktp .*	*ʿAnatu* a shoulder-cut.

bhm . ygʿr . ṯġr (12) *bt . ỉl .*	The doorman of ʾ*Ilu*'s house yells at them,
pn . lm . rlb[7] *. tʿdbn* (13) *nšb .*	That they should not prepare a *nšb*-cut for a dog!,
l ỉnr . tʿdbn . ktp	Not prepare a shoulder-cut for a hound.
(14) *b ỉl . ảbh . gʿr .*	He also yells at ʾ*Ilu*, his father;[8]
yṯb . ỉl . k⸢r⸣ (15) *ả⸢šk⸣[rh]*	ʾ*Ilu* takes a seat and calls together[9] his drinking [group],
ỉl . yṯb . b mrzḥh	ʾ*Ilu* takes his seat in his drinking club.
(16) *yš⸢t⸣ . [y]⸢n⸣ . ʿd šbʿ .*	He drinks wine to satiety,
trṯ . ʿd škr	New wine to drunkenness.
(17) *ỉl . h⸢l⸣k . l bth .*	ʾ*Ilu* heads off to his house,
yštql . (18) *l ḥẓrh .*	Arrives at his courts.
yʿmsn . nn .	*Ṯukamuna-wa-Šunama*
ṯkmn (19) *w šnm .*	Bear him along.
w ngšnn . ḥby .	ḤBY meets him,[10]
(20) *bʿl . qrnm . w ḏnb .*	He who has two horns and a tail,
ylšn (21) *b ḫrỉh . w ṯnth .*	Knocks him over in his feces and his urine.
ql . ỉl . km mt	ʾ*Ilu* falls as though dead,
(22) *ỉl . k yrdm . ảrṣ .*	ʾ*Ilu* falls like those who descend into the earth.
ʿnt (23) *w ʿṯtrt . tṣdn .*	ʿ*Anatu* and ʿ*Aṯtartu* go off on the hunt,
⸢*š---*⸣[...] (24) *q⸢d⸣š . bʿ⸢-⸣*[...]	[...]QDŠ[...]
....	
(25') [ ]⸢*n*⸣ *. d*[...]	[...]
(26') [*ʿṯ*]⸢*t*⸣*rt . w ʿn*⸢*t*⸣[...]	[...] ʿ*Aṯtartu* and ʿ*Anatu* [...]
(27') ⸢*w*⸣ *bhm . tṯṯb .* ⸢*-m*⸣*dh*[...]	And in them she brings back [...].
(28') *km . trpả . hn nʾr*	When she would heal him, he awakes.

(29') *d yšt . l lṣbh . šʿr klb*	What is to be put on his forehead:[11] hairs of a dog.

(30') ⸢*w*⸣ *riš* . *pqq* . *w šrḫ*	And the head of the PQQ and its shoot[12]
(31') *yšt ảḫdh* . *dm zt* . *ḫr*⸢*p*⸣*ảt*	he is to drink mixed together with fresh olive oil.[13]

Consultation of *Ditānu* with a View to Healing

52. RS 24.272

This brief text, of which the only named actors are divine, contains three main sections: (1) the narrative frame (lines 1–4); (2) the response to the messenger (*tʿny*, line 5); (3) the words the messenger is to carry (lines 5–16), divided into two subsections with a second narrative introduction separating the two (*w yʿnynn dtn*, lines 13–14). The principal problems are: (1) the state of the text (especially lines 5–10, where the reading of several words is hypothetical); (2) the identification of *ảdn ỉlm rbm*, "the father of the many gods," who seeks the consultation; (3) the meaning of some words (e.g., *bnt*, line 8) and phrases (in particular, line 15).

The second of these problems merits discussion here. If the phrase *ỉlm rbm* refers to the royal inhabitants of the netherworld (cf. text 56 [RS 24.257], according to which the deceased kings were divinized), then the "lord" would be one of the important figures of that world, perhaps *Rašap*, *Milku*, or *Yariḫu* (who spends the daylight hours in the netherworld)—certainly not the solar deity, who is feminine in Ugaritic. Because this text is in prose rather than in poetry, it is also possible that *ảdn* here designates the "father," as in letters in the Ugaritic language, rather than a nonspecific "lord." If such be the case, the reference can only—in our present state of knowledge of the Ugaritic texts—be to *ʾIlu*, who in text 22 (RS 1.002) bears the title of *ảb bn ỉl*, "the father of the sons of *ʾIlu*." The reference in RS 15.039:1–2 (Virolleaud 1957: text 90) *bt ỉlm rbm*, "temple of the great gods," may be to the temple of *ʾIlu,* in which others of the "great gods" were also worshiped. According to that scenario, *ʾIlu*'s visit to a lower-ranking god would be an indication not so much of humility on *ʾIlu*'s part as of *Ditānu*'s powers of healing. In either case, the "child" mentioned in line 3, with no form of identification, would be the petitioner's child, and *Ditānu*'s words (lines 5–22) would be addressed to the practitioners of healing spells in the petitioner's house. Unfortunately, we have no mythological material that would permit us to place this snippet in a larger context and to identify the protagonists.

The purpose of the "ruling" or "decision" that is sought (lines 3, 12) is not stated in the narrative introduction, and it only comes out in the messages from *Ditānu:* the child is ill and in need of healing by divine intervention (*ḫlh*, "his illness," in line 10 refers back to *yld*, "the child," and *mr,* "bitterness," in line 16 also refers to the illness). The latter term may indicate that the illness is in fact poisoning by snake bite, for *šmrr*, "that which causes bitterness," derived from the root MR(R), "to be bitter," is a descriptive term for serpent venom in text 53 (RS 24.244). In terms of the literary structure of this text, one will note the use of myrrh (*mr*, line 5, partially restored in line 7) in causing the "bitterness" (*mr*, line 16) to disappear.

In spite of the core of the text being placed in the mouth of a god, the entire text seems to be in prose, rather than in poetry, an extremely rare feature of texts of a mythological nature. The practical aspect of this text appears to lie in the instructions from *Ditānu*, and the text does not, therefore, have the neat separation of the mythological and practical aspects that was visible in the previous text. On this analysis, *Ditānu*'s prescription for the healing of a sick (divine) child would have been the model for similar human cases. Though the attempt has been made to identity the function of this text as specifically necromantic (e.g., Loretz 1993: 289–93), one wonders if *Ditānu*'s nature as an ancestor of the dynasty is sufficient to warrant so specific a classification. There is no reason to doubt, on the other hand, that the story served as a model for consulting the quasi-mythological head of the dynasty in the case of illness striking the young heir to the throne (and, perhaps, by extension, in the case of any infant). It would thus be *Ditānu*'s status as head of the dynasty that makes of him an oracle for healing as much as his status as one of the *Rapaʾūma*, which some have emphasized (see the recent summary of views in Brown 1998, esp. p. 144).

Text	***Translation***
Obverse	
(1) *k ymǵy . ảdn*	When the lord/father of the
(2) *ỉlm . rbm . ʿm dtn*	many gods reaches *Ditānu*
(3) *w yšảl .* ⸢*m*⸣*ṯpṭ .* ⸢*y*⸣*ld*	and asks of him a ruling for the child,
(4) *w yʿny . nn .* ⸢*dtn*⸣	*Ditānu* answers him:
(5) *tʿny . n*⸢*ảd*⸣ *.* ⸢*mr*⸣ *. q*⸢*ḥ*⸣	"You are to reply: 'A skin-bottle of myrrh take
(6) *w št .* ⸢*b*⸣ [.]⸢*bt ḥrn*⸣ *. t*⸢*rḥ*⸣	and put it in the house of *Ḥôrānu;*[14] a new *trḥ*-bottle

(7) *ḫdṯ m[r] . ⸢q⸣ḥ [.] w š⸢t⸣*	of myrrh take and put it
(8) *b bt . ⸢bʿ⸣l . bnt . q⸢ḥ⸣[ ]*	in the house of *Baʿlu*; take *bnt*
(9) *w št . b bt . w prʿ[t]*[15]	and put it in the child's house and it will bring
(10) *hy . ḫlh . w ymǵ[ ]*	his illness to a head.[16] Your messenger has
(11) *mlảkk . ʿm dt⸢n⸣*	reached *Ditānu*,
(12) *lqḥ mṯpṭ*	he has received the ruling.'"
(13) *w yʿny . nn*	*Ditānu* answers him
(14) *dtn . btn . mḥ⸢y⸣*	further: "Cleanse (lit. "wipe") the house:
(15) *l dg . w l kl⸢b⸣*	no more fish and no more dog!
Lower Edge	
(16) *w ảṯr . ỉn . mr*	And thereafter the "bitterness" will disappear."

Ḥôrānu and the Mare: Ridding the Land of Serpents

53. RS 24.244

One of the best-preserved of the larger Ugaritic tablets dealing with religious topics, this text operates on the mythological level. The principal female protagonist is an equid whose origins are cosmological and who converses with the sun and, through the latter's intermediary, with twelve of the other principal deities of the Ugaritic pantheon. That such a figure, otherwise unknown in Ugaritic mythology, would play so important a role in the text may be taken as an indication that the real concern of the text is with the flesh-and-blood equids of Ugarit and, by plausible extension, with their human owners. Such an interpretation appears more plausible than attempting to place the literary work on a higher mythological plane by attempting to identify the mare with one of the principal Ugaritic goddesses (on such attempts, see Dietrich and Loretz 2000: 390–92): this mare is not the goddess depicted as standing on an equid's back (Leclant 1960) but a literary representation of concern for the equid expressed in terms of the mother's concern.

The structure of the text is clear: (1) Appeals to the divinities (lines 1–60); (2) *Ḥôrānu*'s intervention (lines 61–69); (3) *Ḥôrānu*'s marriage proposal (lines 70–76). The first section is broken down into twelve subsections describing the appeals to each of twelve deities, of which only the last, *Ḥôrānu,* is capable of acting effectively. This last deity's powers are underscored, somewhat ironically, by the recent discovery that two of the divinities named here as ineffectual in dealing with serpents were in their earthly manifestations possessors of horses: the administrative text RS 86.2235:16'–17' lists rations distributed for the horses of *Rašap* and of *Milku ʿAṯtarti,* who appear in this text in paragraphs VI and IX.[17]

Ḥôrānu is an important figure in prophylactic magic at Ras Shamra and is actually named as such in one of the Ugaritic incantations (see text 49 [RIH 78/20]). He is, however, presented in this text in mythological terms, and, in terms of genre, the text itself is to be classified as (para-) mythological rather than incantatory. There is, however, a conventional incantatory phrase embedded in the mare's appeal to the twelve deities (lines 4–6, *mnt* ... *ḫmt,* and in each of the following eleven paragraphs). On this interpretation of the text as a whole and of the passage in lines 4–6, see Pardee 1988a: 206–8; Pardee 1997e; Pardee 2000b: 63, 64.

One of the principal interests of this text is that the commissioning of the message to each of the divinities consulted in the twelve-part first thematic section (lines 1–60) names not only the divinity but also that divinity's principal seat of reign. These are widespread and provide a tour of much of the then-known world: from Crete (Caphtor) to central Anatolia (*Bibitta*) to central Syria (*Larugatu*) to upper Mesopotamia (Tuttul, Mari) to northern Transjordan (*ʿAṯtartu*) to back near home (Mount *Ṣapunu*); two are expressed in traditional mythological terms (*ʾIlu*'s home is "at the headwaters of the two rivers, at the confluence of the deeps"; that of *Šaḫru-wa-Šalimu,* i.e., "Dawn-and-Dusk," is said to be in "the heavens"); three are uncertain either as to localization (*ʾInbubu*—the name is known from mythological sources but the geographical identification is disputed) or as to identification (ḤRY, MṢD). Virtually the same cast of divine characters appears again in the following text (RS 24.251, text 54), but, with the sole exception of *Milku* in *ʿAṯtartu,* they are not there geographically defined. Because of the wide geographical purview of this text, and, implicitly, of text 54, it is necessary to remain very cautious about exploiting any one element (e.g., *Milku*'s location in Transjordan) to the exclusion of the others in attempting to fix Ugaritian ethnic or religious origins. At least on the basis of present data, a cautious explanation identifies these elements drawn from far-flung points as inclusions into the local "Amorite" traditions,[18] which can be traced in some cases back more than a millennium and which are thus reflective of a venerable cosmopolitan attitude.

Text	***Translation***
Obverse	
I. (1) *ủm . pḥl . pḥlt .*	The mother of the stallion, the mare,
bt . ʿn . bt . ảbn .	The daughter of the spring, the daughter of the stone,
bt . šmm . w thm	The daughter of the heavens and the abyss,[19]
(2) *qrỉt . l špš . ủmh .*	Calls to her mother, *Šapšu:*
špš . ủm . ql . bl .	"Mother *Šapšu*, take a message
ʿm (3) *ỉl . mbk nhrm .*	To *ʾIlu* at the headwaters of the two rivers,
b ʿdt . thmtm	At the confluence of the deeps:
(4) *mnt . nṯk . nḥš .*	'My incantation for serpent bite,
šmrr . nḥš (5) *ʿqšr .*	For the scaly serpent's poison:
lnh . mlḫš ảbd .	From it, O charmer, destroy,
lnh . ydy (6) *ḥmt .*	From it cast out the venom.'"[20]
hlm . yṯq . nḥš .	Then he binds the serpent,
yšlḥm[21] *. ʿqšr*	Feeds the scaly <serpent>,
(7) *yʿdb . ksả . w yṯb*	Draws up a chair and sits.
II. (8) *tqrủ . l špš . ủmh .*	She again calls to her mother *Šapšu:*
špš . ủm . ql bl	"Mother *Šapšu*, take a message
(9) *ʿm . bʿl . mrym . ṣpn .*	to *Baʿlu* on the heights of *Ṣapunu:*
mnty . nṯk (10) *nḥš .*	'My incantation for serpent bite,
šmrr . nḥš . ʿqšr .	For the scaly serpent's poison:
lnh (11) *mlḫš . ảbd .*	From it, O charmer, destroy,
lnh . ydy . ḥmt .	From it cast out the venom.'"
hlm . yṯq (12) *nḥš .*	Then he binds the serpent,
yšlḥm . nḥš . ʿqšr .	Feeds the scaly serpent,
ydb[22] *. ksả* (13) *w yṯb*	Draws up a chair and sits.
III. (14) *tqrủ l špš . ủh*[23] *.*	She again calls to her mother *Šapšu:*

špš . ủm . ql . bl .	"Mother *Šapšu*, take a message
ʿm (15) *dgn . ttlh .*	to *Dagan* in *Tuttul:*
mnt . nṯk . nḥš .	'My incantation for serpent bite,
šmrr (16) *nḥš . ʿqšr .*	For the scaly serpent's poison:
lnh . mlḫš . ảbd .	From it, O charmer, destroy,
lnh (17) *ydy . ḥmt .*	From it cast out the venom.'"
hlm . yṯq . nḥš .	Then he binds the serpent,
yšlḥm (18) *nḥš . ʿqšr .*	Feeds the scaly serpent,
yʿdb . ksả . w yṯb	Draws up a chair and sits.

IV. (19) *tqrủ l špš . ủmh .*	She again calls to her mother *Šapšu:*
špš . ủm . ql . bl .	"Mother *Šapšu*, take a message
ʿt[24] (20) *ʿnt w ʿ. ṯtrt ỉnbbh .*	to *ʿAnatu-wa-ʿAṯtartu* in *ʾInbubu:*
mnt . nṯk (21) *nḥš .*	'My incantation for serpent bite,
šmrr . nḥš . ʿqšr .	For the scaly serpent's poison:
lnh . ml(22)*ḫš . ảbd .*	From it, O charmer, destroy,
lnh . ydy . ḥmt .	From it cast out the venom.'"
hlm . yṯq (23) *nḥš .*	Then he binds the serpent,
yšlḥm . nḥš . ʿqšr .	Feeds the scaly serpent,
⌜*yʿ*⌝*db ksả* (24) *w yṯb*	Draws up a chair and sits.

V. (25) *tqrủ . l špš . ủmh .*	She again calls to her mother *Šapšu:*
špš . ⌜*ủ*⌝[*m . q*]⌜*l*⌝ *bl .*	"Mother *Šapšu*, take a message
ʿm (26) *yrḫ . lrgth .*	to *Yariḫu* in *Larugatu*:
mnt . nṯk . ⌜*n*⌝[*ḥ*]⌜*š*⌝ *.*	'My incantation for serpent bite,
šmrr (27) *nḥš . ʿqšr .*	For the scaly serpent's poison:
lnh . mlḫš . ảbd .	From it, O charmer, destroy,
lnh . ydy (28) *ḥmt .*	From it cast out the venom.'"
hlm yṯq . nḥš .	Then he binds the serpent,
yšlḥm . nḥš (29) *ʿqšr .*	Feeds the scaly serpent,
yʿdb . ksả . w yṯb	Draws up a chair and sits.

VI. (30) *tqrủ* . *l špš* . *ủmh* .	She again calls to her mother *Šapšu:*
špš . *ủm* . *ql b*[25] . *ʿm* (31) *ršp* . *bbth* .	"Mother *Šapšu*, ta<ke> a message to *Rašap* in *Bibitta:*
mnt . *nṯk* . *nḥš* . *šmrr* (32) *nḥš* . *ʿqšr* .	'My incantation for serpent bite, For the scaly serpent's poison:
lnh . *mlḫš ảbd* . *lnh* . *ydy* (33) *ḥmt* .	From it, O charmer, destroy, From it cast out the venom.'"
hlm . *yṯq* . *nḥš* . *yšlḥm* . *nḥš* . *ʿq*(34)*š*[26] . *yʿdb* . *ksả* . *w yṯb*	Then he binds the serpent, Feeds the scaly serpe<nt>, Draws up a chair and sits.

[27]<———

VII. (34a) *tqrủ* . *l špš* . *ủmh* .	She again calls to her mother *Šapšu:*
špš . *ủm* . *ql bl* . *ʿm* (34b) *ʿṯtrt* . *mrh* .	"Mother *Šapšu*, take a message to *ʿAṯtartu* in *Mari:*
mnt . *nṯk* . *nḥš* . *šmrr* (34c) *nḥš* . *ʿqšr* .	'My incantation for serpent bite, For the scaly serpent's poison:
lnh . *mlḫš ảbd* . *lnh* . *ydy* (34d) *ḥmt* .	From it, O charmer, destroy, From it cast out the venom.'"
hlm . *yṯq* . *nḥš* . *yšlḥm* . *nḥš* (34e) *ʿqšr* . *yʿdb* . *ksả* . *w yṯb*>	Then he binds the serpent, Feeds the scaly serpent, Draws up a chair and sits.

VIII. (35) *tqrủ l špš* . *ủmh* . *špš* . *ủm* . *ql bl* . *ʿm* (36) *ẓẓ* . *w kmṯ* . *ḥryth* .	She again calls to her mother *Šapšu:* "Mother *Šapšu*, take a message To *Ẓiẓẓu-wa-Kamāṯu* in ḤRY.[28]
mnt . *nṯk nḥš* . *šm*(37)*rr* . *nḥš* . *ʿqšr* .	'My incantation for serpent bite, For the scaly serpent's poison:
lnh . *mlḫš ảbd* . *lnh* (38) *ydy* . *ḥmt* .	From it, O charmer, destroy, From it cast out the venom.'"
hlm . *yṯq* . *nḥš* *yšlḥm* . *nḥš* (39) *ʿq* . *šr*[29] . *yʿdb* . *ksả* . *w yṯb*	Then he binds the serpent, Feeds the scaly serpent, Draws up a chair and sits.

IX. (40) ⌜*t*⌝*qrủ l špš . ủmh .*	She again calls to her mother *Šapšu:*
špš . ủm ql . bl .	"Mother *Šapšu*, take a message
ʿm (41) *mlk . ʿṯtrth .*	To *Milku* in *ʿAṯtartu:*
mnt . nṯk . nḫš .	'My incantation for serpent bite,
šmrr (42) *nḫš . ʿqšr .*	For the scaly serpent's poison:
lnh . mlḫš ảbd .	From it, O charmer, destroy,
lnh . ydy (43) *ḥmt .*	From it cast out the venom.'"
hlm yṯq . nḫš .	Then he binds the serpent,
yšlḥm . nḫš (44) *ʿqšr .*	Feeds the scaly serpent,
yʿdb . ksả . w yṯb	Draws up a chair and sits.

X. (45) *tqrủ l špš . ủmh .*	She again calls to her mother *Šapšu:*
špš . ủm . ql bl .	"Mother *Šapšu*, take a message
ʿm (46) *kṯr w ḫss . kptrh .*	To *Kôṯaru-wa-Ḫasīsu* in Caphtor:
mnt . nṯk . nḫš	'My incantation for serpent bite,
(47) *šmrr . nḫš . ʿqšr .*	For the scaly serpent's poison:
lnh . mlḫš . ảbd	From it, O charmer, destroy,
(48) *lnh . ydy . ḥmt .*	From it cast out the venom.'"
hlm yṯq . nḫš	Then he binds the serpent,
(49) *yšlḥm . nḫš . ʿqšr .*	Feeds the scaly serpent,
yʿdb . ksả (50) *w yṯb*	Draws up a chair and sits.

XI. (51) *tqrủ l špš . ủmh .*	She again calls to her mother *Šapšu:*
špš . ủm ql . bl .	"Mother *Šapšu*, take a message
ʿm (52) *šḥr . w šlm šmmh .*	To *Šaḫru-wa-Šalimu* in the heavens:
mnt . nṯk . nḫš	'My incantation for serpent bite,
(53) *šmrr . nḫš ʿqšr .*	For the scaly serpent's poison:
lnh . mlḫš (54) *ảbd .*	From it, O charmer, destroy,
lnh . ydy ḥmt .	From it cast out the venom.'"
hlm . yṯq (55) *nḫš .*	Then he binds the serpent,
yšlḥm . nḫš . ʿqšr .	Feeds the scaly serpent,
yʿdb (56) *ksả . w yṯb*	Draws up a chair and sits.

XII. (57) *tqrủ . l špš . ủmh .*	She again calls to her mother *Šapšu:*
špš . ủm . ql . bl	"Mother *Šapšu*, take a message
(58) *ʿm . ḥrn . mṣdh .*	To *Ḥôrānu* at MṢD:[30]
mnt . nṯk nḥš	'My incantation for serpent bite,
(59) *šmrr . nḥš . ʿqšr .*	For the scaly serpent's poison:
lnh . mlḫš (60) *ảbd .*	From it, O charmer, destroy,
lnh . ydy . ḥmt .	From it cast out the venom.'"[31]

XIII. (61) *b ḥrn . pnm . trǵnw .*	She turns her face to *Ḥôrānu,*
w tṯkl (62) *bnwth .*	For she is to be bereaved of her offspring.
ykr . ʿr . d qdm	He returns to the city of the east,
(63) *ỉdk . pnm . l ytn .*	He heads
tk ảršḫ . rbt	For Great *ʾAraššiḫu,*
(64) *w ảršḫ . ṯrrt .*	For well-watered *ʾAraššiḫu.*[32]
ydy . b ʿṣm . ʿrʿr	He casts a tamarisk from among the trees,
(65) *w b šḥt . ʿṣ . mt .*	The "tree of death" from among the bushes.
ʿrʿrm . ynʿrảh[33]	With the tamarisk he expels it (the venom),
(66) *ssnm . ysynh .*	With the fruit stalk of a date palm he banishes it,
ʿdtm . yʿdynh .	With the succulent part of a reed he makes it pass on,
yb(67)ltm . yblnh .	With the "carrier" he carries it away.[34]
mǵy . ḥrn . l bth .	Then *Ḥôrānu* goes to his house,[35]
w (68) *yštql . l ḥẓrh .*	Arrives at his court.
tlủ . ḥt[36] *. km . nḫl*	The venom is weak as though in a stream,
(69) *tplg . km . plg*	Is dispersed as though in a canal.[37]

XIV. (70) *bʿdh . bhtm . mnt .*	Behind her the house of incantation,[38]

bʿdh . bhtm . sgrt	Behind her the house she has shut,
(71) *bʿdh . ʿdbt . ṯlṯ .*	Behind her she has set the bronze bolt.
ptḥ . bt . mnt	"Open the house of incantation,
(72) *ptḥ . bt . w ủbả .*	Open the house that I may enter,
hkl . w ỉštql	The palace that I may come in."
(73) *tn . km . nḥšm .*	"Give as <my bride-price>[39] serpents,
yḥr . tn . km (74) *mhry .*	Give poisonous lizards as my bride-price,
w bn . bṯn . ỉtnny	Sons of adders as my wife-price."
(75) *ytt . nḥšm . mhrk .*	"I hereby give serpents as your bride-price,
bn . bṯn (76) *ỉtnnk*	Sons of adders as your wife-price."
Left Edge	
(77) *ảṯr ršp . ʿṯtrt*	After *Rašap*, *ʿAṯtartu:*
(78) *ʿm ʿṯtrt . mrh*	To *ʿAṯtartu* in Mari:
(79) *mnt . nṯk nḥš*	My incantation for serpent bite.[40]

Šapšu, with *Ḥôrānu*'s Help, Rids the Land of Serpents

54. RS 24.251

This text is unfortunately nowhere near so well preserved as the preceding text (RS 24.244); indeed the tablet in its present state may contain remnants of only about half the original text. It is nevertheless clear that it also deals with the problem of serpent venom and that essentially the same deities are involved. Here, however, if the preserved portions have been correctly interpreted, *Šapšu* is not just a messenger but plays the principal role: near the beginning of the text, she calls, rather than being called, and, in the partially preserved text on the reverse, her intervention is requested both before and after that of the other gods. *Ḥôrānu* plays an independent role here, but the text is too damaged for us to know what that role was (see lines 29' and 31'). Subsequently (lines 37'–44'), he is named along with the other gods who are asked to eradicate the venom. The circumstances appear to be entirely different from those visible in the preceding text: instead of the victims being equine, an unidentified personage called *Šrǵzz* has been bitten, has collapsed, and is weeping like a child (lines 6-12). According to one interpretation of line 6, *Šrǵzz* would have been an inexpert snake handler or charmer (references in Wyatt 1998: 391–92). None of the characteristic words for snake charming known from RS 24.244 is, however, present in this section, and we must await further evidence on the nature of the events that led to the divine intervention described later in the text. The identification as a historiola appears reasonable, whether *Šrǵzz* be identified as belonging to the human sphere (in which case, the historiola would have a legendary base rather than a mythological one) or, like the mare in RS 24.244, as being of at least semidivine origin.[41] The method of dealing with the serpent venom is also different here: instead of being diluted, it is gathered (ʾSP) by the gods. The damaged state of the end of the text prevents us from knowing how the venom was ultimately eradicated. Because the venom is presented metaphorically as a "fog," the efficacy of the sun's action is nevertheless clear. Is it possible that the invitation to the other gods to participate in gathering the "fog" was ironic and that this text in its original state presented only *Šapšu* as truly capable of dissipating the miasma? If such were the case, the basic presentation would be similar to that of RS 24.244, with *Šapšu* here the main god and *Ḥôrānu* presented as no more powerful than the others. In our present state of knowledge, where *Ḥôrānu* is consistently presented as efficacious against evil, this putative presentation of the god's powers as ineffectual constitutes the major argument against this interpretation. Only a more complete version would allow us to answer such questions.

Text[42]

Obverse

---

(1) [ ]⌜-⌝ . *b*[ ] . *hl*[ ]
(2) [ ]⌜-⌝⌜*r*⌝⌜-⌝ . ⌜*ỉl*⌝*m* . *rbm* . *nʿl*[ ]*mr*
(3) [ ]⌜-⌝[ ]⌜*r*⌝*ṣ* . *bdh* . *ydrm*[ ]*pỉ*⌜*t*⌝ . ⌜*ả*⌝*dm*
(4) [ ]⌜-⌝*ỉṯ*[ ] . *yšql* . *yṯk*[--]⌜-⌝*npbl* . *hn*
(5) [ ]⌜-⌝*ṭ*⌜*b*⌝*t*[43] . *p ẓr* . *p ẓr*⌜-⌝ . *p nḥš*
(6) [ ]⌜*q*⌝ . *nṯk* . *l ydʿ* . *l bn* . *l pq ḥmt*
(7) [ ]⌜-⌝*nh* . *ḥmt* . *w tʿbtnh* . *ảbdy*
(8) [*npl b š*]*r* . *šrǵzz* . *ybky* . *km nʿr*
(9) [*ydmʿ* .] ⌜*k*⌝*m* . *ṣǵr* . *špš* . *b šmm* . *tqrủ*
(10) [*mdʿ ảt*] *nplt* . *y*⌜-⌝[?]⌜-⌝[44] . *mdʿ* . *nplt* . *b šr*
(11) [*š*]⌜*r*⌝*ǵzz* . *w tpky* . ⌜*k*⌝[*m* .] *nʿr* [.] ⌜*t*⌝*dmʿ* . *km*
(12) [*ṣ*]⌜*ǵ*⌝*r* . *bkm* . *yʿny*[ ]⌜-⌝[ ]⌜-⌝ *wth*
(13) [ ]⌜-⌝*nn* . *bnt yš*[ ] . [ ]⌜*h*⌝*lk*

(14) [ ]⸢b⸣ . kmm . l k⸢l⸣[.] ⸢m⸣sp[r]

---

(15) [šp]š . b šmm . t⸢qr⸣ủ . ⸢-⸣[ ]⸢-⸣-rt
(16) [ ]⸢h⸣t⸢m⸣ . ảmn[ ]⸢-⸣[ ]n . ảmr
(17) [ ]⸢-⸣l ytk bl⸢t⸣[ ]⸢-⸣m⸢r⸣ . hwt
(18) [ ]⸢-⸣ . ṯllt . k hn[ ] . k pʿn
(19) [ ]y . yd . nšy . ⸢-⸣[ ]š . l mdb
(20) [ ]h . mḫlpt[ ]⸢-⸣ . ả⸢m⸣r
(21) [ ] . nʿlm . ⸢-⸣[…]
(22) [ ]⸢š⸣ . hn . ảl[…]
(23) [ ]⸢-⸣t . bn . ⸢-⸣[…]
(24) [ ] . ḥ⸢m⸣[t …]
(25) [ ]⸢-⸣[…]

....

Reverse

....

(26') [ ] . ả[…]
(27') [ ]⸢-⸣bt . np⸢š⸣[ ]⸢-⸣

(28') [ ]l šd . ql . ṯ[ ]⸢-⸣t . ảṯr
(29') [ ]ǵrm . y[ ]⸢-⸣rn
(30') [ ]rk . ḥ⸢-⸣[ ]⸢-⸣lk
(31') [ ]sr . n[ ]⸢-⸣ . ḥrn
(32') [ ]sp . ḫph . ḫ⸢-⸣[tỉsp . šp]š . l hrm
(33') [ǵrpl] . ʿl . ảr[ṣ . lản . ỉ]⸢sp⸣[. ḥ]mt
(34') [ỉsp . š]pš . l hr[m .] ⸢ǵ⸣rpl . ʿl . ảrṣ
(35') [tỉsp .]ḥmt . l p[. n]ṯk . ảbd . l p ảk[l]
(36') [ṯmdl .]⸢ả⸣sp . ḥm⸢t⸣[. ỉl .] ⸢ỉ⸣[l]hm . yảsp[.]ḥmt
(37') [ỉsp . š]pš . l ⸢hr⸣[m .]⸢ǵr⸣[p]⸢l⸣ . ʿl . ảrṣ . lản
(38') [ỉsp . ḥ]mt . ỉ[l .] ⸢w⸣ ḥrn . yỉsp . ḥmt
(39') [bʿl .] ⸢w⸣ dgn . ⸢y⸣[ỉ]⸢s⸣p . ḥmt . ʿnt . w ʿṯtrt
(40') [tỉ]sp . ḥmt . y⸢r⸣ḫ . w ršp ḫỉsp[45] . ḥmt
(41') [ʿṯt]r w ʿṯtpr . yỉsp . ḥmt . ẓẓ . w ktṯ[46]
(42') [yỉ]sp . ḥmt . mlk . b ʿṯtrt . yỉsp . ḥmt
(43') [kṯ]r w ḫss . y⸢ỉ⸣sp . ḥmt . šḥr . w šlm
(44') [yỉs]p . ḥmt . ỉsp . ⸢šp⸣š l hrm . ǵrpl . ʿl ảrṣ
(45') [ảs]⸢p⸣t . ḥmt . l p [. n]ṯk . ảbd . l p . ảkl . ṯmdl
(46') [ ]l . bl . tbḥ[ ]⸢-⸣tzd . ʿrq . dm

(47') [ ] . ʿr⌜q⌝[. š]pš
(48') [ ]⌜-⌝[ ]n . mšḫt . kṯpm . ảkṯn
(49') [ ]⌜-⌝n⌜-⌝[ ]⌜-⌝ṭ b ym . tld

Upper Edge

(50') [ ]b⌜r⌝y[ ]
(51') [ỉ]lm . rb⌜m⌝[ ]⌜-⌝ š⌜-⌝
(52') [ ]t . nš . b⌜-⌝[ ]mt[ ]
(53') [ ]⌜-⌝ . tmt[ ]⌜k⌝ṯ[ ]
(54') [ ]⌜-⌝ảk⌜l⌝[ ]

Translation

---

(1) [ ]⌜-⌝ . B[ ] . HL[ ]
(2) [ ]⌜-⌝⌜R⌝⌜-⌝ the many gods NʿL[ ]MR
(3) [ ]⌜-⌝[ ]⌜R⌝Ṣ in his hand(s) YDRM[ ]the temples of the man
(4) [ ]⌜-⌝ʾIṮ[ ] YŠQL it bites[--]⌜-⌝NPBL see
(5) [ ]⌜-⌝good, the mouth of flint, the mouth of flint, the mouth of the serpent
(6) [ ]⌜Q⌝ bite(r) does not know, does not understand, does not find[47] the venom
(7) [ ]⌜-⌝N him does the venom and the destructress[48] twists him about.

(8) *Šrǵzz* [falls in prostra]tion,
weeps like a child,
(9) [sheds tears] like a small boy.

Šapšu calls out in the heavens:

(10) ["Why] have [you] fallen O ⌜-⌝[?]⌜-⌝
Why have you fallen in prostration, (11) O *Šrǵzz*?

Why do you weep like a child,
Shed tears like a (12) [sm]all boy?"

Weeping he responds[ ]⌜-⌝[ ]⌜-⌝ WTH
(13) [ ]⌜-⌝NN . BNT YŠ[ ] . [ ] go
(14) [ ]⌜B⌝ the same according to the entire recitat[tion].[49]

---

(15) [*Šap*]*šu* calls out in the heavens: ⸢-⸣[ ]⸢-⸣-RT
(16) [ ]⸢H⸣T⸢M⸣ I will count[ ]⸢-⸣[ ]N a saying
(17) [ ]⸢-⸣L he pours BL⸢T⸣[a sa]ying, a word
(18) [ ]⸢-⸣ a band K HN[ ] like the foot
(19) [ ]Y the hand NŠY . ⸢-⸣[ ]Š to the deep
(20) [ ]H . MH̯LPT[ ]⸢-⸣ a saying
(21) [ ] . NʿLM . ⸢-⸣[...]
(22) [ ]⸢Š⸣ see ʾAL[...]
(23) [ ]⸢-⸣T son ⸢-⸣[...]
(24) [ ] ven[om ...]
(25) [ ]⸢-⸣[...]

....

Reverse

....

(26') [ ] . ʾA[...]
(27') [ ]⸢-⸣BT throa[t]⸢-⸣

(28') [ ]L ŠD . QL . T̲[ ]⸢-⸣T . ʾAT̲R
(29') [ ]mountains Y[*Ḥ*]*ô*⸣*rānu*
(30') [ ]RK Ḥ⸢-⸣[ ]⸢-⸣LK
(31') [ ]SR . N[ ]⸢-⸣ *Ḥôrānu*
(32') [ga]thers on its shore[50] H̯⸢-⸣[ ]
[You must gather, O *Šap*]*šu*, on the mountains (33') [the fog],
On the lan[d of the Mighty One ga]ther the [ve]nom.[51]

(34') [Gather, O *Ša*]*pšu*, on the mountain[s the f]og,
On the earth (35') [you must gather][52] the venom.

From the mouth of the [bi]ter destroy,[53]
From the mouth of the devou[rer] (36') [destroy? T̲MDL].

Gather,[54] [O *ʾIlu*], the venom,
All the [go]ds, may they gather the venom.

(37') [Gather, O *Ša*]*pšu*, on the mountain[s the f]o[g],
On the land of the Mighty One (38') [gather the ve]nom.[55]

May *ʾI*[*lu*] and *Ḥôrānu* gather the venom,
(39') May [*Baʿlu*] and *Dagan* [ga]ther the venom,
[May] *ʿAnatu* and *ʿAt̲tartu* (40') [ga]ther the venom,
May! *Yariḫu* and *Rašap* gather the venom,

(41') May [ʿA*ṯta*]*ru* and ʿ*Aṯtapar* gather the venom,
[May] *Ẓiẓẓu* and *Kam*[!]*āṯu* (42') [ga]ther the venom,
May *Milku* in ʿ*Aṯtartu* gather the venom,
(43') May [*Kôṯa*]*ru* and *Ḫasīsu* gather the venom,
[May] *Šaḫru* and *Šalimu* (44') [gathe]r the venom.[56]

Gather, O *Šapšu*, on the mountains the fog,
On the earth, (45') [O gathe]rer of venom.[57]

From the mouth of the [bi]ter destroy,
From the mouth of the devourer destroy[?] ṮMDL.

(46') [ ]L . BL . TBḤ[ ]⸢-⸣will not increase the flow of blood
(47') [ ] the flo[w of *Ša*]*pšu*
(48') [ ]⸢-⸣[ ]N destruction, the thicknesses I will tear
(49') [ ]⸢-⸣N⸢-⸣[ ]⸢-⸣Ṭ on the day you/she gives birth

Upper Edge

(50') [ ]B⸢R⸣Y[ ]
(51') [ ]the numerou[s g]ods[ ]⸢-⸣ Š⸢-⸣
(52') [ ]T . NŠ . B⸢-⸣[ ]MT[ ]
(53') [ ]⸢-⸣ . TMT[t]ear[ ]
(54') [ ]eat/devour[ ]

Notes

1. A new text in which the god *Ḥôrānu* plays, as here in texts 53 and 54, an important role is RS 92.2016 (to be published in Caquot and Dalix forthcoming). Unfortunately, that text is too fragmentary to allow a solid decision as to its content and hence its genre.

2. The West Semitic *marziḫu* is a social institution with the following noncultic characteristics: (1) it groups a dozen or so individuals; (2) membership is transmittable to heirs; (3) the place of meeting is noncultic (see text 60 [RS Varia 14]); (4) the principal activity when the group meets is the drinking of wine; (5) bloody sacrifice is not practiced in the *marziḫu*. Thus, though each *marziḫu* appears to have been devoted to a particular deity, and though cultic personnel could be members, the institution itself is neither cultic nor located in a holy place. For a comparison of the West Semitic *mrzḫ* with similar associations in the Near East, see O'Connor 1986. On the absence of systematic orgiastic, mortuary, or sacrificial activity at the *marziḫu* (the claim that all three are characteristic of the *marziḫu* may be found in a single sentence in del Olmo Lete and Sanmartín 1998: 191), see Pardee 1988a: 54–57, 176–77 and 1996a: 277–79. An additional

argument against the function of the *marziḫu* as being primarily mortuary has occurred to me since these formulations were published: one would expect the mortuary cult to be organized along family lines, as indeed appears to be the case with the royal mortuary cult, judging from the few indications that we have (see texts 24 and 56 [RS 34.126 and RS 24.257/RS 94.2518]). The data available on the *marziḫu* indicate, however, that the membership of a given *marziḫu* was not drawn from a single family (O'Connor 1986 explicitly contrasts family organizations with that of the *marziḫu*).

3. It is out of the question that the so-called Temple aux Rhytons at Ras Shamra may have been "the temple of El" (e.g., Wyatt 1998: 404) for reasons indicated in Pardee 1996a: 280 and 2000b: 55, though it may have been the meeting place of a *marziḫu*-group (see below on text 60).

4. The appearance of *dbḥ* here is illustrative of the pitfalls of translation: normally "sacrfice" denotes what humans do for divinities, not what divinities do for themselves. The use of *dbḥ* here reflects, therefore, the literal meaning of the root, viz., "to slaughter (an animal by slitting its throat)."

5. The literary link between *Yariḫu* the dog in the first part of the text and the use of hairs of a dog in the second is clear, for such links constitute one of the principal literary characteristics of the "para-mythological" texts. It does, however, remain a mystery why it is the principal lunar deity of Ugarit who plays this role. The allusion may constitute a polemic against another ethnic group whose principal deity was lunar (Pardee 1988a: 39–42). I note that the principal deity of the Eblaite cult ({DINGIR.NI-da-KUL/BAL}) had as one of his principal seats *Larugatu*, the home of *Yariḫu* according to text 53 (RS 24.244:26); unfortunately, the nature of the Eblaite deity remains unelucidated (Archi 1993: 10–11). The only serious attempt at accounting for *Yariḫu*'s role here was Cooper's (1991: 833–35), who linked the moon god's role as judge in the underworld with his view of the *marziḫu* as a mortuary feast—the *ỉlm* in line 2 would be the gods of the underworld. Because there is no reason so to identify the gods invited to the feast, because everything speaks against the *marziḫu* being a mortuary feast, and because *Yariḫu*'s role is anything but that of a judge according to the text itself, such an explanation appears of dubious value.

6. Because the order of mention of these two goddesses is not fixed in this text (in line 22, the order is reversed), they appear not yet to have fused into a true "double-deity." In text 53 (RS 24.244), however, one encounters *ʿAnatu-wa-ʿAṯtartu*, whose seat of residence is in one place, and *ʿAṯtartu* who lives in a different place.

7. Read {k[!]lb}.

8. Apparently for allowing the behavior that has just been the object of reproof. The "doorman" is here identified as a son of *ʾIlu*, which explains how a lowly doorman could reprove exalted *ʾIlu*. The son is plausibly *Šunama* who, with his brother *Ṯukamuna*, was at hand to help his father home when the latter left the drinking session (lines 18–19).

9. The next-to-the last sign of line 14 is a well-preserved {k}, and the last is one that consists of a total of five wedges, all rather clearly horizontals, though the lower edge of the sign has suffered some damage.

10. ḤPY is as yet not identified with certainty (see Wyatt 1998: 411 n. 38); an identification with the Egyptian Apis-bull (an identification first suggested by M. Liverani), who played the role of psychopomp ("bearer of souls [to the underworld]"), is philologically and historically plausible (Pardee 1988a: 60–62).

11. Again without a new collation of the tablet, Dietrich and Loretz (1998: 179, 191; 2000: 413, 478) reject a reading based on collation (Pardee 1988a: 15, 20), in this case a word divider after {lṣbh}; they thereby prefer Dietrich, Loretz, and Sanmartín 1976: 120 over Dietrich, Loretz, and Sanmartín 1995: 130. Any resemblance between this word divider and a {ẖ} must, however, be judged purely superficial. In addition to the purely epigraphic perspective, it may be remarked that this reading destroys the literary link between *Yariḫu* the dog in the first part of the text and the "hair of the dog" in the prose recipe (see above, n. 5 to this section), for in this reading and interpretation the "dog" is eliminated (*ḫš ʿrk lb*, "zubereiteten Thymian(?) . . . Leib").

12. The form of presentation here, similar to that of the hippiatric texts, indicates that PQQ is plausibly identified as a plant.

13. The term for "olive oil" here is not the prosaic *šmn* of the ritual texts, but *dm zt*, "blood of the olive tree."

14. The restoration of *Ḥôrānu* is far from certain, but plausible; in any case the presence of a divine name here appears likely.

15. A trace of the {t} may be visible (see Pardee 1988a: 181).

16. Whatever the precise function of the myrrh may be in the sanctuaries, the independent pronoun *hy* in line 10 shows that it is the last item named, the *bnt*, that is the active agent of PRʿ, "to excel over, to bring to culmination."

17. RS 86.2235 will be edited in Bordreuil and Pardee forthcoming a. For preliminary statements regarding the horses belonging to *Rašap* and *Milku ʿAṯtarti*, see Caquot 1986; Bordreuil 1987: 298; idem 1990: 12; Pardee 1987: 31 (correct "quinze paniers" in line 17' to "cinq jarres"); idem 1988b; Yon et al. 1987: 187.

18. On the "Amorite" origins of the Ugaritic language, of the royal family, and of the Ugaritic onomastic tradition, see Pardee 1988a:173–76, 1997g, h, and forthcoming d, e.

19. The precise interpretation of this line of ancestors is unknown: "heavens and abyss" are unknown as a pair of deities, though each of the elements is known, *šmm* in the double deity *ảrṣ-w-šmm*, *thm* as a common noun designating the primeval sea of fresh water (*CTA* 23:30; cf. Hebrew *tᵊhōm*). The forms of the latter that appear as a divine name in these and the mythological texts are *thmt* and *thmtm*, plausibly plurals (the singular form, corresponding to *Tiāmat* in the Babylonian creation story, appears in a vocabulary text—cf. Huehnergard 1987: 184–85). "Spring-and-stone" are unknown elsewhere as divinities (in *CTA* 3 iii–iv,

the pairing is *ʿṣ . . . ảbn*, "wood . . . stone"). The comparison of "heavens and abyss" with "earth-and-heavens" and "mountains and abysses" in RS 24.643 and the parallel deity lists (see texts 1, 3, and 12) seems to indicate, however, that these pairs express cosmological origins in this text.

20. This bicolon, repeated to each of the gods invoked, constitutes the only properly incantatory element of the text. Because below *Ḥôrānu* refuses to undertake this particular act, one must conclude that this text is implicitly critical of standard snake-charming incantations. From a structural perspective, either the reaction of *ʾIlu* and the ten following deities is not described or else the following tricolon describes it. Wyatt adopts the former analysis (1998: 379–80 n. 10). I prefer the latter because it is precisely this verse that is replaced by *Ḥôrānu*'s effective reaction described in lines 61–69 (this interpretation is also adopted by Parker in Parker et al. 1997: 220). Wyatt's reference to the omitted paragraph after line 34 in support of his belief that this tricolon was inadvertently omitted from the *Ḥôrānu* paragraph is invalid because the former error was caught and corrected (see note to lines 34a–e and lines 77–79). Because these verses in the following paragraphs are not marked for feminine gender when the divinity is female, the subject of the verbs in the final tricolon of each of the first eleven paragraphs must in all cases be *mlḫš*, "charmer."

21. The word *nḫš* is present at this point in all following paragraphs and is hence to be inserted after {yšlḥm}.

22. Read {y<ʿ>db}.

23. Read {ủ<m>h}.

24. Read {ʿm!}.

25. Read {b<l>}.

26. Read {ʿqš<r>}.

27. Lines 77–79 indicate that a paragraph omitted in the inscription of the tablet is to be inserted here; see translation of those lines below. The precise division into five lines first proposed in Pardee 1978: 78–81 is, of course, hypothetical, since the precise distribution of the repeated words varies from one paragraph to another.

28. This place is as yet unidentified.

29. Read {ʿqšr}.

30. As a common noun, *mṣd* may mean "fortress"; it is uncertain whether such is the meaning here or whether this is a presently otherwise unknown name of a city. To cite the analogy of "heavens" in the preceding paragraph in favor of the interpretation as a common noun is not totally convincing, for there is only one set of heavens but many fortresses exist.

31. This name apparently reflects the Hurrian name for the Tigris, though a city so named is unknown from presently available sources.

32. *Ḥôrānu*'s special status in this text is expressed by the omission here of the tricolon present in the preceding eleven paragraphs in which the standard snake-

charmer's response was depicted. Functionally speaking, that paragraph, where ineffectiveness was the theme, is replaced by the second principal section of this text (lines 61–69), where *Ḥôrānu*'s peculiar talents are the theme.

33. Read {ynʿrn$^{!}$h}.

34. As is appropriate in a magical rite, each of the acts is expressed by a punning formula; the last plant named has not yet been identified botanically. For a generic reference to the use of wood in magical rites, see above, text 48 (RS 92.2014:3). One will note that the reference to the date palm properly places this action in Mesopotamia, where *Ḥôrānu* has just traveled, and the other plants are probably, therefore, also to be understood as those of that region. This displacement to the east is apparently a nod to the efficacy of Mesopotamian magic. See Wyatt 1998: 385–86 for references to the earlier literature and for a defense of his interpretation, not implausible, of the three terms designating the agents in lines 66–67 as parts of the tamarisk rather than as separate types of plants.

35. I.e., back to MṢD.

36. Read {ḥ<m>t}.

37. The venom is as powerless as if diluted in the Tigris and in its canals and streamlets.

38. Because the only incantation mentioned to this point is the mare's, we may conclude that the new paragraph marks a change of scene, back to the mare's house; alternatively, she has shut herself up in *Ḥôrānu*'s house while he was traveling. The following three paragraphs contain a dialogue between *Ḥôrānu* and the mare: the god asks for entry, the mare requires marriage, the god responds with a promise of (devenomized) snakes as the bride-price.

39. Restore plausibly {tn . km . <mhry> nḥšm}, with repetitive parallelism of *mhr* (cf. Hebrew *mōhar*, "bride-price"), or another word for "gift."

40. This correction is to be interpreted as meaning: "After (the paragraph dealing with) *Rašap*, (insert a paragraph dealing with) *ʿAṯtartu*, (of which the operative phrase will be:) to *ʿAṯtartu* in Mari; (then continue with the rest of the paragraph on the pattern of the other paragraphs:) My incantation for serpent bite (etc.)." See above, where, according to this instruction, the omitted paragraph is inserted as lines 34a–e.

41. The identification of the text as (para-)mythological in nature implies the rejection of its classification as an incantation (as, for example, is recently claimed by del Olmo Lete and Sanmartín 1998: 176 n. 7)—what holds for text 53 (RS 24.244) holds in all probability for this text as well (see Pardee 2000b: 63).

42. Because of the state of the tablet, only a few lines can with certainty be set out as poetry. The translation below is, therefore, laid out according to the lines of the text except in those cases where a poetic division is possible. I have left all untranslated signs in the text to make it easier for the reader to determine exactly what is translated and what is not. The reader should also note that I have included in the transliterated text all of the restorations reflected in the translation, including some rather hypothetical ones. For a more conservative text and

all the proper reservations regarding the restorations, see Pardee 1988a: 230–33, 238–39, 248–53.

43. The reading here of {ḥ[m]t} (Wyatt 1998: 392) is out of the question: the {ṭ} is perfectly preserved and the lower wedge of {ḥ} has not "been overwritten by a word-divider" (as claimed by Wyatt, ibid.); moreover, the left side of the {b} is preserved and cannot belong to {m}. The first occurrence of the word for "venom" in this text, is, therefore, in line 6 rather than here.

44. Because we do not know the correct reading of the two traces of signs after {y}, and for that reason do not know the width of the two signs partially preserved, it now appears safer to me to indicate that a third sign may have totally disappeared between the two traces (in my transliteration [1988a: 230], I indicated only a blank space between two half-brackets, with the remark [p. 234] that it was "peu probable" that a third sign had disappeared).

45. Read {y!·ỉsp}.

46. Read {km!·t̲}.

47. I know of no verb PQ meaning "remove" (Wyatt 1998: 392). See Pardee 1988a: 244 and n. 56.

48. *ảbdy* appears to be derived from the root ʾBD, "to destroy," to which the archaic feminine ending *-ay* has been attached.

49. Because of the state of the text, the precise meaning of this scribal directive for repetition is unknown. Because none of the deities of text 53 (RS 24.244) has yet been named (at least in the present state of the text), it is uncertain whether this directive refers here to a repetition before each of the deities on the pattern of text 53; in any case, because of the new way in which these divinities are presented below (grouped, sometimes artificially, in pairs, without a geographical designation), it seems unlikely that the repetition would have been part of a visit to each deity.

50. There is no doubt whatever that the third sign of this word is {h}, not {p} (contra Wiggins 1996: 342).

51. For the rationale behind the various restorations and interpretations of this passage, see Pardee 1988a: 248–51. The varying lengths of the restorations at the beginnings of lines 33'–37' proposed there constitute a problem and indicate the necessity of some changes, for which see remarks in following notes (several of the changes reflect the proposals of Wiggins 1996: 342–43—if, however, text 53 may be taken as an example, the stichometry proposed by Wiggins cannot be admitted). Here the venom is presented as "fog" or a "dark cloud" (*ǵrpl* is cognate with Hebrew *ʿărāpel*—see Cohen 1995). It is clear that the sun is particularly apt to dissipate the venom in that form, but the origin of the metaphor itself is unknown. Though it is partially true that "the imagery of darkness and thick fog correlates in biblical poetry with evil" (Levine and Tarragon 1988: 508), it is a big step from there to employ "fog" as a metaphor for "venom." It is also uncertain who the "Mighty One" is from whose land the venom is to be gathered, but it is difficult to solve that problem by reading {lản ḥmt}, "the power of the venom," for

that reading is ruled out by considerations of space in both lines 33' and 37'–38' (in order to maintain this tempting solution, Wyatt has paid no attention to the problems of restoration here and actually emended the text in line 45' [1998: 393–94]). Finally, the analysis of the form *ỉsp* as an imperative is based on the assumption that the verb had a *yaqtil*-prefix conjugation, as in Akkadian, rather than *yaqtul*- as in Hebrew.

52. I now judge that the restoration of {lả̀n . ỉsp}, proposed in Pardee 1988a: 248, is too long, and I propose that the word *lản* was omitted not only in line 45' but here also. This hypothesis suggests that the word *lản* was present in the first and third instances of this verse (lines 34'–35', 37'–38'), absent in the second and fourth (here and lines 44'–45'); it gains in attraction by providing a difference between this verse and the previous one (in 1988a: 248 n. 80, I entertained the idea that what I had reconstructed as a verbatim repetition might have come about through dittography). If {lản} is removed here, then the restoration of {ỉsp} alone is a bit short; on that basis, I further posit that the verb forms of the first verse were reversed here, producing a chiastic structure. Of course, these restorations are no less hypothetical than were my former proposals (see Pardee 1988a: 248–49), but they do fit the space better and provide a better set of verses.

53. Because the form of the word that appeared above with the plausible meaning "feminine destroyer" (line 7) was *ảbdy*, whereas here and in line 45' we encounter *ảbd*, the best parallel appears to be with the brief incantation in the preceding text, where *ảbd* appears in a similar formula (text 53 [RS 24.244], lines 5–6 and repeated in the following paragraphs) as a D-stem imperative (against the translation of *ảbd* here in del Olmo Lete 1992a: 250; 1999a: 372 as "*perdición*/ruin," in Wyatt 1998: 393–94 as "venom"). The four signs left untranslated at the end of this verse have to date not received an explanation satisfying to all. By analogy with the verse from text 53 to which allusion has just been made, one would expect the signs to hide a verb and an object: *ṯm dl*, "do something destructive to something poisonous" (parallel to *ydy ḥmt* in the other text). But no convincing explanation of these putative words has been proposed (proposals indicated in Pardee 1988a: 251 n. 95) and in line 45' the space between the {m} and the {d} is well preserved with no word divider present. The present translation assumes that *ṯmdl* is the object of the verb ʾSP, which would not have been repeated in the second colon of the verse (for a possible etymology, see del Olmo Lete 1992a: 250 n. 130; 1999a: 372).

54. As nearly as the state of the text allows us to tell, the verb ʾSP is expressed in the D-stem only in this bicolon, which appears to refer generically to *ʾIlu* and the gods (*ỉlhm* may designate specifically the gods of *ʾIlu*'s immediate family, as the generic plural is *ỉlm* elsewhere in Ugaritic; compare the usage in the sacrificial texts of *ỉlhm* and *bʿlm*). {⸢ả⸣sp} in line 36' cannot go with the preceding verse (Wyatt 1998: 393) because the verb ʾSP is in all other verses expressed in the first colon, and here the space in the following lacuna is insufficient to contemplate restoring this or any other verb as well as the two subjects required of the

bicolonic structure (cf. Wyatt 1998: 393 n. 16). I adopt the reading {⸢ả⸣sp} here (D-stem imperative), rather than {[y]⸢ả⸣sp} purely because of the space that appears to be available in the lacuna.

55. Two imperative forms of ʾSP are here reconstructed purely for reasons of space.

56. The structure of this list as pairs of deities has led to some differences with respect to the deities of text 53 (RS 24.244), though the order followed there is essentially preserved here. All the deities to whom the message was sent according to the first twelve paragraphs of text 53 are present here except the *ʿAṯtartu* of Mari, replaced here (apparently because *ʿAṯtartu* was already named in line 39' and in order to maintain the structure of two divine names per line) by the double deity *ʿAṯtaru-wa-ʿAṯtapar*. The two-deities-per-line rule was broken in line 42' because the preceding and following deities in the list were already double; this was apparently not viewed as serious because the name of *Milku*'s place of residence was identical to a divine name. The other important difference is that *Ḥôrānu* is here a member of the first pair rather than coming at the end of the list. In the other text, the last place represented a culmination, the preceding deities having shown themselves to be ineffectual, whereas here *Ḥôrānu* enjoys the place of honor next to *ʾIlu*. One can think of two reasons for this: (1) the two-deities-per-line rule required *ʾIlu* to have a partner and (2) the function of this text appears not to be to praise the powers of *Ḥôrānu* above those of the other gods but to show him working in cooperation with them. Unfortunately, the state of the rest of the text prevents us knowing *Ḥôrānu*'s role elsewhere in the story. In order to underscore the structure of this unit, I have translated the conjunction *w* everywhere as "and," whether the two deities are incidentally associated here or, judging from other texts, constitute a "double deity" (such as *ʿṯtr w ʿṯtpr*, *ẓẓ w kmṯ*, *kṯr w ḫss*, *šḫr w šlm*).

57. The second form of ʾSP is certainly not the same as in line 33', the only other case where the verb is partially preserved (there is not space in the lacuna to restore {t} as well as {ḥ} in line 33'). Because *ỉsp*, well preserved in the preceding line, appears to be an imperative, I have difficulty in accepting that the purpose of *ảspt* is to express narratologically that the act of gathering is complete (Wyatt 1998: 394 "gather . . . you have gathered"). If it be granted that *ảbd* in the following verse is also an imperative (see note above to this word), then lines 35'–45' form a partial chiastic structure (ABC—D—C'A').

X

Rites Including Divine Participation

THE FOLLOWING TWO TEXTS are presented separately from the historiolae because they appear, in their damaged state, to lack the "story" that bears the message in the texts presented in the previous section. In the first text, several deities are invited to participate in a feast; then there is a long lacuna followed by a description of what the first deity addressed is capable of doing for the king. The second consists of fragmentary references to a musical rite followed again by a lacuna, then a list of the deceased and divinized kings of Ugarit. If the association of the two texts on the tablet was meant to express a literary association, the deceased kings must somehow have participated in the rite, either directly, as in text 24 (RS 34.126), or indirectly by the simple recitation of their names. As will be suggested below, it is not implausible, though unprovable from data presently available, that these texts may have been redacted on the occasion of the entombment of *Niqmaddu* III and the assumption of the throne by *ʿAmmurāpiʾ*, the last king of Ugarit.

A Divine Drinking Rite and a Blessing

55. RS 24.252

The first two sections of this text address two deities at some length; then, judging from the appearance of the verb *yšt*, "may he drink," in lines 10 and 13, other deities appear to receive more briefly stated invitations. The operative verbal form, just cited, is a third-person jussive that urges each deity named to "drink," though the object of the verb is never stated (contrast the drinking of *ʾIlu* and the other deities in text 51 [RS 24.258], where the beverages are named). For this reason, the verb may be ŠT, "to put," in the passive: "X-deity is established"; in this case, the text would be referring to some sort of establishment of these deities. I prefer the former interpretation because of the excellent parallels for deities participating in drinking feasts and because of the lack of specificity in the verb ŠT as to what kind of establishment would be so designated.[1] Because of the apparent focus on drinking, this text may reflect the presence of the various deities named in their *marziḫus*; or the rite in question could reflect the Ugaritic version of the Mesopotamian *kispu*.[2] But in the absence of specific indications such as those in the preceding text (RS 24.251), and because of the differences of genre between that text and this one, either cultic/literary identification of this text is for the present beyond certainty.[3] In any case, the form of this text is, strictly speaking, neither that of the hymn, nor that of the prayer;[4] rather it appears to be an invitation to the deities invoked to join in a feast at which *Rāpiʾu*, the first deity named, is described as requesting of *Baʿlu* that he transmit the powers of the *Rapaʾūma* to the living king. According to this interpretation, the text would be that of a rite by which the transfer of these powers is effected; there may well have been a prayer in the central section that has disappeared, that is, between the invitation to the feast and the description of its outcome, but that is only a hypothesis. Because no royal name appears in the text, a specific setting for this text can only be a matter of speculation, but two primary possibilities present themselves: (1) the rite would have been regularly repeated to assure the king's ongoing success; (2) it could have been used only as a *rite de passage* from one king to another. In either case, it would be a rite parallel with the following text in which the deceased kings are apparently feted in an explicit manner. Indeed, it is possible to hypothesize that both these texts were part of a series of rites associated with the passage from *Niqmaddu* III to *ʿAmmurāpiʾ*, the last known king of Ugarit. Of this series only one text, RS 34.126 (text 24), includes the names of the deceased king and his successor. If such be the case, this text would have been associated with the accession ceremonies of *ʿAmmurāpiʾ*, for its burden is clearly that of assuring the ongoing line, whereas the following text may have been more closely associated with the burial ceremonies of *Niqmaddu*, for its concerns appear to be uniquely with the deceased members of the royal line.

Text	***Translation***
Obverse	
(1) [*hl*]*n* . *yšt* . *rpủ* . *mlk* . *ʿlm* .	Now[5] may *Rāpiʾu*, king of eternity,[6] drink,

w yšt (2) [*ỉl*] ⸢g⸣*ṯr . w yqr .*	May he drink, the god mighty and noble,
ỉl . yṯb . b ʿṯtrt	The god who dwells in *ʿAṯtartu*,
(3) *ỉl ṯpṭ . b hdrʿy .*	The god who rules in *Hadraʿyi*,[7]
d yšr . w yḏmr	Who sings and makes music,[8]
(4) *b knr . w ṯlb .*	With lyre and flute,
b tp . w mṣltm .	With drum and double-sistrum,
b m(5)*rqdm . d šn .*	With ivory castanets,
b ḥbr . kṯr . ṭbm	Among the goodly companions of *Kôṯaru*.
(6) *w tšt . ʿnt . gṯr .*	May *ʿAnatu*-of-Might also drink,[9]
bʿlt . mlk .	Lady of kingship,
bʿ(7)*lt . drkt .*	Lady of sovereignty,
bʿlt . šmm . rmm	Lady of the High Heavens,
(8) [*ʿ*]⸢*n*⸣*t . kpṯ .*	*ʿAnatu*-of-the-*kupṯu*-hat,
w ʿnt . dỉ . dỉt .	*ʿAnatu*-of-the-wing, the kite,
rḥpt (9) [*b šm*]⸢*m*⸣ *rm .*	Soaring in the heavens on high,[10]
ảklt . ʿgl ṯl[11] *. mšt*	Who devours the calf of *ʾIlu* at the feast,
(10) [*ỉ*]⸢*m*⸣*r . špr .*	[...] the comely lambs.
w yšt . ỉl (11) [...]	May the god [...] also drink,[12]
[...]⸢-⸣*n . ỉl ǵnṯ . ʿgl ỉl*	[...] the god ǴNṮ, the calf of *ʾIlu*
(12) [ ]⸢-⸣*d . ỉl . šdy ṣd mlk*	[...] the god *Šaddayyu*, hunter of MLK,[13]
(13) [ ]⸢-⸣ *. yšt . ỉlh*	[...] May *ʾIlāhu* drink
(14) [ ] ⸢-⸣*ỉṯmh*	
(15) [ ]⸢*r*⸣*š*⸢*p*⸣[...]	*Rašap*

....

Reverse

....

(16') [ ] ⸢-⸣*mǵy*	[...]ARRIVE
(17') [ ]⸢*n*⸣*drh*	[...]his vow
(18') [ ]	
[*tštk . yả*]*rš . l bʿl*	Your success he will ask of *Baʿlu*,[14]

(19') [*w l ỉrštk . y*]*mǵk* .	To what you have requested he will bring you;
rpủ mlk (20') [*ʿlm . ymǵy*]*k* .	*Rāpiʾu*, king of eternity, will bring you
l tštk . l ỉršt(21')[*k*]	To your success, to what you have requested,
[*b yd* .]*rpỉ . mlk ʿlm* .	By the power of *Rāpiʾu*, king of eternity,
b ʿz (22') [*rpỉ* .] ⌜*m*⌝*lk . ʿlm* .	By the strength of *Rāpiʾu*, king of eternity,
b ḏmrh . b l(23')[*ảnh*] .	By his power, by his might,
b ḥtkh . b nmrth .	By his paternal care, by his divine splendor.[15]
l r(24')[*p*]*ỉ . ảrṣ . ʿzk* .	Your strength will be that of the *Rapaʾūma* of the earth,
ḏmrk . lả(25')*nk* .	As will be your power, your might,
ḥtkk . nmrtk .	Your paternal care, your divine splendor,
b tk (26') *ủgrt* .	Within Ugarit
l ymt . špš . w yrḫ	For the days of *Šapšu* and *Yariḫu*,
(27') *w nʿmt . šnt . ỉl*	For the goodly years of *ʾIlu*.

Rites Involving the Royal Shades of the Dead

56. RS 24.257/RS 94.2518

Because of the list of royal names on the reverse of RS 24.257, the texts it bears have attracted a great deal of attention. The damage that the tablet has suffered is such, however, that its interpretation is fraught with difficulties, in particular as regards the three following points: (1) the obverse is so badly damaged that its content and genre are uncertain; (2) the loss of the bottom of the tablet has removed the evidence for the link between the texts on the obverse and the reverse and for the original length of the king list on the reverse as presently preserved; (3) though better preserved, the reverse is so badly damaged that many of the names have been lost.

The recent publication of a similar list in syllabic script, attested in four exemplars, three of which are complete, requires a total revamping of our views of the Ugaritic king list (in Arnaud 1998, one will find a photograph of the text provided below, RS 94.2518). I will provide first a brief outline of what we thought we knew about this list based on RS 24.257, then discuss the revisions required by the syllabic versions.

Because the shape of the original tablet RS 24.257 may only be estimated and because we do not know exactly where on the tablet the list began, the number of names on the Ugaritic list may only be the object of surmise. In my re-edition of the tablet, I posited that the most plausible number was around fifty, assuming that the height of the tablet would have been about half again that of its width (a common form) and that the list would have begun at the top of the reverse (1988a: 173–75). Any number beyond thirty was, however, entirely hypothetical.[16] The last king in the right-hand column, *Yaqaru*, was thought to be the first of the royal line, whose royal seal was still used in the fourteenth-thirteenth centuries. The editor of the seal (Nougayrol 1955: XLI–XLII) suggested that it might date to the eighteenth or nineteenth century B.C.E. As for the structure of the list, only three data were thought to be of real importance: (1) the identification of the last name in the right-hand column with the *Yaqaru* of the dynastic seal was thought to indicate that the list was in reverse order; (2) the presence of a partially preserved vertical line between the two columns on the reverse left no doubt that the text was actually inscribed as two separate columns, not as a single column with facing entries (in the latter format, the standard scribal procedure is either to inscribe a horizontal line between each entry on the line or else to leave the space blank between the two entries); (3) because the text on the obverse was written across the width of the tablet, the two-column arrangement on the reverse may have been thought to have proceeded from left to right; that is, the left column was entirely inscribed before the column on the right was begun.[17] It appears necessary to abandon the first of these hypotheses, but the other two still hold.

The principal problem in comparing the new texts with the Ugaritic version is that the former are inscribed in a single column on tablets devoted entirely to the king list, and *Yaqaru* appears not in last position but is the twentieth of twenty-six names. There is simply no easy way to harmonize the two sets of data. Arnaud assumes that, because his lists are complete, they represent complete lists of the Ugaritic kings, from the first so identified, a certain *ʾUgarānu*, to the king immediately after whom the list would have been prepared, that is, the *Niqmēpaʿ* who reigned early in the thirteenth century (Arnaud 1998: 157); moreover, the Akkadian and Ugaritic lists would have been identical, or nearly so (ibid., pp. 153–54, 157[18]). *Yaqaru*, who appears near the end of the list, would not have lived in the eighteenth or nineteenth century, but in the fifteenth (ibid., p. 163). The Ugaritic list would have been in two columns, intended to be read from right to left. The problem with this view is that it obliges Arnaud to assume that the left-hand column of RS 24.257 held only six names. Because he believes it certain that the poorly preserved names in col. I, lines 20'–22', correspond to three of these six names, he is further obliged to conclude that the top of the left column contained "un texte quelconque, et non des noms royaux" (p. 156), that is, any kind of text except a list of royal names. Structurally speaking this must be described as unlikely, viz., that a single list would have been inscribed in two columns, with twenty names in the first column, six in the second, with fourteen lines of something else positioned in the middle of the list, that is, after the first fourteen names and before the last six. If, for example, the list had been divided into two sections with a rite of some kind between the two, the text would in all likelihood have been arranged otherwise on the tablet. Moreover, with a list of kings numbering only twenty-six, there is no reason to believe that the scribe would have begun writing his list on the right side of the tablet—unless there is a strict literary and graphic continuity from obverse to reverse, a scribe will usually begin inscribing his columns from left to right.

A more likely scenario, it appears to me, is this:

(1) The Ugaritic and Akkadian texts overlapped but were not identical.

(2) The Ugaritic text is to be read from left to right, as is expected (see above) and as is indicated by the fact that the last line of the left-hand column impinges on the space of the right-hand column and the latter begins, therefore, slightly to the right of the left margin that was followed in the preceding lines.[19]

(3) In agreement with the new Akkadian texts, and therefore in disagreement with the preceding consensus on order of writing, the Ugaritic king list was written in descending rather than ascending order; that is, *Yaqaru* reigned later than the kings whose names precede his.

(4) Instead of containing only six names, the left-hand column contains a list as long as that of the right-hand column, and that list must, therefore, have contained a whole series of names of kings who preceded *ʾUgarānu:* there is general agreement that some of these names appear in text 24 (RS 34.126) and that the dynastic line must have gone at least all the way back to the mythical *Ditānu*.[20] It is some or all of these names that would have preceded *ʾUgarānu* and been inscribed in the left column.

(5) *Yaqaru*, as Arnaud posits, would not have reigned in the eighteenth/nineteenth century, but more recently, though that time can only be estimated.[21]

(6) The Ugaritic list either differed from the Akkadian one in ending with this *Yaqaru* or, as appears more likely, the last six names were inscribed on the left edge of the tablet, which has completely disappeared. This argument from silence is not as arbitrary as it may seem: the fact that the writing on the top edge of the tablet touches the horizontal line marking the beginning of the text on the obverse is a sufficient basis for the hypothesis, for when the Ugaritic scribes had filled all available space on the obverse, the lower edge, the reverse, and the upper edge, they habitually turned to the left edge and placed the end of the text there. Unfortunately, because of the uncertainty regarding the size of the lacuna caused by the disappearance of the lower portion of this tablet (see introduction), it is impossible to determine whether the right column began with the first name on the Akkadian list or if other names preceded that one. My original hypothesis, based on a reconstruction of the shape of the tablet, that each column would have borne twenty-six names (Pardee 1988a: 173), would mean that six names preceded that of *ʾUgarānu* in the right column. But such considerations are very hypothetical, and there is no reason why *ủgrn* could not have been the first name in the second column. The preserved traces at the bottom of the left column do not allow for a shorter reconstruction of the two columns, viz., one in which any part of the sequence provided by the first eight names on the Akkadian list would be placed at the end of that column. The comparison of the Akkadian and Ugaritic texts shows, therefore, that the original Ugaritic list plausibly bore a minimum of forty-six names (20 + 20 + 6); a larger number is possible, depending on the original height of the tablet and/or on where the transition took place from the type of text attested on the obverse to the list itself.

(7) Another possibility is that the Ugaritic list did not end with the *Niqmēpaʿ* who reigned early in the thirteenth century, but continued down through the *Niqmaddu* whose funerary rite was recorded on text 24 (RS 34.126): this would have involved only three more names, and there is no reason to doubt that the space on the left edge of the tablet was sufficient to bear nine names. If this text reflects one of the rites carried out in connection with the funeral of this *Niqmaddu* and the coronation of *ʿAmmurāpiʾ*, such an up-dating is plausible.[22] According to this hypothe-

sis, the original Ugaritic list of divinized kings would have borne a total of forty-nine names (20 + 20 + 9).

(8) The obvious weak point of this interpretation is that the traces of writing in the left column of the Ugaritic texts are in two cases (lines 21' and 22') most plausibly restored as names that correspond to names common in later times—hence Arnaud's hypothesis that these names correspond to the those that follow *Yaqaru* in the Akkadian text.[23] Names of a demonstrably recent type would, therefore, according to my hypothesis, have preceded those at the head of the Akkadian list, some of which are of a more archaic type. This weakness does not appear, however, to be as important as those criticized above. Indeed, the name *Rapʾānu*, which appears in third position in the Akkadian list, is attested in the later periods (Nougayrol 1968: 41–259), though it is not used later as a royal name. This may be taken as an indication that the royal names common from the seventh name on in the Akkadian list could have also occurred earlier. These would in turn have been preceded by names even more archaic than those in RS 94.2518:1–3 if the *Rapaʾūma* named in RS 34.126 were named in RS 24.257.

The new Akkadian texts appear also to disambiguate a feature of the Ugaritic list which the Ugaritic writing system left unclear: the second word of each entry appears to be in the genitive, and the meaning of each is, therefore, "the god of (the king in question)" (Arnaud 1998: 159).[24] I have never known[25] what that means precisely, but the syntax now appears clear and is seen to match that of similar texts from Ebla.[26] The syntax has been taken as indicating that something is done for the particular god of each king (Schmidt 1994: 69–70). Though the concept of the personal god is certainly an ancient one, I do not see how it can apply here, for the implication of that interpretation is either that all the kings had the same personal god (what then would be the sense of the rite?) or that they had different personal gods, none of whom is named (Is it plausible that the rite would have been in honor of a long list of unnamed gods?). Because the departed kings certainly belonged to the *Rapaʾūma*, the denizens of the netherworld, and because one may plausibly hypothesize that they were designated as *Malakūma*, that is, "kings," a name that actually figures on both of the long deity lists provided above (text 1 [RS 1.017:33]; text 3 [RS 92.2004:42]), there is no reason to doubt that the deceased king became a part of the divine (though the realm of this segment of the divine was the netherworld); hence there is no particular reason to shy away from the interpretation of *ỉl* as expressing this fact explicitly.[27] Though one must be careful about appealing to relatively rare grammatical phenomena, the fact that the first element of these formulae is a common noun and the second a proper noun leaves open the analysis of the syntax as that of the "genitive of identification," of the type *nᵊhar pᵊrāt*, "the river Euphrates," or *bat yᵊrūšalayim*, "girl Jerusalem," in Hebrew. The translation according to that analysis would be "the god (who is) *Yaqaru*, etc."

One feature of the new Akkadian texts may be taken as an indication that these texts at least were related to sacrificial rites. I refer to the check mark to the right of each entry (Arnaud 1998: 168). A similar set of marks is found in the right margin of RS 20.024 (the Akkadian version of text 1) and in the left margin of RS 24.264+ (the second Ugaritic version of text 1)[28] that is, the deity lists for which a link with sacrificial texts is proven explicitly (see above, texts 1 and 12). If RS 24.257 does not reflect a *kispu*-rite (present evidence does not allow a certain decision on that point, but the content of the text on the obverse at least does not provide a confirmation of the *kispu* interpretation[29]), RS 94.2518 may plausibly do so, by the very fact of the indicators of ritual usage. It must now be recognized, therefore, that the (at least partial) identity of RS 94.2518 and RS 24.257 reverse makes the hypothesis that RS 24.257 reflects some aspect of a *kispu*-like rite more plausible, in spite of the formal problem that arises from linking the text on the obverse with the deity list. Only further textual data can tell us whether RS 24.257 obverse reveals a new aspect of the *kispu*-rite or a very different rite in which the departed kings also take part.

The text on the obverse of RS 24.257 is divided into paragraphs by horizontal lines, but no line is complete. The vocabulary is repetitive, and the language may have been poetic, but this is impossible to determine with certainty. Two musical instruments are named, the lyre and the drum, both of which are included in the list of instruments on which *Rāpiʾu* would make music according to the preceding text. If the two texts on the tablet were literarily related, one may posit a rite characterized by music in favor of the departed kings. One function of each entry would, then, be to state that the king in question had, by the appropriate rite (e.g., text 24 [RS 34.126]), joined the *Rapaʾūma* and become a god.

It is uncertain who the "Good One" is in the text on the obverse of RS 24.257, but making it the parallel term to *tp* appears implausible to me (del Olmo Lete 1992a: 122, 1999a: 177–78) because the word is used elsewhere in a musical context to describe the performer (*CTA* 3 i 19, parallel with *ṭb*), not as a substantive for the performance. It is more plausible that *nʿm* refers to an individual, perhaps the divine *Rāpiʾu/Milku* (Pardee 1988a: 171), since he is both king of the dead and a musician (see text 55 [RS 24.252]). On the other hand, the idea that the reference may be to a dead king is attractive. If there was on the original tablet a notice that the verses were to be repeated, the repetition could have been for each of the kings (Wyatt 1998: 400 n. 7), and each in turn would have been the Good One.[30] In any case, the text may reflect a musical rite in honor of the deceased kings,[31] perhaps repeated regularly, perhaps repeated only on the death of a king. In the latter case, the text would plausibly reflect a rite parallel to the funerary rite text 24 (RS 34.126), and the Good One would be the recently deceased *Niqmaddu* III, while the musician may have been *Rāpiʾu*, as in the preceding text.

A. RS 24.257

Text	***Translation***
Obverse	
————	
(1) [...]⸢-⸣ *w rm tph*	[...] and high is his drum[32]
(2) [...]*lủmm l nʿm*	[...] peoples, for the Good One.
————	
(3) [...]⸢*w*⸣ *rm ṯlbm*	[...] and high is the double-pipe[33]
(4) [...]*pr l nʿm*	[...]PR, for the Good One.
————	
(5) [...]⸢-⸣*mt w rm tph*	[...]⸢-⸣MT[34] and high is his drum
(6) [...]*ḥb l nʿm*	[...]ḤB, for the Good One
(7) [...]*ymǵy*	[...]arrives.
————	
(8) [...]⸢*r*⸣*m ṯlbm*	[... and h]igh is the double-pipe
(9) [...]⸢*ʿ*⸣*m*	[... for the Go]od One.
————	
(10) [...]*ḥ nʿm*	[...]Ḥ Good One.
————	
(11) [ ]⸢-⸣[...]	
....	
Reverse[35]	
....	

Col. I

(12') [ ]	
(13') [ ]	
(14') [ ]	
(15') [ ]	
(16') [ ]⸢-⸣	
(17') [ ]	
(18') [ ]⸢-⸣[ ]	
(19') [ ]⸢*p*⸣[ ]	
(20') [ ]*d*[ ][36]	
(21') [*ỉl nq*]*mpʿ*	the god who is *Niqmēpaʿ*,
(22') [*ỉl ʿm*]*ṯtmr*	the god who is *ʿAmmiṯtamru*,

Upper Edge

(23') [ ]⸢*d*⸣	
(24') [ ]	
(25') [ ]	
(26') [ ]⸢*q*⸣	

Col. II

(27') [*ỉl*]⸢--⸣[...]	[the god who is]⸢--⸣[...],
(28') [*ỉl ʿm*]⸢*ṯ*⸣*tm*⸢*r*⸣	the god who is *ʿAmmiṯtamru*,
(29') [*ỉl n*]*qmpʿ*	the god who is *Niqmēpaʿ*,
(30') *ỉl mpḫ*[37]	the god who is *Mapḫû*,
(31') *ỉl ỉbrn*	the god who is *ʾIbbīrānu*,
(32') *ỉl yʿḏrd*	the god who is *Yaʿḏurraddu*,
(33') *ỉl nqmpʿ*	the god who is *Niqmēpaʿ*,
(34') *ỉl ỉbrn*	the god who is *ʾIbbīrānu*,
(35') [*ỉ*]⸢*l*⸣ *ʿmrpỉ*	the god who is *ʿAmmurāpiʾ*,
(36') [*ỉl*] *nqmpʿ*	the god who is *Niqmēpaʿ*,
(37') *ỉl ỉb*⸢*r*⸣[*n*]	the god who is *ʾIbbīrānu*,

Upper Edge

(38') *ỉl nqmp*⸢*ʿ*⸣	the god who is *Niqmēpaʿ*,
(39') *ỉl ỉbrn*	the god who is *ʾIbbīrānu*,
(40') *ỉl nqmd*	the god who is *Niqmaddu*,
(41') *ỉl yqr*	the god who is *Yaqaru* . . .[38]

B. RS 94.2518

This syllabic text is provided separately here because, with respect to RS 24.257 reverse, it corresponds to the syllabic column of texts 1 and 3 but is not, because of the various problems associated with the nature and form of the two texts, so easily reducible to a parallel column. Because the text consists formally of a list of divine names, it could—perhaps should—have been presented with the texts in section I. I have not so classified it for two reasons: (1) the most obvious is because it overlaps in part with RS 24.257 of which the text on the obverse does not belong to the category of deity lists; (2) perhaps of less importance is the fact that the deities of this list are divinized kings, who belong to a different stratum of the divine society from that of the deities named in the lists in section I. On the possibility that this text may contain the names of the dead and divinized kings honored in a ritual of a type similar to the Mesopotamian *kispu*, see the introduction.

Text[39]	***Translation***
(1) DINGIR ^{m}*ú-ga-ra-na*	The god who is *ʾUgarānu*,
(2) DINGIR ^{m}*am-qú-na*	the god who is *ʿAmqūnu*,
(3) DINGIR ^{m}*rap-a-na*	the god who is *Rapʿānu*,
(4) DINGIR ^{m}*lim-il*-LUGAL	the god who is *Lim-Il-Šarri*,[40]
(5) DINGIR ^{m}*am-mu-ḫa-ra-ši*	the god who is *ʿAmmuḫarrāšī*,[41]
(6) DINGIR ^{m}*am-mu-ša-mar*	the god who is *ʿAmmuṯamar*,[42]
(7) DINGIR ^{m}*a-mis-tam-ri*	the god who is *ʿAmmiṯtamru*,[43]
(8) DINGIR ^{m}*níq-me-pa*	the god who is *Niqmēpaʿ*,
(9) DINGIR ^{m}*ma*-AB-*i*	the god who is *Maphû*,[44]
(10) DINGIR ^{m}*i-bi-ra-na*	the god who is *ʾIbbīrānu*,
(11) DINGIR ^{m}KAR-^{d}IŠKUR	the god who is *Yaʿḏuraddu*,
(12) DINGIR ^{m}*níq-me-pa*	the god who is *Niqmēpaʿ*,
(13) DINGIR ^{m}*i-bi-ra-na*	the god who is *ʾIbbīrānu*,
(14) DINGIR ^{m}*am-mu-rap-i*	the god who is *ʿAmmurāpiʿ*,[45]
(15) DINGIR ^{m}*níq-me-pa*	the god who is *Niqmēpaʿ*,
(16) DINGIR ^{m}*i-bi-ra-na*	the god who is *ʾIbbīrānu*,
(17) DINGIR ^{m}*níq-me-pa*	the god who is *Niqmēpaʿ*,
(18) DINGIR ^{m}*i-bi-ra-na*	the god who is *ʾIbbīrānu*,
(19) DINGIR ^{m}*níq-ma-du*	the god who is *Niqmaddu*,
(20) DINGIR ^{m}*ya-qa-ri*	the god who is *Yaqaru*,
(21) DINGIR ^{m}*i-bi-ra-na*	the god who is *ʾIbbīrānu*,

(22) DINGIR ᵐ*níq-ma-*ᵈIŠKUR	the god who is *Niqmaddu*,
(23) DINGIR ᵐ*níq-me-pa*	the god who is *Niqmēpaᶜ*,
(24) DINGIR ᵐ*a-mis-tam-ri*	the god who is *ᶜAmmiṯtamru*,
(25) DINGIR ᵐ*níq-ma-*ᵈIŠKUR	the god who is *Niqmaddu*,
(26) DINGIR ᵐ*níq-me-pa*	the god who is *Niqmēpaᶜ*.

Notes

1. Del Olmo Lete, the champion of this interpretation, takes ŠT, "to put," as designating the "deification of the king" (1999a: 185–86; 1992a: 127). This reads a good deal, however, into the verb ŠT and assumes an unwarranted relationship between the "king/*Milku*," *Gaṯaru*, and *Yaqaru* (according to this interpretation, the phrase *rpủ mlk ᶜlm* is applied to any newly deceased king, who becomes a shade, a king in the underworld, a *gaṯaru* [another term for a shade, in del Olmo Lete's view], and a *Yaqaru* [who was believed to be the first king of the dynasty, though that has recently been disproved—see text 56, RS 24.257/RS 94.2518]). I take the terms *gṯr* and *yqr* as adjectives; the first evokes by paronomasia the qualities of the deity *Gaṯaru*, but neither expresses an explicit identification (Pardee 1988a: 93–94—now to be modified by the new data showing that *Yaqaru* was not the founder of the Ugaritic dynasty). Del Olmo Lete's translation of {gṯr w yqr} as "*Gaṯaru Yaqaru*," apparently intended to mean "the shade *Yaqaru*," does not give sufficient weight to the conjunction between the two terms and is, in any case, rendered out of date by the new data on the makeup of the Ugaritic king list.

2. On these possibilities, see Pardee 1996a: 276–77.

3. Because of the absence of links in the West Semitic texts between the *marziḥu* and the *kispu* as we know the latter from Mesopotamian texts, I prefer to view the two institutions as separate until more specific data appear (Pardee 1996a). The Mesopotamian texts present the *kispu* as a rite in honor of the departed ancestors, while the characteristics of the *marziḥu* are basically noncultic (see above, introduction to text 51 [RS 24.258]).

4. Pardee 1988a: 118 and 2000b: 63; Wyatt fuses the two genres by calling the text a "hymnic prayer" (1998: 395).

5. Some palliate the problem of a missing direct object for the verb *yšt* by restoring {[y]n}, "wine," here, but the space in the lacuna calls for the restoration of two signs, not just one.

6. This deity, otherwise unknown from the Ugaritic texts, is shown by his place of residence, indicated in the following verse, to be identical with *Milku* (see here text 53 [RS 24.244:40–41] and text 54 [RS 24.251:42']). This datum is sufficient to rule out identifications with other deities (bibliography in Brown 1998:

139–41). *Rāpiʾu* thus appears to be a title of *Milku*, designating him as head of the *Rapaʾūma*, he the "healer" (*qātil*), they the "healthy" (*qatal*). These vocalizations are, however, hypothetical, extrapolated from extra-Ugaritic attestations. If there is anything to them, *Milku* as god of the underworld would be the one responsible for the underworld existence of the dead. His title of "king of eternity," *malku ʿālami*, is both a pun on his name and a reference to the atemporality of the afterlife.

7. The identification of these two places goes back to Margulis 1970; the link between the two, so strongly reminiscent of *ʿAshtoret* and *ʾEdreʿi* in the Hebrew Bible (e.g., Deut 1:4; Josh 12:4), leaves little doubt that the seat of *Rāpiʾu/Milku*'s rule was situated to the northeast of the Sea of Galilee (see now Niehr 1998).

8. One of the principal wordplays in this text is that between D̲MR, "to make music" here (cf. Hebrew *zimmēr*) and D̲MR, "(protective) power," in lines 22' and 24' (an old West Semitic word preserved in Hebrew in the proper name *Zimrī*). The principal link between the two sections as preserved is, of course, provided by the name and title *Rāpiʾu malku ʿālami*. It is morpho-syntactically possible that *Rāpiʾu* is here the object of the song (the construction is attested in Hebrew), rather than the singer; that would require either that the following forms be passive or that they have an unstated subject ("one sings, they sing"). Like *Kôṯaru*, however, whose workshop is in the netherworld, *Milku* may be a musician; the purpose of the formulation would be to present the royal lot in the netherworld as a happy one.

9. None of the forms under which *ʿAnatu* is described here are known elsewhere in Ugaritic specifically as titles, but all fit in with data from other sources; e.g., Rameses II called her the Lady of the Heavens; the *kupṯu*-hat is probably a reference to the Egyptian Atef crown (*kpṯ* cannot refer to dominion, Hebrew KBŚ, as some have thought, because /ṯ/ does not correspond to Hebrew /ś/); according to the *Baʿlu* Cycle *ʿAnatu* claims to have defeated the calf of *ʾIlu* (*CTA* 3 iii D 41); etc. As *ʿAnatu* is feted in text 18 (RS 1.005) in company with *Gaṯaru*, *Šapšu*, and *Yariḫu*, so here she appears immediately after *Rāpiʾu-Milku*, moreover, the two deities of these first two sections are both qualified by forms of the root GṮR.

10. Either {rm} is used adverbially, as here translated, or the text is faulty and to be read {rm<m>}, i.e., as an adjective agreeing with *šmm*, giving the phrase "high heavens" (the idiom that is attested in line 7).

11. A circle around this {*ṯ*} may be interpreted as indicating an error; read plausibly {ỉ!.l}.

12. Because the text gradually disappears from this point on, it is impossible to ascertain the meaning of several of the following words and phrases, e.g., what deity is designated by {ỉl (11) [...]}, whether {ǵnṯ} is a divine name or an epithet, what the "calf of *ʾIlu*" is doing here again, etc.

13. If *Šaddayu* is correctly identified as a forerunner of biblical *Šadday*, the

characterization as "hunter" would appear to show that the name means "he of the field/steppe" (*šadû*, "field"); if such be the case, the Hebrew divine name would have been borrowed from another West Semitic dialect, for "field" in Hebrew is *śādeʰ* (i.e., with *śin* rather than *šin*—the two phonemes have coalesced in Ugaritic). It is uncertain whether MLK designates a deity or a place; if the former, the character of *Milku* identifies that of *Šaddayu* as chthonic.

14. As with most restorations as extensive as those in this verse, these must be considered hypothetical; they are based on words that appear in the following verses, however, a reasonable procedure given the high level of repetition in the rest of the text as it is preserved. If *bˁl* is indeed the divine name and not the title meaning "master," the deity appears to be serving as intermediary between *Rāpiʾu* and the king (the assumed referent of the suffix *-k*, "your," in the following lines): his intervention allows the qualities evoked in lines 21'–23' to pass to the king (lines 23'–25') ensuring his success. The phrase *btk ủgrt*, lit. "in the midst of Ugarit," in lines 25'–26', and the spectrum of qualities named, including "paternal care," indicate that the function of these virtues was not for the king's private glorification but to enable him properly and effectively to rule his people. That these virtues were to continue as long as sun and moon and *ʾIlu* himself indicates that they were not seen as benefiting a single king, but the entire line: when the present living king joined the *Rapaʾūma* he would, in turn, take up the role of assuring the transmission of these virtues on to his successor.

15. The letter RS 18.113A+B appears to contain a variant of this word (the basic proposal goes back to Rainey 1974: 188) as well as a variant of the phrase *mlk ˁlm* here in line 1: line 9 of the letter reads *nmry mlk ˁlm*, which may be interpreted as meaning ". . . the splendor of eternal kingship" (Dijkstra 1999: 158). If this interpretation of the letter be correct, an official of the king of Ugarit writing from Cyprus was pronouncing a blessing whereby he implies that his king did indeed participate in the divine/royal virtues which, according to this text, were mediated by *Baˁlu* (for more details on this interpretation of RS 18.113A+B, see Pardee forthcoming f as well as my re-edition of the Ugaritic letters, in preparation).

16. Pardee 1988a: 173–74. Dietrich assumes the number of "36" with no substantiating arguments (1996: 34, 37–38).

17. If an entire tablet is inscribed in columns, the usual order is left to right on the obverse, right to left on the reverse, though there are exceptions, particularly in the case of two-column administrative texts.

18. "RS 34.126" in the ninth line from the top of p. 157 appears to be a typographical error for "RS 24.257."

19. See photograph and hand-copy in Pardee 1998a: 168.

20. For a brief discussion and comparison of the Ugaritic and Akkadian sources, see Arnaud 1998: 156–57, 170–73. On *Ditānu*, see above, texts 24 and 52 (RS 34.126 and RS 24.272).

21. There is a text written under a king *Yaqaru* (RS 16.145, published by Nougayrol 1955: 169), and there is no reason, other than the editor's dating of the so-called dynastic seal where *Yaqaru* is named (ibid, pp. XLI–XLII) to date this text so early as the eighteenth or nineteenth century. Because of his early dating of the seal, Nougayrol took the *Yaqaru* of RS 16.145 to be an honorific name of a later king (p. XXXVIII), but there is no parallel for such a usage and the hypothesis may not be retained. The problem remains of the dynastic seal, which has not, to my knowledge, been the object of a new art-historical analysis since Nougayrol made his proposal. I wish to thank C. Roche for pointing out RS 16.145 to me and for discussing with me the problem of the relationship between the new king list and the Ugaritic version; much of the scenario presented here came out of that discussion.

22. Another possibility, though I consider it less likely, was proposed by Arnaud (1998: 157), viz., that the Ugaritic list was shorter than the Akkadian versions, stopping with the fourteenth-century *Niqmaddu,* who is named twice in text 24 (RS 34.126:12 and 26). Because the "king list" of RS 34.126 is an abbreviated one that includes only segments of the complete list (the "ancient *Rapaʾūma*" named as a category, *Ditānu* and four other very archaic names, and the two kings *ʿAmmiṯtamru* and *Niqmaddu*), while the list of RS 24.257 is by any hypothesis more complete and by the hypothesis presented here even more complete than RS 94.2518, there is no particular reason why one would expect this list to have ended with the fourteenth-century *Niqmaddu*.

23. His hypothesis does, however, involve the restoration of four other lines where the traces represent only a single partially preserved sign, and one of these restorations requires a correction: what I took to be the last sign in line 19' clearly shows two tips of horizontal wedges, requiring the reading {p} (or perhaps {h, ỉ}), but Arnaud's theory requires reading the sign as {r} followed by {n}, i.e., {[ỉb]⌜r!⌝[n]} (1998: 156), a proposal that I cannot consider plausible. Finally, there appears to be the trace of a sign that would belong to a seventh line at the bottom of the left column, one more than Arnaud's hypothesis requires.

24. I retain prudent language here because, though most names show what is most plausibly taken as genitive or oblique endings, one does not, viz., {níq-ma-du}, in line 19.

25. Pardee 1988a: 173 n. 25.

26. For a defense of the genitival explanation and a comparison with the Ebla texts, see Schmidt 1994: 15–20, 69–70.

27. Arnaud accepts this interpretation of the list (see the title of Arnaud 1998), but does not provide an explanation of how to get there from the syntactic structure of the text he publishes.

28. For the latter, see remarks in Pardee 2000a: 659; for the former, Nougayrol 1968, text 18.

29. Pardee 1988a: 176-78 ; 1996a: 276.

30. Note that the space in the break is not long enough to accommodate a text in which a single verse of the original text would have been devoted to each name on the following list; also against this version of the hypothesis is the presence of variation from verse to verse; note in particular the verse that ends in a verb (line 7). Because a text of several lines has disappeared, however, it is not impossible that motifs other than musical ones, such as eating and drinking, may have appeared as the rite went on (compare *CTA* 3 i).

31. The best parallels presently known for such a rite appear to come from Mesopotamia (Dijkstra 1979: 210).

32. RM is an intransitive verb and cannot, therefore, mean "raise up," i.e., "play" the instrument in question (Wyatt 1998: 400 n. 6); it may, on the other hand, be used quasi-metaphorically for "praise," i.e., "high is he" stated nonagentially for "someone places him high by praise" (so del Olmo Lete 1999a: 178). Formally *tpẖ* could mean "you (or she) shall see" (ibid.), as in the incantation text 50 (RS 22.225), but the apparent parallelism with *ṯlbm* in alternating verses belies that interpretation, especially in light of the preceding text, where *tp* and *ṯlb* appear side by side in the list of instruments played by *Rāpiʾu*.

33. Because the percussion instrument is in the singular, we might expect there to have been only one corresponding wind instrument. This renders attractive the suggestion to analyze *ṯlbm* as a dual designating a double-pipe (Koitabashi 1998: 375).

34. It is tempting to read here {⸢d⸣ mt} with Dietrich, Loretz, and Sanmartín 1995: 128 (cf. idem 1976: 119) and to translate "who has died" (so del Olmo Lete 1992a: 122; 1999a: 178; Wyatt 1998: 400)—in which case the reference would be specifically to a recently deceased king. I hesitate simply because of the state of the tablet and our resultant uncertainty about its real message.

35. In my re-edition of this text (1988a: ch. V), I attempted in my transliteration to reflect the total situation on the reverse of this tablet by not inserting line numbers for the right-hand column. Because that mode of transliteration is, however, open to misinterpretation, i.e., the assumption that the scribe has listed the names in pairs in what was in effect a single column, I now insert line numbers for the second column. (See introduction for the arguments in favor of the text having been inscribed in two separate columns.)

36. The {d} is certain (see copy in Pardee 1988a: 168), and the insistence on reading {[ảrḫl]b} here can only be based on presuppositions as to the length/structure of the list. In Wyatt's detailed exposition of the problem (Wyatt 1998: 401–2 n. 10), only the explicit epigraphic methodology is to be criticized: he refers to a "colour slide" as the basis for his own option, whereas my reading was based on autopsy and has been confirmed by another direct examination of the tablet (Schmidt 1994: 67). Methodologically speaking (see Pardee 1998a and forthcoming a), a reading based on autopsy may only be plausibly refuted by someone who has in turn reexamined the tablet.

37. Dietrich, Loretz, and Sanmartín 1976: 119 read the name as {ʿmph} (correcting the {ỉ} to {h}), and I followed this reading in my re-edition of the text, though I did mark the reading of the {ʿ} as uncertain (1988a: 166). Because no such name is known, it has been taken as a scribal error for {⌜ʿ⌝m<r>pỉ[!]}. RS 94.2518 does not, however, support that hypothesis, and it is probably necessary to read {mph}, without the {ʿ} (see below, note to RS 94.2518:9).

38. For the hypothesis that the remaining six names inscribed on RS 94.2518, or a greater number of names, would have been written on the left edge of this tablet, see introduction, points 6 and 7.

39. Each entry consists of the logogram for "god" (which corresponds, of course, to *ỉl* in the Ugaritic text), followed by the single vertical wedge used as a determinative for human males (here represented by 'm'), then by the name itself, which may be spelled either phonetically or with a logogram for one or more of the elements of the name.

40. If this name has the meaning that Arnaud proposes, viz., "Lim is the divine king" (1998: 160), or some other such meaning, such as "Lim is the god of the king," it would belong to the East Semitic naming tradition, where three-element names are common, rather than to the West Semitic tradition, where such combinations are extremely rare. The spelling *il* for "god" also indicates East Semitic, for, in Ugaritic, one would not expect the "absolute" state, i.e., with Ø case vowel, in either construction.

41. This vocalization reflects Arnaud's analysis (1998: 159) of the second element as the common West Semitic word for "artisan, maker, builder." The name would mean "the Divine Uncle is my maker."

42. This name should correspond to the traces at the top of the right-hand column of RS 24.257. Though I took the vertical wedge visible there as the lower wedge of {ỉ} and the trace to the right as that of the type of wedge that has its head to the right, it would bear checking to see whether the vertical might not be that of a {m} and the trace before that of the last wedge of {š} or the right tip of {ṯ} (if the root is ṮMR) or of {ḏ} (if the root is ḎMR)—though my copy does not favor the latter hypothesis [1988a: 168]). The name as registered in the syllabic script is previously unattested in Ugaritic; it may contain the verbal element ṮMR, "to guard," rather than ḎMR, "to protect," the basis for the name in the following line. Its meaning would be "the Divine Uncle has guarded (this child)."

43. Both the syllabic script and the corresponding entry in RS 24.257 represent this name in its developed form *ʿAmmiṯtamru*. As the seal of *ʿAmmiṯtamru* II shows, the common form represents a simplified pronunciation of the original form, *ʿAmmīyiḏtamru*, in which the sequence /īyi/ simplifies to a single /i/ and the /ḏ/ loses its voicing by assimilation to the following unvoiced /ṯ/ (see Bordreuil and Pardee 1984).

44. Arnaud addresses the problems of reading and comparing this name with the corresponding Ugaritic entry (1998: 160), which has been taken to be {ỉl}

⌜ˁ⌝mph} (RS 24.257:30'). The sign {AB} may represent either *ab* or *ap*, and, if there be any connection between the two names, the Ugaritic writing speaks in favor of *ap*, but no analysis of the name is clear. In spite of the fact that I copied the lower tip of a {ˁ}, I now consider that reading dubious because the tip of a wedge as copied does not correspond to the form of {ˁ} elsewhere in this text (see Bordreuil and Pardee forthcoming b). The {h} at the end appears certain, however, for no trace of the lower wedge of {ỉ}, which was quite large in the hand of this scribe, is visible. If the {ˁ} were not there, the comparison of the two writings would indicate a vocalization /maphu/, which is not a known name and is not easily interpreted by etymology. Arnaud considered explaining the form {ˁmph} by the root PHY, "to see" (1998: 160), but no other proper name is based on this verb. If the reading {mph} be correct, one could consider a vocalization /maphû/ based on Arnaud's identification of the root. In spite of the lack of onomastic attestations, the religious significance of the verb would be illustrated by the "contemplation rituals" examined above (texts 19–21). The name would be hypocoristic and mean something like "(the child is) a vision (of such-and-such a deity)" or "(such-and-such a deity is my) vision (i.e., the one I contemplate in worship)." Cf. *ʾēl rᵒʾīy* in Gen 16:13.

45. In another of the new texts, this name is written {am-mu-rap-pì} (Arnaud 1998: 154). As the editor points outs (ibid., p. 159), these variant spellings show that the third syllable was long and that the scribe wished to note the presence of /ʾ/. The vocalization of the name as /ˁammurāpiʾ/, "the divine uncle is a healer," is thus now finally confirmed by evidence from Ugarit itself.

XI

A Myth That Explains a Ritual Practice

THOUGH I SUSPECT that two other texts found in the "House of the Priest with Lung and Liver Models" may have had a similar function (RS 24.245 and RS 24.263), only in the text presented here is the key word preserved that may explain the origin of the text. All three of these texts belong to a fairly homogeneous lot that included not only the "para-mythological" texts presented in the two preceding chapters, but many ritual texts as well (all those translated above from the twenty-fourth campaign and several others judged too fragmentary for inclusion in this work). Two of the texts include extracts from known and unknown mythological texts (this one and RS 24.245), while RS 24.263 is a small fragment from the bottom edge of a tablet that bears a text known from the Baal cycle (*CTA* 3 E 1–3; 4 i 4–17, iv-v 45–55). The mystery of the first two texts, and perhaps of the third in its original state, is why the scribe joined on a single tablet a "new" text and a text "known" from the Baal Cycle—"known" is here placed in quotation marks to express the fact that the scribe may not have known the versions of these myths that we know, those inscribed by the famous scribe *ʾIlīmilku*, but the oral version current in his school (as is indeed indicated by the important variants when these "known" texts are compared with the *ʾIlīmilku* versions).[1] The motivation for the creation of text 57 (RS 24.293) may be found in its very last line: for all the difficulties that the interpretation of the "new" text on this tablet presents (caused both by its content and by its poor state of preservation), it does contain the word *rgbt,* which, in no small part because of the parallel term *ảbn*, "stone," must itself mean "clod of dirt," the very same word that appears in text 8 (RS 24.256:4), where a "bowl of *rgbt*" is prescribed as an offering to *Baʿlatu-Bahatīma*. I have been unable to explain the origin of the ritual practice (cf. 1988a: 162–63), though hints exist (RGB is expressed as a quality of *Baʿlu* and of *Liʾmu* in text 4 [RS 24.246:16, 24] and in RS 19.039:28' *rgbt* appears in a broken context where *Baʿlu* is mentioned[2]). In the "new" fragment of a mythological text attached here to the "known" text, the *rgbt* features as a weapon by which someone, probably *Baʿlu* because of the title *zbl*, defeats the rapacious *Môtu*. The appearance of "clod(s)" in a ritual text would be based on a practice functionally similar, therefore, to the use of the "weapons by which the weather deity defeated the sea deity" in rites at Mari.[3] The mystery remains, however, of exactly what the "clod" was that *Baʿlu* used to defeat *Môtu*.

57. RS 24.293

Text	***Translation***
Obverse	
(1) *w yʿny . bn* (2) *ỉlm . mt .*	*Môtu*, the son of *ʾIlu*, responds:
npš[ ] (3) *npš . lbỉm (4) thw .*	My "throat" is the "throat" of a lion in the waste,
w npš (5) *ảnḫr . b ym*	Yea the "throat" of the *ʿAnḫaru* in the sea;[4]
(6) *brkt . -šbšt* (7) *k rủmm .*	It attaches itself to the pool as do wild bovids,
hm (8) *ʿn . k d̲d . ảylt*	Even to the spring as does a herd of deer.
(9) *mt . hm . ks . ym*(10)*sk . nhr*	*Naharu* himself mixes my cup,
hm (11) *šbʿ . ydty . b ṣʿ*	Even my seven portions in a bowl.
(12) [ ]⸢*š*⸣*bʿ rbt*	[...]seven/satiety, many/ten thousand
(13) [ ]. *qbẓ . t̲m*⸢*t*⸣	[...] QBẒ there
Lower edge	
(14) [ ]⸢-⸣*m . ẓbm . t̲r*	[...]⸢-⸣M gazelles, a bull
Reverse	

(15) [ ]*bn . ỉlm* (16) ⸢*m*⸣[*t* .] *šmḫ* .	*Môtu*, the son of *ʾIlu*, he has effaced,
p ydd (17) *ỉl* [.] *ǵzr*	Yea the hero, the beloved of *ʾIlu*,
(18) *b ả*⸢*b*⸣*n . ʿz* .	With the stone of the Strong One,
w (19) *rgbt . zbl*	With the "clod" of the Prince.

Notes

1. For the possibility of re-dating *ʾIlīmilku*, see below, n. 10 to "Conclusions."
2. This text was edited by Virolleaud in 1965 (text 1); there has never been any doubt about the reading (cf. Dietrich, Loretz, and Sanmartín 1995: text 1.92:31), though the broken context makes interpretation difficult.
3. Durand 1993; Bordreuil and Pardee 1993a.
4. The precise identification of the sea-creature known as the *ʾanḫaru*, "snorter," is debated. See Bordreuil and Briquel-Chatonnet forthcoming.

XII

Administrative Texts

MANY OF THE NEARLY one thousand known administrative texts include data of interest for the history of cultic practice at Ugarit.[1] I have chosen for inclusion here two that are entirely devoted to the sacrificial cult and one that deals with the social institution known as the *marziḫu*—the latter is of interest because each *marziḫu*-group seems to have had a divine patron. The first is the most informative because it provides the administrative background for one aspect only—wine consumption—of a series of rites some of which are known from the prescriptive sacrificial texts. The second appears to deal with a type of tax.

Wine for Royal Sacrificial Rites

58. RS 19.015

This text is of special interest, in spite of its mundane subject matter, because it provides a precious list of cultic ceremonies explicitly identified as *dbḥ mlk*, "royal sacrificial rites." In some cases, it is possible to make a specific identification with a text translated above (e.g., *dbḥ ṣpn*, line 3, with text 12 [RS 24.643:1–12] or *ỉl bldn*, line 6, with text 23 [RS Varia 20]), sometimes only a general connection is clear (e.g., *tzǵm*, line 4, or *ỉlỉb*, line 5), while sometimes there is no connection with known ritual practice (e.g., {ḫlủ . dg}, line 12). The text deals exclusively with supplies of wine furnished by a series of towns within the kingdom of Ugarit. Because wine is mentioned relatively rarely in the prescriptive ritual texts as a specific offering to a deity, this wine was probably intended for the feast that followed or accompanied the sacrifice in the narrow sense of the word.

Text	***Translation***
Obverse	
(1) *yn . d . ykl . bd .* ⸢*r*⸣[...]	Wine which is to be consumed under the supervision of [...][2]
(2) *b . dbḥ . mlk* ———[...]	during the royal sacrificial rites (lit. "sacrifices of the king"):[3]
(3) *dbḥ ṣpn*	the sacrifices of *Ṣapunu;*
(4) ⸢*t*⸣*zǵm*	the *tzǵ*-sacrifices;
(5) ⸢*ỉ*⸣*lỉb*	the sacrifices for *ʾIluʾibī;*
(6) ⸢*ỉ*⸣*l bldn*	the sacrifices for the Gods-of-the-Land;
(7) [*p*]*dry . bt . mlk*	the sacrifices for *Pidray* (in) the royal palace;[4]
(8) [-]*lp . ỉzr*	the sacrifices for/of [-]LP ʾIZR;
(9) [-]*rz*	the sacrifices for/of [-]RZ;[5]
(10) *k . tʿrb . ʿṯtrt . šd . bt* ⸢*. m*⸣*lk*	the sacrifices for when *ʿAṯtaru-Šadî* enters the royal palace;
(11) *k . tʿrbn . ršpm . bt . mlk*	the sacrifices for when the *Rašapūma* enter the royal palace;
(12) *ḫlủ . dg*	the sacrifices for/of ḪLʾU DG;[6]
(13) *ḥdṯm*	the sacrifices of the new moons;[7]
(14) *dbḥ . bʿl - - - - . k . tdd . bʿlt . bhtm*	the sacrifices for *Baʿlu*; the sacrifices for when *Baʿlatu-Bahatīma* arises;[8]
(15) *b . ǵb . ršp . ṣbỉ*	the sacrifices in the sacrificial pit of *Rašap Ṣabaʾi;*
(16) [ ]⸢*m*⸣*m*	[ ]⸢M⸣M;[9]
Lower Edge	
(17) [ ]⸢- .⸣ *ỉln*	[ ]⸢-.⸣ ʾILN;
(18) [ ] *. ṣmd* [.] *r*[-]⸢*š*⸣*pd*⸢--⸣[...]	[ ] . ṢMD [.] R[-]⸢Š⸣PD⸢--⸣[...];
(19) [ ]⸢-⸣	[ ]⸢-⸣;
(20) [-]⸢-⸣[--]*ʿlt*	[-]⸢-⸣[--]ʿLT.[10]

Reverse

---

(21) *lb⸢n⸣m* —— [.] *ʿšr . yn*	*Labnuma*: ten *kd*-measures of wine,[11]
(22) *ḫlb . gngnt . ṯlṯ . y*[*n*]	*Ḫalbu Ganganati:* three *kd*-measures of wine,
(23) *bṣr . ʿšr . yn*	*Baṣiru:* ten *kd*-measures of wine,
(24) *nnủ* —— [.] *ảrbʿ . yn*	*Naniʾu*: four *kd*-measures of wine,
(25) *šql* —— *ṯlṯ . yn*	*Šuqalu:* three *kd*-measures of wine,
(26) *šmny* —— *. kdm . yn*	*Šamnaya*: two *kd*-measures of wine,
(27) *šmgy* —— *. kd . yn*	*Šamēgaya*: one *kd*-measure of wine,
(28) *hzp* —— *. tšʿ . yn*	*Hizpu:* nine *kd*-measures of wine,
(29) ⸢*b*⸣*ỉr* ——*. ʿšr* [.] ⸢*mṣ*⸣[*b*]⸢-⸣*m ḫsp*	*Biʾru*: ten *kd*-measures of *mṣb*-wine, [X-number] of *ḫsp*-wine,[12]
(30) ⸢*ḫ*⸣*pty* —— *. kdm* ⸢*. mṣ*⸣[*b* ...]	*Ḫupataya*: two *kd*-measures of *mṣb*-wine [...],
(31) ⸢*ả*⸣*gm* —— *. ảrbʿ* ⸢.⸣ *m*⸢*ṣ*⸣[*b* ...]	*ʾAgimu:* four *kd*-measures of *mṣb*-wine [...],
(32) *šrš* —— *. šbʿ . mṣb*[...]	*Šurašu:* seven *kd*-measures of *mṣb*-wine [...],
(33) *rqd* —— *. ṯlṯ . mṣb .* ⸢*w*⸣ . ⸢-⸣[...]	*Raqdu:* three *kd*-measures of *mṣb*-wine and [...],
(34) *ủḫnp* —— *. ṯṯ* — *. mṣb*	*ʾUḫnappu:* six *kd*-measures of *mṣb*-wine.

---

(35) *tgmr .* ⸢*y*⸣*n . mṣb . š*[...]	Total of the *mṣb*-wine: s[eventy-four *kd*-measures]
(36) *w . ḫs*[*p .*] *ṯn . kbd*[...]	and of *ḫsp*-wine: two and [X-DECADES *kd*-measures].[13]

An Oil Tax for *Baʿlu* of Aleppo

59. RS 24.292

If the word *ʿrk* is correctly identified as cognate with Hebrew *ʿerek*, which refers to an evaluation in view of a tax and to the tax established thereby, this text is an administrative note registering the payment of amounts of oil for the cult of *Baʿlu-Ḫalbi* by five individuals. Text 11 (RS 24.249:18') may refer to the formal presentation of such a tax to *Baʿlu* as part of a sacrificial ritual.

Text	***Translation***
Obverse	
(1) *ʿrk . bʿl*	ʿRK-taxes for *Baʿlu* of
(2) *ḫlb* [.] *dt . l yt*⸢*n*⸣	Aleppo that were properly paid
(3) *šm*⸢*n*⸣	in oil by
(4) *mnḫm*	*Munaḫḫimu*,
(5) *ủbyn*	*ʾUbbiyānu*,
(6) *bdn bn . t*⸢*ḫ*⸣[...]	*Badunu*, son of T⸢Ḫ⸣[...],
(7) *ʿmyn*	*ʿAmmuyānu*,
(8) *ảḫršp .* ⸢*b*⸣[...]	*ʾAḫīrašap*, s[on of X].

A Contract for a *Marziḫu* Meeting Place

60. RS [Varia 14]

In text 51 (RS 24.258), we have already seen *ʾIlu* convene his *marziḫu* and the essentially noncultic nature of the institution was described there. The fact that each *marziḫu*-group had a patron deity, however, places the phenomenon on the margin of religious ritual: though bloody sacrifices characteristic of the temple cult were not a part of the *marziḫu*-ceremony, it is not implausible to assume that wine, the principal commodity dispensed in these ceremonies, was at the meetings of the group poured out in libation to the patron deity. This is the best preserved of the Ugaritic administrative texts that reveal the economic and legal side of the institution. There are also three well-preserved Akkadian texts that deal with property holdings by such groups: in RS 15.088 and RS 15.070 (Nougayrol 1955: 88, 130) the topic is, as in this text, houses owned by *marziḫu*-groups, while RS 18.001 (Nougayrol 1956: 230) recounts the regulation of vineyard holdings between two such groups that are identified as located in different towns on the southern border of the kingdom.

Text	***Translation***
Obverse	
(1) *mrzḫ*	The drinking-club

(2) *d qny*	that *Šamumānu*
(3) *šmmn*	established
(4) *b . btw*[14]	in his house:
(5) *w št . ỉbsn*	he has set aside the storeroom
(6) *lwm . wm . ảg*	for them.[15] "Now if I should
(7) *rškm .*	evict you
(8) *b . bty*	from my house,
(9) *ksp ḫmšm*	silver in the amount of fifty shekels

Lower Edge

(10) ⸢*ỉ*⸣*sʿ*	I shall pay."[16]

Reverse

(11) *w šm.mn*[17]	Furthermore, *Šamumānu* will be
(12) *rb . ảl . ydd*	the president. No man of the drinking-club
(13) *mt . mrzḥ*	may arise
(14) *w yrgm . l*	and say to
(15) *šmmn . tn .*	*Šamumānu*: "Give back
(16) *ksp . t̠ql d ʿmnk*	the silver in the amount of one shekel that is in your keeping."[18]
(17) *t̠qlm . ysʿ*	If that should occur, the man must pay two shekels of silver.
(18) *ypḫ . ỉḫršp*	Witnesses: *ʾIḫīrašap*,
(19) *bn . ủd̠rnn*	son of ʾUD̠RNN,
(20) *w . ʿbdn*	and *ʿAbdīnu*,

Top Edge

(21) *bn . sgld*	son of *Sigilda*.

Notes

1. For a general discussion of the contribution of the administrative texts to our understanding of the Ugaritic cult, see del Olmo Lete and Sanmartín 1998.

2. The restoration {⸢r⸣[b khnm]}, "chief priest," i.e., the person who was appointed by the royal administration to be in charge of the royal functionaries of the priestly class, is plausible though not certain.

3. The function of the horizontal line extending from {mlk} to the break is unclear: because a total is indicated explicitly in lines 35–36, one may doubt that

such was the case here, though it is possible that a grand total of *kd*-measures may have been given here, whereas the total below is broken down into the two (or three) specific types of wine named in the text.

4. Because the phrase *pdry bt mlk* occurs in RS 24.300:13'–18', a text judged too fragmentary to be included here, there must be a correspondence between this designation and the rite originally laid out on that tablet. A much better preserved text in which *Pidray* is the principal divine participant is text 28 (RS 24.291). The king is the principal human participant in this rite, but the phrase *pdry bt mlk* does not occur in that text. It is plausible that this entry and RS 24.300:13'–18' are abbreviated references to the rite of which more details are provided in text 28.

5. The restoration {[p]rz] is suggested by text 26 (RS 24.255:1, 5).

6. The meaning of the first word is unknown; that of the second is uncertain ("fish" or something totally different?); and it is also uncertain whether the two terms constitute the compound name of a rite or whether each designates a separate rite.

7. Nothing in the text permits a decision as to whether *ḥdṯm* here is dual or plural, i.e., whether these supplies of wine were for two months or for a longer period.

8. This line may contain the double designation of a single rite or two individual rites. (The erased signs between the two entries clearly indicate some hesitation on the part of the scribe, but they do not constitute hard evidence for one interpretation or the other of the line as a whole.) Because none of the sacrificial ritual texts translated above furnishes details on either term, it is not possible to reach a certain conclusion on this point. The root NDD, "arise," is unattested in the offering texts.

9. The presence in line 4 of *tzǵm*, a type of sacrifice expressed in the plural, suggests restoring here the well-known sacrificial term {[šl]⌜m⌝m}, "the peace-offerings."

10. The second sign, partially preserved, could be {b}, and this entry may, therefore, have contained, like lines 3 and 14, the word *dbḥ*.

11. In the administrative texts, *kd* is the standard term designating a container and a measure of wine; as is frequent in those texts, the word itself appears only when the number of measures is "one" (line 27) or "two" (line 26). The volume of the *kd* is unknown, but may have been in the neighborhood of 22/23 liters. The towns named in lines 21–34 are all known as belonging to the kingdom of Ugarit, and they are situated both in the plain south of Ugarit and in the hilly areas to the east and to the north.

12. Though the meaning of the terms *mṣb* and *ḥsp* is unclear in both cases—usages elsewhere do not establish their meaning and no etymological explanation is totally convincing—the terms probably refer to different types of wine defined by the grape varieties or by the vinification process. According to one hypothesis, the references might be, on the one hand, to wine made from the juice that flows from the weight of the grapes themselves and from light pressing, on the other to

wine made from the heavier and more tannic juice that comes from pressing the skins, pips, and stalks.

13. Given the structure of lines 21–34, where the entries in lines 21– 28 consist of *yn* only and the word *mṣb* does not appear until the first entry where *ḫsp* appears, the formulation in line 35 could mean either "total of *yn*-wine (and) of *mṣb*-wine" (i.e., there are three types, of which the first two are joined) or "total of *mṣb*-wine," where *mṣb* serves as the qualifier only in contrast with *ḫsp* (i.e., there are two types of wine). In any case, the total in modern terms would probably have been superior to 2,000 liters (at least 96 *kd*-measures x 22.5 liters per measure = 2,160 liters).

14. The principal graphic problem in this text is the presence of {w} in two places where one would certainly expect {h} (here and in {lwm}, line 6) and in a third case where one might have expected a form with {h} or {ʾ} ({wm} for {w hm} or {w ỉm}, line 6). While the third case might reflect actual pronunciation (/wahimma/ or /waʾimma/ → /wimma/), the other two cases are not susceptible of such an explanation. One notes the absence of {h} in the text and wonders if the scribe was simply having a bad day. The expected writings are {bth}, {lhm}, and perhaps {hm} or {ỉm} (or {whm}/{wỉm}).

15. The verb ŠT is not specific enough to tell us whether the text is dealing with the creation of a new *marziḫu* society, or whether an existing group is transferring its meeting place. Though there is no proof that the so-called Temple aux Rhytons that has been excavated in the "Centre de la Ville" was the meeting place of a *marziḫu* group (Yon 1996), I find the hypothesis plausible, and, if so, it provides an excellent model for a large room in a residential part of town having been dedicated to such a special usage.

16. The importance of the contract between *Šamumānu* and the other members of the *marziḫu* may be gauged by the importance of this potential fine: fifty shekels is a large amount of money, enough to purchase a herd of animals (a sheep went for less than a shekel) or a wardrobe of fine garments.

17. Misplaced word-divider between {m} and {n}.

18. Other than the graphic problems discussed in n. 14, this line contains the only significant problem of the text: What is the shekel that a member is asking the president to "give," apparently to return? The obvious superficial answer is that each member was required to pay a one-shekel fee to help pay for the wine consumed at the gatherings of the society; this stipulation would then be that under no circumstances could a member reclaim his fee. If the generally accepted reading of RS 16.179 (Virolleaud 1957: text 88) be correct, wine intended for temples and nonsacred persons was obtainable at the rate of 14 5/6 *kd*-measures for 52 shekels or about 6.4 liters per shekel (14.83 x 22.5 = 333.7 liters ÷ 52 = 6.4). Hence, by the hypothesis just advanced, each member's shekel could have purchased roughly that amount. Unfortunately, we have no data on how often these groups met and can only gauge consumption very generally—Was the goal to drink, to get drunk, or to get really drunk?

Summary and Conclusions

IN A SIX-PART APPENDIX to my edition of the ritual texts, I outline the data derivable from these texts for each and every cultic act performed according to these texts (Appendix IA), for the deities named (Appendix IB), for the categories of cultic activity (Appendix IC), for the content of the sacrifices and offerings (Appendix ID), for times (Appendix IE), and for places (Appendix IF). These data will be briefly summarized here. (The reader is referred to these appendices for an assemblage of the raw data and to the chapter of conclusions for a more extensive presentation and discussion of these data.)

It should be clear to the reader who has perused the texts presented above that those in part II are most relevant for an inquiry based on all the types of data just mentioned, though the texts in part I, especially those that are tied directly to the sacrificial rituals (texts 1 and 3), are of inestimable importance, for they provide, however tenuously, a link between the sacrificial cult and the ideology that lay behind it. The importance of the texts in part II is that, by their quasi-administrative nature, they provide concrete data on the concrete assets that were committed to the various divinities named.[1] They are not explicitly economic in nature, but they provide the same sort of data as would economic texts in that they refer to actual cultic ceremonies: though they are prescriptive rather than descriptive, there is no reason to doubt that they were carried out as described, that the sacrifices and offerings named were in fact presented as prescribed.[2] I entertain no illusions about the value of the figures provided below in the section of these conclusions devoted specifically to the sacrificial rituals: a corpus so small and made up of tablets that have virtually all suffered damage in various degrees cannot by its very nature provide statistically reliable data. It does nevertheless appear legitimate to state here what the data are in their present state and to draw some general conclusions based on these data. The reader and future researchers must simply be aware that the discovery of a single tablet could change the statistical structure that emerges from the present data. This fact is perhaps best illustrated by text 23 [RS Varia 20]): if this text from clandestine digging at the site had not been made available for study (Bordreuil and Pardee 1993b) by its proprietor, the hierarchy of deities established by number of offerings received by each would have been significantly different. The same thing could happen again on the same scale; the discovery of a major new archive of religious texts could occasion even more significant changes.

The Gods and the Offerings Presented to Them

In the full range of texts of the category presented here in parts I–VIII, one encounters 234 different deities, 178 of which are specifically indicated in the sacrificial rituals as recipients of offerings. A total of 2,509 offerings, of all types, are ascribed to these divinities.[3] Because of the damaged state of the texts, the beneficiary of a given offering is frequently not known; the total number of offerings mentioned is 3,052, which may be reduced to 2,873 if 179 offerings mentioned in the texts as devoted to two or more divinities are counted only once. Forty-nine of the 178 deities named as offering recipients receive ten or more sacrifices; the total of the sacrifices offered to these divinities is 2,192, which represent 87 percent of the offerings made to divinites of which the name is known. Here is the list of those divinities:[4]

Alphabetical Order[5]		***Numerical Order***	
ˀib	14* betrothal gifts	*ˁṯtrt šd*	377 (+ *n* ?) offerings
ˀiy	10 offerings	*bˁl ṣpn*	266 (+ *n*) offerings
ˀil	60 offerings	*ˀilhm*	163* offerings
ˀilm (kbkbm)	35 offerings	*bˁlm*	142* offerings
ˀil tˁḏr bˁl	27 offerings	*ˀilˀib*	126 (+ *n*) offerings
ˀilˀib	126 (+ *n*) offerings	*ṣpn*	92 (+ *n*) offerings
ˀilh	10 offerings	*bˁl ˀugrt*	71 (+ *n*) offerings
ˀilhm	163* offerings	*ˀil*	60 offerings
ˀilt mgdl	24 offerings	*bˁl*	50* (+ *n*) offerings

ảmšrt	22 offerings
ỉn ảtn	10 offerings
ỉn ṯln	12* offerings
ỉnš ỉlm	41 (+ *n*) offerings
ảrṣy	19 (+ *n* ?) offerings
ảṯrt	18* (+ *n*) offerings
bʿl	50* (+ *n*) offerings
bʿl-m	32 offerings
bʿl ủgrt	71 (+ *n*) offerings
bʿl ṣpn	266 (+ *n*) offerings
bʿlm	142* offerings
bʿlt b(h)tm	26 offerings
gṯrm	11 offerings
ḫyr	45 offerings
dgn	41 (+ *n* ?) offerings
dr ỉl w pḫr bʿl	25 offerings
ym	28 offerings
yrḫ	46* (+ *n* ?) offerings
kzǵ/kḏǵ	11 offerings
kmrb/kmrw	10 offerings
kṯr	40 offerings
šlm	10 offerings
špš	12* offerings
nbdg	12 offerings
nkl	15 offerings
ʿnt	36 offerings
ʿnt ḫbly	24 offerings
ʿnt ṣpn	11 offerings
ʿṯtrt	22 offerings
ʿṯtrt ḫr	11 (+ *n* ?) offerings
ʿṯtrt šd	377 (+ *n* ?) offerings
pdry	10 offerings
prgl ṣqrn	15 offerings
ṣpn	92 (+ *n*) offerings
ršp	18 offerings
ršp ḥgb	10 offerings
ršp [...]	23 offerings
ṯkmn w šnm	14* offerings
ǵlmt	34 offerings
ṯṯb	11 (?) offerings

yrḫ	46* (+ *n* ?) offerings
ḫyr	45 offerings
ỉnš ỉlm	41 (+ *n*) offerings
dgn	41 (+ *n* ?) offerings
kṯr	40 offerings
ʿnt	36 offerings
ỉlm (kbkbm)	35 offerings
ǵlmt	34 offerings
bʿl-m	32 offerings
ym	28 offerings
ỉl tʿḏr bʿl	27 offerings
bʿlt b(h)tm	26 offerings
dr ỉl w pḫr bʿl	25 offerings
ỉlt mgdl	24 offerings
ʿnt ḫbly	24 offerings
ršp [...]	23 offerings
ảmšrt	22 offerings
ʿṯtrt	22 offerings
ảrṣy	19 (+ *n* ?) offerings
ảṯrt	18* (+ *n*) offerings
ršp	18 offerings
nkl	15 offerings
prgl ṣqrn	15 offerings
ỉb	14* betrothal gifts
ṯkmn w šnm	14* offerings
špš	12* offerings
nbdg	12 offerings
ỉn ṯln	12* offerings
gṯrm	11 offerings
kzǵ/kḏǵ	11 offerings
ʿnt ṣpn	11 offerings
ʿṯtrt ḫr	11 (+ *n* ?) offerings
ṯṯb	11 (?) offerings
ỉy	10 offerings
ỉlh	10 offerings
ỉn ảtn	10 offerings
kmrb/kmrw	10 offerings
šlm	10 offerings
pdry	10 offerings
ršp ḥgb	10 offerings

Perhaps the most interesting feature of this list is the importance of the manifestations of *Baʿlu*: *Baʿlu Ṣapunu* is effectively at the head of the list (see n. 3 to this section) and several more manifestations of the deity appear below, with a total of some 561 offerings. Though *ʾIlu* is high on the list, his sixty offerings pale in comparison. The facts (1) that *ʾIlu* is mentioned in a fairly large number of texts (some fifteen offering texts as well as the deity lists) and (2) that he is usually ascribed a single offering may be interpreted as meaning that his nominal prestige was high, though this translated into a relatively small economic investment. The very fact of the prestige is enough, however, to discount attempts to make of him a *deus otiosus* in Ugaritic religion.

Offerings and Offering Types

Ninety-two different objects are mentioned as offerings, many only once and some unidentifiable. Here is a list of objects of which ten or more units are offered:

Alphabetical Order[5]		***Numerical Order***	
ảlp, "male bovid"	267*	*š*, "male ovid"	680* (+ *n*)
ảp, "snout"	15	*šʿrt*, "wool"	500 (units)
gdlt, "female bovid"	192 (+ *n*)	*ảlp*, "male bovid"	267*
ḫrṣ, "gold"	50* (shekels)	*dqt*, "female ovid"	198* (+ *n*)
dqt, "female ovid"	198* (+ *n*)	*gdlt*, "female bovid"	192 (+ *n*)
dṯt, "*dṯt*-grain"	105* (measures)	*ṣỉn*, "ovicaprid"	114
yn, "wine"	38 (+ *n*) (measures)	*dṯt*, "*dṯt*-grain"	105* (measures)
kbd, "liver"	16	*ksm/ks̀m*, "emmer-wheat"	105* (measures)
ksm/ks̀m, "emmer-wheat"	105* (measures)	*ʿṣr*, "bird"	85 (+ *n*)
ksp, "silver" (cf. *nskt ksp*)	20 (shekels)	*lb*, "heart"	72*
š, "male ovid"	680* (+ *n*)	*rkb rtn*, '?'	53
šʿrt, "wool"	500 (units)	*ḫrṣ*, "gold"	50* (shekels)
lb, "heart"	72*	*yn*, "wine"	38 (+ *n*) (measures)
mtnt, "kidney, loin"	10 (+ *n* ?)	*npš*, "neck"	28

npš, "neck"	28	*ksp*, "silver" (cf. *nskt ksp*)	20 (shekels)
ʿṣr, "bird"	85 (+ *n*)	*kbd*, "liver"	16
ṣỉn, "ovicaprid"	114	*ảp*, "snout"	15
rkb rtn, '?'	53	*ṯʾt*, "female ovid"	15*
ṯʾt, "female ovid"	15*	*mtnt*, "kidney, loin"	10 (+ *n* ?)

The disparities are obvious: body parts alongside whole animals, different units and measures. Nevertheless the preponderance of animal offerings, virtually all of which were in fact bloody sacrifices, is obvious, and the same preponderance emerges from a calculation based on all available data: ovids/caprids make up 33% of the total, bovids 15%, birds 3%, and body parts mentioned independently of a given animal sacrifice another 3%, for a total of 54%. The other categories are: garments/tissues (19%), vegetal products (6%), precious metals (2%), various implements (less than 1%), donkeys (less than 1%), with the balance made up of unidentifiable items or items of which the name is destroyed in the text. The low percentage of precious metals does not change significantly if one calculates relative market value: the metals offered were worth only about 4% of what the animals were worth (about two hundred shekels of silver versus some five thousand shekels). Assertions that one sometimes encounters to the effect that Ugaritians gave large amounts of silver and gold to their gods are thus shown by the texts to be unfounded.

Though well over twenty different terms appear in these texts describing cultic acts, there were four principal types, judging by the numbers of offerings recorded in the texts (for further coverage, see below): the *šalamūma*, the "peace-offering"; the *šurpu*, which probably designates the holocaust or burnt-offering (Hebrew *ʿōlāʰ*); the *šanūpatu*, which corresponds etymologically to Hebrew *tᵊnūpāʰ* and probably functioned similarly, as a "presentation-offering," and the *ṯaʿû*, of which the precise function is uncertain but which may have been an expiation sacrifice. In addition, the general term DBḤ, which etymologically denotes the slaying of a sacrificial victim, seems occasionally to have been used as a category of sacrifice; that is, it appears in sequential contrast to one of the above terms. The *šalamūma* and the *šurpu* were the most frequent, accounting for nearly three-quarters of all offerings explicitly categorized in the texts themselves. Gauging the relative importance of these two types according to numbers and contents of offerings shows that the peace-offering involved approximately five times more animals than the holocaust, and this in spite of the fact that both types were offered to about the same number of divinities. On the other hand, female animals, which were in general offered less frequently than males (the ratio is 1 : 2.6), were more commonly offered as holocaust offerings than as peace-offerings. One may infer that the female, more valuable for reproduction, was offered less often but that when such an offering was made, the tendency was to send the entirety up to the deity as smoke. Though liquid offerings, such as oil and wine, are mentioned fairly frequently, there is only one reasonably clear reference to a libation offering, that of oil (text 13 [RS 24.266:25']). It is thus difficult to say how common was the offering of such liquids; functionally, the libation would have corresponded to the *šurpu* burnt offering, that is, one that was consumed by the deity alone.

Though none of the texts at our disposal describes in any specific way the carrying out of any given rite, the rather high percentage of offerings that consisted of garments and textiles leads to the question of to what extent the Ugaritic cult was one of "care and feeding" the divinities in question. This mode of cultic practice, in which a daily theater was acted out that consisted of feeding and clothing the divine effigies on the model of human behavior, is best known from Egyptian religion and is thought to be characteristic of the Mesopotamian and Anatolian systems as well (Oppenheim 1964: 192–98; McCarthy 1969). The fact that so many textile products were presented to the deities in the Ugaritic cult would seem to indicate either that the cult statues were clothed and that these garments were changed fairly often or that the clothing of their priestly representatives was provided by this cultic fiction. There can be little doubt that the animal sacrifices and the vegetal offerings were considered at some level to provide the gods with food, for such a view is characteristic of many ancient sacrificial systems (for example, in addition to Egypt, Mesopotamia, and Anatolia just cited, ancient Greece: see Detienne and Vernant 1979); the question that remains for the Ugaritic cult is to what extent the divine meal was acted out, the best-known models at the two extremes being the Egyptian, on the one hand (regular presentations of complete meals), and that represented in the final text of the Hebrew Bible, on the other, where most such details have been partially demythologized.

Cultic Acts

Though bloody sacrifice is the essential act of the Ugaritic cult, a series of nonsacrificial acts is prescribed in these texts, the most obvious of which is perhaps the presentation of offerings of a nonbloody nature (see above for these). Some of the cultic acts are sacrificial or offertory in nature: the two clearest cases are the *šurpu* and the *šalamūma*, though fully half of the attested terms probably express or presuppose a bloody sacrifice. One very specific term, *šʿly*, expresses the presentation to a divinity of an offering intended to become a permanent possession of the divinity: attested are two inscriptions on memorial stelae and another on a votive offering consisting of a lion-headed vase (sections IV and V). Other terms designate major events of a *sui generis* nature of which sacrifice is only a part: the clearest and best-attested categories are the "entry" rites, the "contemplation rites," and the cultic processions. Yet others may be described as adjuncts to a sacrificial rite, for example, prayer (the two extant examples have been translated in section VII) and song (no text of a specifically cultic song is presently attested in Ugaritic). Communal acts of which sacrifice was not a part, of which the gathering of a *marziḫu* is the clearest example, are thus ritual in nature (i.e., a ceremonial system, religious or otherwise) though not cultic (specifically religious rites)—the offering of libations at the *marziḫu*, which is plausible though not proven, does not transform this meeting into a cultic act in the narrow sense of the term any more than does an "invocation" pronounced before an otherwise secular event in modern society.

Times and Places

The ritual calendar was indubitably lunar, for all temporal indications are to the day of the lunar month or to parts thereof. Twenty-one days of the month are mentioned in the sacrificial ritual texts (presently unattested are the 2nd, the 4th and 5th, the 12th, the 23rd and 24th, the 27th, the 29th and the 30th[6]). There are good reasons to believe that the month was divided according to the quarters of the moon. There are some indications that each "week," that is, the quarter-division of the lunar month, had its series of rites.[7] Though the texts presently available indicate that sacrifices were offered at every new moon, by far the most important of the "weekly" rites in terms of assets expended was that of the full moon.[8] One may infer from certain nonexplicit indications that the solstices and equinoxes had their rituals, but no other aspect of the solar year has left a trace in the Ugaritic ritual texts. Finally, as we have seen, not all the sacrificial rites presently attested are presented in a chronological framework; among those for which no date is indicated are the important rites of "entry" of a deity into the royal palace and the rites of "contemplation" of a deity by the king.

The only term for "temple" used in these texts was *bêtu*, "house," plus the name of the divinity. Six such names are attested, of which the two most important are *bêtu ʾili*, "the house of *ʾIlu*," and *bêtu baʿli ʾugarit*, "the house of *Baʿlu* of Ugarit." The latter is plausibly identified with the Temple of Baal excavated at Ras Shamra during the early years of excavation, whereas the identification of the former is disputed. The find of stelae devoted to *Dagan* in proximity to this other temple earned it the name of Temple of *Dagan*, but a "house of *Dagan*" is never named in the texts, and some have identified this temple as the *bêtu-ʾili*, "the house of *ʾIlu*/the god." The two major temples excavated at Ras Shamra have recently been reconstructed as temple towers (Yon 1994: 424; idem 1997: 116–25). Most sacrifices would have taken place in the courtyard located at the entrance to the temple, but some smaller ones may have been offered on the flat roof of the tower. No "house of *Baʿlu*" or "houses" for the other manifestations of *Baʿlu* are mentioned in the texts. But we have seen that these *Baʿlu* deities all received sacrifices; did that occur always in the "house of *Baʿlu* of Ugarit," or did each have his "own house"? The other temples are those of more obscure deities, such as *ʾilatu* and *baʿlatu ba(ha)tīma rāmīma*, "the lady of the high houses"; one such temple is clearly within the royal palace, the *bêtu ʾilīma kabkabīma*, "the house of the star-gods" (see text 18 [RS 1.005]) and another may well have been, the *bêtu ʾili bêti*, "the house of the god of the house," who was in all probability the tutelary deity of the royal household. In addition to these "houses," four terms are used that refer to what one might call "chapels," constructions smaller than a "house" that could be either located within larger temples or small independent sanctuaries. These are (1) the ḪMN, a cultic term that has been much studied in recent years, (2) the ʿD, a sort of "inner room," (3) the *ʿaliyyu*, an "upper (room)," and (4) the *qudšu*, a term that corresponds semantically to "sanctuary" (QDŠ, "holy," is the rough equivalent of Latin *sanctus*, from which the word "sanctuary" is derived), used once for an inner portion of one of the temples, the *bêtu ʾili bêti*, "the house of the god of the house." There is also a *qudšu ʾili*, "sanctuary of *ʾIlu*," but nothing in the text permits its localization. The "altar" is not named frequently, only six times in three texts, two of which are quasi-duplicates. The enigmatic *ǵabbu*, perhaps a sort of sacrificial pit, is named four times in two texts. Finally, the *bêtu malki*, probably the royal palace, not the temple of the deity *Milku*, appears fairly frequently without the explicit mention of the temple or chapel in which the cultic event occurred. Cultic events are said to have taken place at the *gabbu* (with /g/, not /ǵ/) of the palace, some sort of a raised structure of which the ideology is uncertain, in the "garden," at the "threshing floor," and at an "altar" not explicitly linked with a given temple or chapel.

The Scientific Texts

In spite of being linked to the sacrificial cult by the use of the basic verb DBḤ, the practical scientific texts are formally and functionally different from those of the prescriptive and descriptive sacrificial ritual texts: formally in that they describe individual acts of sacrifice, rather than corporate ones, and in that they do not correspond to any of the standard types of sacrifices (*šalamūma*, *šurpu* . . .); functionally in that, instead of constituting an institutionalized context for the daily care and feeding of the divinities, they were perceived as devices for determining the will of the gods in precise circumstances. The divinatory manuals represent, at least in theory, compendia of individual cases which provided the diviner with a body of information on which to base his reading of a given phenomenon.

The data on divinatory practice at Ugarit have largely to do with extispicy, more specifically with hepatoscopy, the examination of the liver of an animal that has been sacrificed to make its internal organs available for examination. This was a well-developed "science" in Mesopotamia, where manuals and model livers prepared for instructional purposes are known.

The manuals from Ugarit reveal a broader spectrum of divinatory practice, ranging from malformed human and animal births to dreams. Judging from the few remains that have come down to us, it is not unlikely that the Ugaritic scribes were acquainted with the full range of Mesopotamian divinatory science in the stage it had reached in the late second millennium B.C.E., though that question must remain open as must the much more difficult one of knowing whether the full range of Mesopotamian divinatory practice had its devotees at Ugarit.

Because of the identity of general form and function between the Ugaritic and Mesopotamian texts, and because of the demonstrated antiquity of several of the sub-genres in Mesopotamia, it has generally been assumed, by myself and by others who have worked on these texts, that the Ugaritic versions are translations of unattested Akkadian originals. As I have worked through all these texts, however, I have been struck not only by the absence of specific correspondences in the attested Akkadian tradition but also by the general purity of the Ugaritic language: there are very few Akkadian loanwords and no obvious calques on Akkadian words, expressions, or syntactic structures. It appears necessary to conclude that the Ugaritic divinatory manuals reflect an old West Semitic tradition; how old can only be a matter of speculation at this point. The absence of Mesopotamian examples that show the "general-overview" format of the Ugaritic texts, in any case, precludes fixing the West Semitic borrowing to a known point in the Mesopotamian stream of tradition. And the general absence in the present archaeological picture of tablets in any language that predate the Late Bronze Age at Ugarit means that there are no local textual data available by which to solve the local problem. The primary feature of the Ugaritic texts that can be cited as a possible indication of date by comparison with the Mesopotamian tradition is the relative simplicity and brevity of the apodoses; the later the text in the Mesopotamian tradition, the more likely it is that the apodoses will be long and complicated. By this criterion, the Ugaritic tradition should date to the Old Babylonian or perhaps the Kassite period.

While recognizing the impossibility of dating the Ugaritic tradition, I would be remiss if I did not state that the characteristics of the scientific texts that I have cited fit well into the perception growing in some minds that the early West Semitic contributions to culture have been eclipsed by the preponderance of textual data pouring out of Mesopotamia. Without saying or even wishing to hint that the Amorites invented science, it would not be at all improper to hypothesize that their role in the spread of divinatory practice and compendia of knowledge may have been greater than hitherto suspected.

Because of these multiple uncertainties regarding the age, the origin, and the place in local thought of these "scientific" texts, it is as yet difficult to evaluate their place in the intellectual and cultural world of Syria-Palestine. In any case, because of the clear connections with the thought-world of Mesopotamia and the present tenuous state of the evidence for the spread of this "science" into Palestine, it is difficult to determine to what extent it is valid to cite them as background to the Bible.

Incantations

Virtually unknown a few years ago, the Ugaritic incantatory tradition is now attested by the three texts translated above. These have provided us with sufficient data to begin saying something about the formal and thematic features of this genre. The fact that all three are in a rather loose form of poetry makes it likely that this formal characteristic was common in incantations (compare the similar cases of the first-millennium examples in the Phoenician language from Arslan Tash [Pardee 1998c]). On the other hand, we can expect the thematic palette to have been as broad as any other in the ancient world; should new examples be discovered, therefore, we may expect to find there techniques for warding off means of attack by sorcery different from those that are presently attested.

The Ritual Texts in Mythological Form

In this collection of texts revelatory of religious practice in Ugarit, I have included most of the presently known texts that appear to contain a specific link between mythological and practical elements.[9] I have classified these as historiolae and as more narrowly cultic. Two of the former, texts 53 and 54 (RS 24.244 and RS 24.251), show by their preoccupation with venomous reptiles a direct link with the incantation text 48 (RS 92.2014); the first also contains a dialogue which may reveal that the text may have functioned as a sort of libretto for a sort of cultic theater. Another (text 51 [RS 24.258]) is on the fringe of cultic practice in that it contains a recipe for alcoholic collapse after imbibing too freely in the *marziḫu*, while the last (text 52 [RS 24.272]), if read correctly, makes a direct link between certain cultic practices and the recovery from illness of a child. One of the more narrowly mythological texts (RS 24.293, text 57) appears to provide the literary background for a specific cultic phenomenon, the offering of a bowl containing clods of dirt, while the two others (texts 55 and 56 [RS 24.252 and RS 24.257) portray royal ancestors and their patrons participating in rites that involve music and the drinking of wine. Because of certain links with the one known funerary ritual (text 24 [RS 34.126]), it appears plausible that these latter represent some of the rites surrounding the burial of a Ugaritic king; if so, they may represent either a long tradition that was repeated in the case of every royal decease or the specific form of a broader tradition elaborated for a particular set of funerary rites. In either case, it is tempting to link these texts with the passing of *Niqmaddu* III and the assumption of the throne by his successor, *ʿAmmurāpiʾ*.

These poetic texts, including text 24 (RS 34.126), which was translated with the prescriptive sacrificial ritual texts because of its explicitly sacrificial component, may be said to constitute literary productions fully as remarkable as the great mythological texts discovered during the first years of the exploration of Ras Shamra. Their explicit or implicit link with the cult provides further proof (after *CTA* 23, discovered in 1930) not only that the cult did not consist only of sacrifice, prayer, and song, but that there was apparently such a thing as cultic theater—though the extent and the modalities of this acting out of mythological themes are presently unknown. What it is possible to say with regard to the cultic texts is that they provide no evidence for the theatrical reenactment of the major mythological texts as a regular part of the royal cult.[10] Though such may have occurred on a regular or irregular basis, this form of cultic theater has left no traces in the ritual texts. Indeed all evidence for such practices comes from the mythological (*CTA* 23) or paramythological texts (RS 24.244, text 53) themselves. Either such cultic theater was separate from the regular sacrificial cult, therefore, or else the writers of the ritual texts felt no need to indicate at what point in a series of rituals the cultic enactment was to take place.

Unanswered Questions

Without wishing to appear in the least ungrateful for the wealth of detail provided by these texts on cult and ritual in Late Bronze Ugarit, the only significant source of such data in a West Semitic language predating the Hebrew Bible, I must nevertheless observe that the types of data provided are very limited in number and that they provide little or no information regarding many aspects of Ugaritic religious practice. Four areas may be mentioned as particularly important: (1) liturgy (What was the precise form of each cultic act, for example, of the care and feeding of the divinities alluded to above?); (2) economy (Who really received what from the offerings?); (3) politics/society (virtually all these rites proceed from and reflect the royal cult and ideology—What was the form of the nonroyal cult? What was the real role of the priests in the royal cult and in the nonroyal cult?); (4) theology (What meaning did the Ugaritians themselves, whether king, priest, or commoner, ascribe to the rites in which they participated or which they witnessed?). Though one may extrapolate from other cultures to reach conclusions regarding these aspects of the Ugaritic cult (e.g., Lipiński 1987: 23–27), the great number of unknowns make it impossible to move beyond generalities. For example, though it may indeed be a general rule that the priest lives from the altar (Lipiński 1987: 23 ; idem 1988: 138–42), the Ugaritic data allow us to assert no more than that it is plausible that such was also the case at Ugarit; there are, in any case, no explicit data on how the various offerings were divided among the various participants in any given rite.

Ugarit and the Bible

The present work is intended only as one source among others for an up-dated "Ugarit and the Bible," not as that work nor even as a finished chapter of such a work. In this final set of conclusions, therefore, I will only outline some of the similarities and differences that have struck me as I completed the edition of the texts and as I have prepared this very different English version.

Similarities

• The most striking set of similarities is provided by those terms that are either etymologically related to corresponding Hebrew terms (DBḤ, "sacrifice" [noun and verb with the derived noun *madbiḫu*, "altar"]; *šalamūma*, "peace-offering"; *šanūpatu*, "presentation-offering") or that reflect similar usage (*šurpu*, "burnt-offering," comparable to the Hebrew *ʿōlāʰ*), along with the general identity of the sacrificial victims (bovids, ovid/caprids, birds). Two principal caveats are, however, necessary: (1) identity or similarity of vocabulary may not be taken as indications that practice and ideology were the same; (2) several terms in both corpora have no certain correspondence in the other (some of these are indicated below at "differences").

• The Hebrew Bible condemns child sacrifice and no certain reference thereto appears in the Ugaritic texts (the reference to a "firstborn" sacrifice in text 13 [RS 24.266:31'] does not necessarily refer to a human firstborn).

• Neither the dog nor the pig is sacrificed in either society (because the puppy figured in certain Hittite sacrificial rites, such a sacrifice may show up at Ugarit, but it is not yet attested).

• Another joint absence is reference to the sacrifice of wild animals.

• Both corpora make reference to perfumed oil, but the usages thereof may have been different: the biblical references are explicitly with regard to oil intended to be burnt in lamps, whereas the destination is not stated in the Ugaritic texts, leaving open the question of whether the oil may have been used primarily for anointing.

• Though stated explicitly only for the king in the Ugaritic texts, the requirements for bodily purity are similar in the two corpora.

• The basic architectural vocabulary is similar (*bt* + DN, "temple of DN"; *qdš*, "sanctuary") but there are also many differences (see below).

• The fertility cult so dear to the heart of older generations of Hebrew and Ugaritic scholars shows up clearly in neither corpus; the sexual depravity that some have claimed to be characteristic of the Canaanite cult in general[11] has left no trace in any of the Ugaritic texts translated above (unless one considers the possibility of a *hieros gamos* in text 28 [RS 24.291] to constitute such a trace).

• At Ugarit, as in Israel, the *marziḫu* was not a primarily cultic institution, as is proven for Israel by the fact that Amos and Jeremiah reprove certain forms of behavior associated with the *marzēᵃḥ*, rather than condemning it as a place of false worship.[12] The extrabiblical evidence shows that it was a religious institution only in the sense that each *marziḫu*-group appears to have had a patron deity to whom libations may have been made. In both societies, it was a social institution of which the function was to bring a limited number of males together as a drinking society. There is no evidence from either corpus that the society was primarily mortuary in nature or that one of its primary functions was to provide its members with sexual activity. Neither body of texts provides evidence in favor of the hypothesis that either the *marziḫu* or any of the cultic institutions mentioned in them was the meeting place of *eros kai thanatos*.

• Neither in the Bible nor in the Ugaritic texts does one find explicit references to a new year festival similar to the Babylonian *akītu* festival, with its ritual dethronement and reenthronement of the king. In both cultures, the festival appears to have been primarily a harvest festival featuring a ritual use of "booths" representing the annual erection of temporary dwellings in the fields during the harvest season. According to the Ugaritic version, these booths were set up on the roof of a temple or palace and were ritually inhabited by the gods.

• Just as the Ugaritic ritual texts show virtually no influence from the Akkadian language and relatively little from Mesopotamian religion (the adoption of various Mesopotamian deities into the West Semitic pantheon is the clearest evidence of such influence), most Mesopotamian influences on Israelite cultic practice appear to be late, in fact to reflect Neo-Assyrian hegemony in the region.[13] The Ugaritic texts show more influence from Mesopotamian "science," though, as we have seen, much of this influence may be centuries older than the Late Bronze texts at our disposal; the Mesopotamian literary and scribal traditions adopted by the scribal class at Ugarit in their original syllabic form appear, on the other hand, to reflect a more direct influence.[14] The occasional find in Palestine of a Mesopotamian "scientific" or literary text indicates that we may only need await the discovery of a more extensive archive to witness a situation more comparable in these respects to the one at Ugarit.

Differences

- Perhaps the most basic literary difference is to be found in the different genres represented in the two corpora. Most of the Ugaritic ritual texts consist of two principal types: the prescriptive rituals in prose and the poetic texts that reflect various phenomena that stand outside of but in organic relationship with the regular sacrificial cult. Less well attested but of no less importance are the deity lists, the memorial and *ex voto* inscriptions, and the divinatory texts. Despite certain superficial similarities, the biblical texts are quite different: the cultic texts reflect a reasoned literary presentation of what are described as the historical situations in which the Israelite cult was prescribed by God to Moses and in that literary context many details as well as certain theological motivations were provided—both categories of information are almost entirely lacking in the Ugaritic texts. The cultic psalms show certain formal similarities to some of the Ugaritic poetic texts, but the themes, in particular the mythological and narrative elements of the historiolae, are vastly different. With the exception of the traditions regarding the Urim and Thummim, explicit divinatory material has virtually been eradicated from the Hebrew Bible, as have incantations—which does not, of course, preclude the use of the Ugaritic texts to discover traces of or allusions to such practices in the Hebrew Bible, whether their earlier verbal form was entirely oral or in some cases perhaps inscribed as at Ugarit.

- Surely the most obvious difference is the severe pantheon reduction visible in the Hebrew Bible, where, instead of over two hundred theonyms, some seven divine names are permissibly used and these seven were seen, at least in the final redaction of the text, as alternate forms and epithets rather than as distinct divinities.[15] Though the date of inception of Hebrew monotheism is uncertain, the fact remains that there are only traces of polytheism visible in the Hebrew Bible in contrast with the full-blown Ugaritic polytheism,[16] and such traces are even fewer in the biblical texts that refer to cultic practice than in the poetic material.

• In spite of the current uncertainty in biblical circles regarding the origins of Israelite religion, it appears fairly clear that its archaic features and some of its most important constituent features reflect southern Canaanite religion, including whatever may have been going on in the Edomite area when Israel was coming together, while the corresponding features of Ugaritic religion reflect older "Amorite" connections. Such a statement is not meant to deny the overlap between the Ugaritic and biblical religions (not to mention Phoenician religion) in both cultic practice and mythological traditions; but the fairly large number of links, both in pantheon and in cultic practice, between Ugarit and the Amorite civilizations of the early second millennium, best known from the Mari texts, and the absence of many of these links in Israelite religion as visible in the Hebrew Bible (donkey sacrifice, the *pagrû* rite, the "entry" rite)[17] must be judged significant. If the early West Semitic civilization constituted a continuum of which the Canaanites were the southern extremity and the eastern Amorites the northeastern extremity, the relative geographical positions of Israel and Ugarit may be said to be reflected in their religions: we would not expect all aspects of cultures so geographically widespread to be identical, no matter how similar their ethnolinguistic origins may have been.

• Alongside the many similarities of a general and specific nature between the Ugaritic ritual texts and the Hebrew Bible and to a lesser extent with the other Northwest Semitic cultures, the important difference constituted by the major Hurrian component in the Ugaritic cult must be stressed. The presence of Hurrian texts, of Hurrian-Ugaritic bilingual texts (translated above as texts 25–28), and of Hurrian terms in the Ugaritic cultic vocabulary makes this ethnosocial component second only to the West Semitic one in importance. Judging from the absence of such terms in the first-millennium Northwest Semitic texts, it appears unlikely that the Hurrian influence reached Canaan in the second millennium with anything like the importance it obviously had at Ugarit—it is difficult to envisage that the relics of such an influence would have been eradicated so thoroughly from both language and practice.

• As we saw above, certain of the principal sacrificial terms are identical or similar in the two corpora of texts, while others are different, principally the *ṯaʿû*-sacrifice, the mortuary-sacrifice designated by the word *pagrû*, the cultic feast referred to by the root ʿŠR, and certain rites that have no explicit parallel in the biblical texts, such as the "contemplation" and "entry" rites. In addition to these Semitic terms must be mentioned the Hurrian terms *ủṯḫlm* and *tzǵ*. Viewed from the biblical perspective, the important function there of the sacrificial system as serving to cleanse (ṬHR) or to expiate (KPR) sin (ḤTʾ) and iniquity (ʿWN) is largely missing from the Ugaritic record. Of the roots mentioned, only one occurs in these texts, viz., ḤTʾ in text 22 (RS 1.002)—cf. also the mention of ḤTʾ // RŠʿ in the incantation text 49 (RIH 78/20). These occurrences show, however, that the concept of ridding from sin was not alien to the cult, nor was the concept of sin//evil as being at the origin of bodily suffering. But either because of the genre differences mentioned above or because of differences of ideology, or both, the preoccupation with sin and cleansing therefrom characteristic of the Hebrew texts is not visible in Ugaritic.

• The blood and the fat of sacrificial victims, of great importance in the sacrificial system of the Hebrew texts, are entirely absent from the Ugaritic texts.[18] This may reflect the different genres, that is, the Ugaritic texts prescribe the principal features of certain rites of which the details would have been known to the practitioners, whereas the literary perspective of the biblical texts requires that many details be stated explicitly. It may be assumed from the use of the verb DBḤ in Ugaritic that the shedding of sacrificial blood had ideological importance and must, therefore, have been regulated. But, because of the silence of the Ugaritic texts on these details, we have no way of determining the concrete facts and *a fortiori* the ideology behind them. Based on other points of contact with Palestinian and Arabian religious beliefs, one may speculate that the importance of blood in Ugaritic ritual practice was somewhere between the Mesopotamian and Israelite views, viz., that the sacrificial system was essentially one of "care and feeding" of the gods, but the proper disposal of the blood may also have had a role.

• Certain organs specifically mentioned as sacrifices in the Ugaritic texts, in particular the "heart" (*libbu*), the "kidneys/loins" (*matunatāma*), the "snout" (*ʾappu*), and the "throat" (*napšu*) are not mentioned or do not have the same precise meaning in the Hebrew Bible.

• The donkey-sacrifice (text 22 [RS 1.002]) is absent from the Bible, though, if the flesh of the animal was not eaten, there is no obvious ideological reason why it could not have been practiced (in general, however, the biblical cult allowed only the sacrifice of animals that were also admissible as food, and not even all of those: game, for example, was not admitted at the divine table).

• Another absence from the Ugaritic texts as compared with the Hebrew is a specific mention of incense, though at least some of the perfumed oil mentioned above may have been used in lamps and functioned to provide both light and sweet-smelling smoke. As with the blood and the fat, the absence of specific mention may reflect only the differences of genre between the two corpora (i.e., the Ugaritic priests would have known what was to be offered as incense and when it was to be offered); again, however, the absence of details on this topic from the Ugaritic texts means that the question must be left open.

• It seems highly likely that much of the wine mentioned in text 58 (RS 19.015) was actually consumed by the participants in the various sacrificial feasts outlined in that text. According to one biblical passage, imbibing wine was actually forbidden for priests[19] and the only cultic use that is mentioned is as a libation.[20]

• Though the biblical texts prescribe the garments to be worn by the priests, the regular offering of textiles, intended to clothe either the deities or the priests or both, that is characteristic of the Ugaritic texts is not a part of the biblical system.[21]

• Certain architectural terms appear in the Ugaritic texts that are absent or rare, in any case not terms of primary importance, in the Hebrew Bible, for example, the *ʿaliyyu*, "upper room," the ʿD-room, the ḪMN-sanctuary, the mound(-room) (*gb*), and the "opening" (*ủrbt*). In addition to these different terms must be mentioned the proliferation of sanctuaries characteristic of the Ugaritic polytheistic cult: though relatively few are actually mentioned in the texts, the existence of multiple sanctuaries, some explicitly located in the royal palace, constitute an important difference from the radical cult centralization (i.e., not only to one town but to one building within that town) that is presented as the ideal in the final redaction of the Hebrew Bible.

• The Ugaritic cultic calendar is purely lunar, without the development of an unbroken sequence of seven-day weeks characteristic of the biblical cultic legislation.

• Because the king was, according to the implicit ideology of the Ugaritic texts, the principal cultic actor, he was required to pass regularly from the "profane" sphere of his daily functions as king to the cultic and back again. Though the passage to the cultic sphere is expressed only as purification (RḤṢ + *brr*), the return to the "profane" is expressed by the root ḤL(L), with a good Hebrew cognate. The differences lie in the primary role played by the king (a role that is attributed to the priests in the pentateuchal legislation, though the king's primacy shows up occasionally in the historical texts[22]) and in his regular passage back and forth from the sacred to the profane (according to biblical legislation, the priests belonged to the sacred sphere and were required to be able to distinguish the sacred from the profane). As an aside, it must be observed that the use of the root ḤL(L) to designate the king's departure from his cultic responsibilities indicates that whatever "sacredness" was attributed to kingship in general was not identical to cultic sacredness.

- The primacy of the king in the Ugaritic texts at our disposal has resulted in the virtual absence from those texts of references to the cultic personnel who actually performed the sacrificial and other cultic acts. From the ritual texts themselves, we know of a *qdš*, "holy person," whose role it is to sing, but we know nothing about what other roles the persons played who belonged to this category. One cultic official mentioned in these texts but absent from the Bible is the *ṯāʿiyu,* who, etymologically at least, would have been primarily involved in the *ṯaʿû*-sacrifice. Unfortunately, all we really have to go by is this etymology, of which the real meaning is uncertain and which may not, in any case, correspond to the official's true or full functions. In the administrative texts the *qdšm* are mentioned, as are the "priests" (*khnm*), but these texts say nothing about their function.[23] The term *ṯʿy* has not yet appeared in the occupation lists, and it is not yet clear exactly where this officiant fit into the Ugaritic socioeconomic system. The great scribe *ʾIlīmilku* describes himself as "the *ṯāʿiyu*-official of *Niqmaddu*" and student of *ʾAttānu-purulini*, who was *rb khnm* and *rb nqdm*, "chief of the priests, chief of the cultic herdsmen" (for a defense of this interpretation of the terms, see Pardee 1997a: 273). That the *khnm* had an administrative function appears clear from the likely equivalence in the mind of the Ugaritic scribes between *khn* and Akkadian *šangû*, "(temple) administrator." The equivalence of the two terms is deduced from the sequence *qadšu–šangû* in the Akkadian text RS 17.131:26–27 (Nougayrol 1970: 85–87, text 93), for the *qdšm* and *khnm* are usually named side by side in the Ugaritic occupation lists. It appears legitimate to conclude from the very inclusion of the cultic categories *khnm*, *qdšm*, and, probably though not certainly, *nqdm* in the occupation lists that these officials were more narrowly functionaries of the royal administration than were the *kōhᵃnīm* as described in the Hebrew Bible.

Judging simply from the biblical usage of this term, we would expect the Ugaritic *khnm* to have been directly involved in the various liturgies and not to have functioned only as administrators. It may be argued (Leithart 1999) that the basic role of the *khn* in both societies was to be in charge of a god's house and the god's well-being. With such a perspective, one would expect (1) the daily activities of the *khnm* to have varied according to rank, and (2) the precise roles of the *khnm* and other cultic functionaries to have varied from one society to another across the ancient West Semitic world. To determine these roles with precision at Ugarit requires, however, additional data.[24] Though to a lesser extent, the same is no doubt also true for early Israel because the comparatively more abundant biblical sources are relatively late and reflect to varying degrees the concerns of the time of redaction. The role of the *qdš* in both societies is equally uncertain: the identification of the *qādēš* in the Bible as a male prostitute appears at the least tendentious and there is no evidence that the Ugaritic *qdšm* had such a function. Because prostitution was not limited in the ancient world to the sacred variety and because male sacred prostitution was even rarer, it appears unlikely from a historical perspective that such was the Israelite *qādēš*'s role: the identification may reflect the ascendance of the *kōhᵃnīm* to power and subsequent denigration of their rivals rather than the true, or at least the exclusive, function of the *qᵊdēšīm*. As to the basic meaning of the term *qdš*, the Akkadian and Hebrew forms are unequivocally stative in form, and I see no reason to doubt that the Ugaritic term was also formally stative. The *qdš* is grammatically therefore, whatever his social role may be, "the holy one," neither "the sanctified one" (del Olmo Lete and Sanmartín 1998: 181 "'geheiligte' Menschen") nor the "consecrator" (Vita 1999: 474).

• Finally, the mortuary cult does not show up so clearly in the Ugaritic texts as some would have us believe. That there was a mortuary cult of the divinized royal ancestors is becoming clearer (see texts 55 and 56), but corresponding data for the common people are still largely absent, as are details on the precise form of the cult in either social setting. If the *ʾInāšu ʾIlīma* represent deceased humans, either in general or as a segment thereof (royalty, for example), that compound deity is the only representative of the dead to appear regularly in sacrificial rituals. Other texts indicate, however, that the belief in intervention by divine ancestors was an important feature of Ugaritic religion (see here texts 52 and 55), as it was for the opponents of the biblical legislators and prophets.

Though the Ugaritic texts at our disposal represent the royal perspective, we probably should not doubt that commoners relied on receiving strength from their ancestors much as did the kings.

Notes

1. "A way to ascertain the relevance of a god in the cult is to compare the number of quotations refering [*sic*] to him in the economic documents registering the deliveries of goods" (Archi 1993: 11).

2. Caquot 1979: 1403, and Niehr 1999: 109 have described the function of these texts as "*aides-mémoires*," i.e., as lists put down to enable the priest properly to carry out the various liturgies for the period prescribed. As such, the intention of the writer certainly has economic repercussions, if we assume that these intentions were followed reasonably closely by the clergy who were responsible for carrying them out.

3. In order that the numbers indicated in connection with sacrifices might be as conservative as possible, wherever the actual number is broken I have counted that token as "1." It is certain, therefore, that the actual number was higher. I have also counted each item as mentioned in the text, irrespective of the unit of count or measure assumed in the text: seven bulls are counted as seven offerings, seven (shekels of) silver as seven offerings. Once again, the reason for the procedure was to remain as objective as possible given that the measure/weight is usually not indicated and that the relative value of the various commodities is very difficult to determine. But following this method has certainly introduced some misleading relationships between the divinities, the most striking of which is the placement of *ʿAṯtartu Šadî* at the head of the hierarchy of divinities according to numbers of offerings received, for this ranking is owing entirely to the fact that this goddess once received 300 unnamed units of wool (text 12 [RS 24.643:20]), which must, in order to maintain consistency, be counted as 300 offerings, in spite of the fact that the unit of measure was probably the shekel and the total value of the 300 units was not, therefore, very great. For an attempt to calculate relative economic value, see below, on cattle versus precious metals.

4. The order used here and in other charts below organized in "alphabetical order" is that of the Ugaritic abecedaries.

5. The asterisk in the following list indicates a number of offerings indicated in the text as devoted to two or more divinities; "*n*" indicates that a number has disappeared from one or more texts, "*n* ?" that a number may have disappeared from one or more texts.

6. The thirtieth day of the month is mentioned in the lunar-omen text 44 (RS 78/14) but is not yet attested in a prescriptive ritual.

7. The quotation marks are meant to imply that there is no indication whatso-

ever from the Ugaritic texts that a system of weeks had been imposed on that of the lunar month. In other words, each month would be divided according to the lunar quarters, but the weekly pattern would be broken by the irregularity of the lunar cycle, which oscillates between twenty-eight and a half and twenty-nine and a half days (in round figures).

8. Only one ritual text passes explicitly from a rite taking place before the full moon to one taking place thereafter (text 13 [RS 24.266]): see list in Pardee 2000a: 160.

9. The most important such text omitted here is *CTA* 23, the story of *Šaḫaru-wa-Šalimu*. The reader who wishes to consult my interpretation of that most interesting text will find it in Pardee 1997b.

10. Those interested in the interrelationship of myth and cult should also be aware that the possibility is now being aired—and I stress that it is for now only a possibility—that the famous scribe of the principal Ugaritic myths, *ʾIlīmilku*, lived near the end of the kingdom, viz., in the late thirteenth/early twelfth century (Dalix 1996; Pardee 1997a: 241 n. 3), rather than a century or more earlier, as was previously thought to be the case. Should this redating prove correct, the paradigm that held for nearly seven decades, in which the mythological texts were dated to the dawn of writing in alphabetic cuneiform while the rituals texts were later, would, of course, have to be abandoned (for a tentative statement along these lines, see Niehr 1999).

11. E.g., "The more I studied pre-Israelite Religion, the more I was amazed with its utter depravity and wickedness" (Oldenburg 1969: ix).

12. Jer 16:5; Amos 6:7.

13. It is, nevertheless, necessary carefully to distinguish between authentic ancient West Semitic practice and first-millennium Assyrian influence; for the particular case of Ugaritic vocabulary having to do with "magic," see Pardee 1997i: 367–68).

14. Arnaud 1982: 107; 1999.

15. For a discussion of the seven acceptable names for the divine, see Pardee 1988d.

16. It should be clear that I see little evidence in the Ugaritic texts for de Moor's vision of a "crisis of polytheism" at the end of the Late Bronze Age (1997).

17. It is not impossible that an allusion to rites of the same type as the PGR-rites known from Mari and Ugarit is present in Lev 26:30 and Ezek 43:7 (bibliography in de Moor 1995: 6 n. 28). The PGR is proscribed in both texts cited, while the modality of the entry rites as described above (introduction to text 18) has not been preserved in the biblical tradition.

18. It was suggested, purely as a hypothesis, that the blood of certain sacrifices may have been poured into the *ǵb*, "sacrificial pit" (see glossary).

19. Lev 10:9.

20. Exod 29:40, etc.

21. See, e.g., 2 Kgs 23:7.

22. E.g., 1 Sam 13:9–12; 2 Sam 6:12-19; 24:25; 1 Kgs 3:15.

23. On these two categories of cultic personnel, see del Olmo Lete and Sanmartín 1998: 177–81.

24. I would query, therefore, two aspects of Lipiński's otherwise very useful overview of the Ugaritian clergy (1988): (1) Though he may be correct that "in Ugarit as well as in other ancient Near Eastern societies, priests were the principal officiants of divine services and their main function, as cultic officials, consisted in performing ritual ceremonies in the temples" (p. 126), we as yet have no direct proof from the Ugaritic texts that it was indeed the *khnm* who performed these tasks, as the rest of the article assumes. (2) Very legitimately, Lipiński concentrates on the textual data to elucidate the social role of the priests, but most of these data, to the extent that they are at all explicit regarding economic details, reflect primarily the "upper crust" of the priestly corps—it is likely that this corps had several levels, with the top members far better off than those situated at the bottom and with those at the various levels performing different functions according to their rank. As regards the role of the *khn*, see Tarragon's more cautious statement (1980: 134–35).

Concordance of Text Numbers

Text and Excavation Number	Edition	KTU/CAT
1. RS 1.017	*CTA* 29	1.47
RS 24.264+	*Ug* 7 pp. 1–3	1.118
RS 20.024	*Ug* 5 N 18	
RS 24.643:1–9	*Ug* 5 V 9	1.148
2. RS 6.138	*CTA* 48	1.74
3. RS 24.643 *verso*	*Ug* 5 V 9	1.148
RS 92.2004	RSO XIV 22	
RS 26.142	*Ug* 5 N 170	
4. RS 24.246	*Ug* 5 V 14	1.102
5. RS 4.474	*CTA* 30	1.65
6. RS 1.009	*CTA* 36	1.46
RS 24.253	*Ug* 5 V 13	1.109
RS 24.284	*Ug* 7 pp. 135–38	1.130
7. RS 24.248	*Ug* 7 pp. 39–41	1.104
8. RS 24.256	*Ug* 7 pp. 21–26	1.112
9. RS 24.276	*Ug* 7 pp. 138–40	1.126
10. RS 24.298	RSO XII 58	1.138
11. RS 24.249	*Ug* 5 V 12	1.105
12. RS 24.643	*Ug* 5 V 9	1.148
13. RS 24.266	*Ug* 7 pp. 31–39	1.119
14. RS 24.250+	*Ug* 7 pp. 26–30	1.106
15. RS 1.003	*CTA* 35	1.41
RS 18.056	*CTA* pp. 136–38	1.87

Text and Excavation Number	*Edition*	*KTU/CAT*
16. RS 24.260	*Ug* 5 V 11	1.115
17. RS 1.001	*CTA* 34	1.39
18. RS 1.005	*CTA* 33	1.43
19. RS 19.013	*PRU* V 5	1.90
20. RIH 77/2B^{+}	*Syria* 56 (1979) 297–99	1.164
21. RIH 77/10B^{+}	*Syria* 56 (1979) 299–301	1.168
22. RS 1.002	*CTA* 32	1.40
23. RS [Varia 20]	*Sem* 41–42 (1993) 42–53	1.162
24. RS 34.126	RSO VII 90	1.161
25. RS 24.254	*Ug* 5 L pp. 507–8	1.110
26. RS 24.255	*Ug* 7 pp. 140–43	1.111
27. RS 24.261	*Ug* 5 L pp. 499–504	1.116
28. RS 24.291	*Ug* 7 pp. 41–44	1.132
29. RS 1.019	*CTA* 39	1.48
30. RS 13.006	*PRU* II 154	1.79
31. RS 15.072	*PRU* II 153	1.80
32. RS 6.021	*Syria* 16 (1935) 177–80	6.13
33. RS 6.028	*Syria* 16 (1935) 177–80	6.14
34. RS 25.318	*Ug* 7 pp. 147–54	6.62
35. RS 24.312	*Ug* 6 pp. 173–74	1.141
36. RS 24.323	*Ug* 6 pp. 172–73	1.142
37. RS 24.326	*Ug* 6 p. 174	1.143
38. RS 24.327	*Ug* 6 p. 175	1.144
39. RS 24.654	RSO XII 69	1.155
40. RS 24.277	*Ug* 6 pp. 165–72	1.127
41. RS 12.061	*PRU* II 162	1.78
42. RS 24.247^{+}	*Ug* 7 pp. 44–60	1.103 + 1.145
43. RS 24.302	*Ug* 7 pp. 60–62	1.140
44. RIH 78/14	*Syria* 57 (1980) 352–53	1.163
45. RS 18.041	*PRU* V 158	1.86
46. RS 24.266:26'–36'	*Ug* 7 pp. 31–39	1.119
47. RS 24.271	*Ug* 5 V 10	1.123
48. RS 92.2014	RSO XIV 52	
49. RIH 78/20	*Syria* 57 (1980) 346–50	1.169
50. RS 22.225	*CRAI* 1960 pp. 182–84	1.96
51. RS 24.258	*Ug* 5 V 1	1.114

Text and Excavation Number		*Edition*	*KTU/CAT*
52.	RS 24.272	*Ug* 5 V 6	1.124
53.	RS 24.244	*Ug* 5 V 7	1.100
54.	RS 24.251	*Ug* 5 V 8	1.107
55.	RS 24.252	*Ug* 5 V 2	1.108
56.	RS 24.257	*Ug* 5 V 5	1.113
	RS 94.2518	Arnaud 1998	
57.	RS 24.293	*Ug* 5 V 4	1.133
58.	RS 19.015	*PRU* V 4	1.91
59.	RS 24.292	*Ug* 7 pp. 143–44	4.728
60.	RS [Varia 14]	AnOr 48 (1971) 37–49	3.9

Excavation Number	*Text*	*Edition*	*KTU/CAT*
RIH 77/2B+	20	*Syria* 56 (1979) 297–99	1.164
RIH 77/10B+	21	*Syria* 56 (1979) 299–301	1.168
RIH 78/14	44	*Syria* 57 (1980) 352–53	1.163
RIH 78/20	49	*Syria* 57 (1980) 346–50	1.169
RS 1.001	17	*CTA* 34	1.39
RS 1.002	22	*CTA* 32	1.40
RS 1.003	15	*CTA* 35	1.41
RS 1.005	18	*CTA* 33	1.43
RS 1.009	6	*CTA* 36	1.46
RS 1.017	1	*CTA* 29	1.47
RS 1.019	29	*CTA* 39	1.48
RS 4.474	5	*CTA* 30	1.65
RS 6.021	32	*Syria* 16 (1935) 177–80	6.13
RS 6.028	33	*Syria* 16 (1935) 177–80	6.14
RS 6.138	2	*CTA* 48	1.74
RS 12.061	41	*PRU* II 162	1.78
RS 13.006	30	*PRU* II 154	1.79
RS 15.072	31	*PRU* II 153	1.80
RS 18.041	45	*PRU* V 158	1.86
RS 18.056	15	*CTA* pp. 136–38	1.87
RS 19.013	19	*PRU* V 5	1.90
RS 19.015	58	*PRU* V 4	1.91

Excavation Number	*Text*	*Edition*	*KTU/CAT*
RS 20.024	1	*Ug* 5 N 18	
RS 22.225	50	*CRAI* 1960 pp. 182–84	1.96
RS 24.244	53	*Ug* 5 V 7	1.100
RS 24.246	4	*Ug* 5 V 14	1.102
RS 24.247+	42	*Ug* 7 pp. 44–60	1.103 + 1.145
RS 24.248	7	*Ug* 7 pp. 39–41	1.104
RS 24.249	11	*Ug* 5 V 12	1.105
RS 24.250+	14	*Ug* 7 pp. 26–30	1.106
RS 24.251	54	*Ug* 5 V 8	1.107
RS 24.252	55	*Ug* 5 V 2	1.108
RS 24.253	6	*Ug* 5 V 13	1.109
RS 24.254	25	*Ug* 5 L pp. 507–8	1.110
RS 24.255	26	*Ug* 7 pp. 140–43	1.111
RS 24.256	8	*Ug* 7 pp. 21–26	1.112
RS 24.257	56	*Ug* 5 V 5	1.113
RS 24.258	51	*Ug* 5 V 1	1.114
RS 24.260	16	*Ug* 5 V 11	1.115
RS 24.261	27	*Ug* 5 L pp. 499–504	1.116
RS 24.264+	1	*Ug* 7 pp. 1–3	1.118
RS 24.266	13	*Ug* 7 pp. 31–39	1.119
RS 24.266:26'-36'	46	*Ug* 7 pp. 31–39	1.119
RS 24.271	47	*Ug* 5 V 10	1.123
RS 24.272	52	*Ug* 5 V 6	1.124
RS 24.276	9	*Ug* 7 pp. 138–40	1.126
RS 24.277	40	*Ug* 6 pp. 165–72	1.127
RS 24.284	6	*Ug* 7 pp. 135–38	1.130
RS 24.291	28	*Ug* 7 pp. 41–44	1.132
RS 24.292	59	*Ug* 7 pp. 143–44	4.728
RS 24.293	57	*Ug* 5 V 4	1.133
RS 24.298	10	RSO XII 58	1.138
RS 24.302	43	*Ug* 7 pp. 60–62	1.140
RS 24.312	35	*Ug* 6 pp. 173–74	1.141
RS 24.323	36	*Ug* 6 pp. 172–73	1.142
RS 24.326	37	*Ug* 6 p. 174	1.143
RS 24.327	38	*Ug* 6 p. 175	1.144
RS 24.643	12	*Ug* 5 V 9	1.148
RS 24.643:1-9	1	*Ug* 5 V 9	1.148
RS 24.643 *verso*	3	*Ug* 5 V 9	1.148

Excavation Number	*Text*	*Edition*	*KTU/CAT*
RS 24.654	39	RSO XII 69	1.155
RS 25.318	34	*Ug* 7 pp. 147–54	6.62
RS 26.142	3	*Ug* 5 N 170	
RS 34.126	24	RSO VII 90	1.161
RS 92.2004	3	RSO XIV 22	
RS 92.2014	48	RSO XIV 52	
RS 94.2518	56	Arnaud 1998	
RS [Varia 14]	60	AnOr 48 (1971) 37–49	3.9
RS [Varia 20]	23	*Sem* 41–42 (1993) 42–53	1.162

KTU/CAT	*Text*	*Excavation Number*	*Edition*
1.39	17	RS 1.001	*CTA* 34
1.40	22	RS 1.002	*CTA* 32
1.41	15	RS 1.003	*CTA* 35
1.43	18	RS 1.005	*CTA* 33
1.46	6	RS 1.009	*CTA* 36
1.47	1	RS 1.017	*CTA* 29
1.48	29	RS 1.019	*CTA* 39
1.65	5	RS 4.474	*CTA* 30
1.74	2	RS 6.138	*CTA* 48
1.78	41	RS 12.061	*PRU* II 162
1.79	30	RS 13.006	*PRU* II 154
1.80	31	RS 15.072	*PRU* II 153
1.84	22	RS 17.100A+B	*CTA* pp. 134–36
1.86	45	RS 18.041	*PRU* V 158
1.87	15	RS 18.056	*CTA* pp. 136–38
1.90	19	RS 19.013	*PRU* V 5
1.91	58	RS 19.015	*PRU* V 4
1.96	50	RS 22.225	*CRAI* 1960 pp. 182–84
1.100	53	RS 24.244	*Ug* 5 V 7
1.102	4	RS 24.246	*Ug* 5 V 14
1.103	42	RS 24.247+	*Ug* 7 pp. 44–60
1.104	7	RS 24.248	*Ug* 7 pp. 39–41
1.105	11	RS 24.249	*Ug* 5 V 12
1.106	14	RS 24.250+	*Ug* 7 pp. 26–30
1.107	54	RS 24.251	*Ug* 5 V 8

KTU/CAT	*Text*	*Excavation Number*	*Edition*
1.108	55	RS 24.252	*Ug* 5 V 2
1.109	6	RS 24.253	*Ug* 5 V 13
1.110	25	RS 24.254	*Ug* 5 L pp. 507–8
1.111	26	RS 24.255	*Ug* 7 pp. 140–43
1.112	8	RS 24.256	*Ug* 7 pp. 21–26
1.113	56	RS 24.257	*Ug* 5 V 5
1.114	51	RS 24.258	*Ug* 5 V 1
1.115	16	RS 24.260	*Ug* 5 V 11
1.116	27	RS 24.261	*Ug* 5 L pp. 499–504
1.118	1	RS 24.264+	*Ug* 7 pp. 1–3
1.119	13, 46	RS 24.266:26'–36'	*Ug* 7 pp. 31–39
1.123	47	RS 24.271	*Ug* 5 V 10
1.124	52	RS 24.272	*Ug* 5 V 6
1.126	9	RS 24.276	*Ug* 7 pp. 138–40
1.127	40	RS 24.277	*Ug* 6 pp. 165–72
1.130	6	RS 24.284	*Ug* 7 pp. 135–38
1.132	28	RS 24.291	*Ug* 7 pp. 41–44
1.133	57	RS 24.293	*Ug* 5 V 4
1.138	10	RS 24.298	RSO XII 58
1.140	43	RS 24.302	*Ug* 7 pp. 60–62
1.141	35	RS 24.312	*Ug* 6 pp. 173–74
1.142	36	RS 24.323	*Ug* 6 pp. 172–73
1.143	37	RS 24.326	*Ug* 6 p. 174
1.144	38	RS 24.327	*Ug* 6 p. 175
1.145	42	RS 24.247+	*Ug* 7 pp. 44–60
1.148	1, 3, 12	RS 24.643	*Ug* 5 V 9
1.155	39	RS 24.654	RSO XII 69
1.161	24	RS 34.126	RSO VII 90
1.162	23	RS [Varia 20]	*Sem* 41–42 (1993) 42–53
1.163	44	RIH 78/14	*Syria* 57 (1980) 352–53
1.164	20	RIH 77/2B+	*Syria* 56 (1979) 297–99
1.168	21	RIH 77/10B+	*Syria* 56 (1979) 299–301
1.169	49	RIH 78/20	*Syria* 57 (1980) 346–50
3.9	60	RS [Varia 14]	AnOr 48 (1971) 37–49
4.728	59	RS 24.292	*Ug* 7 pp. 143–44
6.13	32	RS 6.021	*Syria* 16 (1935) 177–80
6.14	33	RS 6.028	*Syria* 16 (1935) 177–80
6.62	34	RS 25.318	*Ug* 7 pp. 147–54

Edition	*Text*	*Excavation Number*	*KTU/CAT*
AnOr 48 (1971) 37–49	60	RS [Varia 14]	3.9
Arnaud 1998	56	RS 94.2518	
CRAI 1960 pp. 182–84	50	RS 22.225	1.96
CTA 29	1	RS 1.017	1.47
CTA 30	5	RS 4.474	1.65
CTA 32	22	RS 1.002	1.40
CTA 33	18	RS 1.005	1.43
CTA 34	17	RS 1.001	1.39
CTA 35	15	RS 1.003	1.41
CTA 36	6	RS 1.009	1.46
CTA 39	29	RS 1.019	1.48
CTA 48	2	RS 6.138	1.74
CTA pp. 136–38	15	RS 18.056	1.87
PRU II 153	31	RS 15.072	1.80
PRU II 154	30	RS 13.006	1.79
PRU II 162	41	RS 12.061	1.78
PRU V 4	58	RS 19.015	1.91
PRU V 5	19	RS 19.013	1.90
PRU V 158	45	RS 18.041	1.86
RSO VII 90	24	RS 34.126	1.161
RSO XII 58	10	RS 24.298	1.138
RSO XII 67	22	RS 24.650B	1.153
RSO XII 69	39	RS 24.654	1.155
RSO XIV 22	3	RS 92.2004	
RSO XIV 52	48	RS 92.2014	
Sem 41–42 (1993) 42–53	23	RS [Varia 20]	1.162
Syria 16 (1935) 177–80	32	RS 6.021	6.13
Syria 16 (1935) 177–80	33	RS 6.028	6.14
Syria 56 (1979) 297–99	20	RIH 77/2B+	1.164
Syria 56 (1979) 299–301	21	RIH 77/10B+	1.168
Syria 57 (1980) 346–50	49	RIH 78/20	1.169
Syria 57 (1980) 352–53	44	RIH 78/14	1.163
Ug 5 L pp. 499–504	27	RS 24.261	1.116
Ug 5 L pp. 507–8	25	RS 24.254	1.110
Ug 5 N 18	1	RS 20.024	
Ug 5 N 170	3	RS 26.142	
Ug 5 V 1	51	RS 24.258	1.114

Edition	*Text*	*Excavation Number*	*KTU/CAT*
Ug 5 V 2	55	RS 24.252	1.108
Ug 5 V 4	57	RS 24.293	1.133
Ug 5 V 5	56	RS 24.257	1.113
Ug 5 V 6	52	RS 24.272	1.124
Ug 5 V 7	53	RS 24.244	1.100
Ug 5 V 8	54	RS 24.251	1.107
Ug 5 V 9	1, 3, 12	RS 24.643	1.148
Ug 5 V 10	47	RS 24.271	1.123
Ug 5 V 11	16	RS 24.260	1.115
Ug 5 V 12	11	RS 24.249	1.105
Ug 5 V 13	6	RS 24.253	1.109
Ug 5 V 14	4	RS 24.246	1.102
Ug 6 pp. 165–72	40	RS 24.277	1.127
Ug 6 pp. 172–73	36	RS 24.323	1.142
Ug 6 pp. 173–74	35	RS 24.312	1.141
Ug 6 p. 174	37	RS 24.326	1.143
Ug 6 p. 175	38	RS 24.327	1.144
Ug 7 pp. 1–3	1	RS 24.264+	1.118
Ug 7 pp. 21–26	8	RS 24.256	1.112
Ug 7 pp. 26–30	14	RS 24.250+	1.106
Ug 7 pp. 31–39	13, 46	RS 24.266	1.119
Ug 7 pp. 39–41	7	RS 24.248	1.104
Ug 7 pp. 41–44	28	RS 24.291	1.132
Ug 7 pp. 44–60	42	RS 24.247+	1.103 + 1.145
Ug 7 pp. 60–62	43	RS 24.302	1.140
Ug 7 pp. 135–38	6	RS 24.284	1.130
Ug 7 pp. 138–40	9	RS 24.276	1.126
Ug 7 pp. 140–43	26	RS 24.255	1.111
Ug 7 pp. 143–44	59	RS 24.292	4.728
Ug 7 pp. 147–54	34	RS 25.318	6.62

Bibliography

Archi, A.

1993 "How a Pantheon Forms: The Cases of Hattian-hittite [*sic*] Anatolia and Ebla of the 3rd Millenium [*sic*] B.C." Pp. 1-18 in *Religionsgeschichtliche Beziehungen zwischen Kleinasien, Nordsyrien und dem Alten Testament. Internationales Symposion Hamburg 17.-21. März 1990,* edited by B. Janowski, K. Koch, and G. Wilhelm. OBO 129. Freiburg: Universitätsverlag; Göttingen: Vandenhoeck & Ruprecht.

1994 "Studies in the Pantheon of Ebla." *Or* 63: 249–56.

forthcoming "Formation of the West Hurrian Pantheon: The Case of Išḫara." In *Recent Developments in Hittite Archaeology and History: Papers in Honor of Hans G. Güterbock,* edited by K. A. Yener and H. A. Hoffner. Winona Lake, IN: Eisenbrauns.

Arnaud, D.

1982 "Une lettre du roi de Tyr au roi d'Ougarit: Milieux d'affaires et de culture en Syrie à la fin de l'âge du Bronze Récent." *Syria* 59: 101–7.

1994 "Relecture de la liste sacrificielle RS.26.142." *SMEA* 34: 107–9.

1998 "Prolégomènes à la rédaction d'une histoire d'Ougarit II: Les bordereaux de rois divinisés." *SMEA* 41: 153–73.

1999 "Scribes et belles-lettres." *MdB* 120: 54–55.

Attridge, H. W., and R. A. Oden, Jr.
1981 *Philo of Byblos, the Phoenician History: Introduction, Critical Text, Translation, Notes*. CBQMS 9. Washington, D.C.: The Catholic Biblical Association of America.

Bordreuil, P.
1987 "Découvertes épigraphiques récentes à Ras Ibn Hani et à Ras Shamra." *CRAI*: 289–301.
1990 "À propos de Milkou, Milqart et Milkᶜashtart." *Maarav* 5–6: 11–21.

Bordreuil, P., and F. Briquel-Chatonnet
forthcoming "Tiglath-phalasar Ier a-t-il pêché ou chassé le *naḫiru*?" *Topoi*.

Bordreuil, P., and A. Caquot
1980 "Les textes en cunéiformes alphabétiques découverts en 1978 à Ibn Hani." *Syria* 57: 343–73.

Bordreuil, P., and D. Pardee
1984 "Le sceau nominal de ᶜAmmīyid̲tamrou, roi d'Ougarit." *Syria* 61: 11–14.
1989 *La trouvaille épigraphique de l'Ougarit: 1 Concordance*. Ras Shamra–Ougarit V/1. Paris: Éditions Recherche sur les Civilisations.
1991 "Les textes ougaritiques." Pp. 139–72 in *Une bibliothèque au sud de la ville,* edited by P. Bordreuil. Ras Shamra–Ougarit VII. Paris: Éditions Recherche sur les Civilisations.
1993a "Le combat de *Baᶜlu* avec *Yammu* d'après les textes ougaritiques." *MARI* 7:63–70.
1993b "Textes ougaritiques oubliés et 'transfuges.'" *Sem* 41–42: 23-58.
1995 "L'épigraphie ougaritique: 1973–1993." Pp. 27–32 in *Le pays d'Ougarit autour de 1200 av. J.-C. Actes du Colloque International, Paris, 28 juin-1er juillet 1993,* edited by M. Yon et al. Ras Shamra–Ougarit XI. Paris: Éditions Recherche sur les Civilisations.
1999–2000 "Catalogue raisonné des textes ougaritiques de la Maison d'Ourtenou." *AuOr* 17–18: 23–38.
forthcoming a "Les textes alphabétiques en ougaritique." Ras Shamra–Ougarit XIV. Paris: Éditions Recherche sur les Civilisations.

forthcoming b "Un nouveau membre de la famille royale d'Ougarit?" *J.-L. Cunchillos Festschrift.*

Bounni, A., J. Lagarce, and E. Lagarce

1998 *Ras Ibn Hani, I. Le palais nord du Bronze récent, fouilles 1979–1995, synthèse préliminaire.* Bibliothèque Archéologique et Historique 151. Beirut: Institut Français d'Archéologie du Proche-Orient.

Brown, M. L.

1998 "Was There a West Semitic Asklepios?" *UF* 30: 133–54.

Caquot, A.

1978 "Correspondance de ʿUzzin fils de Bayaya (RS 17.63 et 17.117)." Pp. 389–98 in *Ugaritica VII.* Mission de Ras Shamra 18. Bibliothèque Archéologique et Historique 99. Paris: Mission Archéologique de Ras Shamra; Leiden: Brill.

1979 "La littérature ugaritique." Cols. 1361–1417 in *Supplément au Dictionnaire de la Bible* 9. Paris: Letouzey et Ané.

1986 "Séance du 4 juillet.' *CRAI*: 437–39.

Caquot, A., and A.-S. Dalix

forthcoming « RS 92.2016 » Ras Shamra–Ougarit XIV. Paris: Editions Recherche sur les Civilisations.

Catagnoti, A., and M. Bonechi

1998 "Magic and Divination at IIIrd Millennium Ebla, 1. Textual Typologies and Preliminary Lexical Approach." *SEL* 15: 17–39.

Charpin, D., and J.-M. Durand

1986 "'Fils de Simʾal': Les origines tribales des rois de Mari." *RA* 80: 141–83.

Cohen, C.

1995 "The Basic Meaning of the Term עֲרָפֶל 'Darkness.'" *HS* 36: 7–12.

1996 "The Ugaritic Hippiatric Texts: Revised Composite Text, Translation and Commentary." *UF* 28: 105–53.

Cooper, A.

1991 Review of Pardee 1988a. *JAOS* 111: 833–36.

Coote, R. B.

1974 "Ugaritic *ph(y)*, 'See.'" *UF* 6: 1–5.

Dalix, A.-S.

1996 "Ilumilku, scribe d'Ougarit au XIIIe siècle avant J.-C." Thesis Paris IV and Institut Catholique de Paris.

De Jong, T., and W. H. Van Soldt
1987–88 "Redating an Early Solar Eclipse Record (KTU 1.78). Implications for the Ugaritic Calendar and for the Secular Accelerations of the Earth and Moon." *JEOL* 30: 65–77.

del Olmo Lete, G.
1992a *La religión cananea según la liturgia de Ugarit: Estudio textual*. Aula Orientalis Supplementa 3. Sabadell: Editorial AUSA.
1992b "Un conjuro ugarítico contra el "mal ojo' (KTU 1.96)." *Anuari de Filologia* 15: 7–16.
1996 "Once again on the 'Divine Names' of the Ugaritic Kings. A Reply." *AuOr* 14: 11–16.
1998 "A Ritual for the Country's Salvation, KTU 1.162: A Reappraisal." Pp. 164–73 in *Boundaries of the Ancient Near Eastern World: A Tribute to Cyrus H. Gordon*, edited by M. Lubetski et al. JSOTSup 273. Sheffield: Sheffield Academic Press.
1999a *Canaanite Religion According to the Liturgical Texts of Ugarit*. Translation of 1992a by Wilfred G. E. Watson. Bethesda: CDL Press.
1999b "The Offering Lists and the God Lists." Pp. 305–52 in Watson and Wyatt, eds., 1999.

del Olmo Lete, G., and J. Sanmartín
1998 "Kultisches in den keilalphabetischen Verwaltungs- und Wirtschaftstexten aus Ugarit." Pp. 175–97 in *"Und Mose schrieb dieses Lied auf": Studien zum Alten Testament und zum Alten Orient: Festschrift für Oswald Loretz zur Vollendung seines 70. Lebensjahres mit Beiträgen von Freunden, Schülern und Kollegen*, edited by M. Dietrich and I. Kottsieper. AOAT 250. Münster: Ugarit-Verlag.

de Moor, J. C.
1971 *The Seasonal Pattern in the Ugaritic Myth of Baʿlu According to the Version of Ilimilku*. AOAT 16. Kevelaer: Butzon & Bercker; Neukirchen-Vluyn: Neukirchener Verlag.
1995 "Standing Stones and Ancestor Worship." *UF* 27: 1–20.
1997 *The Rise of Yahwism: The Roots of Israelite Monotheism*. Revised and enlarged Edition. Leuven: Leuven University Press and Peeters.

Detienne, M., and J.-P. Vernant
1979 *La cuisine du sacrifice en pays grec*. Paris: Gallimard.

Dietrich, M.
1996 "Aspects of the Babylonian Impact on Ugaritic Literature and Religion." Pp. 33–47 in Wyatt, Watson, and Lloyd, eds., 1996.

Dietrich, M., and O. Loretz
1997 "Der Charakter der Göttin ʿAnat: *ʿnn* und weitere Schreibfehler in KTU 1.96." *UF* 29: 151–60.
1998 "'Siehe, da war er (wieder) Munter!' Die mythologische Begründung für eine medikamentöse Behandlung in KTU 1.114 (RS 24.258)." Pp. 174–98 in *Boundaries of the Ancient Near Eastern World: A Tribute to Cyrus H. Gordon*, edited by M. Lubetski et al. JSOTSup 273. Sheffield: Sheffield Academic Press.
2000 *Studien zu den ugaritischen Texten:* I, *Mythos und Ritual in KTU 1.12, 1.24, 1.96, 1.100 und 1.114*. AOAT 269/1. Münster: Ugarit-Verlag.

Dietrich, M., and O. Loretz, eds.
1995 *Ugarit: Ein ostmediterranes Kulturzentrum im Alten Orient. Ergebnisse und Perspektiven der Forschung*. Band I, *Ugarit und seine altorientalische Umwelt*. ALASP 7. Münster: Ugarit-Verlag.

Dietrich, M., O. Loretz, and J. Sanmartín
1976 *Die keilalphabetischen Texte aus Ugarit*. AOAT 24/1. Kevelaer: Butzon & Bercker; Neukirchen-Vluyn: Neukirchener Verlag.
1995 *The Cuneiform Alphabetic Texts from Ugarit, Ras Ibn Hani and Other Places (KTU: second, enlarged edition)*. ALASP 8. Münster: Ugarit-Verlag.

Dijkstra, M.
1979 "Some Reflections on the Legend of Aqhat." *UF* 11: 199–210.
1999 "Ugaritic Prose." Pp. 140–64 in Watson and Wyatt, eds., 1999.

Donner, H., and W. Röllig
1966, 1968, 1969 *Kanaanäische und aramäische Inschriften*. 3 vols. Wiesbaden: Harrassowitz.

Durand, J.-M.
1989 "L'assemblée en Syrie à l'époque pré-amorite." Pp. 27–

44 in *Miscellanea Eblaitica, 2,* edited by P. Fronzaroli. Quaderni di Semitistica 16. Florence: Università di Firenze.

1993 "Le mythologème du combat entre le dieu de l'orage et la mer en Mésopotamie." *MARI* 7: 41–61.

Ford, J. N.

1998 "'Ninety-Nine by the Evil Eye and One from Natural Causes': KTU^2 1.96 in its Near Eastern Context." *UF* 30: 201–78.

Fox, J.

1998 "The Ugaritic Divine Epithet *ybmt limm* and the Biblical *ʾēmîm*." *UF* 30: 279–88.

Frankfurter, D.

1995 "Narrating Power: The Theory and Practice of the Magical Historiola in Ritual Spells." Pp. 457–76 in *Ancient Magic and Ritual Power,* edited by M. Meyer and P. Mirecki. Religions in the Graeco-Roman World 129. Leiden: Brill.

Freu, J.

1999 "La fin d'Ugarit et l'empire hittite: Données nouvelles et chronologie.' *Sem* 48: 17–39.

Gianto, A.

1995 Review of del Olmo Lete 1992a. *Or* 64: 144–46.

Hallo, W. W.

1999 "A Ugaritic Cognate for Akkadian *ḫitpu?*" Pp. 43–50 in Ki Baruch Hu: *Ancient Near Eastern, Biblical, and Judaic Studies in Honor of Baruch A. Levine,* edited by R. Chazan, W. W. Hallo, and L. H. Schiffman. Winona Lake, IN: Eisenbrauns.

Hallo, W. W., and K. L. Younger, Jr., eds.

1997 *The Context of Scripture*. Vol. I, *Canonical Compositions from the Biblical World*. Leiden: Brill.

Herdner, A.

1963 *Corpus des tablettes en cunéiformes alphabétiques découvertes à Ras Shamra-Ugarit de 1929 à 1939*. Mission de Ras Shamra 10. Bibliothèque Archéologique et Historique 79. Paris: Imprimerie Nationale, Geuthner.

Holloway, S. W.

1998 "KTU 1.162 and the Offering of a Shield." *UF* 30: 353–61.

Huehnergard, J.
1987 *Ugaritic Vocabulary in Syllabic Transcription*. HSS 32. Atlanta: Scholars Press.

Koch, K.
1993 "Ḫazzi-Ṣafôn-Kasion: Die Geschichte eines Berges und seiner Gottheiten." Pp. 171-223 in *Religionsgeschichtliche Beziehungen zwischen Kleinasien, Nordsyrien und dem Alten Testament. Internationales Symposion Hamburg 17.–21. März 1990,* edited by B. Janowski, K. Koch, and G. Wilhelm. OBO 129. Freiburg: Universitätsverlag; Göttingen: Vandenhoeck & Ruprecht.

Koitabashi, M.
1998 "Music in the Texts from Ugarit." *UF* 30: 363–96.

Laroche, É.
1968 "Documents en langue hourrite provenant de Ras Shamra." Pp. 447–544 in *Ugaritica* V. Mission de Ras Shamra 16. Bibliothèque Archéologique et Historique 80. Paris: Imprimerie Nationale, Geuthner.

Leclant, J.
1960 "Astarté à cheval d'après les représentations égyptiennes." *Syria* 37: 1–67.

Leichty, E.
1970 *The Omen Series Šumma Izbu*. TCS 4. Locust Valley, NY: Augustin.

Leithart, P. J.
1999 "Attendants of Yahweh's House: Priesthood in the Old Testament." *JSOT* 85: 3–24.

Levine, B. A., and J.-M. de Tarragon
1988 "'Shapshu Cries out in Heaven': Dealing with Snake-Bites at Ugarit (*KTU* 1.100, 1.107)." *RB* 95: 481–518.
1997 "The Patrons of the Ugaritic Dynasty (KTU 1.161) (1.105)." Pp. 357–58 in Hallo and Younger, eds., 1997.

Lewis, T. J.
1989 *Cults of the Dead in Ancient Israel and Ugarit*. HSM 39. Atlanta: Scholars Press.
1996 "The Disappearance of the Goddess Anat: The 1995 West Semitic Research Project on Ugaritic Epigraphy." *BA* 59: 115–21 with cover photograph.

Lipiński, E.
1978 "Ditanu." Pp. 91–110 in *Studies in Bible and the Ancient Near East Presented to Samuel E. Loewenstamm on His Seventieth Birthday*, vol. I, edited by Y. Avishur and J. Blau. Jerusalem: Rubinstein.
1981 "Aḫat-milki, reine d'Ugarit, et la guerre du Mukiš." *OLP* 12: 79–115.
1987 "Société et économie d'Ugarit aux XIVe–XIIIe siècles avant notre ère." Pp. 9–27 in *Histoire économique de l'antiquité. Bilans et Contributions de savants belges présentés dans une réunion interuniversitaire à Anvers/Antwerpen, Universitaire Fakulteiten Sint-Ignatius,* edited by T. Hackens, P. Marchetti. Université Catholique de Louvain, Institut Supérieur d'Archéologie et d'Histoire de l'Art, Document de travail n° 22. Louvain-la-Neuve: Séminaire de Numismatique Marcel Hoc, Collège Erasme.
1988 "The Socio-Economic Condition of the Clergy in the Kingdom of Ugarit." Pp. 125–50 in *Society and Economy in the Eastern Mediterranean (c. 1500-1000 B.C.). Proceedings of the International Symposium Held at the University of Haifa from the 28th of April to the 2nd of May 1985,* edited by M. Heltzer and E. Lipiński. OLA 23. Leuven: Peeters.

Loretz, O.
1993 "Nekromantie und Totenevokation in Mesopotamien, Ugarit und Israel." Pp. 285–318 in *Religionsgeschichtliche Beziehungen zwischen Kleinasien, Nordsyrien und dem Alten Testament. Internationales Symposion Hamburg 17.-21. März 1990,* edited by B. Janowski, K. Koch, and G. Wilhelm. OBO 129. Freiburg: Universitätsverlag; Göttingen: Vandenhoeck & Ruprecht.
1998 "Eblaitisch *Larugatu* = ugaritisch *lgrt*. Traditionen der *Yariḫ*-Verehrung in Ugarit." *UF* 30: 489–96.

Margulis, B.
1970 "A Ugaritic Psalm (RŠ 24.252)." *JBL* 89: 292–304.

McCarthy, D. J.
1969 "The Symbolism of Blood and Sacrifice." *JBL* 88: 166–76.

Meyer, J.-W.
1987 *Untersuchungen zu den Tonlebermodellen aus dem Alten Orient*. AOAT 39. Kevelaer: Butzon & Bercker; Neukirchen-Vluyn: Neukirchener Verlag.
1993 "Die Eingeweideschau im vor- und nachexilischen Israel, in Nordsyrien und Anatolien." Pp. 531–46 in *Religionsgeschichtliche Beziehungen zwischen Kleinasien, Nordsyrien und dem Alten Testament. Internationales Symposion Hamburg 17.-21. März 1990,* edited by B. Janowski, K. Koch, and G. Wilhelm. OBO 129. Freiburg: Universitätsverlag; Göttingen: Vandenhoeck & Ruprecht.

Niehr, H.
1998 "Herkunft, Geschichte und Wirkungsgeschichte eines Unterweltsgottes in Ugarit, Phönizien und Israel." *UF* 30: 569–85.
1999 "Zu den Beziehungen zwischen Ritualen und Mythen in Ugarit." *JNSL* 25/1: 109–36.

Nougayrol, J.
1955 *Le Palais Royal d'Ugarit III: Textes accadiens et hourrites des archives est, ouest et centrales*. Mission de Ras Shamra 6. Paris: Imprimerie Nationale, Klincksieck.
1956 *Le Palais Royal d'Ugarit IV: Textes accadiens des archives sud (Archives internationales)*. Mission de Ras Shamra 9. Paris: Imprimerie Nationale, Klincksieck.
1968 "Textes suméro-accadiens des archives et bibliothèques privées d'Ugarit." Pp. 1–446 in *Ugaritica* V. Mission de Ras Shamra 16. Bibliothèque Archéologique et Historique 80. Paris: Imprimerie Nationale, Geuthner.
1970 *Le Palais Royal d'Ugarit VI: Textes en cunéiformes babyloniens des archives du Grand Palais et du Palais Sud d'Ugarit*. Mission de Ras Shamra 12. Paris: Imprimerie Nationale, Klincksieck.

O'Connor, M.
1986 "Northwest Semitic Designations for Elective Social Affinities." *JANES* 18: 67–80.

Oldenburg, U.
1969 *The Conflict Between El and Baʿal in Canaanite Religion*. Supplementa ad Numen, Altera Series: Dissertationes ad historiam religionum pertinentes 30. Leiden: Brill.

Oppenheim, A. L.
1964 *Ancient Mesopotamia. Portrait of a Dead Civilization.* Chicago: University of Chicago Press.

Pardee, D.
1978 "A Philological and Prosodic Analysis of the Ugaritic Serpent Incantation *UT* 607." *JANESCU* 10: 73–108.
1987 "La vie sur des tablettes." *MdB* 48: 29–31.
1988a *Les textes para-mythologiques de la 24ᵉ campagne (1961).* Ras Shamra–Ougarit IV. Paris: Éditions Recherche sur les Civilisations.
1988b "A New Datum for the Meaning of the Divine Name Milkashtart." Pp. 55–68 in *Ascribe to the Lord: Biblical & Other Studies in Memory of Peter C. Craigie,* edited by L. Eslinger and G. Taylor. JSOTSup 67. Sheffield: JSOT Press.
1988c "Troisième réassemblage de RS 1.019." *Syria* 65: 173–91.
1988d "An Evaluation of the Proper Names from Ebla from a West Semitic Perspective: Pantheon Distribution According to *Genre*." Pp. 119–51 in *Eblaite Personal Names and Semitic Name-Giving: Papers of a Symposium held in Rome July 15-17, 1985,* edited by A. Archi. Archivi Reali di Ebla, Studi I. Rome: Missione Archeologica Italiana in Siria.
1991 "The Structure of RS 1.002." Vol. II, pp. 1181–96 in *Semitic Studies in Honor of Wolf Leslau on the Occasion of his Eighty-fifth Birthday November 14th, 1991,* edited by A. S. Kaye. Wiesbaden: Harrassowitz.
1992 "RS 24.643: Texte et Structure." *Syria* 69: 153–70.
1993 "RS 1.005 and the Identification of the *g̱trm*." Pp. 301–18 in *Ritual and Sacrifice in the Ancient Near East: Proceedings of the International Conference Organized by the Katholieke Universiteit Leuven from the 17th to the 20th of April 1991,* edited by J. Quaegebeur. OLA 55. Leuven: Peeters.
1995 Review of M. Dietrich and O. Loretz, *"Jahwe und seine Aschera": Anthropomorphes Kultbild in Mesopotamien, Ugarit und Israel. Das biblische Bilderverbot.* UBL 9. Münster: UGARIT-Verlag, 1992. *JAOS* 115: 301–3.
1996a "*Marziḫu*, *Kispu*, and the Ugaritic Funerary Cult: A

Minimalist View." Pp. 273–87 in Wyatt, Watson, and Lloyd, eds., 1996.

1996b "L'ougaritique et le hourrite dans les textes rituels de Ras Shamra–Ougarit." Pp. 63–80 in *Mosaïque de langues, mosaïque culturelle: Le bilinguisme dans le Proche-Orient ancien. Actes de la table-ronde du 18 novembre 1995 organisée par l'URA 1062 "Études Sémitiques,"* edited by F. Briquel-Chatonnet. Antiquités Sémitiques 1. Paris: Maisonneuve.

1997a "The Baʿlu Myth (1.86)." Pp. 241–74 in Hallo and Younger, eds., 1997.

1997b "Dawn and Dusk (1.87) (The Birth of the Gracious and Beautiful Gods)." Pp. 274–83 in Hallo and Younger, eds., 1997.

1997c "Ugaritic Extispicy (1.92) (RS 24.312, RS 24.323, RS 24.326, RS 24.327, RS 24.654, RS 24.277)." Pp. 291–93 in Hallo and Younger, eds., 1997.

1997d "Ugaritic Dream Omens (1.93) (RS 18.041). Pp. 293–94 in Hallo and Younger, eds., 1997.

1997e "Ugaritic Liturgy Against Venomous Reptiles (1.94) (RS 24.244)." Pp. 295–98 in Hallo and Younger, eds., 1997.

1997f "A Ugaritic Incantation Against Serpents and Sorcerers (1.100) (1992.2014)." Pp. 327–28 in Hallo and Younger, eds., 1997.

1997g Review of *Ugarit and the Bible: Proceedings of the International Symposium on Ugarit and the Bible, Manchester, September 1992,* edited by George J. Brooke, Adrian H. W. Curtis, and John F. Healey. UBL 11. Münster: Ugarit-Verlag. *JAOS* 117: 375–78.

1997h "Ugaritic." Pp. 262–64 in *The Oxford Encyclopedia of Archaeology in the Near East*, vol. V, edited by E. Meyers. New York: Oxford University Press.

1997i Review of Schmidt 1994. *JSS* 42 (1997) 362–68.

1998a "Remarks on J.T.'s 'Epigraphische Anmerkungen.'" *AuOr* 16: 85–102.

1998b "A Brief Reply to G. del Olmo Lete's Reply." *AuOr* 16: 255–60.

1998c "Les documents d'Arslan Tash: Authentiques ou faux?" *Syria* 65: 15–54.

2000a *Les textes rituels*. Ras Shamra–Ougarit XII. Paris: Éditions Recherche sur les Civilisations.

2000b "Ugaritic Studies at the End of the 20th Century." *BASOR* 320: 49–86.

2001 "Ugaritic Science." Pp. 223–54 in *The World of the Aramaeans: III, Studies in Language and Literature in Honour of Paul-E. Dion,* edited by P. M. M. Daviau, J. W. Wevers, and M. Weigl. JSOTSup 326. Sheffield: Sheffield Academic Press.

forthcoming a "A Brief Reply to J. Tropper's 'Probleme." *AuOr*.

forthcoming b Review of P. Merlo, *La dea Ašera: La dea Ašratum–Aṯiratu–Ašera. Un contributo alla storia della religione semitica del Nord*. Mursia: Pontificia Università Lateranense, 1998. *JNES*.

forthcoming c "Ivoires inscrits de Ras Shamra–Ougarit, connus et inconnus." Ras Shamra–Ougarit XIV.

forthcoming d "Canaan." In *Companion to the Hebrew Bible,* edited by Leo Perdue.

forthcoming e "Ugaritic." *Morphologies of Asia and Africa,* edited by Alan Kaye.

forthcoming f "Ugaritic Letters." In *The Context of Scripture,* edited by W. W. Hallo and K. L. Younger, vol. III.

forthcoming g "Épigraphie et structure dans les textes administratifs en langue ougaritique: Les exemples de RS 6.216 et RS 19.017." *Orientalia*.

Pardee, D., and N. Swerdlow

1993 "Not the Earliest Solar Eclipse." *Nature* 363/6428: 406.

Parker, S. B., ed.

1997 *Ugaritic Narrative Poetry*. SBLWAW 9. [Atlanta:] Society of Biblical Literature, Scholars Press.

Pitard, W. T.

1994 "The 'Libation Installations' of the Tombs at Ugarit." *BA* 57: 20–37.

Prechel, D.

1996 *Die Göttin Išḫara: Ein Beitrag zur altorientalischen Religionsgeschichte*. ALASP 11. Münster: Ugarit-Verlag.

Rainey, A. F.

1974 Review of *Ugaritica* V. Mission de Ras Shamra 16. Bibliothèque Archéologique et Historique 80. Paris: Imprimerie Nationale, Geuthner. *JAOS* 94: 184–94.

Rochberg, F.
1999 "Empiricism in Babylonian Omen Texts and the Classification of Mesopotamian Divination as Science." *JAOS* 119: 559–69.

Shedletsky, L., and B. A. Levine
1999 "The *mšr* of the Sons and Daughters of Ugarit (KTU2 1.40)." *RB* 106: 321–44.

Schmidt, B. B.
1994 *Israel's Beneficent Dead: Ancestor Cult and Necromancy in Ancient Israelite Religion and Tradition.* FAT 11. Tübingen: J. C. B. Mohr (Paul Siebeck).

Singer, I.
1999 "A Political History of Ugarit." Pp. 603–733 in Watson and Wyatt, eds., 1999.

Smith, M. S.
1998 "A Potpourri of Popery: Marginalia from the Life and Notes of Marvin H. Pope." *UF* 30: 645–64.

Tarragon, J.-M. de
1980 *Le culte à Ugarit d'après les textes de la pratique en cunéiformes alphabétiques.* Cahiers de la Revue Biblique 19. Paris: Gabalda.

Tropper, J.
1997 "Aktuelle Probleme der ugaritischen Grammatik." *UF* 29: 669–74.
2000 *Ugaritische Grammatik.* AOAT 273. Münster: Ugarit-Verlag.

Van der Toorn, K., B. Becking, and P. van der Hoorst
1999 *Dictionary of Deities and Demons in the Bible.* Second extensively revised edition. Leiden: Brill; Grand Rapids: Eerdmans.

Van Soldt, W.
1995 "Babylonian Lexical, Religious and Literary Texts and Scribal Education at Ugarit and Its Implications for the Alphabetic Literary Texts." Pp. 171–212 in M. Dietrich and O. Loretz, eds., 1995.

Virolleaud, C.
1957 *Le Palais Royal d'Ugarit II: Textes en cunéiformes alphabétiques des archives est, ouest et centrales.* Mission de Ras Shamra VII. Paris: Imprimerie Nationale, Klincksieck.

1960 "Un nouvel épisode du mythe ugaritique de Baal." *CRAI* 180–86.

1965 *Le Palais Royal d'Ugarit V: Textes en cunéiformes alphabétiques des archives sud, sud-ouest et du petit palais.* Mission de Ras Shamra 11. Paris: Imprimerie Nationale, Klincksieck.

1968 "Les nouveaux textes mythologiques et liturgiques de Ras Shamra (XXIVe Campagne, 1961)." Pp. 545–95 in *Ugaritica* V. Mission de Ras Shamra 16. Bibliothèque Archéologique et Historique 80. Paris: Imprimerie Nationale, Geuthner.

Vita, J.-P.

1999 "The Royal Family, Administration and Commerce." Pp. 467–75 in Watson and Wyatt, eds., 1999.

Watson, W. G. E., and N. Wyatt, eds.

1999 *Handbook of Ugaritic Studies.* Handbuch der Orientalistik, Abteilung 1: Der Nahe und Mittlere Osten, Band 39. Leiden: Brill.

Wiggins, S. A.

1996 "Shapsh, Lamp of the Gods." Pp. 327–50 in Wyatt, Watson, and Lloyd, eds., 1996.

Wyatt, N.

1995 "The Significance of ṢPN in West Semitic Thought: A Contribution to the History of a Mythological Motif." Pp. 213–37 in Dietrich and Loretz, eds., 1995.

1998 *Religious Texts from Ugarit: The Words of Ilimilku and his Colleagues.* The Biblical Seminar 53. Sheffield: Sheffield Academic Press.

Wyatt, N., W. G. E. Watson, and J. B. Lloyd, eds.

1996 *Ugarit, Religion and Culture: Proceedings of the International Colloquium on Ugarit, Religion and Culture, Edinburgh, July 1994. Essays Presented in Honour of Professor John C. L. Gibson.* UBL 12. Münster: Ugarit-Verlag.

Xella, P.

1979–80 "Le dieu Rashap à Ugarit." *Les Annales Archéologiques Arabes Syriennes* 29–30: 145–62.

1981 *I testi rituali di Ugarit.* I, *Testi.* Studi Semitici 54. Rome: Consiglio Nazionale delle Ricerche.

Yon, M.

1994 "Ougarit et ses relations avec les régions maritimes

voisines (d'après les travaux récents)." Pp. 421–39 in *Ugarit and the Bible: Proceedings of the International Symposium on Ugarit and the Bible, Manchester, September 1992,* edited by George J. Brooke, Adrian H. W. Curtis, and John F. Healey. UBL 11. Münster: Ugarit-Verlag.

1996 "The Temple of the Rhytons at Ugarit." Pp. 405–22 in Wyatt, Watson, and Lloyd, eds., 1996.

1997 *La cité d'Ougarit sur le tell de Ras Shamra*. Guides Archéologiques de l'Institut Français d'Archéologie du Proche-Orient 2. Paris: Éditions Recherche sur les Civilisations.

Yon, M., J. Gachet, and P. Lombard

1987 "Fouilles de Ras Shamra-Ougarit 1984–1987 (44e–47e campagnes)." *Syria* 64:171–91.

Yon, M., M. Sznycer, and P. Bordreuil, eds.

1995 *Le pays d'Ougarit autour de 1200 av. J.-C. Actes du Colloque International, Paris, 28 juin-1er juillet 1993*. Ras Shamra–Ougarit XI. Paris: Éditions Recherche sur les Civilisations.

Glossary

1. Cultic Terms

ʿD-room. In the Kirta text, the *ʿd*-room is where the hero's throne is located, and it may have been the same room in the "house" of a divinity.

altar. As in Hebrew, the word is derived from the root meaning "to sacrifice" (*mdbḥ*, pl. *mdbḥt*) and designates the place where the sacrifice was offered to the deity.

arise. As the designation of a sacrificial feast, the verb NDD, "to arise," occurs only as part of the designation of a feast in text 58 (RS 19.015:14) for which the corresponding prescriptive ritual has not been preserved.

ascend. Where the end point is indicated, the act of ascension (ʿLY) is always to a sanctuary or to a part thereof, e.g., an altar.

ʿRK-taxes. By comparison with Hebrew *ʿerek*, the word *ʿrk* in text 11 (RS 24.249:18') and text 59 (RS 24.292:1) may refer to a type of tax.

bird. The generic term is *ʿṣr;* the sacrifice is primarily for chthonic deities.

bull. *ảlp*, an adult male bovid, probably noncastrated when offered to a deity; *ỉbr*, with the same meaning, appears only in the poetically expressed prayer in text 13/46 (RS 24.266).

burnt-offering. The Ugaritic term is derived from the root ŠRP, "to burn"; perhaps functionally the equivalent of the Hebrew *ʿōlā*ʰ, though both the details of practice and the theology may have been very different.

consume. The verb is KLY, "to disappear, be depleted, be consumed," usually in a passive form, denoting various comestibles used in sacrificial feasts.

contemplation rituals. Those in which the king "looks upon" (PHY) a deity.

cow. *gdlt*, literally "large female (animal)."

***dabḥu*-sacrifice.** The verb DBḤ (< ḎBḤ) is the most generic term for an offering to a deity but is sometimes used as the technical term for a sacrificial category (see also "sacrifice").

day. *ym*, cognate with Hebrew *yōm*; reference to a day of the month is usually by an ordinal number alone, e.g., *b ḫmš*, "on the fifth (day)"; "next day" is *ʿlm*, literally, "thereupon"; "day after next" is *ʿlm ʿlm*. May refer either to the sunlight hours or to the calendar day, which probably began at sundown.

donkey. The sacrifice of the *ʿr*, "donkey," is extremely rare in these texts (two occurrences); historically it is linked with the establishment of agreements between ethnic groups.

dove. *ynt*, cognate with Hebrew *yōnāh;* "city-dove" (*ynt qrt*) may denote specifically a domesticated dove.

DṮT-grain. Uncertain meaning; perhaps either wild grain or green stalks.

dwellings. *mṯbt*, from the root YṮB, "to sit, to dwell," occur in multiples of four and eight; are erected for deities; seem to correspond functionally to the Hebrew *sukkōt*, "booths," of the new year festival.

emmer. *kśm*, a high-quality wheat (cf. Hebrew *kussemet*).

enter, entry-offering. The verb ʿRB is used to designate the passage of a divinity into a new environment and the festival that accompanied it (see text 18 [RS 1.005] and parallels cited there); in text 58 (RS 19.015:10, 11), mention is made of the "entry" rite by a full verbal phrase ("when DN enters"); the noun *mʿrb* appears to be attested in text 15 (RS 1.003:19 [restored]/RS 18.056:21); in RS 1.003 it may have been part of a compound designation of a type of offering.

ewe. Conventional translation of *dqt*, "small female (animal)"; in theory may designate either a ewe or a nanny.

fall. In a few texts, an apparently intransitive form of QL, "to fall," is used to express the sacrifice of bulls.

feast. Cultic feast (*ʿšrt* or *ʿšr*) offered to a deity (the verb *ʿšr* is sometimes used); of uncertain cultic function, though it may be made up in part or in full of *ṯʿ*-sacrifices.

firstborn. Appears only in the poetically expressed prayer in text 13/46 (RS 24.266), where the first letter is restored: {[b]kr}. If the restoration is correct, the reference is probably to a firstborn animal sacrifice.

fish. An extremely rare component of offerings: one text mentions *sbšlt* *dg*, perhaps "fish soup" (text 14 [RS 24.250+:22]); this may be the meaning of the second word in *ḫlủ dg*, the partial or entire name of a "royal sacrificial feast" (text 58 [RS 19.015:12]).

flames. *ủrm*, appears to function both descriptively (text 17 [RS 1.001:8]) and as a technical term for a type of offering (text 13 [RS 24.266:13]).

flour. *qmḫ*, in addition to grain, the offering of ground flour is attested in text 15 (RS 1.003/RS 18.056).

food. *ảkl*, from the root ʾKL, "to eat," perhaps denoting grains generically.

foodstuffs. *šlḫmt*, apparently a general term, derived from LḤM, "to eat."

free (of cultic obligations). *ḫl*, cognate with Hebrew ḤLL, designates the transition from the holy state required for participation in the cult to the normal, non-cultic state; also attested transitively (texts 13 and 16 [RS 24.266:23' and RS 24.260:6], translated "purify"); has no negative connotation in these texts.

full moon. See moon.

ǴR. A sacrificial installation of unknown composition, perhaps of a geographical nature (either "hill" or "low place" are possible etymological interpretations).

heart. *lb*, cognate with Hebrew *lēb*; certainly the bodily organ; as a sacrifice, appears only as a "roast-offering"; also used in the phrase "speak according to one's heart" (text 15 [RS 1.003:52–53]).

ḪLʾU. An otherwise unknown sacrificial feast named in text 58 (RS 19.015:12); may be a compound name *ḫlủ dg*, of which the second element may be the word for "fish."

ḪMN-sanctuary. The term has been identified in recent years as designating an architectural entity, but its precise nature and function are still unknown.

honey. *nbt*, a rarely attested offering.

ḤTP-offering. Attested only in the poetically expressed prayer in text 13/46 (RS 24.266); function unknown. For a comprehensive coverage of the data on this offering, see Hallo 1999.

ʾIPD-garment. Cognate with Hebrew *ʾēpōd*, "ephod," though the exact description of the garment is unknown.

king. As in Hebrew and Phoenician, *mlk;* the primary participant named in these texts.

lamb. *ỉmr*, an extremely rare sacrifice, only attested once in these texts as such.

libation offering. *mtk,* from the root NTK, "to pour," only attested once (text 13 [RS 24.266:25']), where (olive-)oil is the offering poured out. The root ŠQY appears also to denote some form of libation, literally "drinks (viz., of the god)," in text 16 (RS 24.260:11).

liver. *kbd*, cognate with Hebrew *kābēd*, one of the body-part sacrifices.

loin. *mtnt*, cognate with Hebrew *motnayim*, one of the body-part sacrifices.

moon. *yrḫ*, cognate with Hebrew *yārēaḥ;* "new moon" is expressed by the word *ḥdṯ* alone, literally "newness," in the phrase *ym ḥdṯ*, "day of the new moon"; the plural *ḥdṯm* in text 58 (RS 19.015:13) designates a series of "royal sacrificial feasts" extending over an unknown number of months; "full moon" is expressed by *mlảt*, literally, "fullness," also with the word for "day" (*ym mlảt*, "day of the full moon"); in terms of sacrifices offered, the new moon festival was less important than that of the full moon.

mortuary sacrifice. *pgr* (see introduction to texts 32, 33 [RS 6.021, RS 16.028]).

mound(-room). The precise meaning of the term *gb* is uncertain, but it may designate an artificial mound with symbolic value raised within one of the palace sanctuaries (its only occurrence is in text 18 [RS 1.005:1]).

myrrh. *mr*, cognate with Hebrew *mōr*, is the one spice that is designated by name in these texts; it is usually used to spice "(olive-)oil." The general expression is *šmn rqḥ* "oil perfumed (with unnamed spices)."

neck. *npš*, cognate with Hebrew *nepeš*, one of the body-part sacrifices.

new moon. See moon.

night. *ll*, cognate with Hebrew *laylāh*; used in contrast with preceding daylight hours.

offer. In the prescriptive rituals, verbs are rare, and the various offerings are usually designated nominally by their technical term. In the texts describing ritual acts, the verb YTN, "to give," is attested (texts 30, 31 [RS 13.006, RS 15.072]), apparently for presenting an offering (though a divine recipient is not expressed as the indirect object). In the memorial and *ex voto* texts (texts 32–34) the causative stem of ʿLY, literally "to cause to ascend," is used for the offering/ presentation of these objects (cf. the corresponding Akkadian verb *šūlû*, used at Mari for the presentation of a gift to a human recipient).

oil. *šmn*, cognate with Hebrew *šemen*; normally olive oil, a fairly frequent offering; sometimes perfumed; attested once (text 13 [RS 24.266: 24'–25']) as a libation. The word also appears as a divine name.

opening. *ủrbt*, cognate with Hebrew *ʾarubbāh;* place of sacrifice in these texts; precise form and location unknown.

outfit. *npṣ(m)*, never defined in these texts, but in the mythological texts the term designates a complete outfit or "accouterment," e.g., that of a warrior.

peace-offering. Cognate with Hebrew *š^{ə}lāmīm* and formally identical, i.e., the form is plural (*šlmm*) as in Hebrew: literally "a sacrifice (productive) of well-being." The latter was probably produced by the sacrificial meal being taken in common with other humans and in communion with the deities to whom it is offered.

presentation-offering. *šnpt*, cognate with Hebrew *t^{ə}nūpā^{h}*, the precise set of acts expressed by *šnpt* and its function are unknown.

purify. See free.

QDŠ-official. The professional title is well known from the administrative texts as appearing in conjunction with the *khnm*, "priests," but it appears only once (text 8 [RS 24.256:21]) in the ritual texts, where his role is to sing. N.B. The word *khn*, "priest," does not appear even once in the ritual texts. For a discussion of these two terms, see "Conclusions."

ram. *š*, cognate with Hebrew *śeh*, probably primarily ovids, though caprids cannot be excluded in any given case.

recitation. *dbr*, "word," usually used with a form of the root ṮB, "to return"; the contents of the recitation are never indicated in detail.

rectitude. Ugaritic *mšr;* the third of the major themes in text 22 (RS 1.002); the same word also occurs as a divine name.

roast-offering. Ugaritic *rmṣt* (< RMḌ); the cultic function of the sacrifice is uncertain.

royal palace. The scene of many rites, though to date no sanctuary has been identified within the palace itself; perhaps the sanctuaries were located in the royal area located to the north of the palace, where a "Hurrian sanctuary" and other constructions possibly identified as chapels have been discovered.

sacrifice. The most common term for sacrifice is DBḤ (< ḎBḤ), used as a noun or a verb; in the Hurrian-Ugaritic bilinguals, the corresponding Hurrian term is *ảṯḫlm*; in the administrative text RS 19.015 (text 58), several rites that correspond entirely or partially to a prescriptive ritual text are termed *dbḥ;* from this text and other indications, it is clear that DBḤ designated both the act of sacrifice and the feast that accompanied the offering to the deity; etymologically, DBḤ expresses the cutting of the throat of the sacrificial beast and the center-piece of the *dbḥ*-feast would thus be the sacrificial victim.

sacrifice (Ṯᶜ-). The *ṯᶜ*-sacrifice has no Hebrew equivalent; on the basis of etymology, it may refer to a "(sacrificial) gift"; its function may be expiatory (see text 22 [RS 1.002]).

sacrificial pit. *ǵb*, meaning uncertain, though may be etymologically identified with a "pit" or "depression." It was certainly a place where sacrifices were presented, rather than a type of sacrifice, for these sacrifices could be categorized by standard terms (*tzǵ* and *šrp* are attested). Perhaps a place where the blood of the sacrifices—never specifically mentioned in these texts—was poured out.

same. *kmm*, denotes repetition of a preceding series of sacrifices, usually under a new sacrificial category, e.g., as peace-offerings when the previous series consisted of burnt-offerings.

sanctuary. *qdš*, cognate with Hebrew *qōdeš*; one of several possible interpretations of these consonants.

Ṣapunu. One of the sacrificial feasts named in text 58 (RS 19.015); the rite is known from text 12 (RS 24.643:1-12); the rite is linked with the mountain (and the deified mountain) by the same name, but the precise form of the link is uncertain.

sheep/goats. The term *ṣi̇n*, like the Hebrew cognate *ṣō(ʾ)n*, denotes the mixed herd of sheep and goats. In the sacrificial rites, *ṣi̇n* functions as the plural of *š*, "ram."

sing. Though relatively rare, the root ŠR appears in nominal and verbal forms to express the performance by professional singers of song as part of the cult; a *qdš*-official is also required once to sing.

slaughter. Translation of NKT in texts 22 (RS 1.002 and parallels) and of the derived term *mkt* in text 29 (RS 1.019:15); of ṬBḪ in text 31 (RS 15.072).

snout. *a̓p*, cognate with Hebrew *ʾap;* "nose"; one of the body-part sacrifices; usually linked with the offering of a "neck."

spring. An unidentified spring of water, real or artificial, where sacrifices were offered.

stela, sacred. *skn*, an old Amorite word for a standing stone of a sacred nature; at Mari, sacrifices were occasionally said to be offered to the *sikkannu*.

sunrise. *ṣbu̓ špš*, literally, "(at) the coming forth of the sun (from the nether world where it has spent the night)," is attested less frequently than is "sunset."

sunset. *ᶜrb špš*, literally, "(at) the entering of the sun (into the nether world)," typically marks the end of a cultic sequence, in no small part because it probably also marked the passage from one day to the next; usually followed by a statement of liberation from further cultic obligations and from the holy state required for participation in the cult.

ṯāʿiyu-priest. An officiant who took his title from the ṯʿ-offering. Apparently a very high function and not a simple occupation or profession, for it does not appear in the lists of such occupations. The scribe of the major mythological texts, *ʾIlīmilku*, was a *ṯāʿiyu*-priest (*CTA* 6 vi 56).

***tarūmatu*-offering.** Corresponds etymologically to the Hebrew *təʳrūmāʰ*, though the set of acts exptressed by *trmt* and its function in the Ugaritic cultic system are not known.

temple. Normally corresponds to *bt*, "house," usually in a compound phrase *bt*-DN, "house of a deity," though the divine name is occasionally missing, either through omission in the original or through damage to the tablet.

time(s). *pảm*(*t*), partially cognate with Hebrew *pʿm;* designates number of repetitions of a cultic act.

TZǴ-sacrifice. A category of sacrifice of unknown function; the term is of Hurrian origin.

upper room. *ʿly*, a noun from the root ʿLY, "to be high." It is known that the two principal sanctuaries on the acropolis were constructed as towers several stories high (Yon 1997: 116–20); but the palace itself would have had a minimum of two stories, and the presence of the word *ʿly* does not necessarily imply, therefore, that a given rite was occurring on the acropolis.

wash oneself clean. *rḥṣ brr*, the verb "to wash," in a reflexive stem, plus a verbal adjective from the root BRR, "to be bright, clean, pure"; enacted by the king preparatory to participation in the cult.

wine. Not mentioned particularly often as an offering but text 58 (RS 19.015), administrative in nature, shows that large quantities of wine were used in the feasts that accompanied the sacrificial rites named in that text.

2. Deities

***ʾAdamma*.** Goddess commonly associated with *Kubaba*.

ʾALʾIT. Deity of unknown origin and characteristics.

***ʾAllani*.** Deity apparently identical to *Allatum*, Mesopotamian goddess of the underworld.

ʿAmmu. "The divine paternal uncle"; appears in these texts only in the compound divine name *ʿAmmutāru*, "the divine paternal uncle has returned," where it is likely that *ʿAmmu* is the epithet of a known divinity, rather than a divine name in the narrow sense of the word.

ʾAmrur. Attested in these texts only in text 47 (RS 24.271:26') as the second element of the binomial *Qudšu-wa-ʾAmruru*; this double deity is known from the *Baʿlu* Cycle as the messenger(s) of *ʾAṯiratu*.

ʾAMŠRT. Unidentified deity in text 23 (RS [Varia 20]).

ʿAnatu. Tomboy goddess, *Baʿlu*'s chief ally in the mythological texts; from text 53 (RS 24.244:20) we learn that the goddess's seat of residence was, as in the mythological texts, the mountain *ʾInbubu*, of unknown geographical location.

ʿAnatu Ḫablay. A manifestation of *ʿAnatu* of uncertain meaning, perhaps "*ʿAnatu* (who has) mutilated (herself in mourning for *Baʿlu*)."

***ʿAnatu*-ḤLŠ.** Manifestation of *ʿAnatu;* meaning of second element unknown.

***ʿAnatu* of *Ṣapunu*.** A manifestation of *ʿAnatu* formally parallel to *Baʿlu* of *Ṣapunu*, though of much rarer occurrence.

***ʿAnatu*-SLZ/Ḫ.** Unidentified manifestation of *ʿAnatu*.

***ʿAnatu-wa-ʿAṯtartu*.** In text 53 (RS 24.244:20), these two names function to designate a true double deity, for there the two names together occupy a single slot, *ʿAṯtartu* another; this same text identifies the seat of residence as identical to that of *ʿAnatu* in the mythological texts, i.e., the mountain *ʾInbubu*.

***ʾArde(ni)*.** Hurrian city god.

ʾArṣay. Known from the mythological texts as one of *Baʿlu*'s daughters; the name means "earthy."

ʾArṣu-wa-Šamûma. "Earth-and-Heaven(s)," a double deity who appears after the manifestations of *Baʿlu* in the first of the major deity lists (text 1) but immediately after *ʾIluʾibī* in the second principal list (text 3); practically speaking, this double deity appears only in the ritual texts, for where the two names appear in the mythological texts the order of mention is *šmm . . . ảrṣ;* in the ritual texts, the double deity appears only in the two principal deity lists and in the ritual connected to them (see texts 1, 3, and 12).

Assembly-of-the-Gods (*pḫr ỉlm*). Corresponds formally to the *pḫr bʿl*, which, however, only occurs as the second element of the compound theonym *dr ỉl w pḫr bʿl* (see below at "Circle . . ."); composition unknown.

Assembly-of-the-Sons-of-*ʾIlu* (*mpḫrt bn ỉl*). A grouping of *ʾIlu*'s offspring that is presented as a divine entity different from the *dr bn il*, "the Circle of the Sons of ʾ*Ilu*." The two terms probably represent socio-political strata within ʾ*Ilu*'s family.

ʾAṯiratu. Chief wife of ʾ*Ilu* and mother of the gods; corresponds to Asherah in Hebrew.

ʾAṯtabi. God of war of the western Hurrians but of Syrian origin (Archi 1993: 10).

ʿAṯtapal/ʿAṯtapar. Variant forms of a theonym that occurs only as the second element of the double name *ʿAṯtaru-wa-ʿAṯtapal/r*; from the few data available, *ʿAṯtapal/r* would appear to be little more than a form of *ʿAṯtaru*, though the origins of the variant forms remain uncertain.

ʿAṯtartu. Goddess corresponding to Ishtar in Mesopotamian religion and to Astarte in modern terminology. In the west, male and female hypostases of the deity are attested; these were identified, respectively, with the evening star and the morning star. *ʿAṯtartu*'s seat of residence according to text 53 (RS 24.244: 78 [cf. line 34b]) was in Mari, where a temple devoted particularly to her has been excavated.

ʿAṯtartu-Ḫurri. The manifestation of *ʿAṯtartu* known from the land of *Ḫurru*, etymologically the land of the Hurrians, but used more broadly, especially by the Egyptians, as a term for northern Syria/ southeastern Anatolia.

ʿAṯtartu-Šadî. The syllabic version of this name, where the second element is translated by *ṣēru*, "steppe land," shows that this is the nonurban manifestation of *ʿAṯtartu*, though the precise meaning of the term and the precise function of the hypostasis are unknown (Nougayrol [1956] 121 saw a long-term link between this goddess and the Ugaritic dynasty; judging from the etymology alone, the link may have gone back to a time when their forefathers had not yet adopted the urban life).

ʿAṯtaru. *ʿAṯtaru* is the male counterpart to *ʿAṯtartu* (see preceding entries); he is known from the mythological texts as the god of the flat earth and hence, perhaps, as the god of irrigation.

ʿAṯtaru and ʿAṯtapal (or ʿAṯtapar). A double deity joining two whose characteristics were very similar; the second element is already known in the third millennium and a Hurrian manifestation thereof, *Ashtabi*, is identified with *ʿAṯtaru* in the syllabic versions of the two principal deity lists presented above.

ʿAṯtaru-Šadî. Male equivalent of *ʿAṯtartu-Šadî;* known only from text 26 (RS 24.255).

Auxiliary-Gods-of-*Baʿlu*. *ỉl tʿd̲r bʿl*, literally, "the gods of the helping of *Baʿlu*"; a group that receives sacrifices as a single entity; deities associated with *Baʿlu* but of unknown composition.

***Baʿalūma*.** Offerings are occasionally ascribed simply to *bʿlm*, unnamed multiple manifestations of *Baʿlu* (cf. deity lists 1 and 3, where several manifestations of *Baʿlu* are listed without specification). N.B.: the writing {bʿlm} may reflect either this plural (/baʿalūma/) or the singular with "enclitic"-*m* (/baʿluma/).

***Baʿlatu-Bahatīma*.** Literally, "the lady of the houses," apparently a female equivalent of *ʾIlu-Bêti*, but whose sphere may have been larger: the plural "houses" rather than "house" may indicate that she was the goddess of the entire royal area while *ʾIlu-Bêti* was more specifically the dynastic god. In text 15 (RS 1.003/RS 18.056) a goddess appears whose name is written {bʿlt btm rmm}, "the lady of the high houses"; it is uncertain whether {btm} is a mistake for {bhtm} and whether she is identical with *Baʿlatu-Bahatīma*. It is also uncertain whether *Baʿlatu-Bahatīma* is the title of a well-known deity or whether her title is her name and she is an independent goddess. If one prefers a synthetic approach, the two titles might refer to a single goddess and that goddess might be *ʿAnatu*, for, according to text 55 (RS 24.252:7), that goddess bears the title of *baʿlatu šamīma ramīma*, "the lady of the high heavens." Others prefer the "lady of the palace" to be *ʾAt̲iratu*, because of her status as head wife of *ʾIlu*.

***Baʿlu*.** Weather god and hence responsible for vegetal fertility, hero of Ugaritic mythology, and one of the principal deities worshiped in the cult (cf. Hebrew *baʿal* and modern Baal); appears in the ritual texts under seven hypostases, some local, some defined by characteristics; in the principal deity lists (texts 1 and 3) *bʿlm*, "another *Baʿlu,*" designates an undefined hypostasis; in the deity list on the reverse of text 4 (RS 24.246), there are four hypostases of *Baʿlu* that are formed of the divine name and a predicating element.

***Baʿlu-Kanapi*.** "*Baʿlu*-of the-wing," a once-named manifestation of *Baʿlu* as a winged deity, probably specifically comparable to Egyptian Seth.

***Baʿlu* of Aleppo (*bʿl ḫlb*).** Because of the ancient fame of the weather deity of Aleppo, it is probable that *bʿl ḫlb* corresponds to that deity, rather than to a more local manifestation (viz., *Baʿlu* of one of the toponyms of the kingdom of Ugarit of which *Ḫalbu* is the first or the unique element).

***Baʿlu* of *Ṣapunu*.** "The *Baʿlu* of Mount *Ṣapunu*," one of the principal manifestations worshiped at Ugarit; probably identified with the

Baʿlu of the myths whose seat of reign according to text 53 (RS 24.244:9) was located on Mount *Ṣapunu;* the mountain name corresponds to *ṣap̱ōn* in Biblical Hebrew, the mountain itself to modern Jebel el-ʿAqra, located some 75 kilometers north of Ugarit.

***Baʿlu* of Ugarit.** The manifestation of *Baʿlu* who was identified particularly with the city of Ugarit; among the more frequently named deities and the beneficiary of many offerings; one of very few named possessors of a temple (*bt bʿl ủgrt*—the simple phrase *bt bʿl* does not occur in the ritual texts, though it does occur in the "para-mythological" text RS 24.272, text 52); this temple corresponds plausibly to the so-called *Temple de Baal* excavated at Ugarit (Yon 1997: 118–20).

***Baʿlu*-RʿKT.** Only occurs once (text 13 [RS 24.266:2]), apparently as a manifestation of *Baʿlu*, but the text is damaged and the second element unexplained.

Bittu-Bêti. "The daughter of the house," of unknown identification.

Circle-of-*ʾIlu* and Assembly-of-*Baʿlu*. The two elements of this double deity, each element of which is itself a collective, are *dr ỉl*, a distinct grouping of gods, perhaps *ʾIlu*'s "grandsons" to an unknown number of generations, and *pḫr bʿl*, another group of which the membership is unknown. The two groups appear in these texts only as a compound deity that receives a single sacrifice, always that of a cow.

Circle-of-the-Sons-of-*ʾIlu* (*dr bn ỉl*). A grouping of *ʾIlu*'s offspring that is presented as a divine entity different from the *mpḫrt bn ỉl*, "the Assembly of the Sons of *ʾIlu*."

***Dadmiš*.** A goddess of healing; of obscure origin.

***Dagan*.** Known from the mythological texts only as the father of *Baʿlu*, perhaps genealogically his half-brother and stepfather (Pardee 1997a 263 n. 190); appears before *Baʿlu* in the two principal deity lists but this precedence is not always observed in the sacrificial lists that do not reflect the known deity lists; according to text 53 (RS 24.244:15), his principal seat of residence was *Tuttul* (a city located on the river Baliḫ in upper Mesopotamia), a feature that is already attested in the third-millennium Ebla texts (Archi 1993: 9).

***Daqqītu*.** A goddess of probable Semitic origin but best known from Anatolian sources, where she was associated with the weather deity—she belongs to the same group, therefore, as *Pidray*.

***Didānu/Ditānu*.** The divinized eponymous ancestor of the clan of Kirta; apparently played the same role, whether genealogically or by association, for the reigning dynasty at Ugarit.

Door-bolt. Appears only in the second major deity list (text 3) and the corresponding offering list (text 12 [RS 24.643:42]); the Ugaritic entry is destroyed.

ʾEne ʾAttanni. Hurrian deity "the god, the father"; each element corresponds to the two elements of *ʾIluʾibī*, but the relationship between the two words is different in the two languages; appears in singular and plural forms.

ʾEya. Hurrian form of Mesopotamian Ea; the latter is identified with *Kôṯaru* in the deity lists.

Ǵalmatu/Ǵalmatāma. Singular and dual forms; the word is etymologically cognate with Hebrew *ʿalmāh*, "young girl," but of uncertain attachment in the divine sphere.

Ǵalmu. Masculine equivalent of preceding.

Gaṯarāma/Gaṯarūma. The form may be dual or plural; group of uncertain composition though one of the members is plausibly *Ǵaṯaru* himself (see next entry).

Gaṯaru. Identified on comparative grounds as a chthonic deity of vegetation and warfare.

ǴNṮ. Deity of uncertain identification who appears only in text 55 (RS 24.252).

Gods-of-*Labana*. Appears only in the second major deity list and the corresponding offering text (see text 3), where the third sign of the geographical term is missing in the Ugaritic version, making the precise Ugaritic form uncertain; appears to correspond to Lebanon.

Gods-of-Men and Gods-of-Women. Appears only in the second major deity list and the corresponding offering list (text 3), where the restoration of the Ugaritic is uncertain.

Gods-of-the-City (*ỉl qrt*). Appears only in the second major deity list and the corresponding offering list (text 3); partially restored in Ugaritic; the name designates a compound entity that receives a single sacrifice; the presumption that the city is Ugarit awaits confirmation.

Gods-of-the-Land (*ỉl bld* and *ỉl bldn*). The word *bld*(*n*) in this title refers to the "native country"; the longer formula occurs as descriptive of a group of deities (texts 58 and 23 [RS 19.015:6 RS Varia 20:1]) whereas the shorter, if correctly reconstructed in RIH 78/4:3 (not translated here), functions as a collective recipient of a single offering.

Gods-of-the-Land-of-Aleppo (*ỉl ddmm*). *Dadmum* is an old Amorite designation of the land around Aleppo (Durand 1989: 29–30).

Haddu. The old West-Semitic weather deity; identified with *Baʿlu* whose name began as a title of *Haddu* ("master, lord, proprietor"); appears in these texts only in the hypostases formed by the divine name and a verbal form, "*Haddu* is generous" (*ygbhd*) and "*Haddu* is magnanimous" (*ydbhd*), both in text 4 (RS 24.246:15, 22).

Ḫasīsu. "The skilled one"; appears in these texts only as the second element of a binomial with *Kôṯaru*.

Ḫazi. North-Syrian/Anatolian equivalent of *Ṣapunu* in deity lists (Koch 1993).

ḤBY. An apparently divine or semi-divine entity that, according to text 51 (RS 24.258), meets *ʾIlu* on the way from his *marziḥu* to his living quarters.

Ḫebat. Important Hurrian goddess; identified with *Pidray* in deity lists.

Ḫiyyāru. Best known as a month name, rarely attested as a deity.

ḪMN. See above, ḪMN-sanctuary. May sometimes designate a deity (text 27 [RS 24.261]); uncertain whether the divinized sanctuary or an unrelated divinity.

ḪNNǴD. Hurrian plural divine entity.

Ḥôrānu. Deity of magic and exorcism.

Ḫudena/Ḫudellurra. Hurrian goddesses of conception and birth (correspond to Ugaritic *Kôṯarātu*); the two entities appear sometimes joined, sometimes separately.

ʾIbbu. Feminine lunar deity of uncertain origin; best known from the Betrothal of Nikkal text (Parker, ed., 1997, text 24); appears in these texts only in text 26 (RS 24.255). *ʾIbbu* would appear, on the basis of these two texts, to be a feminine correspondent to male *Yariḫu* and to be of West Semitic origin. In the Betrothal of Nikkal text, the deity of Mesopotamian origin bears the double name *Nikkal-wa-ʾIbbu*, indicating a desire there to assimilate the eastern and western manifestations of the lunar goddess.

ʾIlāhu and ʾIlāhūma. Singular and plural of the divine name known in Hebrew as *ʾᵉlōᵃh* (Eloah); the plural (cf. Hebrew *ʾᵉlōhīm*) seems at least in some cases to be a designation of *ʾIlu*'s sons by *ʾAṯiratu*.

ʾIlatāma Ḫāniqatāma. "The two strangling goddesses"; of uncertain identification; perhaps rough equivalents of later *Lilith* and modern "crib death," but the basis for their duality remains unexplained.

ʾIlatu. Formally, the feminine of *ʾIlu*; uncertain whether an independent deity or simply a title for one of the known goddesses.

ʾIlatu-ʾASRM. "The Goddess of ʾASRM"; the meaning of the second element is unknown.

ʾIlatu-Magdali. "The Goddess of the Tower"; more specific identification unknown.

ʾILŠ. Deity of unknown characteristics who appears only in text 15 (RS 1.003/RS 18.056).

ʾIlu. According to the mythological texts, *ʾIlu* (cf. Hebrew *ʾēl* and modern El) was the father of the gods and their executive director; in the deity lists, he is preceded by *ʾIluʾibī;* dwells at the sources of the cosmic waters; in the deity list on the reverse of text 4 (RS 24.246) and in the sacrificial ritual text 14 (RS 24.250+), there are several hypostases of *ʾIlu* that are formed of the divine name and a predicating element.

ʾIlu-Bêti. "The God of the House," probably the tutelary deity of the palace and of the dynasty; if he is to be identified with a deity whose name is known, it would be *Haddu*.

ʾIluʾibī. Literally, "the god of the father," apparently referring to the ancestral head of *ʾIlu*'s family and hence of all the gods; first-named deity in both of the primary deity lists and hence the theogonic "first cause"; according to text 58 (RS 19.015:5), there was a sacrificial rite devoted to this deity, but the text outlining the rite has not survived.

ʾInāšu-ʾIlīma. Literally, "the mankind of the gods," perhaps "men (who have become) divine," a designation of the dead, either limited to royalty or inclusive of the entire population; it is the principal term, virtually the only term, used in the ritual texts to refer to the dead; receives sacrifices as a collecive entity.

ʾIšḫara. Mesopotamian/Anatolian form of *ʾUšḫaraya*.

Kamāṯu. Appears only in the binomial *Ẓiẓẓu-wa-Kamāṯu;* corresponds to the deity vocalized as *Kᵊmōš* in the Masoretic tradition of the Hebrew Bible (English Chemosh); principal deity of the Moabites in the first millennium B.C.E.

Kasʾa. Appears only paired with the moon deity *Yariḫu* (text 47 [RS 24.271:6]); cognate with Hebrew *keseʾ* and with similar terms in other Semitic languages designating a phase of the moon, but the traditions are not unanimous as to which phase is so designated.

Keldi. Hurrian deity.

Kinnāru. The divinized lyre; *knr* also appears as a common noun in text 55 (RS 24.252).

Kôṯarātu. Seven goddesses presented in one of the deity lists (text 3) as offspring of *ʾIlu*; their role in the universe is to foster conception and birth.

Kôṯaru. Known from the mythological texts as the chief craftsman deity; allusions in the main mythological texts and especially text 55 (RS

24.252) show that he also had, like his functional equivalents Enki and Hephaistos, strong underworld connections; appears alone and as a binomial with *Ḫasīsu*; according to text 53 (RS 24.244:46), the principal seat of residence of *Kôṯaru-wa-Ḫasīsu* was Caphtor, or Crete (the mythological texts ascribe two residences to the double deity, Caphtor and Memphis).

Kubaba. Goddess best known from Hittite sources, though of northern Syrian origin.

Kuḏuǵ/Kuzuǵ. Hurrian lunar deity; identified with *Yariḫu*.

Kulitta. Like *Ninatta*, lady in waiting to *Ṯaʾuṯka*.

Kumarbi/Kumarwi. Hurrian deity of high standing; identified with Dagan, *ʾIlu*, and Enlil.

Liʾmu. Rarely attested deity; plausibly a manifestation of *Baʿlu/Haddu;* attested in these texts only in the hypostasis "*Liʾmu* is awesome" (*yrgblỉm*, text 4 [RS 24.246:22]).

Maḏ(ḏ)ara. Appears only in the second major deity list and the corresponding offering list (text 3); the vocalization is provided by the syllabic version, but the meaning of the name is hypothetical at this point.

Malakūma. Deceased "kings" of the line to which the kings of Ugarit believed themselves to belong; this divine entity appears in the two principal deity lists (texts 1 and 3) but in neither of the sacrificial rituals that follow the order of these lists (text 12 [RS 24.643:1-9, 23-45]); may be the object of a libation offering in text 13 (RS 24.266:24'–25').

Mêšaru. "Rectitude, uprightness"; appears as a divine name in these texts only in RS 24.271:14 (text 47), as the second element of a binomial with *Ṣidqu*, "righteousness"; cf. the common noun in RS 1.002 (text 22), translated "rectitude."

Milku. Underworld divinity; because the name is from the same root as *malku*, "king," may be the ruler of the underworld; according to text 53 (RS 24.244:41), his seat of reign was *ʿAṯtartu*; a manifestation of this deity, known as *Milkaštart*, became an important Phoenician-Punic deity.

Mountains-and-Waters-of-the-Abyss (*ǵrm-w-thmt*). The syllabic "translation" (RS 92.2004:29 [text 3]) shows that *thmt* is a plural and that the term refers to the fresh water ocean underlying the earth (cf. Hebrew *tᵊhōm*, with the same meaning).

Môtu. The name means "Death," and the deity's realm is the underworld;

this deity is completely absent from the sacrificial texts but does appear in a mythological fragment the function of which was perhaps to explain a ritual practice (text 57).

Naharu. "River," *Yammu*'s cohort in the mythological texts; apparent ally of *Môtu* in text 57 (RS 24.293).

NGH. Divinity in text 47 (RS 24.271), here classified as a prayer; probably from the Semitic root NGH that denotes "brightness."

Nikkal. West-Semitic form of the Sumerian goddess Ningal, wife of the lunar deity Nanna and mother of the solar deity Utu.

Ninatta. Like *Kulitta*, lady in waiting to *Ṯaʾuṯka*.

Nubadig. Hurrian deity of unknown function.

Piḏaḏapḫi. Hurrian goddess of unknown characteristics.

Pidar. Masculine form of following; characteristics unknown.

Pidray. Known from the mythological texts as one of *Baʿlu*'s daughters; the name means "fatty"; according to RS 19.015:7 (text 58), a sacrificial feast existed in her honor (this feast may be the object of RS 24.300:13'–18' [not translated here], perhaps also of RS 24.291 [text 28]); viewed as Ugaritic equivalent of Hurrian *Ḫebat*.

PRGL-ṢQRN. Unidentified entity to whom sacrifices for the first day of the new year are offered (RS 1.003:50 [text 15]).

PRZ(N). Element of Hurrian divine name expressed in two forms, as "the lord of PRZ(N)" and as "the god of PRZ(N)"; meaning unknown.

QLḤ. Deity of unknown characteristics; appears only in text 15 (RS 24.260).

Qudšu. Attested as a divine name only in RS 24.271:20' and 26' (text 47), in the latter case in the form of the binomial *Qudšu-wa-ʾAmrur*; this double deity is well known from the mythological texts,where the two serve as the personal attendants and messengers of *ʾAṯiratu*.

Rapaʾu, Rapaʾūma. The technical term for the dead in the underworld; scholars are divided as to whether the term is to be understood intransitively (the "healthy ones" or the like, perhaps euphemistic) or transitively ("healers," "invigorators"); my vocalization reflects the former interpretation. The singular is used for a member of the group and, perhaps with a different vocalization, for the eponymous head of the group, probably as a title of another deity (see RS 24.252 [text 55]).

Rašap. Chief deity of the underworld; appears in several manifestations (see following entries) that may be referred to by the plural form of the divine name (as in RS 19.015:11 [text 58]); may correspond to

Mars in the classical view of things, both as deity of warfare and as the divinity corresponding to the planet (see RS 12.061 [text 41] and *Rašap-Ṣabaʾi*, below).

Rašap-Bibitta. The manifestation of *Rašap* particular to the Anatolian city of *Bibitta*; this manifestation is indicated specifically in RS 24.244 (text 53).

Rašap-Guni. The manifestation of *Rašap* particular to the Syrian city of *Gunu*.

Rašap-Ḥagab. A manifestation of *Rašap*; meaning of second term uncertain.

Rašap-ʾIdrippi. A manifestation of *Rašap* known only from the second major deity list and the corresponding offering list (text 3); identification unknown.

***Rašap*-MHBN.** Ditto.

***Rašap*-MLK.** Ditto, though MLK could be either a place name or identify the deity as royal.

Rašap-Ṣabaʾi. Attested only as part of the title of a sacrificial feast in RS 19.015:15 (text 58); usually taken as meaning "*Rašap*-of-the-Army" and as a reflection of the warlike character of *Rašap*.

RMŠ. Deity rarely named and whose characteristics are unknown.

Šaddayyu. If correctly interpreted and vocalized, an early attestation of the deity known as *Šadday* in the Hebrew Bible.

Šaggar-wa-ʾIṯum. A double deity who appears only in the second major deity list and the corresponding offering list (text 3); on a comparative basis, the deities should have lunar connections and be responsible for the fertility of the flocks; *Šaggar* may go back to third-millennium *Šanagaru* (Archi 1994: 252–56).

Šaḫru-wa-Šalimu. "Dawn and Dusk"; in these texts, *Šaḫru* appears only as the first element of a binomial with *Šalimu*; according to RS 24.244 (text 53), the principal residence of the double deity is appropriately "the heavens."

Šalimu. The last deity named in various lists; appears alone and as the second element of a binomial with *Šaḫru;* if this is the same deity as the one whose birth is recounted in *CTA* 23, his place in the lists reflects his status as the youngest of *ʾIlu*'s sons, borne by a wife other than *ʾAṯiratu*, indeed one who was human rather than divine.

Šamnu. Deity whose name corresponds to the common noun meaning "(olive-)oil."

Šapšu. The sun deity, of feminine gender at Ugarit; both the divine name and the common noun (designating a time of day) appear in these texts; because the sun constantly travels through the cosmos, she is the perfect messenger to visit various gods in their principal residences (RS 24.244 [text 53]).

***Šapšu-Pagri*.** A manifestation of the sun deity that may express her role as psychopomp ("Šapšu-of-the-corpse," i.e., as the one who enables corpses to gain the underworld). The sun disappeared into the earth every night and reappeared every morning and was thought to be passing through the underworld during the night.

***Ṣapunu*.** The mountain of the gods located north of Ugarit which was itself divinized (Koch 1993); seat of residence of one of the principal manifestations of *Baʿlu*; for the vocalization /ṣapunu/, rather than the traditional /ṣapānu/, see Wyatt 1995: 213–16.

ŠBR. Perhaps, if the reading is correct, an epithet of *Teṯṯub* in text 28 (RS 24.291:6).

***Ṣidqu*.** "Righteousness"; in these texts, appears only in RS 24.271:14 (text 47) as the first element of a binomial with *Mêšaru*.

Sons of *ʾIlu*. A discrete divine entity in text 5 (RS 4.474:1); part of a compound divine entity, "Father-of-the-Sons-of-*ʾIlu*" (*ảb bn ỉl*), that serves as a title of *ʾIlu* in text 22 (RS 1.002).

ŠR. Poorly attested deity whose characteristics are unknown (see discussion in Pardee 1997b: 276–77 n. 13).

***Šrǵzz*.** The injured party in text 54 (RS 24.251); uncertain where this being stands on the scale from human to divine.

SRR. Divinity in text 47 (RS 24.271), here classified as a prayer; meaning of name uncertain.

Star Gods. *kbkbm*, literally "stars." A sanctuary in the palace was called the "House of the Star Gods."

***Tagi*.** Hurrian deity.

***Ṯalan(ni)*.** Hurrian deity, meaning/function unknown; appears in singular and plural forms.

***Ṯarraṯiya*.** Known only from the second major deity list and the corresponding (text 3) sacrificial list; judging from the offering he receives and his position in the list, this is a previously unattested weather deity (or manifestation of *Baʾlu*, in Ugaritic terms).

***Ṯarrumannu* and *Ṯarrumannūma*.** Divinity, perhaps of Anatolian origin, where the deity is presented in bovine form; appears in these texts in singular and plural forms.

***Taʾuṯka*.** Hurrian goddess equated with West-Semitic *ʿAṯtartu*.

***Teṯṯub*.** Hurrian weather deity; identified with *Baʿlu*.

Ṯimegi(ni). Hurrian solar deity.

Tirāṯu. Cognate with Hebrew *tîrôš* and certainly a wine-god (see "Wine, New" in subject index).

Ṯukamuna-wa-Šunama. The youngest of *ʾIlu*'s sons by *ʿAṯiratu*.

ʾUšḫarâ Ḫulmiẓẓi. A manifestation of *ʾUšḫaraya* in reptilian form.

ʾUšḫaraya. Chthonic goddess who appears as *Išḫara* in Anatolia and in Mesopotamia (Prechel 1996); belonged to the Hurrian pantheon but was of Syrian origin (Archi 1993: 10; full treatment in Archi forthcoming); her principal spheres of influence were divination, oaths, and justice.

ʾUṯḫatu. The divinized censer; appears in both principal deity lists (texts 1, 3), but is omitted from the offering list that corresponds to the first (RS 24.643:9 [text 12]).

Yammu. Sea deity, enemy of *Baʿlu* in the mythological texts.

Yariḫu. Moon deity, masculine gender; from RS 24.244 (text 53) we learn that *Yariḫu*'s principal seat of residence was *Larugatu*, a town known otherwise only from Eblaite texts.

***Yariḫu*, Kassite.** *yrḫ kṯy* represents a manifestation of the moon deity *Yariḫu* that was designated as being of Kassite origin.

Ẓiẓẓu-wa-Kamāṯu. *Ẓiẓẓu* appears only in this binomial with *Kamāṯu;* the "meaning" of the name *Ẓiẓẓu* and the function of the deity are both unknown.

Indexes

1. Deities and Other Extraordinary Beings

2. Personal Names

3. Place Names, Including Gentilics

4. Subjects

request (*ảrš, ỉršt*, verb and noun): 7 line 1; 26 lines 19–20
return (*ṯb*): 15 A 41; 15 B 44 [restored]
right (side/hand) (*ymn*): 42 line 26', 28' [restored], 35'
rise (said of moon) (*ʿly*): 44 lines 2, 4, 6 [restored]
rise (said of sun) (*ṣbủ*): 8 line 14; 15 A 47, 53; 15 B 51 [restored]
rod (*ḫṭ*): 49 lines 5, 14
roof (gg): 15 A 50
room (*ʿd-*): 13 line 9
room, upper (*ʿly*): 9 line 19'; 14 line 14; 15 A 46; 15 B 50

sacrifice (*ảṯḫlm*): 25 line 1; 26 lines 3, 8; 27 lines 3, 9, 10; 28 line 4
sacrifice, sacrificial liturgy (*dbḥ*, verb and noun): 12 line 1; 13 lines 8, 13; 15 A 20, 39, 50; 15 B 22, 43; 16 line 1; 17 line 17; 20 lines 1, 3; 22 lines 15', 23', 32', 40', 41'; 23 line 1; 24 line 1; 27 line 1; 29 lines 2 [restored], 13; 30 line 7; 40 lines 1', 3', 7', 9', 12', 22'
sacrifice (*ṯʿ*, verb and noun): 6 A 1; 6 C 4; 13 line 11; 17 line 1; 19 line 23; 22 lines 6', 23', 32', 40', 41'; 24 lines 27–30
sacrifice (*tzǵ-*): 11 lines 13', 21'
sacrifice, mortuary (*pgr*): 32 line 2; 33 line 1
sacrificial consultation (*dbḥt*): 36 line 1
sacrificial pit (*ǵb*): 11 lines 1', 3', 21'
same (*kmm*): 6 A 15; 6 B 11, 28; 12 lines 11–12; 15 A 29 [restored], 33; 15 B 32 [restored], 36; 19 line 4; 20 lines 5, 7, 8; 21 lines 3, 10, 13; 28 lines 16, 21, 24
sanctify (*šqdš*): 13 lines 30', 31'
sanctuary (*ḫmn-*): 7 line 16; 8 lines 3, 8; 14 lines 13, 14; 20 line 1; 29 line 12
sanctuary (*qds*): 7 line 12; 13 lines 6, 33'; 14 line 13; 16 line 7; 49 line 8
sandal (*šản, šỉnm*): 20 line 2; 29 line 5; 45 line 27'
scale (*mzn*): 18 line 5
scatter (*prš*): 42 line 53'
scorpion (*ʿqrb*): 48 lines 5, 7
seat/lodge (*mṯbt*): 7 line 21 [emended]; 15 A 51
see (*ḥdy*): 40 line 27'
see (*pḫy*): 44 line 12'
seek out (*bqr*): 41 line 5
seize (*ảḫd*): 40 line 23'; 42 lines 7, 17
serpent (*bṯn*): 48 lines 4, 6; 49 line 3
servant (*ʿbd*): 30 line 3
servant-girl (*ảmt*): 45 line 18'
set (said of sun) (*ʿrb*): 6 A 9; 8 line 9; 9 line 22'; 13 lines 4, 23'; 15 A 47; 15 B 52, 56; 28 line 27; 41 line 2
set aside (*ảṣl*): 14 line 25
seven(th) (*šbʿ*): 8 lines 7, 10, 26; 9 line 20'; 11 line 5'; 12 line 19; 13 lines 1, 22'; 14 line 21; 15 A 47, 52; 15 B 51; 18 lines 7, 8, 26; 20 line 15'; 24 line 30; 25 line 11; 26 lines 16, 17
seventeenth (day) (*šbʿt ʿšrt*): 8 line 29; 13 lines 4–5
shade (*ẓl*): 24 line 1
shear (*gz*): 31 line 5
sheep/goats (*ṣỉn*): 11 line 4'; 14 lines 13, 29; 18 line 7; 42 line 1; 45 line 14
shekel (*ṯql*): 8 lines 3, 12; 15 A 38 [restored]; 15 B 42; 18 lines 10, 12, 13, 15; 19 line 11
shield (*qlʿ*): 23 line 2
short (*qṣr*): 42 line 39'
silver (*ksp*): 8 lines 4, 12; 11 line 22'; 15 A 38–39 [restored]; 15 B 42 [restored]; 18 line 12; 19 line 3; 20 line 4; 21 lines 3, 9
sin (*ḫṭả*): 22 lines 19', 22', 23'; 49 line 5
sing (*šr*, verb and nouns): 8 line 21; 14 lines 15–16
sit (*yṯb*): 15 A 7; 15 B 7
sixteenth (day) (*ṯṯ ʿšrt*): 8 lines 27–28
six(th) (*ṯṯ, ṯdṯ*): 9 line 18'; 15 A 45; 15

veil (*ỉzr*): 27 line 9
vow (*nḏr/mḏr*): 13 line 30'; 40 line 2'

wall (*ḥmyt*): 13 line 27', 36'; 22 line 18', 26' [restored], 36'
wash (*rḥṣ*): 6 A 10; 6 B 2; 8 lines 10, 16; 11 line 19'–20'; 13 line 5; 14 line 26; 15 A 3 [restored]; 15 B 3, 55
weapon (*mrḥy*): 42 line 7, 47'; 43 line 10'
weep (*bky*): 24 lines 13, 15
well-being (*npy*): 22 lines 1'–2', 9'–10', 18'–19', 26'–28', 35'–36'
well-being (*šlm*, verb and noun): 13 line 24'; 24 lines 31–34; 47 line 1 [restored], 2, 3, 28'–30', 33'.
wine (*yn*): 8 line 13; 15 A 23; 15 B 24 [restored]
wipe (*mḥy*): 15 A 7 [restored], 54; 15 B 8
woman/wife (*ảṯt*): 16 line 8; 22 line 36'; 40 line 24'; 43 lines 1' [restored], 3 [restored]', 5', 7', 9'; 45 line 30'
wood (*ʿṣ*): 42 line 2; 48 line 3
wool (*šʿrt*): 12 line 20
word (*hwt*): 48 line 9, 10
word (interpretation?) (*rgm*): 45 lines 2, 7
work(er) (*mʿbd*): 45 line 23'

year (*šnt*): 45 lines 1, 2, 5
yellow-green (*yrq*): 44 line 4
yoke (*ṣmd*): 5 line 14
young man, youth (*ǵzr*): 35 line 1

5. References to the Hebrew Bible

Genesis
1:4 50 n. 16
1:5, 8 17, introduction
16:13 56 n. 44

Exodus
29:40 Conclusions, n. 20

Leviticus
10:9 Conclusions, n. 19
17 31, introduction
26:30 Conclusions, n. 17

Deuteronomy
1:4 55 n. 7
12:15–16 31, introduction
28:38 42 n. 5

Joshua
12:4 55 n. 7

1 Samuel
13:9–12 Conclusions, n. 22

2 Samuel
6:12–19 Conclusions, n. 22
24:25 Conclusions, n. 22

1 Kings
3:15 Conclusions, n. 22
19:19–21 33 n. 5

2 Kings
23:7 Conclusions, n. 21

Isaiah
33:17 22 n. 117

Jeremiah
16:5 Conclusions, n. 12

Ezekiel
27:3, 4, 11 22 n. 117
28:7, 12, 17 22 n. 117
31:8 22 n. 117
43:7 Conclusions, n. 17

Amos
5:22 24 n. 130
6:7 Conclusions, n. 12

Zechariah
9:17 22 n. 117

Psalm
50:2 22 n. 117

Lamentations
2:15 22 n. 117

Writings from the Ancient World

Edward F. Wente, *Letters from Ancient Egypt,* 1990.

Harry A. Hoffner, Jr., *Hittite Myths,* 1991; second edition, 1998.

Piotr Michalowski, *Letters from Early Mesopotamia,* 1993.

James M. Lindenberger, *Ancient Aramaic and Hebrew Letters,* 1994.

Martha T. Roth, *Law Collections from Mesopotamia and Asia Minor,* 1995; second edition, 1997.

William J. Murnane, *Texts from the Amarna Period in Egypt,* 1995.

Gary M. Beckman, *Hittite Diplomatic Texts,* 1996.

John L. Foster, *Hymns, Prayers, and Songs: An Anthology of Ancient Egyptian Lyric Poetry,* 1996.

Simon Parker et al., *Ugaritic Narrative Poetry,* 1997.

Dennis Pardee, *Ritual and Cult at Ugarit,* 2002.